Democracy in the Woods

STUDIES IN COMPARATIVE ENERGY
AND ENVIRONMENTAL POLITICS

Series editors: Todd A. Eisenstadt, American University, and Joanna I. Lewis,
Georgetown University

Democracy in the Woods

*Environmental Conservation and Social
Justice in India, Tanzania, and Mexico*

Prakash Kashwan

OXFORD
UNIVERSITY PRESS

OXFORD
UNIVERSITY PRESS

Oxford University Press is a department of the University of Oxford. It furthers the University's objective of excellence in research, scholarship, and education by publishing worldwide. Oxford is a registered trade mark of Oxford University Press in the UK and certain other countries.

Published in the United States of America by Oxford University Press
198 Madison Avenue, New York, NY 10016, United States of America.

Library of Congress Cataloging-in-Publication Data
Names: Kashwan, Prakash, author.
Title: Democracy in the woods : environmental conservation and social justice in India, Tanzania, and Mexico / Prakash Kashwan.
Description: New York, NY : Oxford University Press, 2017. | Includes bibliographical references and index. | Description based on print version record and CIP data provided by publisher; resource not viewed.
Identifiers: LCCN 2016042200 (print) | LCCN 2016023452 (ebook) | ISBN 9780190637392 (Updf) | ISBN 9780190637408 (Epub) | ISBN 9780190637385 (hardcover : alk. paper)
Subjects: LCSH: Environmental protection—Political aspects—India. | Environmental protection—Political aspects—Tanzania. | Environmental protection—Political aspects—Mexico. | Social justice—India. | Social justice—Tanzania. | Social justice—Mexico. | Peasants—Political activity—India. | Peasants—Political activity—Tanzania. | Peasants—Political activity—Mexico.
Classification: LCC GE190.I4 (print) | LCC GE190.I4 K37 2017 (ebook) | DDC 363.700954—dc23
LC record available at https://lccn.loc.gov/2016042200

1 3 5 7 9 8 6 4 2
Printed by Sheridan Books, Inc., United States of America

To

Saroj

For your unwavering support and unbounded love.

CONTENTS

LIST OF FIGURES

LIST OF TABLES

LIST OF ACRONYMS

ALAPA	Association for Law and Advocacy for Pastoralists
BINGOs	Big international NGOs
BJP	Bharatiya Janata Party
BRICS	Brazil, Russia, India, China, South Africa
C4	Consultative Council on Climate Change
CAU	Convenio de Accion Unitaria
CBFM	community-based forest management
CBNRM	Community-based Natural Resource Management
CCM	Chama Cha Mapanduzi
CCRO	Certificate of Customary Rights of Ownership
CDI	*Comisión Nacional para el Desarollo de los Pueblos Indigenas*: National Commission for the Development of Indigenous Peoples
CHADEMA	Chama cha Demokrasia
CICC	*Comisión Intersecretarial de Cambio Climático*: Inter-Ministerial Climate Change Commission
CIFOR	Center for International Forestry Research
CM	Chief Minister
CNC	*Confederación Nacional Campesina*: National Peasant Confederation
CNI	National Congress of Indigenous Organizations
CNPA	National 'Plan of Ayala' Coordinator
CNTA	Chotanagpur Tenancy Act
CODESRIA	The Council for the Development of Social Science Research in Africa
CONAFOR	*Comisión Nacional Forestal*: National Forestry Commission
CONASUPO	*Compania Nacional de Subsistencias Populares*: National Basic Foods Company
CONEVAL	*Consejo Nacional de Evaluación de la Política de Desarrollo Social*: National Council for Evaluation of Social Development Policy
CONASIL	*Confederación Nacional de Organizaciones de Silvicultores*: National Confederation of Organizations of Silviculturists

COP	Conference of Parties
CORDS	Community Research and Development Services
CPI	Global Corruption Perception Index
CPM/CPI(M)	Communist Party of India - Maoist
CRI	Cattle Ranching Incorporated
CSD	Campaign for Survival and Dignity
CSE	Center for Science and Environment
CVAP	*Comité de Vigilancia Ambiental Participativa*: Environmental Watchdog Committees
CVL	Certificate of Village Land
FAPTAUX	*Fábricas de Papel Tuxtepec*: Tuxtepec Paper Factories
FBD	Forestry and Beekeeping Division
FCA	Forest Conservation Act
FCPF	Forest Carbon Partnership Facility
FONAFE	*Fondo Nacional de Fomento Ejidal*: National Ejidal Development Fund
FRA	Forest Rights Act
FRC	Forest Rights Committee
GDP	Gross Domestic Product
GEF	Global Environmental Facility
HoR	House of Representatives
IFA	Indian Forest Act
IPCC	Intergovernmental Panel on Climate Change
IUCN	The International Union for Conservation of Nature and Natural Resource
JFM	Joint Forest Management
JMM	*Jharkhand Mukti Morcha*: Jharkhand Liberation Front
KHAM	Kshatriya, Harijans/Dalits, Adivasis, and Muslims
MBC	Mesoamerican Biological Corridor
MDP	Multidimensional Poverty
MKURABITA	Property and Business Formalisation Programme
MoEF	Ministry of Environment and Forests
MoTA	Ministry of Tribal Affairs
MP	Member of Parliament
NAC	National Advisory Council
NAFTA	North Atlantic Free Trade Agreement
NAPCC	National Action Plan on Climate Change
NCA	Ngorongoro Conservation Area
NCAA	Ngorongoro Conservation Area Authority
NCCSC	National Climate Change Steering Committee
NCCTC	National Climate Change Technical Committee
NCFRA	National Committee on Forest Rights Act

NDA	National Democratic Alliance
NGO	Nongovernmental organizaton
NPA	Nature Protected Area
OBC	Ortello Business Corporation
PA	*Procuraduria Agraria*
PAs	Protected Areas
PAN	*Partido de Acción Nacional*: National Action Party
PES	Payment for Ecosystem Services
PESA	Panchayat (Extension to the Scheduled Areas) Act 1996
PIDER	*Programa de Inversión de Desarrollo Rural*: Integrated Investment Program for Rural Development
PMO	Prime Minister's Office
PRI	*Partido Revolucionario Institucional*/Institutional Revolutionary Party
PROCEDE	*Programa de Certificación de Derechos Ejidales y Titulación de Solares Urbanos*: Program for Certification of Ejido Land Rights and the Titling of Urban Housing Plots
PROFEPA	*Procuraduría Federal de Protección al Ambiente*: Federal Attorney of Environmental Protection
PRONASOL	*Programa Nacional de Solidaridad*: National Solidarity Program
PUDR	People's Union for Democratic Reforms
REDD	Reducing Emissions from Deforestation and Forest Degradation
RRI	Rights and Resources Initiative
SAGARPA	*Secretaria de Agricultura, Ganaderia, Desarrollo Rural, Pesca y Alimentacion*: Secretariat of Agriculture, Livestock, Rural Development, Fisheries and Food
SEDATU	*Secretaría de Desarrollo Agrario, Territorial y Urbano*: Ministry of Agrarian, Territorial and Urban Development
SEMARNAT	*Secretaría de Medio Ambiente y Recursos Naturales*: Secretariat of Environment and Natural Resources
SPFE	Society for the Preservation of the Fauna of the Empire
SPILL	Strategic Plan for the Implementation of the Land Laws
SPTA	Santhal Parganas Tenancy Act
STs	Scheduled Tribes
TANAPA	Tanzania National Parks
TANU	Tanganyika African National Union
TFS	Tanzania Forest Services
TSH	Tanzanian Shilling
TVA	Tennessee Valley Authority
UAE	United Arab Emirates
UELC	the Union de Ejidos Lázaro Cárdenas

UNESCO	United Nations Educational, Scientific, and Cultural Organization
UNFCCC	United Nations Framework Convention on Climate Change
UNORCA	*Unión Nacional de Organizaciones Regionales Campesinas Autónomas*: National Union of Autonomous Regional Peasant Organizations
UPA	United Progressive Alliance
USAID	United States Agency for International Development
USD	United States dollar
VLA	Village Land Act of 1999
VLUP	Village Land Use Planning
WMA	Wildlife Management Area
WTO	World Trade Organization
WWF	The World Wide Fund for Nature (formerly, The World Wildlife Fund)
WW I	First World War

PREFACE AND ACKNOWLEDGMENTS

Democracy in the Woods is a study of the triad of democracy, environmental conservation, and social justice—three values that are often seen as being in conflict with one another. Dealing with large-scale and complex processes of environmental change requires prioritization, enactment, and actual implementation of some policies and programs over others. It is a deeply political process, which is closely intertwined with social and political inequalities. The juxtaposition of environmental conservation and social justice is increasingly common, especially in the scholarships on environmental justice and climate justice, but less so in policy debates. In this book I examine how political institutions and political processes mediate the links between environmental conservation and social justice in India, Tanzania, and Mexico. It is worth noting though that the type of political processes that emerge in a country is contingent on the nature and extent of sociopolitical inequalities.

The intractable nature of the key concepts of the triad makes it imperative that I focus on concrete manifestations of democracy, environmental conservation, and social justice. Accordingly, instead of adopting either an abstract and utopian notion of democracy or an extremely narrow and reductionist proxy for it, I emphasize the ways in which interested actors seek to engage with the formal and informal mechanisms of democracy to influence political and policy processes. On the front of environmental conservation, I focus on forest protection and its policy manifestations commonly recognized by national governments and international agencies. Instead of a post-facto evaluation of environmental programs using the criteria of social justice, I consider long-standing forest and land rights conflicts in forested regions as an observable yardstick to measure the extent to which national forestland regimes address questions of social justice in the context of environmental conservation.

To evoke the question of land rights in forested regions is not an argument about the clearing of forests for the sake of land redistributions. Instead, the land rights in questions are related to long-established claims of indigenous and forest-dependent people and are protected by national statutes in each of the three case-study countries. The household land rights of indigenous people remain contested because since colonial times, governments have designated large areas of so-called hinterlands as state forests, national parks, and wildlife reserves. The combination of long-standing but often unsettled land claims in the forest areas is far more common throughout the global South than most readers may realize. More importantly, the multifaceted nature of the issue of forestland conflicts means that it is connected organically, via the actions of forest-dependent people, environmentalists, government agencies, international conservation groups, and bilateral and multilateral agencies, to the contemporary questions of sustainable development, climate change mitigation, and environmental stewardship more broadly. One could not have asked for a more appropriate subject to examine the juxtaposition of the questions of social justice against policies and programs of environmental conservation, which speaks to the by-now well-established arguments about the inherently political nature of environmental policymaking.

My interest in the intersections of social justice and environmental conservation goes back to the four-year period between 1999 and 2003 when I worked for Seva Mandir, a non-governmental organization in India that worked with indigenous and other rural communities in southern Rajasthan (in north-western India), a region which is dominated by large areas of forestlands held under state ownership. More than 20 years before I arrived on the scene, Seva Mandir had formally split into two distinct organizations. One of the major differences between the two contending groups was related to the question of how to engage with the state vis-à-vis the question of forestland conflicts. While the "remain" group sought to engage with the state "constructively" to help promote forest protection, the "leave" group was in favor of challenging the state to wage a more radical land rights movement. As I will show in the following pages, this is not as simple a dichotomy as it may seem at first. My education in this topic continued in the next job I accepted in New Delhi with the Ford Foundation, which supported Ekta Parishad, a not-for-profit group that employs Gandhian philosophy to energize land rights struggles of the poorest people. The opportunity to work closely with Ekta Parishad was instrumental in further fueling my interest in questions of forest and land rights of forest-dependent people.

The training and mentorship of my PhD supervisor Elinor (aka Lin) Ostrom shaped this book in more ways than may be apparent. Lin trained graduate students in methods and frameworks that won her the 2009 Nobel Prize in Economic Sciences, but more importantly, ensured that her students grew up to be analytically disciplined scholars with a genuine respect for methodological pluralism. I have applied those lessons in this book, but have done so in ways and to questions of my own choosing. Lauren M. MacLean taught me how to execute a mixed-methods research strategy and continues to inspire me to this date. Gustavo Gordillo and Leticia Merino, who I knew via the visiting scholars program at the Ostrom Workshop, and my graduate school peer, Gustavo Garcia-López, have been instrumental in kindling my interest in and informing me about Mexico's remarkable history and institutions of community control over natural resources. More recently, David Bray, one of the top experts in Mexican community forestry, has been generous with his time during the several personal visits he made to Storrs-Mansfield. David also kindly connected me to policymakers and patiently vetted my interpretations of Mexican laws and policies. My engagement with countries on the African continent took off in important ways via my involvement with the Responsive Forest Governance initiative led by Jesse Ribot and implemented jointly by the Council for the Development of Social Science Research in Africa (CODESRIA) and the International Union for Conservation of Nature and Natural Resource (IUCN).

The lessons I have learned during various episodes of field research over the years (1997–2014)–during my pre-academia professional engagements with Seva Mandir, Udaipur, and Ford Foundation, New Delhi, and the academic work at Indian Institute of Forest Management Bhopal, Indiana University, Bloomington, and the University of Connecticut, Storrs – have been critical to the development of the arguments in this book. Several years of field research, coupled with the exchange of experiences and insights with colleagues at various stages also prepared me to critically engage with relevant ethnographic research from Tanzania and Mexico. For this, I am grateful to a large number of colleagues, civil society leaders, social activists, government officials, political leaders, village leaders, and hundreds of men and women interlocutors in various places who generously shared their insights, observations, and reflections. To maintain the confidentiality of the names of individuals and places, as warranted under Human Subjects regulations, I have used pseudonyms for individuals and village names. Even though the identity of public officials can be disclosed, considering the sensitivity of the topic, I have maintained anonymity in their case as well.

The following research and travel grants facilitated the research and writing of the manuscript at various stages: The first part of research in India (2009–10) was supported in parts by grants from the International Foundation for Science (grant number: S/4595-1) and the Institute of International Education/ Ford Foundation, New Delhi (number: 1050-0152). University of Connecticut grants, which facilitated literature review, research assistantship, and preparation of manuscript, include the SHARE/Bennett undergraduate awards, the Summer Research Grant of the Economic and Social Rights Group (ESRG) in 2011–12, a book grant from Human Rights Institute (2013), Faculty Large Grant (2013–14), India Studies/Asian & Asian American Studies Institute grant (2016), and the Scholarship Facilitation Fund Awards (2016).

I must make special mention of my University of Connecticut colleagues, Betty Hanson and Mark Healey, whose critical feedback on key chapters allowed me to make the text comprehensible to audiences other than the scholars, policymakers, and activists who routinely engage with the subject matter. A number of individuals read book proposals, chapter drafts, or gave inputs that shaped this research in one way or the other: Arun Agrawal, Antonio Azuela, Amita Baviskar, Mark Boyer, Maria DiGiano, Tomas Frederiksen, Shareen Hertel, David Kaimowitz, Christian Lund, Mathew Mabele, Lanse Minkler, James Murombedzi, Shayla C. Nunnally, Lauren Persha, Amy Poteete, Vasant Saberwal, Cathy J. Schlund-Vials, Lyle Scruggs, Thomas Sikor, Margaret Skutsch, and Cyrus Ernesto ("Ernie") Zirakzadeh. An earlier version of Chapter 7 of this book was published by the MIT Press *Journal Global Environmental Politics* (August 2015, Vol. 15, No. 3, Pages 95–117). Inputs from the special issue editors Mark Purdon and Catherine Boone, and two anonymous reviewers helped sharped the analysis presented there.

The meticulous shepherding of the manuscript through peer review and various stages of production by OUP editor Angela Chnapko and the support of her colleagues Princess Ikatekit and Shalini Balakrishnan ensured the timely production of the book. Last, but the most important, this book would not have been possible without the love and support of my family, especially my wife and soul mate Saroj, who has been the source of my strength, determination, and perseverance. During the three long years that I devoted almost exclusively to researching and writing this book, Saroj compensated for my numerous absences from the play hours of our lovely daughters Zia and Sophia. To Zia, especially, I promise to cook fun recipes and organize games of Monopoly more frequently than I have in the past. My mom would have been very proud to see my first book being published. It is to her values of compassion that I should attribute my interest in the questions of social justice and environmental conservation.

While any project of this scope has to stand on the shoulders of giants and the support of many colleagues, only I am responsible for the shortcomings of the text, which I present in the hope of a socially just and environmentally sound world for all of the people who call it their home.

Democracy in the Woods

CHAPTER 1

ↄᐯↄ

The Politics and Political Economy
of Forestland Regimes

Social justice and environmental conservation, two of the most important issues of this day and age, are at odds in many of the world's forested regions. In 2002 and 2003, India's forestry agencies ran a nationwide "eviction campaign" that "cleared" 152,400 hectares of farmlands within the lands designated as state forests.[1] These evictions displaced 150,000 peasant families, with Amnesty International reporting widespread human rights violations.[2] In Tanzania, more recently, armed rangers from Serengeti National Park burned 114 Maasai settlements to the ground in February 2015, with the rangers arguing that the settlements were located within the park's boundaries. While the government agencies justified their actions for the sake of advancing conservation goals, local residents in the forested regions of India and Tanzania—whose livelihoods depend on peasant farming, pastoralism, and the use of forest produce for subsistence—argue they have lived in these areas for generations.[3] As serious as these incidents are, they are unfortunately not exceptions.

The forested regions that international conservation groups have designated as biodiversity hotspots are also social and political flashpoints, with

---

1. Drèze 2005; Bijoy 2008.
2. Other reports suggested that the evictions affected 168,000 families. See T.K. Rajalakshmi, "Fatwa raj is over: Interview with Brinda Karat, CPI(M) leader and Member of the Rajya Sabha," *Frontline, Volume 23—Issue 26 Dec. 30, 2006-Jan. 12, 2007.* http://www.frontline.in/static/html/fl2326/stories/20070112003201100. htm; "Forced evictions target adivasi," *Amnesty International Australia,* April 27, 2007, http://www.amnesty.org.au/news/comments/1160/.
3. Benjaminsen et al. 2013.

insecure land tenure, high levels of poverty, enduring power asymmetries, and histories of state control and repression.[4] Worldwide, an estimated 750 million indigenous and other forest-dependent peasants claim customary and de facto land rights, which national forestry and wildlife agencies do not accept as legitimate (see Appendix I).[5] These land rights conflicts often lead to violence: Global Witness reported that 908 people in 35 countries died between 2002 and 2012 because of their work on "environment and land issues."[6] Clearly, these numbers represent only a tiny fraction of fatalities linked to forestland conflicts, which occur on a routine basis in major forested countries (see Appendix II for a list of violent conflicts throughout the world).[7] Additionally, land-related conflicts often have exacerbated civil conflicts in a number of countries, including the Naxalite insurgency in India, the Zapatista rebellion in Mexico, and the Rwandan genocide, among others.[8] These conflicts have intensified as national forestry agencies and international conservation groups have worked to set aside large areas of land exclusively for the provision of environmental goods and services—such as wildlife and biodiversity conservation, biofuels, and forest-based carbon emission reductions.[9] International support for forest and wildlife conservation programs fuel most of the demand for these new enclosures.[10]

The frequency and scope of these land rights conflicts, rooted in state-led defense of forests, call into question the cliché that pits long-term policy goals (such as nature conservation) against short-term electoral considerations. If incumbent governments were driven exclusively by electoral calculus, elected leaders in India and Tanzania would have sought to prevent the bloody conflicts mentioned above in order to avoid the wrath of voters. Instead, these

4. Brechin et al. 2002, p. 42, emphasis added.
5. Seven hundred and fifty million is a conservative estimate by the author based on various reports, including a new report by environmental journalist Fred Pearce, which cites several sources to suggest that "up to 2.5 billion people depend on indigenous and community lands" (Pearce 2016, 7).
6. Global Witness 2014. The reference in the first part of the sentence is to the noted book *Violent Environments*, Peluso and Watts 2001.
7. Van Hoyweghen 1999; Alston et al. 2000. For nuanced discussions of land rights violations as one of the root causes of the Marikana mines conflict in South Africa, which led to the death of 44 miners in a police shooting, see Tropp 2003; Malaika wa Azania, "Marikana is actually about 'stolen' land." *The Sunday Independent*, July 5, 2015.
8. Uvin 1996; Collier and Quaratiello 2005; Li 2010; cf. Peluso and Watts 2001; Peluso and Vandergeest 2011.
9. Fairhead et al. 2012.
10. Delegates from 193 countries assembled at the tenth meeting of the Conference of Parties to the Convention on Biological Diversity held in October 2010 in Nagoya, Japan, resolved to bring 17 percent of global landmass under protected areas by 2020. See Convention on Biological Diversity, "TARGET 11—Technical Rationale extended (provided in document COP/10/INF/12/Rev.1)," http://www.cbd.int/sp/targets/rationale/target-11/.

governments proceeded to violently enforce the colonial-era forest boundaries, which government agencies defended as being necessary for forest protection and wildlife conservation. Nationwide mobilization following these incidents forced the Indian government to enact the Forest Rights Act (FRA) of 2006 to address land rights conflicts, even though the act remains poorly implemented.[11] Across the Indian Ocean, as Tanzania's ruling party faced its toughest-ever electoral competition from a united opposition in the 2015 presidential election, its candidate promised to redistribute land and end land conflicts.[12] Since the election, however, the new government has sent mixed signals. While the Land Ministry promised to resolve land conflicts, the Ministry of Tourism and Natural Resources politely refused to be drawn into an ongoing legal battle between the Maasais and a U.S.-based safari company.[13]

Why do elected governments and political leaders often respond to the tensions between competing local and global demands regarding forestlands in a manner that contradicts expectations associated with populist politics? And what impacts do their decisions have on social justice and environmental conservation? This book's comparative analysis of peasant land rights in the forested regions in India, Tanzania, and Mexico shows that political and economic factors are central to explaining the diverging paths of forestland rights and nature conservation regimes. The analytical logic for the choice of case study countries is explained at length in section 1.3, but one important motivation is related to a puzzling divergence over time in the nature of forestland regimes in these three countries. At the beginning of the twentieth century, peasants in these countries' forested regions enjoyed few if any forest and land rights. Mexican peasants and indigenous people were in the worst position with regard to land access and land rights. However, peasant land rights in the country changed significantly during the next hundred years. Mexican peasants today enjoy far greater security of forest and land rights than do their counterparts in India or Tanzania. While Mexico's agrarian revolution of 1910–1917 lent strength to peasants' demands for land redistribution, the revolution did not predetermine the outcomes of forestland regimes in the decades to come, as Chapter 3 demonstrates.

Democracy in the Woods offers political-economic explanations for the remarkable differences in the negotiation of peasant land rights in forested regions of the three case study countries. First and foremost, it shows that

---

11. For discussions of FRA's implementation failures, see NCFRA 2010; Kashwan 2013; Lélé and Menon 2014; Menon and Bijoy 2014; Kumar et al. 2015.
12. Anon., "Tanzania ruling party candidate promises to redistribute unused land, says tycoons are hoarding," *Mail & Guardian Africa*, September 3, 2015, http://mgafrica.com/article/2015-09-06-tanzania-ruling-party-candidate-promises-to-redistribute-unused-land.
13. Katy Migiro, "Maasai locked in Tanzania legal battle with US safari firm, land conflicts grow," Thomson Reuters Foundation. November 11, 2015.

political structures that enable sustained engagement between peasant groups and ruling political parties lead to governments providing statutory protection to peasant land rights in forested regions. Drawing on research from the fields of historical institutionalism, development studies, and comparative politics, I theorize the conditions under which progressive policy reforms are likely to be enacted *and* effectively implemented. Indeed, the nature and extent of engagements between actors in social and political arenas is a product of the political and economic contexts within which forested territories are embedded.

This leads to the second main argument of the book, which connects the history of state-led development in the case study countries to the status of forest and land rights within their national forestland regimes. By "forestland regimes," I mean the configuration of actors, authorities, and institutions that regulate forest and land use, as well as "the formal and informal structure and nature of political power" in forested regions.[14] Contrary to the conventional understanding of conflict between environment and development, this book shows that environmental considerations and economic development may also reinforce one another. Moreover, it shows that the implications of this interaction between economic development and environmental protection for social justice hinge on the nature of political process that mediates these divergent, though not necessarily contradictory, goals.

In the postcolonial era, the imperatives of national development motivated national leaders to centralize control over hinterlands in most countries of Africa and Asia. Over time, national governments designated much of this centrally controlled land as forests and wildlife reserves to secure support from international conservation groups and multilateral agencies.[15] Many postcolonial governments deployed internationally supported nature conservation programs as "development" projects, which brought new opportunities and resources to remote forested regions. While these new resources occasionally benefited forest-dependent people, in most cases, they did more to reinforce the authority, powers, and resources at the disposal of national forestry and wildlife agencies.[16]

Finally, I examine the outcomes of recent efforts to bring about institutional change in forestland regimes in Mexico, Tanzania, and India—efforts that underscore the importance of interactions between national politics and subnational political-economic relations. At the national level, each of these countries has introduced reforms designed to formalize peasant

14. Jayal 2001; Siaroff 2011. See also, Larson and Ribot 2007; Sikor and Lund 2009.
15. Neumann 1992, 1997; Gibson 1999; Schroeder 1999; Thompson and Homewood 2002; Adams and Hutton 2007; Randeria 2007.
16. The title of a recent doctoral dissertation—"Wildlife is Our Oil"—aptly summarizes this aspect of international conservation. See Sachedina 2008.

land rights, and national forestry agencies have offered forest-based carbon emission reduction proposals as part of international negotiations related to climate change mitigation. These national and subnational processes present yet another set of opportunities to test the arguments set forth in this chapter which I do in Chapters 5–7.

This book's emphasis on the political drivers of land rights of forest-dependent peasants draws attention to the highly consequential intersections of social justice and environmental conservation. The timeliness of such an approach is evident in light of the United Nations' recently adopted 2030 Sustainable Development Goals, which include a pledge to protect the rights of all men and women, in particular the poor and the vulnerable, to have "ownership and control over land and other forms of property, inheritance, natural resources."[17] Instead of exploring land rights in isolation, this book situates them within an analysis of the emergence of national forestland regimes and forest policy reforms, which are often at the center of sustainable development campaigns.

1.1 RESEARCH ON FORESTED REGIONS AND FORESTLAND CONFLICTS

Political scientists often describe the hinterlands in developing countries as peripheral regions characterized by a missing state, or as poorly governed "brown spots."[18] But scholars of historical and comparative institutionalism, who examine colonial legacies' impact on postcolonial institutional outcomes, argue against such characterizations.[19] They argue that the unevenness of democratic governance in the hinterlands stems from "strategic logics" that serve political elites' interests and that have important implications for environmental conservation.[20] Radical environmentalists and green political theorists, meanwhile, seek to establish a rationale for the "rights of nature" or "intergeneration environmental human rights."[21] Critics argue that these attempts to promote nature conservation are often "unnecessarily and unfortunately narrow . . . [because they tend] to delimit political contest regarding the appropriate relation of humans to the natural world."[22] A single-minded pursuit of ecological values does not necessarily align with political values such as liberty and equality.[23] These types of considerations are especially relevant

---

17. United Nations General Assembly 2015, 15.
18. O'Donnell 1993.
19. Mahoney 2000, 507; also see Pierson 2000.
20. Boone 2012, 629.
21. Eckersley 1995; Hiskes 2009.
22. Gabrielson 2008, 441.
23. Jayal 2001.

in the Global South, where the project of nature conservation is executed via the state, which is invariably infused with asymmetric distributions of social and political power.[24]

The question of land rights conflicts in forested regions often falls through various disciplinary gaps within academia. For example, the discourses and strategies related to "forest conservation" have deeply shaped the tradition of scholarship focused on the commons. These scholars examine how variation in institutions (specifically forest tenure) coupled with rules and norms of local collective action affect the outcomes of local forest protection and management.[25] By emphasizing the agenda of *forest* protection and conservation, however, scholars focusing on the commons sidestep some of the most contentious issues regarding forested landscapes, such as land conflicts between forest-dependent people and government forestry agencies.[26] Agrarian studies scholars who examine peasant land rights, meanwhile, do not usually study land rights in forested regions, and anthropologists who address questions of farming within forested regions examine the issue mainly from social and cultural perspectives.[27] Scholars working in the tradition of historical anthropology and history of forestry engage with the politics of forestry laws and policies, broadly understood, but their goal is to illuminate debates about state-society dynamics centered on questions of forest management and forest conservation.[28]

One of the main groups of scholars focusing on the competing use of forests are political ecologists, who draw attention to the intimate connections between environmental conservation and social and political injustices.[29] Forest policy and institutions are often geared toward centralizing control over forested landscapes, which contain minerals and other economically and strategically important natural resources. National governments also seek to control the hinterlands to ward off insurgencies at a society's political margins.[30] I build on the scholarship of political ecologists and historians to trace the history of forestry regimes in India, Tanzania, and Mexico.[31] Additionally, I address an important gap in political ecology literature, which pays relatively

24. Saberwal 2000.
25. Ostrom 1990, 2005; Agrawal 2001a; Coleman 2009; Poteete et al. 2010.
26. For such critiques of the commons scholarship, see Peluso 1992; Dove 1993; Johnson 2004; Ribot et al. 2006; Larson and Ribot 2007.
27. Exceptions include Sikor 2006b.
28. Rangarajan 1996a; Sivaramakrishnan 2000; Klooster 2000. Notable exceptions include Baviskar 1995; Agrawal and Sivaramakrishnan 2000; Li 2001; Haenn 2006; Borras 2006.
29. Colchester 1994; Baviskar 1994, 1995; Peluso and Vandergeest 2001. For a legal perspective on the problem, see C. Singh 1986; Pathak 1994.
30. Vandergeest and Peluso 1995; Roth 2004.
31. Prominent works by historians and historical anthropologies include Neumann 1997, 2001; Rangarajan 1996a; Sivaramakrishnan 1999; Sunseri 2005.

little attention to the domestic political processes through which subaltern groups seek to challenge unjust forestland regimes.[32]

Despite various gaps in existing scholarship, each type of scholarship discussed above draws attention to the role of the state in influencing the politics and the socially discriminatory outcomes of nature conservation. Because there is considerable variation in how social actors engage with the state, I develop a political economy of institutions framework to structure this inquiry into how the differences in state-society engagements shape forestland regimes and outcomes of institutional change in this arena. This framework brings together analytical tools borrowed from historical institutionalism, development studies, and political science with additional insights from the fields of environmental history and political ecology.

1.2 THEORETICAL FRAMEWORK: POLITICAL ECONOMY OF INSTITUTIONS

A framework enables a researcher to identify key variables, factors, processes, and relationships relevant to a specific inquiry.[33] It helps organize inquiries that rely on different theories for explaining outcomes at a specific analytical level (micro, meso, or, macro). The political economy of institutions framework follows in the footsteps of scholars who bridge historical institutionalism with rational choice institutionalism, thereby bringing together inductive and deductive methods to complement one another.[34] Institutional analysis is especially suitable for the inquiry in this book because institutions connect the past to the present, global and national processes to subnational political and economic relations, and abstract sociopolitical values to concrete outcomes that individuals care about.

The most popular definition of institutions describes them as "the rules of the game" that shape the "opportunities and constraints individuals face" in any given situation.[35] Studies of institutions have been instrumental in developing theories of collective action, property rights, environmental governance, and political and economic reforms.[36] On the other hand, some scholars criticize rational choice institutionalism for failing to account for historical

---

32. See, for instance, Ribot and Peluso 2003; Sundberg 2003; Forsyth 2008. For exceptions, see Saberwal 1999, 2000; Chhatre and Saberwal 2005; Chhatre 2008; Peluso et al. 2008.
33. Ostrom 2007; Schlager 2007.
34. Hall and Taylor 1996; Bates et al. 2000; Thelen 1999; Katznelson and Weingast 2005; Mahoney and Thelen 2010; for a critique of this approach, see Weyland 2002.
35. North 1990; Ostrom 2005, 5.
36. Olson 1965; March and Olsen 1996; Agrawal 2005a; MacLean 2010; Ostrom 1990, 2005, 2010.

and political contexts and the role that social forces play in shaping institutional outcomes.[37] A common thread running through these critiques of institutionalism is that this form of analysis neglects questions of power relations. Critics argue that while institutional analysis examines societal concerns that are deeply *political*, including competitive allocation of scarce resources via government policies and programs, it remains "distinctly apolitical."[38]

The political economy of institutions framework developed here goes beyond institutional analysis's focus on formal rules, and instead accounts for both formal and informal rules, norms, and laws that systematically influence institutional outcomes in the presence of significant differences of social and political power. The framework also accounts for popular politics and other mechanisms that are central to the articulation of popular interests in the policymaking arena.[39] The processes and outcomes of past political mobilizations, as well as the impact of state welfare programs, also influence individual and group responses to the proposals for institutional change. It is necessary to formally integrate these factors into institutional analysis (as opposed to considering them as exogenous contextual factors) since they reshape the preferences, expectations, and aspirations of individuals and groups of individuals, thereby fundamentally altering social and political interactions.

The nexus of formal and informal institutions, actors, and agencies is especially relevant for studies of political institutions, as political institutions are binding in nature and empower winners of institutional battles to impose their preferences on the rest of the society.[40] This is true of even the most successful democracies, but it is especially true in many developing countries.[41] Politically influential actors in developing countries enjoy gatekeeping powers, which allow them to ensure selective application and enforcement of the law to serve vested interests. Such abuses of the rule of law compel marginalized groups to develop defensive adaptations—i.e., the "weapons of the weak," informal negotiations, and clientelistic exchanges.[42] Over time, marginalized groups may come to accept these defensive engagements with political elites and political institutions as the "normal" way of pursuing ends that are critical to their lives. Such "institutionalization of the informal" acts as a diffused but depressing vector of power, which can be overcome only through large-scale and sustained social and political mobilization.[43] The links between

---

37. J. Knight 1992; Moe 2005; Teichman 2012.
38. Mulé 1999, 149.
39. In this book, I follow Partha Chatterjee's use of the phrase "popular politics" to refer to mass engagement with formal politics, including electoral politics, while excluding communitarian and neo-traditionalist populism. See Chatterjee 2011.
40. Moe 2005.
41. Harriss et al. 1995.
42. Scott 1985.
43. See Hyden 1980; Corbridge et al. 2005.

institutions and actors thus contribute to specific behavioral patterns, which in turn influence the expectations and aspirations that socially and politically marginalized groups bring to institutional arenas accessible to them.

Going beyond the dichotomies of cooperation and resistance, and the broad-stroke structural views of winners and losers based on the ideal-type expectations of the right or the left, this book examines the concrete ways in which colonial history, postcolonial developmentalist states, and popular engagements with the state shape land rights regimes within forested land-scapes, which are also the prime sites of nature conservation. The discussion that follows elaborates on three specific elements of political economy of institutions framework. First, I situate political institutions as important forces in and of themselves and examine the manner in which they shape prospects for institutional change. Even so, instead of producing a structuralist narrative, I follow the state in society approach of Joel Migdal and map how social and political forces contribute to the evolution of property regimes, policies, and institutions.[44] In the second part of the framework, I engage with scholarship on popular politics to theorize state-society engagements from an institutional political economy perspective. Part three develops the concept of the mechanisms of intermediation, which facilitate well-mobilized groups' articulation of interests within the political and policy processes.

Political Institutions and the State

Formal political institutions, including constitutions and laws adopted in the immediate aftermath of successful independence movements, create a political environment conducive for promoting egalitarian social, economic, and political orders.[45] Such progressive ambitions embedded in national political institutions not only motivate activists to pursue mass mobilization, they are also central to both the symbolic and legal struggles often witnessed in post-colonial societies.[46] Political institutions' transformative potential inheres as much in these institutions' statutory authority as it does in social and political forces that drive progressive outcomes in practice.[47] However, because of continued imbalances of political and economic power, most postcolonial societies have failed to realize the potential enshrined in their national constitutions.

How does one make sense of these two very distinct faces of political institutions? On the one hand, there are the promises of a constitutional

---

44. Migdal et al. 1994; Migdal 2001; Jayasuriya 2005.
45. See Randeria 2006 for an analysis of progressive statutes related to affirmative action included in the Indian Constitution.
46. Hertel 2015.
47. Crawford and Lijphart 1995.

democracy, and on the other, the rough-and-tumble of everyday politics dominated by power cliques, which often frustrates the actualization of entitlements for a majority of citizens. Contemporary theorists of democracy tend to argue for strengthening the institutional fabric in developing countries to bring them on par with Western liberal democracies.[48] This line of argument assumes that the imbalances of power, which make it difficult for ordinary citizens to realize their rights, will not undermine the development of robust institutions. Such assumptions are clearly misplaced. As Catherine Boone argues, the so-called "brown spots of democracy" in developing countries are not an aberration, but rather the result of the uneven distribution of social and political power within a society.[49]

The unevenness and Janus-faced nature of the postcolonial state partly results from the history of political institutions in developing countries. Dozens of countries in Asia and Africa secured their independence in the post–World War II era, a time when the states' control of the commanding heights of economy enjoyed widespread support.[50] One of the first proponents of state control of commanding heights was Vladimir Lenin, who advocated for the nationalization of valuable natural resources in a centralized state apparatus. Marxism-Leninism had significant sway in postcolonial societies.[51] Political elites in these societies justified the state's control over land and other natural resources by arguing that it was necessary for the successful execution of economic development projects, which were the central plank of postcolonial state-making. The institutions of centralized planning and budgeting further reinforced the authority and power of national governments and political leaders.[52] State-building efforts in hinterlands are focused more on the goals of securing territorial control than on building civic infrastructure and rule of law in these regions.[53]

Most analyses of territorial politics focus on cases where postcolonial governments seized legal ownership of forests and pastures that had been used in common by generations of forest-dependent people.[54] However, territorial politics are deeply embedded within broader political and economic struggles that vary across both space and time. In some cases, peasants and other forest-dependent groups stood up for their historical claims, and forced colonial and postcolonial states to recognize historical land tenure regimes.[55]

---

48. O'Donnell 1993; Diamond 1999.
49. Boone 2012.
50. Yergin and Stanislaw 2008.
51. Ruiz 2007.
52. Ferguson 1990; Chatterjee 2004; Baviskar 1995, 2005; Vandergeest and Peluso 1995; Robbins 1998; Scott 1998; Ribot and Peluso 2003.
53. Boone 2012, 629.
54. Sundar 2010.
55. Foweraker and Craig 1990; Sundar 1998; Guha 2002; Agrawal 2005a.

In the postcolonial context, the governments of developing states framed their massive centralization efforts within the tropes of welfare state, which included the methods of "enumerating, regulating, and managing a population."[56] National leaders used the discourses and techniques of welfare state to signal their intent to secure the goals of redistributive justice enshrined in postcolonial constitutions.[57] The nexus of postcolonial politics and territorial politics led to the "significant extension of state activity into new areas of social life."[58] The effects of this extension of the state's reach are visible most clearly in the hinterlands, where the spatial inequalities resulting from territorial politics reinforced intricately layered social, economic, and political inequalities.[59]

By implication, a proper understanding of the drivers and outcomes of institutional change regarding land rights in postcolonial societies, such as the enactment of radical reforms and their often patchy implementation on the ground, requires an examination of the modes and mechanisms through which different social groups engage with political institutions at national, regional, and local levels. This part of theoretical discussion unfolds in two separate steps: (1) addressing the contingent and multifaceted nature of state-society relations via popular politics and (2) discussing the mechanisms of political intermediation.

Negotiating Institutional Landscapes via Popular Politics

In liberal democracies, periodic free and fair elections serve as the main mechanisms that constituents can use to hold elected leaders to account. The hypothesized mechanisms of electoral accountability work through means of retrospective and prospective voting. In retrospective voting, constituents reward (or punish) leaders for their past successes (or failures), while in prospective voting, constituents vote for party platforms they would like to see translated into political and policy solutions in the near future.[60] However, as Partha Chatterjee argues, such a framework of democratic accountability is premised on the ideals of "individual freedoms and equal rights irrespective of distinctions of religion, race, language, or culture," conditions that are rarely met in the Global South.[61] Popular politics in most of the world takes

---

56. T. Mitchell 2002, 3–4.
57. Chatterjee 1993, 2004; Scott 1998.
58. Meadowcroft 2005, 7; Neumann 1995, 2001. Much of the research on territorial politics focuses on the contested relations between national and regional identities and insurgencies. Cf. Jeffery 2008.
59. Mallon 1994.
60. For detailed commentaries about the limitations of these models, see O'Donnell 1998; Przeworski et al. 1999; Kitschelt and Wilkinson 2007.
61. Chatterjee 2004, 4.

on more direct transactional forms and is often identified with clientelistic or patronage politics.[62] Such politics are often intertwined with political and economic relations that are part of local institutional niches dominated by actors and agencies that wield de facto power and authority. These specialized local niches, such as ethnic and caste groups, networks of informal economic activity, and local patron-client relations often coexist with the relatively open spaces in the realms of the state, society, and markets. Marginalized groups use these open spaces to pursue "everyday struggles ... to make a livelihood, sustain a social world and nourish a moral community of some worth and dignity."[63]

This simultaneous existence of multiple spheres of political and economic activity has yet to receive the attention it deserves. Actors who engage in radical demand-making when they are part of a larger, mobilized political group may find themselves outwitted within the localized niches of their everyday lives. The political economy of institutions framework outlined in this chapter facilitates an examination of memberships in multiple and overlapping communities, which has a number of implications for how individuals and groups of individuals behave in different but related settings. Thinking of individuals as members of a community does not negate individual agency. A multiple-memberships approach provides each individual with a portfolio of bonds and relations, but it also provides a variety of resources that individuals can deploy for the advancement of their personal, familial, or group interests. In addition, political communities, which actors in state and society forge by engaging with the "functions and activities of modern governmental systems," are central to popular politics.[64]

While popular politics takes shape within the "authorized processes of exercise of governmental power," its outcomes need not be limited to the "particularlist, contingent and . . . arbitrary resolutions" of state-society negotiations.[65] In many cases, popular politics creates opportunities for articulating demands for statutory and institutional change.[66] Even so, it is equally important not to romanticize the nature and scope of individuals' and families' agency within

---

62. Chatterjee 2004; O'Dwyer 2006
63. Chatterjee 2011, 150.
64. Chatterjee 2004, 3.
65. Chatterjee 2012, 306–308. This has been a point of major contention among the scholars of popular politics. A particularly provocative formulation suggests, "Chatterjee deems *impossible*" the negotiation and movement between "a 'politics by stealth' and a 'politics of rights' . . ." (Bénit-Gbaffou and Oldfield 2014, 283, emphasis added by this author).
66. Foweraker 2001; Gudavarthy and Vijay 2007; Baviskar and Sundar 2008; Avritzer 2009; Gudavarthy 2102; Corbridge and Srivastava 2013; Nilsen 2012; Chandra 2015.

wider social, political, and economic processes. Research about indigenous peasant groups in Chiapas, a hotbed of revolutionary mobilization in Mexico, shows that peasant agency represents neither the atomized autonomous agency often assumed by economists nor the militant activist agency that indigenous rights activists project onto smallholder households.[67] Similarly, Andrew Walker's recent monograph on Thailand's peasant politics, Marcus Kurtz's analysis of rural politics in the context of free market democracy in Mexico and Chile, and Wendy Wolford's monograph on Brazil's land occupation movement all provide evidence about the varied, contingent, and purposive strategies that marginalized groups adopt to pursue their interests within domestic political structures.[68]

The strategic nature of electoral politics means that the outcomes of popular politics are contingent on the bargaining power that political parties, leaders, brokers, and social groups are able to leverage. It is in the interstices of the formal and informal spheres of politics and society that peasants and other marginalized groups develop a constrained and circumspect agency that gains strength over successive iterations of mobilizations.[69] The next section develops the concept of structures of political intermediation to help examine the means and degrees of leverage that marginalized groups wield via popular politics.[70]

Political Intermediation Mechanisms

While the presence of competing interests and stakes is a universal reality, as classical works in economics and political science show, constellations of interests do not translate into aggregate social preferences that can then be translated into policy instruments.[71] The task of transforming disparate social choices into political choices and policies are accomplished via what I refer to as the mechanisms of political intermediation. These mechanisms are a necessary but often ignored companion to citizens' entitlements to civil, political, and procedural rights, which social scientists often consider to be the main determinant of access to political decision-making. Marginalized groups and their advocates often pursue several different means to represent their concerns within a political system. Some of the most important means include autonomous social

---

67. Eisenstadt 2011, 3.
68. Kurtz 2006; Walker 2012; Wolford 2010.
69. Bebbington 2005; Bebbington et al. 2008; Fox 1994, 1996, 2007; Johnson and Forsyth 2002; Newell 2005.
70. This formulation is inspired by Patrick Heller's research on "degrees of democracy." See Heller 2000, 2001, 2009.
71. Arrow 1951; Olson 1965.

and political mobilizations, as well as seeking the support of actors and agencies with significant influence within the political system, such as political parties and leaders.

The outcomes of state-society engagements depend heavily on the type of political intermediation mechanisms that exist in a society. This section focuses on the mechanisms that are directly related to politics, such as politically engaged social movements and mobilizations linked to political parties, since institutional change often requires political and policy interventions.[72] Scholarship on political corporatism serves as an entry point for this discussion.

Corporatism is "a system of interest representation" in which well-organized groups represent specific constituencies and are recognized by the state as such.[73] While corporatism is a well-established idea in the field of labor politics, the concept has often been used with a "pejorative tone and implication," especially in the context of popular sectors.[74] In her analysis of German labor politics, Kathleen Thelen argues that "centralized bargaining" and the codetermination of benefit through negotiations with local arms of corporate organizations are the core elements of a corporatist representation of interests.[75] When applied to constituencies with large memberships, such as labor groups or peasants, corporatist arrangements may facilitate greater participation and a fairer distribution of benefits for constituents with weak individualized bargaining power.[76] Seen as such, corporatist arrangements in popular sectors could produce equalizing and democratizing effects.

Many peasant studies scholars who examine the effects of corporatism in rural and agrarian sectors tend to overemphasize the amount of control that corporatist arrangements grant to political elites. However, such control is invariably partial and the balance of power within corporatist arrangements is often contingent on political context and the strength of grassroots mobilization.[77] The very fact that political elites in some developing countries have invested in setting up corporatist arrangements is indicative that the grassroots mobilization by subalterns compelled these elites to invest in corporatist arrangements that are costly to establish and maintain.[78] The type of political intermediation mechanisms that emerge in any given setting thus depend on the

---

72. See Heller 2001, 2009; Newell and Wheeler 2006; Heller et al. 2007; Eisenstadt 2003, 2011. In the "polity model" proposed by Charles Tilly, social movements-political party links are crucial to the movement's success. See Tilly 1978; Jenkins 1983.
73. Schmitter 1974.
74. Ibid., 86. For a critical engagement with comparative politics scholarship on corporatism, see Wiarda 1996.
75. Thelen 1991, ix.
76. For a similar approach used to examine the political effects of globalization, see Hellwig 2015.
77. Rubin 1990.
78. Rubin 1990.

balance of social and political power, and are a product of a complex set of negotiations between actors and agencies that cut across the state-society divide. An explanation of how the balance of power between social actors, elected leaders, and government agencies shifts over time requires a "dynamic" framework, as Jonathan Fox shows in his work.[79] As the balance of power undergoes temporary or permanent changes over time, political parties will change the way they engage with groups of socially and politically mobilized citizens.[80]

Cross-national analysis shows that "party system institutionalization" is highly and positively related to the representation of public interests, especially in the presence of leftist parties known for the promotion of corporatist structures.[81] Recent scholarship also underlines the role popular politics and party-linked corporatist and clientelistic networks play even in seemingly technocratic policy arenas, such as privatization of service delivery and national fiscal policy.[82] In addition to presenting evidence about the important role that interest group representation plays in influencing institutional and policy outcomes, analysis in the following pages also explains why differences in the strategies of dominant political parties influence state interventions related to the allocation of forested landscapes to competing usage. While it is important to retain a focus on political parties and leaders, I broaden the scope of interest group representation from party-sponsored corporatist organizations or highly structured labor union movements to include also the less structured and more diffuse mechanisms of sociopolitical intermediation.

Links between actors and agencies, which bring complementary sets of skills and political resources to the table, are critical to the successful pursuit and realization of progressive political and institutional reforms. A variety of organized groups—including federations of community organizations; social, cultural, and political movements; and networks of nongovernmental organizations—could serve as aggregators and organizers of group interests, as long as they engage with political and policy-making processes. The nature and effectiveness of representation relies on two main factors: first, the strategic contingencies of a political system, which create incentives for different political actors to compete for the privilege of representing hitherto marginalized social interests, and second, the presence of mechanisms of political intermediation that enable representation of interests at national, subnational, and local levels.[83]

A key difference between this book and previous work by policy scientists is the multifaceted nature of political intermediation proposed here. Policy

79. Fox 2005; 2007.
80. For detailed discussions of political theories of representation, see Przeworski et al. 1999; cf. Ribot 2004.
81. Luna and Zechmeister 2005; see also Collier and Handlin 2009.
82. See Chandra 2015; Hellwig 2015; Elliott Armijo and Echeverri-Gent 2014.
83. Chhatre 2008, 13; Fox 2007; Bebbington et al. 2008.

scientists often refer to a "policy niche" or "institutional niche," which facilitates collaboration among leaders of popular movements, political entrepreneurs, and supportive policy-makers to seek institutional change.[84] However, the actualization of entitlements and policy reforms through national policy-making arenas is often hampered by the entrenched power imbalances within local institutional niches discussed above.[85] Accordingly, the successful realization of institutional change on the ground requires local political mobilization and active mediation of policy implementation processes.[86] Such political intermediation mechanisms, which ensure the effective realization of marginalized groups' rights, are more likely when elected leaders and ruling parties are faced with strong political competition and have incentives to mobilize local political and state machinery for effective policy implementation. Additionally, this kind of political intermediation is more likely when the ruling party has strong grassroots cadres or can collaborate with socially and politically mobilized nonparty groups that can supply the grassroots cadres needed for effective implementation. The institutional and political contexts of the Global South make it impractical to expect that the poor or racial minorities will benefit from reforms based on a rule of law approach, as such successes are rare even in advanced democracies.[87]

To conclude, the political economy of institutions framework recognizes the historical legacies of colonialism and postcolonial developmentalist state. These legacies shaped the baseline institutions—in this study, national forestland regimes—but the evolution of institutions over time cannot be understood without accounting for the political mediation of competing interests and the stakes of key social and political actors. The political intermediation mechanisms that a society develops over time influence the outcomes of institutional negotiation within the political and policy-making processes. To account for frequent implementation failures, I analyze the linkages between the intermediation mechanisms at the national level (which are instrumental to legal and statutory policy change) from, and the intermediation mechanisms at subnational levels (which influence policy implementation).

1.3 FORESTLAND REGIMES IN INDIA, TANZANIA, AND MEXICO

Forested landscapes may seem like unlikely sites for bitter political and economic struggles, as they conjure up images of lush green landscapes teeming with charismatic carnivores and majestic flora. However, as the

84. See Grindle and Thomas 1989.
85. Cousins 1997; Joshi and Moore 2000; Joshi 2010.
86. See Elmore 1979.
87. Matland 1995.

Intergovernmental Panel on Climate Change (IPCC) explains, for many governments in the Global South, "forest" is primarily a *legal* category applied to large areas of land that may or may not be wooded.[88] For example, the Ministry of Environment and Forests in India defines forest as "an area owned by the Government, notified or recorded as forests in any government records."[89] Researchers have reported a similar process of arbitrary forest expansion in Thailand and explain this as a product of "methodological artifact."[90] Administrative or legal definitions of forests have their roots in the colonial history of India, Tanzania, and most other countries in Asia and sub-Saharan Africa.[91] Colonial governments' multiple interests—related to state-making, maintenance of rule of law, and ensuring a smooth supply of timber to meet their empire's material needs—led to state control of forestlands.[92]

By the first decade of the twentieth century, colonial administrations of India and Tanzania had set aside as state forests and wildlife reserves large areas of land that rural residents had used previously for subsistence, including farming and pasturing. Mexico's colonial history differed on this account. For reasons I discuss in Chapter 2, Spanish colonial rulers did not establish forestry or wildlife reserves in colonial Mexico. In this case, conquistadors usurped large areas of previously common lands, leading to the creation of Mexico's infamous landed estates called *haciendas*. This trend of land concentration continued after independence. Under *Porfiriato*, the regime of President Porfirio Díaz in the late nineteenth and early twentieth century, Mexico witnessed extreme concentration of land in the hands of selected elites and land survey companies. The effects of the *Porfiriato*-era landlessness and poverty persisted in the years and decades to come, including in the early years after the conclusion of Mexican revolution in 1920. The German socialist writer B. Traven, who visited some lumber camps in Chiapas during 1920s, found that "the abuse of [indigenous] workers, often shanghaied from their villages, reached deadly extremes."[93] Environmental historians have documented similar stories about indigenous groups in India and Tanzania.[94]

---

88. Watson et al. 2000.
89. In recent years, the Supreme Court of India has sought to redefine forests to their "dictionary meaning," but those attempts have been contested by the Ministry of Environment and Forests (Lélé 2007). For a similar discussion in the contexts of Vietnam, see Sikor (2006a, 623); for the Philippines, see Waggener (2001, 8); for Cameroon, see Assembe-Mvondo et al. 2014.
90. Leblond and Pham 2014.
91. For an analysis of the issue in Thailand, see Hirsch 1990; For Indonesia, see Fay et al. 2000; Fay and Sirait 2002; for a comparative study of Indonesia, Thailand, and the Philippines, see Fay and Michon 2005; and for an examination of similar land conflicts in Zimbabwe, see Matose 1997.
92. Baden-Powell 1893, 64–68; Adams and Mulligan 2002; Gomez 1985; Sivaramakrishnan 1999; Neumann 1995, 1997, 2000; Rangan and Lane 2001.
93. Joseph et al. 2009, 279.
94. Rangarajan 1996a; Sunseri 2005.

At the beginning of the twentieth century, indigenous and other forest-dependent people in these three countries exercised very little control over lands, forests, and other natural resources they had either lived on or utilized for generations. By 2010, however, rural residents living in the forested regions of these countries experienced remarkable divergences in the security of land rights. Land rights of forest-dependent groups, including agropastoralists, remain insecure in India and Tanzania, although India has made progress in recent years. In Mexico, on the other hand, peasants' land rights are far more secure, with the exception of southern regions of the country that have experienced ongoing armed conflicts.[95]

In each case, the status of peasant land rights in forested regions reflects a specific balance of social justice and environmental conservation. In India, the area of land classified as state forests went up from 40.48 million hectares in 1950–51 to 70.01 million hectares in 2010–2011 (See Table 3.1, p. 58 in Chapter 3). Nearly 6 percent of the country has been set aside as national parks and wildlife sanctuaries. Forest and wildlife preservation, as well as the acquisition of land by central and state governments for large development projects, have led to the displacement of a large number of Adivasis, a term used to describe nearly 600 of India's indigenous groups.[96] Of the 21.3 million people displaced by India's development and forestry projects between 1951 and 1990, more than 40 percent were Adivasis, who constitute a mere 8 percent of India's total population.[97] The Forest Rights Act (FRA) of 2006, which recognizes households' rights to farmlands and homesteads that had been included erroneously within the areas set aside as state forests, has been implemented poorly. By May 2015, nine years after the law came into force, while 1.6 million land rights certificates titles had been approved, more than 2.6 million land claims had been rejected or remain unresolved.[98] In a number of instances, forestry agencies continued to dispossess peasants from land they are entitled to own under the FRA.[99] These outcomes are surprising not only on ethical and legal grounds, but also because of the impact they may have on India's internal security problems. Violations of the FRA are likely to fuel further discontent against the Indian government and increase support for the armed Naxal Rebellion in the country's forested regions, one of the problems the FRA was designed to help resolve.[100] While proponents of exclusionary conservation might defend removing Adivasis from

95. Corbera et al. 2011.
96. Louis 2006.
97. Drèze et al. 1997.
98. Abhijit Mohanty, "Forest Rights Act: Issues and Constraints," June 20, 2016. http://www.adivasiresurgence.com/forest-rights-act-issues-constraints/.
99. Kumar et al. 2015; Read 2015; Ecologist, "India: 'Jungle Book' tribes illegally evicted from tiger reserve," January 14, 2015. http://www.theecologist.org/News/news_round_up/2713128/india_jungle_book_tribes_illegally_evicted_from_tiger_reserve.html.
100. Guha 2007. (MoTA 2014).

their land in the interest of promoting environmental goals, this argument is premised on the negation of a crucial part of the FRA, which recognizes the rights of village assemblies, acting under the statutory authority of local governments, to protect and manage their forests collectively. National forestry agencies have opposed these types of locally controlled conservation regimes, even though emerging evidence suggests that local conservation initiatives of the type FRA recognizes have been fairly successful.[101]

Tanzania—which has one of the world's largest total areas of territory under protected areas (PAs), equivalent to 32 percent of national territory—continues to displace indigenous pastoralists and peasant groups from their ancestral homelands.[102] Overall, forestry and wildlife agencies claim jurisdiction over nearly 40 percent of Tanzania's total landmass; however, as I discuss in Chapter 3, an equally valid interpretation of Tanzania's laws places much of this land under the control of the country's village councils.[103] More importantly, even if Tanzania's local governance laws vest authority over forestlands in the hands of locally elected village councils, the competing claims of forestry and wildlife agencies, backed by the coercive authority of the state, undermine local governments' authority and legitimacy.[104] Such contestations interfere with Tanzania's much publicized forestry decentralization programs promoting village land use planning, community forest management, and apportionment of income and other benefits from the lucrative business of wildlife tourism.[105]

Mexico's land redistributions between the 1930s and 1970s placed half of the country's agricultural land and between 60 to 70 percent of country's forests under the control of organized peasant groups called *ejidos* and *comunidades*, both of which I refer to as "agrarian communities."[106] This more egalitarian distribution of a country's forestlands has come under numerous assaults over the past century, but as the evidence presented in Chapters 3 and 4 show, Mexico's peasant groups and their supporters have defended their rights actively through a combination of social mobilization and political advocacy. Though scholars tend to focus on certain constraints Mexico's agrarian laws place on the exercise of household land rights, these constraints seem burdensome only in comparison to a benchmark of freehold private property rights. In practice, compared with forest-dependent people elsewhere, Mexican peasants enjoy far greater

---

101. Hayes and Ostrom 2005; Kashwan 2013; Seymour et al. 2014.
102. Data on terrestrial protected areas (percent of total land area) based on the World Development Indicators 2014; Neumann 2001.
103. Stevens et al. (2014, 19) use this interpretation of the law to suggest that 63 percent of Tanzania's forests are "community forests," which the government recognizes as such.
104. Wily 2001; Brockington 2007.
105. Nelson 2011.
106. Bray (2013) suggests 60 percent, while Stevens et al. (2014) suggests this figure is 71 percent. Other authors point to the gaps in the data maintained by the National Agrarian Registry. They argue that the percentage of forests owned by agrarian communities is greater than 80 percent (Merino-Perez 2013, 26).

security of land rights. For example, despite 11 percent of Mexico's territory being declared as nature protected areas (NPAs), the country has seen few cases of displacements and evictions.[107] Agrarian communities continue to exercise land rights in 95 percent of lands set aside as NPAs.[108] Table 1.1 summarizes the key features of forestland regimes in the three countries.

How Else Do These Countries Compare?

The stark differences in the history of independence struggles and the status of democracy in India, Mexico, and Tanzania may raise questions about their selection as case studies. Mexico's freedom struggle (and its agrarian revolution in the first two decades of the twentieth century) took the form of violent guerilla campaigns, while in India and Tanzania, nationalist parties spearheaded largely peaceful freedom struggles. These differences in colonial and postcolonial history significantly influenced not only the nature of forestland regimes under discussion in this book, but also the constitution of social and political orders in these societies. First, instead of assuming them away, these differences are part of the analysis in this book. Second, as Chapter 3 shows, an agrarian revolution by itself was not sufficient to trigger large-scale redistribution of forests and forestland to rural communities in Mexico. Instead, Mexico's forestland redistribution resulted from the ongoing power struggle between a relatively well-mobilized, emancipated peasantry and the competing sections of political and economic elite. On the other hand, despite the prominent role agrarian and forestry conflicts played in India and Tanzania's freedom struggles, forest-dependent people in these two countries did not realize the benefits of independence.

India, Mexico, and Tanzania also share some common political and economic characteristics. All three countries share the history of the developmentalist era in which the state shaped societies in profound ways. Although these influences were far from deterministic, political elites in each of these countries professed support for socialist policies.[109] These policies were implemented through local political machines led by the dominant political parties— the *Partido Revolucionario Institucional* (PRI, referred to in English as the Institutional Revolutionary Party) in Mexico, the Congress Party in India, and the Tanganyika African National Union (TANU) in Tanzania. The existence of dominant parties often gives rise to similar types of political-economic

107. Scholars of conservation-related displacements have often pointed to an absence of displacements in Latin America. However, no systematic explanations are available for this regional pattern. See Brockington and Igoe 2006; Igoe 2005; West et al. 2006.
108. An understanding of the differences in the strength of land rights that local residents hold in these countries requires a more detailed analysis, which is offered in the introduction to Part II.
109. Kohli 1987, 2016.

Table 1.1 FORESTLAND REGIMES AND FOREST-DEPENDENT PEOPLE IN CASE STUDY COUNTRIES

	Forested area (km²)	Percent of national territory under forests	Percent of national land under territorial authority of government forestry agencies	Number of forest-dependent people (in millions)	Protected areas (percentage of national wterritory, 2010)	REDD+[3] funding (millions of U.S. dollars)	Carbon stored in community forests (millions of tons)[8]
India	778,424	23.7	23.7[1]	100–300[2]	5.03	$717.5[3]	1,085
Tanzania	352,570	46.0	36.0[4]	35[5]	27.53	$93.5[6] ($46.5 disbursed)	1,268
Mexico	710,000	36.5	5 65[7]	13	11.13	$773.5 ($43.5 disbursed)[6]	1,440

[1] This includes the forests under India's decentralized forest management, which does not devolve substantive management or territorial rights (Sundar 2001).
[2] MoEF (2013, 28): "There are more than 300 million forest dependent people . . . deriving their livelihood and substantial part of their income from forests."
[3] REDD refers to Reducing Emissions from Deforestation and Forest Degradation. A detailed discussion follows in Chapter 7. Voluntary REDD+ Database; based on data submitted by members of the REDD+ partnership to the database. Available at http://reddplusdatabase.org/. Last accessed December 12, 2014.
[4] Ylhäisi 2003.
[5] Projections based on Felix 2015.
[6] REDDX –Tracking Forest Finance database. Available at http://reddx.forest-trends.org/. Last accessed December 10, 2014.
[7] USAID 2010.
[8] Stevens et al. 2014.

networks that link party leaders to local notables.[110] As comparative politics scholars show, the success of dominant parties in the electoral arena often depends on effective clientelistic networks, which facilitate the direct exchange of material incentives in return for continued support from electoral constituencies.[111] The three case study countries also have similar records regarding the core democratic concern of protecting political and civil rights. The Freedom House index, one of the most prominent measures of such rights, rates India as "free," while both Mexico and Tanzania are rated as "partially free." In addition, all three countries have exactly the same Freedom House score for civil liberties.[112]

While there are major differences in the level of economic development in these three countries, these differences narrow down significantly when the forested regions in each of these countries are compared. Researchers at the University of Oxford's Program on Multidimensional Poverty (MDP) report that the level of poverty among indigenous people in India and Mexico is significantly higher than the level for the rest of their respective populations. In fact, poverty among indigenous people in these two countries is identical to levels in sub-Saharan Africa, which includes Tanzania.[113] Mexico's data require a little elaboration. While Mexico is far richer on the whole than India and Tanzania, disaggregated data show a different picture. According to the MDP data from Mexico's National Council for Evaluation of Social Development Policy (CONEVAL), 33.78 percent of indigenous people live in "extreme poverty"—a percentage that goes up to 76.44 percent if one includes the percentage of indigenous people living under conditions of moderate poverty.[114] Mexico's peasant and indigenous populations are much poorer compared with the general population, and with regard to key socioeconomic indicators, they are closer to indigenous and forest-dependent people in the other two case study countries than they are to their middle-class compatriots.

Broadly speaking, the socioeconomic and political contexts of the forested regions in the case study countries are far less distinct than national-level statistics suggest. Even so, the goal is to contextualize the outcomes of interest to this study while accounting for specific features of historical and contemporary contexts. Taken together, the three case study countries represent the range of forestland conflicts and their most-often cited solutions, and demonstrate theoretically relevant variation with regard to key outcomes and explanatory factors. These features of research design allow for a contingent generalization of the study's findings.

110. Kothari 1964; Greene 2008; Magaloni and Kricheli 2010.
111. Kitschelt 2000.
112. Puddington 2015.
113. Hasan Suroor, "Media Hype and the Reality of "New" India," *The Hindu*, July 20, 2010, http://www.thehindu.com/opinion/interview/article523817.ece.
114. De Alba 2012, 11.

1.4 RESEARCH APPROACH AND METHODS

This book explores puzzling divergences and variations in forestland regimes through a theoretically informed comparative analysis. Analysis of variation in land rights within forested regions, amid competing claims of forestry and wildlife agencies, speaks to the larger issue of the tension between the goals of social justice and environmental conservation. Because peasant land rights are often considered "illegal" according to government records, an examination of land rights in forested regions demands a departure from the well-established methods of formal institutional analysis.

The framework outlined above relies on power-oriented institutional analysis, which helps guide an empirical inquiry into a set of politically salient and policy-relevant research questions. This framework helps draw "logically interconnected sets of propositions from which empirical uniformities can be derived."[115] Such an approach is well-suited to address questions that are often referred to as "wicked problems," which cannot be reduced to "optimal solutions."[116] A political and economic analysis of institutions focuses on the interface between the historical legacies attached to specific institutions, the effects of such legacies on contemporary political struggles, and the extent to which participants in these struggles engage with political processes to secure their preferred institutional reforms. In this vein, this book examines three different, but interrelated, institutional outcomes: (1) the divergences in forestland regimes because of colonial and postcolonial developmentalist-era legacies (macro/political economy outcomes); (2) the effects of subnational political mobilization on the demand for and supply of progressive institutional reforms, and their implementation in practice (meso/popular politics outcomes); and (3) the divergences in the national-level policies driven by international efforts related to forest-based climate change mitigation and the implications of these policies for the goals of social justice and environmental conservation (international/policy outcomes). A multilevel inquiry of this type, which spans across temporal and political-administrative boundaries, creates multiple opportunities for the triangulation of research findings related to a limited number of cases.[117] As such, it enables a systematic inquiry into hypotheses drawn from a carefully constructed theoretical framework.

Methodologically, I rely on a combination of contextualized comparative analysis, institutional ethnography, and policy analysis to examine historical and contemporary political processes. Political institutions, coupled with the agency of key actors, jointly shape institutional outcomes.[118] A significant

115. Merton 1949.
116. Rittel and Webber 1973.
117. George and Bennett 2005, 207; Hall 2008.
118. Statistical analysis of village level forestland claims in India, included in Appendix V, supplements the qualitative analysis presented in Chapter 6.

part of this study is based on a decade and a half of research in India (2000–2015), including twenty-four months of intensive field research and data collection from 2008 to 2013. The research in India also included more than 250 interviews with government officials, elected leaders, and activists in Delhi, Gujarat, Madhya Pradesh, and Rajasthan. To supplement the primary data, this book relies on two different types of secondary sources. First, I have culled data about the international scope of the problems regarding conflict-ridden forestland regimes from peer-reviewed scholarly research and publications from international agencies and think tanks. Second, I have traced the evolution of policymaking processes in India, Tanzania, and Mexico through policy documents, news reports, and published research.

The subnational analyses in Chapters 5 and 6 are situated in specific regions with distinctive sociopolitical and economic characteristics. For instance, much of this book's subnational qualitative evidence from India was collected from the state of Gujarat, which is counted among the more developed states in the country. At the same time, however, Gujarat's adivasi areas, including *purvi patti* (the Eastern belt) where my field sites were located, count among the poorest areas in the country.[119] In addition, Gujarat's adivasi areas are closer economically to other states with large populations of Adivasis—Andhra Pradesh, Chhattisgarh, Jharkhand, Madhya Pradesh, and Orissa—than they are to non-adivasi areas within the state of Gujarat.[120] In Mexico, I focus on forestland issues in the central highlands region with very few examples drawn from states such as Oaxaca, which has exceptionally strong community forestry institutions, and Chiapas, which is known for exceptionally strong political mobilization.[121] By not relying on findings from these two states, which are truly exceptional on key variables of interest to this study, this book maintains a focus on the less exceptional and more ordinary settings of Mexico's central highlands.[122] In Tanzania, the study's findings are based mainly on the north and northeastern highlands. Each of these regions in the case study countries is known for conflicts or contestation over questions of forest and land rights, even though they vary in geographic and climatic features.

The book's qualitative analysis of the subnational-level politics related to forestland conflicts relies on the tools of political ethnography.[123] A political ethnographer seeks to solicit insiders' perspectives by practicing a "deeper

119. Shah and Sajitha 2009.
120. Mosse 2010.
121. For an insightful study comparing indigenous mobilization in these two states, see Eisenstadt 2003.
122. As Peter Wilshusen points out in a book review, the problems of representativeness can occur even in studies that focus on specific regions within a country (Wilshusen 2012).
123. Auyero 2006.

sensitivity to actors' subjectivity and to social intersubjectivity."[124] He or she also examines how specific local experiences and intersubjectivities are related to forces and processes that connect actors, agencies, and institutions across multiple social and political arenas.[125] In this sense, political ethnography employed in this book is inherently multi-sited as it "cross-cut[s] dichotomies such as the 'local' and the 'global.'"[126] During my field research in India, I sought to uncover the meanings that individuals and groups of individuals, including elected leaders, attached to institutions relevant to their lives and livelihoods, while also examining how these multifaceted understandings of institutions shaped the processes and outcomes of institutional change.

As Edward Schatz argues, political ethnography entails a "creative tension" between the particularizing impulse of ethnography and the willingness of political inquiry to "bracket aspects of what we see, to simplify for analytic coherence, and to seek to produce generalizations."[127] Such an approach helps examine how political entrepreneurs deploy the power of symbols and ideas to achieve the improbable, as has happened in the political discourses over forestland regimes in Mexico, India, and Tanzania.[128] The method of multi-sited political ethnography employed in this book is especially useful for analyzing institutional change, which is often a result of the ways in which the formal and informal domains of institutions, agency, and politics intersect.[129] The evidence I use in this context emerged from interviews and participant observations in India and immersion and interaction with published ethnographic research from Tanzania and Mexico.

This book's reliance on secondary data creates the risk that important aspects of my case studies' historical and political contexts, which have shaped outcomes at national and subnational levels, are not accounted for properly. However, such risks are more likely in cases when authors take the context for granted, or seek to bracket it by choosing a set of cases they consider to be "most similar." Such risks are minimized in this book through a transparent analysis of the specific features of the historical and contemporary political contexts and their effects on observable outcomes in the three case study countries.[130] The theoretical framework outlined above—which accounts for

124. Schatz 2009: 203.
125. Tilly 2006; Baiocchi et al. 2008.
126. Marcus 1995, 95.
127. Schatz 2009, 306.
128. March and Olsen 1984; Gould 2006; Kubik 2009.
129. Kubik 2009, 133; Kashwan 2016a.
130. For relevant conversations within political science about "analytical transparency" and "process transparency," see Andrew Moravcsik, "One Norm, Two Standards: Realizing Transparency in Qualitative Political Science," The Political Methodologist. January 1, 2015, http://thepoliticalmethodologist.com/2015/01/01/one-norm-two-standards-realizing-transparency-in-qualitative-political-science/.

the contingent effects of social, economic, and political factors—enables the researcher to avoid known errors of interpretation and makes the research output "auditable."[131] Finally, I consulted nearly a dozen scholars and policy experts working in Mexico and Tanzania, whose names are mentioned as part of the acknowledgments, to ensure that this book's analyses of these cases do not run afoul of contextual factors specific to these countries.

1.5 THE PLAN OF THE BOOK AND STRUCTURE OF THE KEY ARGUMENTS

The book is divided into three interrelated parts, each of which addresses research questions at a specific level of analysis. Part I addresses the origins of and divergent changes in forestland regimes in the study countries. Part II analyzes the politics of institutional changes in forestland regimes in these three cases. These analyses yield insights about how the assertions of peasant land rights are embedded in significantly different understandings of state authority in the realm of land relations. Part III applies the broad argument about the political economy of institutions to the contemporary forestry policies and draws implications for the debates about the intersections of social justice and environmental conservation. The sequence of key arguments is summarized in Table 1.2 and discussed below.

The next two chapters (Part I) analyze the origins and divergences of national forestland regimes in in India, Tanzania, and Mexico. While Chapter 2 focuses on analyzing the institutional legacies of colonialism, Chapter 3 analyzes how post-independence economic development efforts shaped the emergence of forestland regimes. Chapter 4 shows that the differences in the political intermediation mechanisms in the case study countries influence the extent to which a country's forestland regimes reflect the interests of forest-dependent groups. Part II, which comprises Chapters 5 and 6, analyzes the counterintuitive outcomes of contemporary interventions related to institutional change in forestland rights. Chapter 5 focuses on the politics of the enactment and implementation of India's Forest Rights Act, while Chapter 6 analyzes the outcomes of formalization of land rights in Tanzania and Mexico. In all three cases, the actual outcomes of reform implementation differed from the outcomes that both the proponents and the detractors of these reforms had predicted. The contradictions between expectations and outcomes point to theoretical gaps in our understanding of institutional change, which this book attempts to address. The two chapters in Part III apply the framework of political

---

131. Ibid. For a discussion of the use of "secondary sources" in ethnography, see Pole and Morrison 2003.

Table 1.2 STRUCTURE OF THE ARGUMENTS

Divergences	Colonial Legacy		Postcolonial		Party-Constituent Links		Divergences in the Outcomes of Institution Reforms		Policy Divergences		
Key dimensions of forestland regimes	Forestry administration	Forestry agencies' territorial authority	Effects of national development on forestland regimes	Status of land reform in forested regions	Nature of corporatist arrangements	Bargaining power of peasant groups	Legal recognition of land rights	The nature of peasant engagement	Inter-bureau checks and balances	Participation of forest-dependent groups	Benefit-sharing arrangements in REDD+
India	Unified	Strong	Centralized	Not pursued	Fragmented and unorganized; Controlled by regional elites	Medium	Yes, but opposed by forestry agencies	Significant but defensive	Nonexistent	Very low	Tactically framed, but aggressive equivocation
Tanzania	Fragmented	Weak	Centralized	Weak	Unified with few grassroots organizations; strongly controlled by top party leaders.	Weak	Yes, but practically discouraged by the state	Weak; reforms expensive and undermined by red tape	Some	Medium	Equivocation
Mexico	Nonexistent	Nonexistent	Decentralized/ Devolved	Extensive	Extensive with numerous grassroots organizations; elite capture, but checked because of inter-elite competition	Strong	Yes, implemented effectively	Extensive and confident engagement	Significant	High	Unequivocal recognition of carbon rights

economy of institutions to offer critical scrutiny of contemporary debates on environmental policy and politics. Chapter 7 analyzes how the national-level political-economic context and the structures of domestic policymaking institutions affect the translation of international policy interventions related to forest-based climate change mitigation into national policy proposals.

The concluding chapter deploys the findings reported in previous chapters to offer critical reflections about the debates regarding political mediation of the equally valued goals of social justice and environmental conservation. It examines how the supposedly neutral concept of "property rights" is applied very differently in policy contexts that favor industries than in ones that favor socially and politically marginalized forest-dependent people. Lastly, Chapter 8 also reflects on the potential for extending this line of inquiry to make interregional comparisons beyond this book's theoretical focus on environmental policy and politics and its geographic focus on India, Tanzania, and Mexico. A key argument is that the two important goals of social justice and environmental conservation are often in conflict because of the manner in which state actors—political elites and government officials—seek to exploit forestry and wildlife conservation programs to secure political and economic goals that they value.[132] Such outcomes are a product of the skewed balance of power in society, a conclusion that speaks to the core concerns of Marxist political economy scholarship. Marxist political economists argue that the forces of capitalism feed on primitive accumulation, a concept that has been expanded recently to show how conservation programs foster primitive accumulation.[133] Others go beyond the Marxist focus on the exploitation of labor as the main source of primitive accumulation; they argue that contemporary capitalism also leads to accumulation by way of dispossessing peasants from means of production.[134] While the conventional argument is that the dispossessed masses would be integrated at the margins of capitalism, Kalyan Sanyal argues that the job of mitigating the adverse consequences of capitalism falls back on the state. To put this in the context of the political economy of institutions framework deployed in this book, even though political institutions do not necessarily protect peasants against dispossession, Sanyal would argue that a state interested in maintaining its legitimacy attempts to rectify the excesses of capitalism after the fact.[135] However, several recent works of

---

132. Consider, for instance, the demand by forest officials in central India that they be given authority to "shoot-at-sight" to control villagers agitating about increasing instances of tiger attacks in the villages adjoining tiger reserves. See Times News Network, "Foresters want powers to shoot violent villagers," August 2015. http://timesofindia.indiatimes.com/city/bhopal/Foresters-want-powers-to-shoot-violent-villagers/articleshow/48650795.cms.
133. Li 2010; Corson 2011; Kelly 2011.
134. Benjaminsen and Bryceson 2012.
135. Sanyal 2007.

scholarship show that instead of merely reacting to the aftereffects of neoliberal economic models imposed from above, legislatures in Latin America and elsewhere proactively negotiated the form and pace of economic reforms.[136] This scholarship suggests that postcolonial states are not only the passive recipients of external influences, but also that their political institutions actively reshape the forces of capitalism as they travel to the margins of the global economy.[137]

This book integrates the two political economy perspectives described above. It shows that the twin agendas of environmental protection and economic development, often pitted in opposition to one another, evolve in a relationship of mutual reinforcement. Moreover, the net effects of such reinforcement are contingent on the structures of intermediation in domestic politics. Such structures provide political spaces in which elites and mass constituencies engage in battles that are partially discursive and partially political-economic in nature. The global community recognizes these contentions, as evident in the recognition of land rights as part of the Sustainable Development Goals adopted recently by the United Nations' General Assembly.[138] Even more importantly, the text of the UN resolution makes it clear that the recognition of land rights is embedded within the broader agenda of sustainable development, which confronts us with the challenges of continuing to think critically about the relationship between the agendas of environmental protection, economic development, and social justice.

136. Coulson 1982; Kingstone 2011, 140–141; Ruparelia et al. 2011; Sinha 2012.
137. Gupta and Sivaramakrishnan 2011; Gidwani and Wainwright 2014.
138. UN General Assembly 2015.

PART I

————— ⌀ᐧᗡ —————

The Origins and Divergences
of National Forestland Regimes

This part offers an explanation for the origins of national forestland regimes and the changes they went through in the postcolonial period in India and Tanzania and in the post-revolutionary period in Mexico. Any serious analysis of contemporary forestry and forestland regime must start with colonialism, which left deep imprints on the institutional architecture of forest management in former colonies. There are rich historical accounts by professional historians about how colonial agendas and administrative structures shaped the legal infrastructure and the core practices of forestry management in each of the three case study countries. However, there are few comparative analyses of forestry history written from a political perspective. Accordingly, Chapter 2 explores how differences in colonial administrations' political and economic incentives and in their collaborations with local chiefs and leaders shaped the legal and administrative structures of forestry management in these three countries. These differences increased during the post-independence era in India and Tanzania. Ironically, Porfirio Diaz who became the president of Mexico in 1876 on the promise to work on realizing the liberal ideals of the constitution of 1857, ended up enacting land laws and policies that led to the dispossession of local residents.[1] For the peasants of Mexico life under *Porfiriato* was not any better than that of their counterparts in Tanzania and India who lived at the time under German and British colonial administration.

The development of a modern nation-state was the principal justification for the continuation of colonial-era forest policies in India and Tanzania and for the introduction of similar policies in post-independence Mexico prior

---

1. Negretto et al. 2000.

to the onset of the revolution in 1910. The politics of nation-building and national development is the central theme of Chapter 3, which explains the post-independence and post-revolutionary divergences in forestland regimes. The failure of the post-independence and post-revolutionary elites to implement effective land reforms led to land conflicts and peasant mobilizations. The nature and intensity of these mobilizations varied significantly, as did dominant political parties' responses. The differences in peasant-party engagements (the subject of Chapter 4) greatly contributed to whether or not national governments recognized and protected peasant land rights in the forested regions.

CHAPTER 2

⟡

Colonialism and the Transformation
of Hinterlands

Hidden beneath the serene landscapes of the hinterlands are complex histories of regimes of access to and control over natural resources. Over the course of the second half of nineteenth century and the first half of twentieth century, colonial governments in Asia and sub-Saharan Africa set aside large territories as state forests, a process which scholars have referred to as the creation of "*political* forests."[1] In so doing, colonial administrations ignored the land rights of forest-dependent peasants, which were established through conventions of de facto use and carried forward through the authority vested in community leaders. The extractive and exploitative nature of the colonial enterprise was the main driver of these transformations in the hinterlands.[2] In this chapter, I examine the variation in the institutions that British, German, and Spanish colonial administrations put in place for the management and exploitation of resources in the hinterlands of the case study countries. Although colonial policies marked a drastic shift in the levels of resource exploitation, native societies' precolonial orders also shaped the impact of the colonial regime.[3] While a detailed examination of precolonial political-economic structures is beyond the scope of this book, the next section offers a concise

---

1. Peluso and Vandergeest 2001, italics added by this author for emphasis.
2. Becker 2001; Neumann 1997, 1998; Peluso and Vandergeest 2001; Rangarajan 1996a.
3. For an examination of how precolonial authority relations shaped the colonial experience, see Gupta 2014; Mamdani 1996; and for arguments about how colonialism represented a clear break from the past, see Gadgil and Guha 1992; Peluso 1992.

introduction to the historical context of pre-colonial land relations in each of the three countries' forested regions.

2.1 AGRARIAN ENVIRONMENTS: THE FOREST FARM INTERFACE IN THE PRECOLONIAL ERA

The photographers of *National Geographic* often produce images of pristine rainforests that seem completely removed from human contact. In reality, few forests would be what they are today without some form of human intervention. The hinterlands in developing countries have long been characterized by a variety of land-use practices—they are "agrarian environments" with complex mosaics of woods, shrubs, and savannahs interspersed among smallholder farms.[4] Contrary to narratives that pit society against nature, agricultural practices and human habitation have often led to the enrichment of soil and the emergence of woodlands in otherwise arid landscapes.[5] In other cases, peasant groups' active management of fire and grazing created savannahs or other specialized landscapes associated with unique populations of plants and wild animals, including charismatic megafauna like tigers and lions.[6]

Despite such complex histories, some reductionist accounts portray precolonial landscapes in Asia, Africa, and Central America as "pristine" and idyllic, while indigenous and other forest-dependent people are portrayed as "ecologically noble savages" and "hunter-gatherers" who do not have to farm.[7] Contrary to such images, which are quite pervasive among conservationists, the people of the hinterlands on all three continents have long practiced agro-pastoralism and forest-based livelihoods, and also have been a part of trade networks and political alliances.[8] Access to forests in these environments was governed by customary norms, which evolved over time into culturally accepted local routines that were often imbued with entrenched inequalities.[9] In all three case study countries, forest-dependent groups also developed collective and household-level systems of land relations, often overseen through customary authority relations. Most agricultural activities were coordinated through this system of household rights embedded within patrilineal relations and obligations. In the "slash-and-burn" or "shifting" (all of which I refer to as "swidden," a term that is used internationally) agriculture practiced in the precolonial

4. Agrawal and Sivaramakrishnan 2000.
5. Leach and Mearns 1996.
6. Saberwal and Rangarajan 2003; Venkataraman 2010.
7. For a review of the debates about the ecologically noble savage, see Hames 2007.
8. Moore 1973; Hardiman 1987; Orlove and Brush 1996; Ruttan and Mulder 1999; West et al. 2006.
9. Mamdani 1996.

era, households occupied and controlled a parcel as long as they farmed it. In the case of sedentary agriculture, parcels of farmland were heritable, mostly in patrilineal forms of succession.[10] The often-cited "customary land tenure" systems of the precolonial era thus comprised a series of household and community rights, which were enforced via social and cultural norms and the hereditary authority of chiefs.

These systems were far from egalitarian. For example, preconquest Mexican societies—Aztec, Maya, and Zapotec—demonstrated sharply unequal sociopolitical hierarchies.[11] Mayan rulers controlled long-distance and regional exchange networks that linked the production and distribution of fine ceramics, jade, shells, and quetzal feathers.[12] Mayan farmers, craftspeople, and local leaders paid tribute to the ruling elites in the form of agricultural produce, corvée, and crafts.[13] Peasants in southern and central Mexico practiced swidden agriculture, which continues even to this day.[14] Conditions and authority relations were very similar in the undulating terrains of Tanganyika, where local populations also practiced swidden farming. Even so, by the beginning of the nineteenth century, peasants of north-eastern Tanzania had developed highly productive and resilient hill-furrow irrigation systems that were a key source of tribute collection by local chiefs.[15] The production of a surplus "worth defending," scholars argue, contributed to the emergence of chieftaincy in the mountains in the north and northeast Tanzania.[16]

Well before the German explorers set foot in the northeastern mountains of Tanganyika in the second half of the nineteenth century, local chiefs had been part of the trade networks fostered by British and Middle Eastern traders based at Zanzibar. The smallest chieftaincies in Tanganyika, such as the one in the South Pare Mountains, engaged in the Indian Ocean trade even before the onset of German colonization. The chiefs bartered food, ivory, and slaves for prestige goods such as livestock, cloth, beads, metals, and aromatic resins, such as copal with a robust export market.[17] These chiefs used cloth distribution ceremonies to maintain and expand hierarchies of patronage. By the middle of the nineteenth century, the central concerns of the political economy of the Shambaa people of the Usambara Mountains had shifted from

10. Håkansson 2008.
11. Flannery and Marcus 1976. Exceptions included the Zapotec-speaking native nobility in the isolated Sierra Zapoteca Mountains of northern Oaxaca, which was poorer and less fortunate, and their level of intra-group inequality was significantly lower (Chance 1996, 477).
12. Demarest 2004, 173.
13. Ibid., 172.
14. Evans 1990; Kleinman et al. 1995; Simonian 1995, 21–22; Faust 2001; Van Dusen 2006.
15. Moore 1973; Neumann 1998; Conte 1999, 2004.
16. Coulson 1982.
17. Håkansson 1998, 263.

tribute collection to competition over trade links, which "helped consolidate many a political system."[18]

In both the Tanzanian and Mexican precolonial hinterlands, the chiefs or local rulers maintained a fair degree of autonomy, which also translated into control over the surpluses generated from the barter trade. The state of affairs was remarkably different in Indian hinterlands, however, where the conditions for stable living and development of political economic institutions did not exist for the forest-dwelling Adivasi populations.

The relationship between Adivasis and the caste society groups that practiced settled agriculture was one of outright hostility. Adivasis were (and are) believed to be at the very bottom of India's social hierarchy, ranked even lower than the so-called untouchables.[19] Indian folk tales and Hindu sacred books portray people of forests as "demons."[20] These sociocultural animosities had roots in Hindu religious practices, but even more importantly became part of political culture. Kautilya, the legendary prime minister of the ancient Gupta dynasty (320 to 550 CE), condemned forest dwellers as troublemakers that could only be controlled through "bribery and political subjugation."[21] The hostility that Adivasis encountered, coupled with their social and political marginalization, often compelled them to migrate, which limited their opportunities to invest in sedentary agriculture.[22] Though they continued to practice swidden agriculture in expansive zones of forests around their areas of residence, most Adivasi groups had taken on fairly settled lives in forested regions by the nineteenth century.[23] This important change enabled the colonial-era rulers to exact taxes and tribute via regional elites, including some tribal kings.

Medieval-era rulers—including the Mughals, who controlled most of northern India from the early sixteenth to the mid-eighteenth century—co-opted regional elites by offering "positions of leadership, authority, and political mediation in state institutions."[24] The system of land revenue collection, known as *Ijara*, was designed specifically to encourage members of dominant farming communities to bring forestland under cultivation. Village intermediaries who brought one-third of the land under cultivation in the leased village would be appointed as the village police Patel, a position with far-reaching powers that we will discuss later in this chapter.[25] Thus, most Adivasi groups had been brought under the jurisdiction of regional rulers via kings or intermediaries who instituted a "regime of annual tribute and imperfect obedience"

18. Sunseri 2009, 14–16.
19. Doniger 2010, 37–39.
20. Bhaduri and Thapar 2009.
21. Thapar 2001: 46. For an extensive analysis, see Ray 1996.
22. Prasad 1999. See also Scott 2009.
23. Chaudhuri 2008; Hardiman 1994.
24. Ludden 1999, 105–6.
25. Bhukya 2013, 102.

from forest people who lived within their jurisdictions.[26] These included the Adivasi kingdoms of the Dangs in the contemporary western Indian state of Gujarat, Berar in central India, and Chota Nagpur in eastern India.

Systems of authority relations within forest peasant groups, with varying levels of organization, also were present in Tanzania and Mexico during the precolonial era. While Tanzanian chiefs had not been subjugated by external rulers until the arrival of the European colonial powers in the late nineteenth century, rudimentary systems of political organization were already present.[27] In Mexico, meanwhile, village groups in pre-conquest Maya and Zapotec civilizations in Mexico lived in well-organized communities. Among the Maya and the Zapotecs, the "landholding village" or *pueblo* was a key unit for social and political organization.[28] Precolonial Tanzania and Mexico were different from precolonial India, however, where regional rulers exercised significant authority over forest-dependent people. These differences in political organization had important implications on how colonial administrations affected the hinterlands. The next section examines the colonial-era apportionment of hinterlands in India and Tanzania, which is followed by a discussion of Spanish colonialism in Mexico.

2.2 COLONIAL CONSTRUCTION OF POLITICAL FORESTS IN INDIA AND TANZANIA

The webs of precolonial authority relations and political organizations (discussed in Section 2.1) were subject to significant changes as colonial rulers began to engage in concerted exploitation of these territories' natural resources. Colonial governments created institutions and organizations to establish control over territories and native populations.[29] The colonial-era institutions of property rights, in particular, relied on a set of theoretical constructs (such as "waste" and "wastelands") that ran counter to colonial notions of productivity and enterprise.

An influential discussion of the notion of "waste" appears in John Locke's treatise "Of Property," in which he outlines the labor theory of property.[30] According to Locke, "Whatsoever then he removes out of the state that nature hath provided, and left it in, he hath mixed his labour with, and joined to it something that is his own, and thereby makes it his property."[31] According

---

26. Sivaramakrishnan 1999, 44.
27. Feierman 1990; Maddox and Giblin 2006.
28. Simpson 1937, 6.
29. Lewis 1998.
30. See Rose 1985.
31. Locke 1690, Chapter 5, section 27.

to this theory, the act of "first possession"—by, say, the European pioneers who migrated to North America—amounts to investment of labor leading to the creation of property rights in nature.[32] Instead of being an armchair theorist, Locke was often out in the colonial field in his role as secretary to both the Lord Proprietors of Carolina (1668–75) and the Council of Trade and Plantations (1673–75).[33] According to his labor theory of property rights, it seems Locke should have asked his English peers to not encroach on the property of the American Indians in North America who, by their very presence in the hinterlands, must have invested some of their labor. Instead, Locke dismissed the prior claims of the Indians who had held the land in "common," with the following rationale:

> ... the provisions serving to the support of human life, produced by one acre of inclosed [sic] and cultivated land, are ... ten times more than those which are yielded by an acre of land of an equal richness lying waste in common. . . . for I ask, whether in the wild woods and uncultivated waste of America, left to nature, without any improvement, tillage or husbandry, a thousand acres yield *the needy and wretched inhabitants* as many conveniences of life, as ten acres of equally fertile land do in Devonshire, where they are well cultivated?[34]

The Lockean labor theory of property was thus premised on the presumed superiority of European practices of intensive husbandry over the lower-intensity practices of "the wild Indian, who (knew) no enclosure."[35] Scholars have argued that Locke's interest in mounting an "economic and ethical defense of England's colonial activities" may have prejudiced him against a fairer view of systems of resource rights prevalent in pre-conquest America.[36] Even so, Locke was not the first member of an elite ruling class to present a political argument in favor of appropriating land from people deemed to be wild and uncivilized. According to the ancient Hindu code of conduct outlined in *Manusmriti* written between 400 BC and 200 AD, the duties of royal authority include protecting the "sacred right of first possession for the people who clear the land, *even if they have taken use of the land away from others—for example, hunters and pastoralists.*"[37] Much later in medieval India, Mughal King Aurangzeb reiterated *Manusmriti*'s tenets on the sacred right of first possession when he declared that "whoever turns (wasteland) into cultivable land

---

32. See Cronon (1983) for a discussion of the similar ideas and ideologies that the early English settlers of New England used to take control of Indian lands.
33. Arneil 1996.
34. Locke 1690, Chapter 5, section 37. Italics added by this author for emphasis.
35. Locke 1690, section 26; see also Rose 1985.
36. Arneil 1996, 60; see also Tully 1994; Bishop 1997.
37. Ludden 1999, 79, emphasis added.

should be recognized as the (owner) and should not be deprived (of land)."[38] Over time, caste groups appropriated Adivasi lands, thereby pushing the Adivasis deeper into the forest, a process that continued well into the nineteenth century.[39]

Locke's prejudiced views about the forest, and about indigenous and peasant groups' claims to land, reinforced similar prejudices among the native elites and left a deep imprint on the nature of the British enterprises in Asian and Sub-Saharan African colonies such as India and Tanzania.

The Political and Economic Drivers of Forest Control in Colonial India

British colonial officers, with their prejudices against forest people, met a receptive audience in India, where agrarian caste groups harbored even stronger prejudices against forest people. According to the colonial adherents of the Lockean philosophy of value and waste (or the Indians who followed the tenets of *Manusmriti*), the "jungly people" who lived in "jungly landscapes" forfeited the natural right of property in land because they failed to produce its highest possible value.[40] British officials regarded much of India's hinterlands as res nullius—i.e., no man's land. The colonial administration set up a separate *baze zameen daftar* (wasteland office) in the late 1780s, with the intention of bringing "wastelands" under productive use and regulating local land relations. Colonial officials had little hesitation in enclosing such lands claimed by itinerant shift-farmers, hunter-gatherers, and pastoralists.[41] Citing the Indian traditions in which conquering rulers took over the conquered territory, one British colonial official remarked, "The right of conquest is the strongest of rights—it is a right against which there is no appeal."[42]

Even though the British were not the only colonial power vying to gain a foothold in India's economy, the British East India Company had a virtual monopoly over trade in large parts of the Indian subcontinent. Moreover, the company *ruled* a significant part of the country until 1857, when Indian soldiers rebelled and refused to work under the command of company officials. Following the rebellion, the British monarchy formally took over the reins of Indian colonial rule. Forced on to the defensive, colonial rulers began assiduously building on the "apparatus of rule" that existed in precolonial times.[43]

---

38. Ibid., 96.
39. Prasad 1998; Ludden 1999.
40. Damodaran 2006, 166.
41. Sivaramakrishnan 1999, 279; Menon 2004. For similar analyses in the context of the Spanish conquest of Mexico, see Melville 1994.
42. Cited in Guha 1983, p. 1884.
43. Gupta 2014.

This process of appropriating pre-existing political and economic structures for colonial purposes was fraught with contingent negotiations between the colonial administration and Indian rulers, including some Adivasi elites.[44]

The British colonial administration built upon the Mughal-era systems of land governance, some of which recognized peasant land rights.[45] British administrators, however, saw settled agriculture as a desirable form of economic development and wanted to promote it through amendments to existing forest policies. Consequently, these colonial officials dubbed Adivasi peasants who practiced various forms of swidden farming as a threat to forests, the hydrological cycle, and to the agricultural productivity of non-Adivasis who practiced settled cultivation in the lowlands.[46] The colonial administration used these justifications to classify large territories in the forested areas as state forests. This policy facilitated the colonial government's fiscal goals, but produced socially discriminatory effects. On the one hand, the colonial administration, driven by the objective of maximizing agriculture taxes, made tenancy rights in India's plains and valleys increasingly more secure. Yet this objective of revenue maximization also led to extensive timber logging, which required the centralization of government authority and control over forests and the dismissal of native claims in forestlands.[47] The net effects of these colonial policies were thus contingent on how different types of colonial property regimes fit into a sharply stratified Indian society.

A plethora of social, economic, and political factors went into the making of British forestry policy in India, which would become the foundation of a global ideology of forest conservation over time. In August 1855, James Ramsay, the Earl of Dalhousie and governor-general of India (1848–56), issued the Charter of Indian Forestry, which declared "annexation a ruling principle."[48] Forests, which were not under private ownership, were deemed to be state property. As Gregory Barton argues, from this "new legal definition of non-private land as state property (and later—nature as state property) grew the policies and practices of [imperial] environmentalism."[49] This forest charter traveled across oceans and temporal milieus to shape British imperial conservation policies across Asia, Africa, and the Americas.[50] The charter also influenced the design of a number of policies in colonial India, such as the Indian Forest Act 1865, the All-India Imperial Forest Service of 1867, and the Forest Act of 1878, the last of which gave the colonial government the authority to reserve any public

---

44. Sivaramakrishnan 1996, 1990.
45. For insights about the effects of the variation in land tenure system on contemporary economic outcomes, see Banerjee and Iyer 2005.
46. Rangarajan 1996b; Sivaramakrishnan 2009; see also J. Scott 2009.
47. Sivaramakrishnan 1999, 279.
48. Barton 2001, 531.
49. Ibid.
50. Barton 2000, 2001; Vandergeest and Peluso 2006.

land, including "wastelands," as state forests.[51] Note that except for some parts of eastern and southwest India—which housed tea, coffee, and rubber estates—commercial plantations were not a major part of British colonial administration in India.[52]

Even though colonial-era forest laws provided for "settling prior rights through negotiated due processes," they mainly functioned as a "*discourse* of rational, systematic, modern legislative process through which the modern state acquires proprietary rights in forests."[53] According to a forest official from the British-India province of Bombay Presidency, "the various government and private rights . . . should be absorbed into the system of Reserved Forests until only one class of government forests remained," under a "system of Reserved Forests."[54] The colonial forestry statutes were used to transform "wastelands" into a territorial jurisdiction devoted to the goals of conserving and sustainably harvesting forests.

In conjunction with these exclusionary forest policies, colonial administrators' racial prejudices prompted them to enact laws aimed to protect, control, and bring about the "improvement" of people of the so-called "wild races."[55] The colonial administration pursued these goals through laws such as the Criminal Tribes Act of 1871. Similarly, the Scheduled Districts Act of 1874 was intended as a process of "reformatory settlement to sedentarize [sic], protect, and civilize wild, unruly subjects of empire."[56] In 1890, the colonial forestry administration created the "Baiga reserve" in central India, meant exclusively for Baiga Adivasis who practiced swidden. As this reserve was created, the Baigas were asked to either settle down as plough cultivators or to work as laborers for the forest department.[57] Ironically, the efforts of colonial administration to settle Adivasis dispossessed them of their lands, with their labor rendered less useful in the confines of the reserve. This was not a coincidence, however.

As important as it was for the colonial administration to secure territorial control, securing an assured supply of labor was also critical to British administrators' forestry operations and their desire to conduct land surveys. Notwithstanding the supposed influence of the Enlightenment on European political culture, the visiting colonial officials relied on an ancient Indian system of compulsory unpaid labor called *begar, veth begar,* or *beth begar.*[58]

---

51. Haeuber 1993a:54; Springate-Baginski and Blaikie 2007, 34.
52. Tucker 1988; cf. Menon et al. 2013.
53. Vasan 2009, 115–16. Italics added by this author for emphasis.
54. Tucker 2012, 21.
55. Krishan 2005: 143.
56. Chandra 2013a, 144.
57. McEldowney 1980; Jewitt 1995.
58. Prasad 2006; Moosvi 2011. For a detailed documentation of dozens of types of bonded and unpaid labor from different parts of the country, see Nagesh 1981.

The burden of begar became so severe that Adivasis in peninsular India fled deep into forests whenever they had the slightest hint of an impending visit by colonial officials.[59] The British also employed the institution of police Patel (mentioned previously) to discipline peasants and to extract unpaid mandatory labor that colonial officials needed for forestry operations and various contingencies.

For more intensive and sustained requirements of labor, the imperial forest department relied on *taungya*, a modified form of Burmese agroforestry. Under taungya, the colonial forestry department permitted registered "squatters" to farm small parcels of land within territories set aside as state forests and cleared of natural-growth forests in preparation for establishing commercial forestry plantations.[60] The licensed squatters were allowed to farm small parcels or to intercrop within the new forest plantations. In return, they were required to contribute their labor for colonial forestry projects at highly discounted rates. After a forestry plantation matured, the taungya participants relocated to a new site.[61] In some of the large forest areas that required consistent labor supplies, "forest villages" comprising clusters of taungya licensees were established. More than 4,500 forest villages, where every household is a tenant of the forest department, exist in India even to this day.[62] Poor and marginalized Adivasis' grudging acceptance of taungya was "the outcome of an antagonistic relationship between an acquisitive colonial power and a threatened indigenous people whose reactions varied from covert resistance to defensive compliance."[63] The colonial officials also incentivized chiefs and police Patels to maintain a consistent supply of taungya and begar labor.

In places where this kind of political maneuvering failed to pacify the "wild races," the colonial administration relied on the power of paramilitary forces such as the Bhil corps in central and western India, who were composed of Bhil Adivasi soldiers led by members of the chiefly families.[64] The corps "freely hunted down and captured their friends and relations who continued to create disturbances, and brought them in for punishment."[65] The colonial administration used membership in the Bhil corps as a means to incorporate chiefs, their families, and other influential clans as the frontline of hinterlands

59. Rangarajan 1996b; Hardiman 1998.
60. The taungya system was practiced throughout colonial Asia and Africa (Peluso and Vandergeest 2001). A modified form of taungya continues to be practiced in Latin America (Larson et al. 2010).
61. Bryant 1994; for a discussion of taungya in Tanzania, see Conte 1999; Sunseri 2005.
62. Press Trust of India, "Centre Asks States to Convert Forest Villages to Revenue Villages," *The Indian Express*, May 2, 2016. http://indianexpress.com/article/india/india-news-india/centre-asks-states-to-convert-forest-villages-to-revenue-villages-2780435/.
63. Bryant 1994, 21.
64. S. Guha 1996; Skaria 1997.
65. Skaria 1997, 736.

administration. Such a dual political-military strategy proved quite effective at pacifying the Adivasis and encouraging many of them to adopt sedentary agriculture, thereby opening up vast areas of hinterlands for colonial appropriation.[66]

The constitution of the colonial forestry regime in peninsular India, which Arun Agrawal explains "relied mainly on [the] exclusion of people, demarcation of landscapes, creation of new restrictions, and fines and imprisonment" was unviable in politically active regions of the Indian Himalayas.[67] The caste society farming groups of the Kumaon region in the north, who also depended significantly on forests, mounted a concerted mass movement against the practices of begar. Farming groups' frequent refusals to cooperate and acts of arson against forest estates forced the colonial government to introduce reforms, and eventually in the year 1921, to abolish the practice of begar in Kumaon.[68] More importantly, prolonged agitation against colonial restrictions on forest use eventually forced the colonial government to enact the Forest Councils Act of 1931, which was designed specifically for the Kumaon region. This act gave the locally elected forest councils wide-ranging powers to set rules, resolve conflicts, and to distribute surpluses from local forest use and management, albeit under the close supervision (and financial control) of colonial forest authorities.[69] Note that the strongest forest rights were granted in precisely the same areas where caste groups enjoyed clearly defined rights to their agricultural lands.

The outcomes in peninsular India were different not because of an absence of resistance against colonial forest policies. On the contrary, Adivasi groups mounted a number of overt rebellions, but regional feudal lords and moneylenders, whom Adivasi groups considered as their principal enemies, became the main targets of these insurgencies.[70] Adivasis of central India also sought the backing of the colonial-era, pro-independence movement leaders of the Indian National Congress (Congress) to launch a forest *satyagrah*, a civil disobedience movement to protest forest laws. However, Congress leadership was distrustful of the consequences of peasant agitations, particularly if such mobilization spilled over into bourgeois representative politics.[71] The forest satyagraha of central India Adivasis illustrated these tensions quite vividly. An influential group of Congress leaders believed that enforcement of imperial forest laws was necessary for the conservation of natural wealth and the protection of agriculture.[72] They also believed that the severe restrictions the

66. Kauffman 1983.
67. Agrawal 2005b, 269.
68. S. Singh 1985; S. Pathak 1991.
69. Chhatre 2003; Agrawal 2005a.
70. Bates 1988; Hardiman 1987, 1994; Prasad 2006; Bhukya 2013.
71. Chatterjee 1993, 160.
72. Prasad 2006.

colonial forest laws imposed on Adivasis' lives and livelihoods did not constitute a valid reason to violate them. Notwithstanding such ambivalence by Congress, the forest satyagrah gained ground and turned into a radical violent mass movement by August 1930. At this point, Congress distanced itself from the movement, with a prominent regional leader reminding the Adivasis that "they were not fighting for mastery over the forest, but for Swaraj [self-rule]."[73]

To conclude, inter-regional differences in the recognition of forest and land rights by the colonial administration mirrored the balance of power within the precolonial Indian society. Relatively better-off individuals and households within the peasant communities enjoyed state privileges in return for their support for the colonial control of forested regions. The enforcement of forest laws via local authorities—such as police Patels and other village leaders, and political actors such as the Congress Party—helped protect the exclusionary colonial forestry regimes. These outcomes were driven, in significant measure, by the social and political marginalization of Adivasis and other forest-dependent peasants within Indian society, which is evident from the comparative analysis of protest movements in the hills of Kumaon and peninsular India. All cases of Adivasi rebellions that led to recognition of forest and land rights in specific pockets, such as the Bastar and Chota Nagpur regions in central and eastern India, resulted from sustained mobilization and violent insurgencies.[74] The colonial-native encounter yielded site-specific outcomes: natives' utilization of defensive adaptations (i.e., "weapons of the weak"), informal negotiations in some places, and the exercise of colonial military power in others. Notwithstanding the differences in specific outcomes, the overall impact of colonial-era policies in India, including that of the freedom movement, was to undermine the political voice of Adivasis and other forest-dependent people.[75] It was on this basis of discriminatory colonization that the edifice of contemporary India's forest regime was founded.

Creation of Political Forests in Colonial Tanganyika

The early period of German colonization in Tanganyika between 1883 and 1902 coincided with what the region's Maasai people refer to as the period of *emutai* (annihilation). This era was marked by epidemics, intense droughts, locust attacks, political upheavals, and plunder for slaves, foodstuffs, and livestock, all of which forced a large number of people to migrate.[76] Taking advantage of the exodus, Germans introduced a number of legislative measures to

73. Prasad 2006, 237, citing a regional newspaper.
74. Sundar 1998, 2009; Upadhyay 2009.
75. Bates 1988; Bhukya 2013.
76. Huijzendveld 2008, 394.

secure control of a sizeable territory in Tanganyika's northern and northeastern regions by the end of the nineteenth century.[77] These legal maneuvers enabled the German East Africa Corporation—founded in 1885 with commercial interests in mining, railroads, and plantations—to capture vast tracts of land. The company's harsh rule, appropriation of land, and forced labor policies led to much native consternation, forcing the German imperial government to assume direct control of Tanganyika in 1891.[78] Among the first German colonial administrators was Eugen Kruger, a professional forester who paved the way for development of German colonial forestry in years to come.[79]

Securing control of forests, land, and labor was the cornerstone of German colonialism in East Africa. While corporations and the colonial administration sometimes purchased land at nominal prices by paying off local chiefs or their families, most land was acquired through trade treaties with these chiefs. As Thaddeus Sunseri explains, the trade treaties also gave the Germans "the sole and unlimited right to exploit mines, rivers, forests, the right to exact tolls and raise taxes, to administer and impart justice, and to maintain an armed presence."[80] The colonial administration transferred large portions of the purchased and acquired territories to settler-owned sisal and coffee estates, though only a small fraction of these lands was ever actually incorporated into plantations. Eighty-nine farms covering an area of 37,720 hectares had been allocated to German settlers by 1910.[81] In 1913, production of sisal—a tropical fiber used in making twine and the German colonial administration's main export product—reached approximately 21,000 tons and was worth £536,000.[82] Even though German rubber plantations in Tanganyika eventually failed, the plantations left behind "islands of private land"—for example, in the riverine lowlands below the Usambaras.[83]

Arguably, the German colonial era's longest lasting legacy in Tanzania is the country's forestry regime, founded with the Imperial Crown Land Ordinance (*Kronlandverordnung*) of 1895. This ordinance gave the German colonial state ownership of all "ownerless" or vacant" land, which included all forested areas previously used by forest-dependent populations. The state in turn could reallocate these lands to settlers. The Wildlife Preservation Ordinance (*Wildschutzverondnung*) enacted in 1896 provided the legal means for establishing wildlife reserves and to support "sport" hunting industry for the Europeans, which colonial conservationists believed went hand in hand

77. Conte 2004, 101.
78. Hughes 1969.
79. Schabel 1990.
80. Sunseri 2009, 21.
81. Neumann 1998.
82. Coulson 1982, 44.
83. Conte 2004, 99.

with the goals of conservation.[84] By 1912, the colonial administration had established a dozen forest reserves in Usambara Mountains alone, leading to the displacement of Mbugu indigenous pastoralist groups, among others. The conversion of vast territories of land into state forests forced people to seek out wage labor opportunities at settler- and native-owned plantations. Groups that lived in the forests were subject to stringent forestry regulations intended to control swidden, fires, and grazing—all of which were seen as damaging to the forest ecosystem. In many cases, the colonial forestry department enforced the regulations with brutality.[85] In addition, the violent repression of the Maji Maji rebellion of 1905 made it less likely that forest peasants would confront the administration openly. Historians attribute this rebellion to colonial policies forcing peasants to grow cotton, the colonial control over copal, ivory, and rubber trades, and the very restrictive forest and wildlife policies that also undermined the authority of headmen and chiefs.[86]

The circumstances described above led to a gradual consolidation of German colonialism from 1891 to 1919, which in turn led to the development of a state-controlled forest estate.[87] By World War I, which put the brakes on German colonialism in Tanganyika, the colonial administration had created a significant territorial infrastructure of forest reserves and legal precedents to preserve its control of the state forests.[88] Even so, the presence of rival trade networks and a settler-led plantation economy meant that Tanganyika's German colonial forestry department did not enjoy quite the same level of territorial control as the British colonial forestry department in India did. Moreover, after the League of Nations removed Tanganyika from German control and placed it under a British mandate in 1922, British colonial policies in the region were subject to monitoring by the league. The Meru land case, a key milestone in Tanzania's struggle for independence discussed later in this chapter, owed its success to the limits that the League of Nations mandate imposed on British colonialism in Tanganyika.[89]

Under the mandate system, British colonial authorities were required to respect "native laws and customs."[90] In practice, however, respect for native rights translated into a system of indirect rule, where the colonial administration exercised control via local indigenous authorities.[91] One of the first concrete manifestations of this approach was the Land Ordinance of 1923,

84. Neumann 1996, 1998; Johansson 2008.
85. Vihemäki 2009.
86. Sunseri 2009.
87. Conte 2004.
88. Ibid.
89. For detailed examination of the case, see Spear (1997) and Neumann (1998), the main sources I have used for the discussion of the case below.
90. Neumann 2000, 120.
91. Mamdani 1996.

which put "native authorities" in charge of administering customary land claims. Even more importantly, the ordinance declared that all land in the colony was to be classified as "public lands" held under the "radical title" (or ultimate ownership) of the British crown.[92] The ordinance also established the duality of property rights institutions: natives' land rights were recognized as customary "rights of occupancy," while settlers' rights were recorded as (state-) "granted" land rights. Because of the complex genealogies of customary land rights, it is often difficult to defend "customary rights of occupancy" in a court of law. "Granted land rights," on the other hand, are often supported by government-backed documentation and are therefore easier to defend.

International advocacy for the conservation of wild fauna also built on the colonial land rights regime in British-administered territories like Tanganyika. In 1928, the Society for the Preservation of the Fauna of the Empire (SPFE) successfully lobbied Britain's secretary of state for the colonies, who, in turn, circulated a confidential letter with plans for the creation of an international agreement to protect wildlife in sub-Saharan Africa.[93] The British colonial administration in Tanganyika later introduced additional restrictions on local access to forests and forest lands through the 1933 Forest Ordinance, the amended Park Ordinance of 1954, and the 1957 Forest Ordinance.[94] The Park Ordinance was especially strict; it curtailed rights of occupants to farm land parcels situated within boundaries of forest reserves that colonial administration determined unilaterally. The SPFE leaders believed that as a "civilized" and educated nation, Great Britain was duty-bound to protect a "natural" Africa.[95] A preference for conservation was justified through "dessicationism"—the now long-discredited thesis that deforestation contributes to poor rainfall and drought, leading to environmental crisis.[96] A direct consequence of the advocacy for nature conservation was to reinforce the colonial administration's powers, as it presumed the role of guardian of wild flora and fauna. The colonial administration used this conservation discourse to further tighten control over native territories.[97]

Even though territorial control was a necessary condition for appropriating colonial surplus, it was not sufficient. As discussed earlier in the context of India, "scientific" forest management and the production of a predictable and marketable surplus from the hinterlands required the mobilization of labor. While forced labor, or corvée operations, were not unheard of in Tanganyika, the colonial government developed a localized form of the taungya (Burmese agroforestry) system discussed earlier. The British colonial

92. Neumann 2000, 120.
93. Ibid., 120.
94. Lovett 2003.
95. Levine 2002, 1045, quotation marks in the original.
96. Saberwal 1998; Mathews 2011.
97. Neumann 1997, 1998.

forestry department actively recruited peasants to live and farm in forest reserves so they could be employed on short notice to tend to tree plantations,
produce charcoal, and craft timber poles for the urban market. During the
1950s, when the forestry department expanded the amount of territory set
aside as state forest by a factor of more than fourteen, the department incorporated the taungya licensees into plans for the development of new forestry
reserves.[98] These colonial proposals were met with a mixed response from
forest peasants.

Left with no alternatives, forest squatters and the chiefs of Rufiji Delta
region sought to appropriate the taungya to their advantage. Over time, these
peasants and chiefs came to see taungya as an instrument to solidify their own
claims on forestland. The chiefs, who were addressed as the "wielders of cer-
emonial axes" because of their authority to regulate forest clearing, appealed
to the colonial administration in 1944 to issue more taungya permits in the
Vikindu and Kisarawe forests. In their petitions, the chiefs referred to the forests as "government bush" (*Pori la Serkali*), thereby indicating an acceptance
of colonial authority to allocate taungya licenses.[99] As the colonial administration sought to assert its control over the Usambara hills, Wambugus—who
were pastoralist immigrants from Kenya's Laikipia plateau—moved in quickly
to assert their claims by planting crops in newly created forest clearings.
However, these strategies worked much better for Wambugus with certain
levels of wealth, sizeable cattle stocks, and greater risk-taking capacity, while
poorer Wambugus were forced to accept the taungya model of farming without secured land rights.[100]

A much higher degree of internal stratification took place among the indigenous groups near Mount Kilimanjaro and Mount Meru, the regions in which
chiefs and their families had started growing coffee on their own initiative.
The educational institutions that European missionaries had founded in this
area beginning in the second half of the nineteenth century primarily benefited local elites, thereby reinforcing the socioeconomic differences among the
people of the hinterlands. The educated coffee-growing local elites did play an
important leadership role, however, as they were the first ones to articulate
the questions of forest and land rights within a broader framework of African
nationalism.[101] These neo-elites also successfully channeled popular discontent
against colonial regulations related to soil and water conservation, decimation
of former grazing grounds, and the appropriation of land for the creation of
settler plantations and forest reserves. The immediate targets of these multiple discontents were the traditional chiefs who, by virtue of their positions

98. Sunseri 2005, 611.
99. Ibid., 620
100. Conte 1999, 300–2.
101. Neumann 1998, 64.

as the colonial administration's local interlocutors, had been complicit in controversial colonial policies.[102] The forest- and land-related grievances forced Tanganyika's elite-led, pro-independence TANU Party to engage with local issues, which gave rise to a "local nationalism" at a time when Julius Nyerere emerged as one of the most vocal advocates of a pan-African nationalism.[103]

Economic anxieties in the aftermath of World War II prompted the colonial administration to respond to European settlers' demands for the establishment of a commercial beef and dairy industry in Tanganyika's northern and northeastern regions. Amid ongoing concerns about the land crisis caused by previous policies designed to promote settler commerce, the colonial administration relocated the indigenous Meru population living in Engare Nanyuki to the dry planes of Kingori (between Mount Meru and Mount Kilimanjaro). This relocation in November 1951 led to the eviction of nearly three thousand Merus, sixty-four deaths, and the loss of thousands of cattle and other livestock. In opposing the move, the Merus mobilized politically under the auspices of the Meru Citizens Union and networked with allies in Nairobi, London, and New York to take their grievances directly to the UN General Assembly. While the Meru pursued their case vigorously, the UN failed to produce any verdict on the case, and thus the British "won by default."[104] In the process, however, the Merus gained confidence to carry on with their struggle throughout the 1950s. Eventually, the territory of Engare Nanyuki was returned to the Merus in the years leading up to Tanzania's independence in 1961, in part because the landscape did not prove suitable for European methods of large-scale mechanized production.

Notwithstanding the Meru land case and numerous other protests, Tanganyika's colonial administration further tightened forest laws during the 1950s. The colonial government amended the Park Ordinance in 1954 to specifically prohibit cultivation by people who occupied parcels within reserved forests. But even while the National Park Board of Trustees wrote in 1955 that the Serengeti region was *"reserved as a natural habitat both for the game and human beings in their primitive state,"*[105] at least eighty-two Maasai families continued cultivating land in the region's Ngorongoro Crater area. The director of national parks argued that occurrence of farming proved that the Maasai had been "adulterated with extra-tribal blood."[106] Eventually, they were evicted through a combination of political maneuvering and coercion. The colonial administration signed a treaty with the resident Maasai, who agreed to give up their land rights in the area set aside as the Serengeti National Park in return for limited land use rights in the Ngorongoro highlands. But this

102. Spear 2003.
103. Sunseri 2007.
104. Spear 1997, 229.
105. Neumann 2000, 124–25, emphasis in the original.
106. Ibid.

treaty was signed by a dozen *laibon*, or traditional medicine men, who did not have the authority to sign the land away on behalf of the Maasai, a majority of whom have always thought of the treaty as a treachery.[107]

The eviction of the Maasai paved way for the 1959 National Park Ordinance (Amended), which the chairman of the National Park Board of Trustees characterized in the following authoritative statement: "Under this ordinance the Tanganyika National Parks become for the first time areas where all human rights must be excluded thus eliminating the biggest problem of the Trustees and the Parks in the past."[108] The ordinance also established the organization now known as Tanzania National Parks (TANAPA).[109] Serengeti became the first national park, leading to the establishment of one of the strongest wildlife conservation regimes in modern history.

The discussion above demonstrates that Tanganyika's forest reserves had their roots primarily in conservationist concerns, which dominated the thinking of an influential group of British colonial elites. While conservation was a concern in India as well, India's imperial forest department focused mainly on securing strong legal and territorial control over large areas, which were devoted to the production of commercially valuable timber. Moreover, India's princely rulers and regional elites collaborated to control local peasant populations. In Tanganyika, on the other hand, a number of factors prevented British colonial administration from securing unchallenged authority over the region's forests. They include the presence of a substantial settler economy, stronger inter-elite competition among Tanganyika's native elite, and the limitations imposed by the League of Nations mandate.[110] Despite these important differences, however, a large number of poor peasants and agro-pastoralists in both India and Tanzania were deprived of their means of subsistence livelihoods when colonial administrations consolidated their control over these colonies' forestlands.

2.3 SPANISH COLONIALISM IN MEXICO

Spanish conquistadors' first forays into the Mexican countryside in the sixteenth century were intended to capture land and natural resources such as timber, which ultimately depleted Mexican Indians' subsistence base.[111] The conquistadors' takeover of land, combined with the estate grants approved by the Spanish crown, led to the emergence of the landed estates in Mexico that

---

107. Nelson and Ole Makko 2005, 128.
108. Neumann 2000, 125.
109. Tanzania National Parks, "Corporate information," http://www.tanzaniaparks. com/corporate_information.html#2.
110. For the data on settler populations, see Lange 2004.
111. Melville 1994.

are often grouped together as *haciendas*.[112] Over time, haciendas emerged as "the most comprehensive institution yet devised for Spanish mastery."[113]

Day laborers called *peones*, who worked the haciendas, were paid either in tokens valid for purchases at hacienda stores or in subsistence farming permits.[114] Haciendas played host to a variety of activities touching upon the entire life of peones, ranging from baptisms to weddings to harvest festivals.[115] Hacienda owners also established an extensive network of intermediaries, often referred to as *caciques*, who managed the peones' lives. Hacienda regimes and exploitative networks of caciques are often singled out as defining aspects of Spanish colonialism, yet haciendas did not enjoy the Spanish crown's unconditional support. The interests of the conquistadors were sometimes at loggerheads with the values and the interests of the Spanish crown.[116]

The philosophy of property rights that the Spanish crown drew upon was remarkably different from the justifications rooted in Lockean property rights that colonial powers used in India and Tanzania. Although a detailed discussion of these differences is beyond the scope of this book, a brief summary follows. The sole authority for the possession of land in the Castilian jurisprudence of property in Spain and in pre- conquest Mexico was the notion that the land was being used for a socially productive purpose.[117] The same philosophy of property rights enshrined in the Brazilian constitution has been instrumental to the success of the landless workers' movement in Brazil.[118] Such norms made the Spanish crown's outlook regarding New Spain qualitatively different from British and German perspectives on colonial administrations in Asia and Sub- Saharan Africa. As early as 1541, King Carlos I declared that all forests, pasturelands, and waters in the New World were held in common. As the wealth and power of the estate owners multiplied during the sixteenth century, the royal administration in Madrid enacted laws to recognize the Indians' rights to town sites called *fundo legal*, which the crown recognized as *ejidos*, or communal property. The crown recoded these protections in *cédulas reales* (royal decrees), which gave legal protection to the establishment of new Indian villages called *pueblos* with sufficient lands for the maintenance of its inhabitants.[119]

112. Lockhart 1969, 527, refers to hacienda as a "scholarly convention." Similarly, Taylor (1974, 388) refers to hacienda as an "abstraction, tacitly taken to symbolize landed society and the colonial heritage of Spanish America."
113. Tutino 1975.
114. Wolf 1969.
115. Tim Street-Porter, "Architecture of Mexico: the hacienda" http://www.mexconnect.com/articles/1928-architecture-of-mexico-the-hacienda.
116. McBride 1923; Ankersen and Ruppert 2006.
117. Ankersen and Ruppert 2006.
118. Wolford 2003.
119. McBride 1923, 123–24.

The Spanish Crown also had material interests aligned with the protection of indigenous property rights. Though many Indian villages were part of the *encomiendas*—a royal grant of authority given to Spanish settlers to collect tribute from indigenous people—many others remained independent and functioned as tribute-paying direct vassals of the king of Spain.[120]

The crown's resolve to protect Indian territorial rights waned during the financial crisis of the 1590s, as Spanish kings began accepting payments in return for the regularization of estate holdings that Spanish settlers had occupied illegally. Even though the percentage of territories regularized in this manner was not very high, these policies created perverse incentives for conquistadors to indulge in land grabs and hope that future financial crises would force the crown to legalize their illegally occupied estates.[121] Economic imperatives drove the colonial promotion of intensive agriculture that the estates were well-equipped to pursue, but noneconomic factors also affected Spanish officials' ability to protect the interest of natives. For example, *milpa,* the swidden farming of maize that the natives practiced, ran counter to the crown's nascent efforts to protect forests, which were motivated by commercial and strategic interests.[122] In addition, familiarity with the pasture-based Castilian economy led Spanish officials to think of ejidos as village grazing lands. However, they failed to appreciate the idea that each village should have a "large stretch of wild and overgrown land," which is how Mexican Indians viewed ejidos.[123]

Perverse incentives inherent in Spanish settlers' methods for extracting natural resources, coupled with the conquistadors' ignorance about the true productive capacity of the pastures in New Spain, led to the degradation of these pastures.[124] Indians and peasants who were deprived of their territories, but were forced to pay tributes and taxes in cash, had few options but to rely on forests for additional income. The dramatic reduction in the size of Indian territories also led to the shortening of swidden cycles, which added to the pressure on remaining forests. In the middle of the eighteenth century, Spain's Bourbon kings recognized the threat to forests and introduced policies to secure control of the colony's timber resources. These policies culminated in a comprehensive colonial forestry law in 1803, which was intended to secure the strategic defenses that the crown needed to prevent foreign powers' access to coastal hardwoods.[125] The Spanish forestry regulations were designed to prevent the transport and sale of timber, not to secure exclusive territorial

120. Ibid.
121. MacLeod 2008, 222–23.
122. Simonian 1995, 36–38
123. MacLeod 2008, 222.
124. Melville 1994.
125. Simonian 1995, 37.

jurisdiction for the crown or its administration, as was the case in colonial forestry policies in Africa and Asia.

In 1813 the Spanish parliament declared that all lands (with or without forests) in the New World would become private property. This decree was intended to promote intensive agriculture and industry, to help citizens without property, and to reward the Spanish pioneers who served the country at home and in the New World. Communal lands used by Indians were excluded from the purview of this decree. Subsequently, oversight of forests was transferred to local officials, thereby foreshadowing "the principal course of Mexican land policy up to the revolution [of 1910]."[126] These colonial policies precluded the creation of a regime of state forests that was an important outcome of the German and British colonial presence in Asia and sub-Saharan Africa.

The Spanish crown's legal protection of Indians' rights is attributed to three key factors. First, while Spain's primary objective in its colonial territories was to exploit gold and other natural resources, it was not the only objective. The political goal of "extending the realm of the crown" and the mission of Christianizing the "pagan nations" of New Spain were also motivating factors. Second, from a purely fiscal perspective, the crown wanted to maximize the number of pueblos that paid tributes to the royal treasury.[127] Pueblos' relative stability also helped maintain the steady, healthy labor force needed for colonial commercial enterprises.[128] Third, neither the pre-conquest Mexican traditions nor the Spanish political system supported the Lockean argument extended by British colonial officials in India that conquest gave the conqueror full rights over the conquered territory.

Two key findings emerge from the discussion of Spanish colonial policies and institutions. First, contrary to the cases of India and Tanzania, Spanish colonialism did not establish a well-organized forestry service or territorial jurisdiction over forest reserves. The net effect of Spanish colonial policies was the concentration of social, political, and economic powers in the hands of local elites and intermediaries. The emphasis on de facto power of local elites, which persisted into the twentieth century in Mexico, has arguably detracted attention from a proper examination of the nature of legal infrastructure put in place during Spanish colonialism. The Spanish crown enacted policies that not only afforded legal protection to Indians, but also reinforced rural and indigenous communities' claims over farmland and the village or the town centers. Third, even though the Spanish crown opposed the traditional milpa system of swidden agriculture in Mexico, the crown did not pursue overzealous anti-milpa measures, as colonial forestry agencies did in India and Tanzania.

126. Simonian 1995, 44.
127. Gomez 1985, 1045–46, 1054–55; McBride 1923, 123–24.
128. Wood 1990.

2.4 CONCLUSION

Agrarian environments—the landscapes that dotted the precolonial societies in India, Tanzania, and Mexico—provided the basis for multiple types of claims on forests, land, and other natural resources. Such claims were tied closely into the local authority relations often dominated by chiefs or local leaders. These authority relations mediated local access to resources and allowed leaders to capture surplus from local production. In all three case study countries, the emergence of European-ruled colonial regimes amounted to a significant shift in the control and exploitation of natural resources in the hinterlands. However, the comparative analysis presented above and summarized in Table 2.1 points to important differences of institutional effects of colonialism.

In both India and Tanzania, the colonial administrations by and large wrote off forest-dependent peoples' claims to land and forests. Such an approach to territories previously used by pastoralists, agro-pastoralists, and forest-based peasant groups was not a mere coincidence. In both India and Tanzania, colonial administrators explicitly drew on the Lockean notions of waste and value to annex territory. In both these cases, the colonial administration justified the takeover of land on the pretext of improving productivity and conserving natural resources. Even more importantly, both of these colonial governments created and then controlled territorially defined and legally enforceable forestland jurisdictions.

The colonial forestry regimes in India and Tanzania differed in two significant ways. First, colonial forestry operations in India constituted a nearly monolithic forestry regime because there were few settlers establishing

Table 2.1 KEY EFFECTS OF COLONIAL RULE IN INDIA, TANZANIA, AND MEXICO

	Settler/ plantation economy	Colonial philosophy of property rights	Agency/actors with territorial control in the hinterlands	Regime of exclusive forest/wildlife conservation	Territorial rights for local communities
India	Weak	Lockean	Forestry service	Strong forestry regime	Not recognized*
Tanzania	Strong	Lockean	Multiple forestry agencies and settler estates	Strong wildlife regime	Not recognized⁺
Mexico	Very strong	Castilian	Haciendas	None	Recognized

* Except in the specific cases in northern India and the cases of active rebellion in peninsular India.
⁺ Except in cases such as the Meru land struggle.

plantations. The colonial forestry department, one of the strongest forestry departments in the world at the time, wielded firm control over the territories set aside as forest reserves, especially in the Adivasi-dominated areas of the hinterlands. On the other hand, forest departments in colonial north India faced stiff competition from the revenue authorities.[129] However, many of these differences have leveled out in independent India, as forest departments have tightened control over any areas that could be brought under the jurisdiction of the forest department.

In Tanzania, on the other hand, the landed estates allotted to European settlers occupied a significant portion of the territories appropriated by the colonial administration. The colonial forest regime in Tanzania was thus more fragmented than the regime in India. Such fragmentation was arguably instrumental in the Merus' eventually regaining their land, a situation that was unimaginable in India.[130] Second, while India's colonial forestry administration focused on securing territorial control for facilitating logging, colonial Tanganyika's forestry laws focused mainly on wildlife conservation. As I show in the following chapters, these differences influenced the forestland regimes in these two countries in the decades following their independence.

Spanish colonialism in Mexico differed from British colonialism in India and Tanganyika on account of the political and economic arguments used to justify colonial control, including the incipient recognition of the *social* functions of property. By abdicating responsibility for forest conservation to local governments, the Spanish parliament precluded the emergence of a strong forestry regime with a broader territorial jurisdiction. This can be explained partly by the fact that Spanish colonial regime ruled Mexico from the sixteenth to the early nineteenth century, long before the agenda of conservation had become part of "empire forestry" in the late nineteenth and early twentieth century. In another importance difference from British colonial practices, Spanish colonial laws in Mexico specifically attempted to secure Indian territorial rights. The conquistadors' and the crown's competing interests—coupled with the Spanish legal regime's acceptance of the integrity of existing indigenous landholding-villages in Mexico—helped protect both the political identity and the territorial organization of villages and towns in the Mexican hinterlands. This was especially true of places such as Oaxaca, where the Spanish colonists did not have a major impact.

129. See Rangan (1997) and Saberwal (1999). In addition, there were some instances of resistance in peninsular India, such as Bastar's Bhumkal rebellion and the rebellion led by Birsa Munda in the Jharkhand (Sundar 1997).
130. In one particular case, adivasi groups in central India forced the colonial forestry department to legally remove the Halon valley part of the landscape from the forest reserve that later became the Kanha National Park (Gaikwad 1995).

There can be no doubt that, legally speaking, the Spanish crown did more in Mexico than the British and German colonial administrations did in India and Tanzania to safeguard indigenous and peasant land rights. While this thesis of colonial difference proposed in this chapter requires further research, a group of sociologists and historians argue that "mercantilist Spain tended to colonize most extensively precolonial regions that were populous and highly developed . . . liberal Britain tended to colonize most extensively precolonial regions that were sparsely populated and underdeveloped . . ."[131] From the vantage point of indigenous and forest-dependent groups, Spanish colonialism left a *relatively* less constraining institutional legacy, compared with the former British colonies, which inherited a legacy of state-led landlordism in the hinterlands.

131. Lange et al. 2006.

ᴄᴠᴚ

Politics of "Development" and National Forestland Regimes

In the final days of European colonialism in Africa, imperial governments acted swiftly to create new forests and wildlife reserves, which led to a "postwar conservation boom."[1] European and American conservationists believed that the only way to save African wildlife from extinction was to create "strict nature reserves" following the recommendations of the 1933 London Convention on the Conservation of Fauna and Flora.[2] In general, European conservationists feared for the future of forests and wildlife in the developing countries that secured independence in the 1950s and 1960s.[3] They believed that newly independent governments were likely to succumb to populist nationalism and give away forests full of a rich diversity of flora and fauna to land-hungry peasants. The condition of land scarcity and poverty in the case study countries at the time would suggest a cause for concern.

When India became independent in 1947, per capita rural landholding stood at 0.92 acre, while more than 60 percent of rural households were either landless or owned land parcels of less than 2.5 acres.[4] Tanzania, meanwhile, might seem like a country with a relative abundance of land, but large areas of its land had been incorporated into colonial plantations and wildlife reserves. Mexico had made great progress on promoting more equitable land

---

1. Neumann 2002.
2. Rogers 2002, 17. Following the independence of the majority of African states, the African Convention on the Conservation of Nature and Natural Resources, signed in Algiers on September 15, 1968, replaced the 1933 London Convention (Klemm and Shine. 1993).
3. Nash 2014 (1967).
4. Haeuber 1993b, 491.

Table 3.1 CHANGES IN LAND UTILIZATION IN INDIA (IN MILLIONS OF HECTARES)

Land use classification	1950–51	1960–61	1970–71	1980–81	1990–91	2000–01	2010–11
Geographical area	328.73	328.73	328.73	328.73	328.73	328.73	328.73
Reporting area for land Utilization statistics (1 to 5)	284.32	298.46	303.75	304.16	304.86	305.19	305.9
Forest	40.48	54.05	63.83	67.46	67.81	69.84	70.01
Not available for cultivation	47.52	50.75	44.61	39.55	40.48	41.23	43.58
Other uncultivated land excluding fallow land	49.45	37.64	35.13	32.31	30.22	27.74	26.16
Fallow lands	28.12	22.82	19.33	24.55	23.37	25.04	24.6
Net area sown	118.75	133.2	140.86	140.29	143	141.34	141.56

Notes: "Other Uncultivated Land" includes two major categories of village common lands: "Permanent Pasture and Other Grazing Land" and "Culturable Waste Land," which is the land available for cultivation, but not cultivated for the last 5 or more years.
Source: Government of India (2014).

distribution since the revolution of 1910, when 0.2 percent of the landowners held 87 percent of the land and 95 percent of rural households were landless.[5] However, according to Mexican conservationists, the country's land redistributions posed a serious threat to its forests.[6]

While each of these countries witnessed deforestation during the period from 1950s through 1980s, most of it was due to the clear-felling of natural forests to make way for commercial plantations and the clearing of land for mega-development projects deemed to be of national interest. Peasant agriculture did not contribute significantly to decimation of forests and wildlife in these countries. At the same time, both India and Tanzania brought large areas of land under the legal category of state forests during this period. Between the early 1960s and 2010, India increased the size of its state forests by nearly 30 percent (see Table 3.1). In Tanzania, meanwhile, an unbelievable 40 percent of the country's landmass is designated as state forests and wildlife reserves. On the other hand, Mexico has redistributed more than 60 percent of its forests to poor peasants.[7] Contrary to the fears that such redistribution

5. Bray 2013, 39; see also Thiesenhusen 1995.
6. Klooster 2003.
7. The estimates vary between 60 percent and 85 percent, possibly because how different authors define "forest."

would lead to decimation of natural wealth, Mexico's community forestry program, which is protected by the statute, is counted among the world's most successful forest conservation programs.[8] The evidence from these case study countries shows that conservationists' fears that populist post-independence land redistributions would lead to the decimation of forests have proven to be unfounded. Governments did not redistribute forestlands in India and Tanzania, and in Mexico, land redistributions did not lead to large-scale clearing of forests.

What explains these counterintuitive outcomes? This chapter demonstrates that the allocation of property rights in the hinterlands is deeply intertwined with the contested meanings and politics of development. I build on previous scholarship to offer a two-fold view of development. "Small" rural development is comprised of state-led social welfare and rural development programs (Section 3.1), while "big" national development (industrial infrastructure, etc.) relies significantly on resources extracted from the hinterlands (Section 3.2). Moreover, I show that developing country leaders have adopted international conservation as an important "development project" that serves specific political and economic goals. The effects of this strategic and instrumental use of conservation projects are contingent on the political context and the extent of peasant mobilization in different countries (Section 3.3).

3.1 LOCAL DEVELOPMENT AND PEASANT WELFARE IN FORESTED REGIONS

The definition and pursuit of development is inherently political. This is particularly true in the hinterlands, where states are often the primary owners of land and other natural resources. Conventional debates pit preservation of the environment against society's pursuit of poverty alleviation and economic development more generally. Departing from these debates, scholars focusing on the politics of natural resources show that the tensions between economic development and the environment are mediated politically.[9] I build on these arguments to show that political elites often use international support for environmental conservation as a strategic tool to pursue their preferred economic and political goals.[10] Furthermore, I argue that the potential for government's strategic and instrumental use of conservation resources to help forest-dependent people and the environment depends on the social and political context within which "development" is negotiated.

---

8. Bray et al. 2005; Bray 2013.
9. Saberwal 1999; Chhatre and Saberwal 2006; Hochstetler and Keck 2007; Bauer 2006; Martinez-Alier 2014.
10. For a related argument, see Ascher 1999.

The Politics of Local Development in India's Hinterlands

Adivasis and other forest-dependent people had a difficult relationship with the Congress Party that spearheaded the mass movement for India's independence, as discussed in Chapter 2. India's first prime minister, Jawaharlal Nehru, acknowledged this tension in his speech at a 1952 Scheduled Tribes and Scheduled Areas Conference. He said that the struggle for freedom was a "great liberating force . . . [but] this experience of hundreds of millions of Indian people was not shared by the tribal folk."[11] While the questions of forest and land rights were part of Nehru's famed *Panchsheel* ("Five Commandments") for tribal development, his ideas about Adivasi development were rooted in a rather simplistic binary of culture versus development.[12] Nehru once told a gathering of Adivasis, "Your old customs and habits are good. We want that they should survive, but at the same time we want that you should be educated and should do your part in the welfare of our country."[13] As the chief architect of the nascent Indian state, Nehru thus promised to protect Adivasi culture in return for persuading Adivasis to "do their part" for the sake of the nation.

The cultural framing of the questions of Adivasi development had several important consequences. First, the privileging of cultural aspects over agriculture and economic development reinforced the patronizing and racialized discourses of protectionism first instituted by the British colonial administration.[14] The colonial-era classification of "backward areas" reappeared in independent India in the form of "scheduled areas"—Adivasi areas that colonial administration governed via the Scheduled Districts Act of 1874. The racially prejudiced colonial-era anthropological research continued through government research institutes established in post-independence India.[15] Second, the government created "income-generation" activities—such as goat-keeping, poultry, and tribal handicrafts—for the stereotyped "backward" Adivasis. The insensitive behavior of bureaucrats, who took their own social and cultural superiority for granted, further marred development programs and normalized petty corruption.[16] Gandhian-inspired social workers sought to "uplift" Adivasis out of their primitive habits that ran contrary to Gandhian values of vegetarianism, abstaining from alcohol, and sexual abstinence.[17] The

11. Nehru 1967.
12. Hardiman 1996.
13. Balmiki Prasad Singh http://www.balmikiprasadsingh.com/Articles/Jawahar_Lal_Nehru.pdf.
14. Corbridge 1988; Chandra 2013a.
15. Bates 1988; Debnath 1999; Rycroft and Dasgupta 2011.
16. Bates 1988; Shah et al. 1998; see also Sainath 1996.
17. Omvedt 2006.

third, and perhaps most important, effect of a cultural framing of the Adivasi question was a total neglect of land reforms in forested regions.

Congress Party leaders used the rhetoric of land reforms to maintain their legitimacy among poor peasants, but in practice, neglected the agenda of land reforms among the Adivasis. Nehru made use of the colonial-era laws related to preventive detention to have leaders of Adivasi land rights movements arrested.[18] Indira Gandhi, who had three terms as Indian prime minister in the period between 1966 and 1984 and was the most populist leader India has produced thus far, argued that land reforms embodied "the most crucial test which our political system must pass in order to survive."[19] Notwithstanding such pronouncements, land reforms were implemented poorly in general, and were entirely neglected in forested areas. As a result, the proportion of Adivasis whom the census identified as cultivators decreased from 68 to 57.5 percent between the first five-year plan period (1951–56) and the fourth (1969–74).[20] Even in states such as Kerala and West Bengal, which implemented agrarian land reforms relatively effectively, the question of forest land conflicts remained unresolved and was even aggravated.[21] The complete failure of land reforms in India's forested regions prompted sociologist Nandini Sundar to characterize the ideological bearings of post-independence India as "property-less socialism."[22] Consequently, forest-dependent people faced dramatically restricted economic opportunities due to lack of land rights, lack of control over forests and other natural resources, poor educational and health facilities, and poor infrastructure in the forested regions. In effect, these policies rendered Adivasis and other marginalized groups as footloose laborers with no economic and political bargaining power.[23]

The peculiar geography of Adivasi habitations, which make them a minority in most of the political constituencies where they live, is one of the main reasons why Adivasis have failed to mount an effective challenge.[24] These multiple constraints have prevented representation of Adivasis and other forest-dependent groups in corporate governance, print and electronic media, and even higher education.[25] The voices of India's poorest people have thus been

18. See Rahul Banerjee, "The Elusive Right to Livelihood," April 29, 2015. http://anar-kali.blogspot.com/2015/04/the-elusive-right-to-livelihood.html.
19. K. Venkatasubramanian, *Planning Commission - Government of India*, n.d., http://planningcommission.nic.in/reports/articles/venka/index.php?repts=m-land.htm.
20. Bates 1988, 242.
21. Bijoy and Raman 2003; Damodaran 2006; Bakshi 2008; Sreerekha 2010.
22. Sundar 2009, 12.
23. Mosse et al. 2002. Baviskar 2004; Mosse 2010.
24. Xaxa 1999, 2001. The Indian state has been reasonably effective at suppressing the challenges that ultra-left guerillas have launched in the form of various Naxalite and Maoist rebellions, even though these conflicts continue even to this day in India's forested heartlands.
25. Robin Jeffrey, "Missing from the Indian newsroom," *The Hindu*, New Delhi, April 9, 2012.

missing from national and state-level policy making processes. The lack of representation of marginalized people, including Adivasis, means the middle classes and political elites shape public opinion about models of economic development that favor the landed and the salaried classes. While activist groups have worked for decades to mobilize socially and politically marginalized groups, including on questions of forest and land rights, these efforts have succeeded only partially, as I discuss in Chapter 4.

Tanzania: Social Stratification in the Home of African Brotherhood

Tanzania's post-independence government—led by the TANU political party and its successor, Chama Cha Mapanduzi (CCM, "Party of the Revolution")— enjoyed a very high level of legitimacy because of the party's role in freedom struggle. Tanzania's first president (and TANU leader) Julius Nyerere emphasized rural development as "the whole strategy of growth—the approach to development, and the prism through which all policies are seen, judged, and given priority."[26] TANU's post-independence policies thus reflected an unwritten social contract rooted in the history of its freedom struggle.[27] Even so, it was not a contract among equals. Nyerere was addressed affectionately as *Mwalimu* ("the teacher") and commanded significant respect, even reverence, across class and ethnic divides. In the Arusha Declaration and TANU's Policy on Socialism and Self-Reliance of 1967, Nyerere outlined the doctrine of *Ujamaa*, or African socialism, defined as the "familyhood and communalism of traditional African society."[28] However, instead of leading to the broad-based economic and political advancement of Tanzanian peasants, Nyerere's socialism produced highly differentiated effects.

Consider the villagization program, arguably the most important of Nyerere's initiatives, which led to the resettlement of nearly 70 percent of the country's entire rural population (an estimated five million people) into centralized Ujamaa villages.[29] A presidential circular of 1969 instructed government departments to direct spending to Ujamaa villages so that peasants willing to move to planned villages stood a "much greater chance of getting a water supply, or a school, or some land in a forest reserve, or whatever they

---

26. Nyerere 1979, 9 cited in S. Fox 2013, 25. Nyerere explicitly de-emphasized the role of industrial and urban development on the ground that a majority of people lived in rural areas (Coulson 1982, 177).
27. Havnevik and Hårsmar 1999.
28. Ibhawoh and Dibua 2003, 62; Hyden 1980; Coulson 1982. For comparable arguments in the Indian context, see Chatterjee 2004, 32–40.
29. Sachedina 2008, 110.

wanted."[30] The program increasingly relied on forced and violent relocations by the mid-1970s. A World Bank report also justified forced villagization, with the idea that Tanzanian peasants could be "required to abide by the rules and to adopt new practices as a condition of receiving new land."[31] In the end, however, the villagization program failed to achieve its main goal of improving the productivity of smallholder agriculture, although it did marginally improve the provision of public services.[32]

But as development studies scholars argue, even apparently failed interventions such as villagization can engender significant social and political consequences.[33] For example, the Villages and Ujamaa Villages Act of 1975 recognized planned villages as incorporated entities with territorial jurisdiction. The laws of local governance that the country enacted in the 1980s and 1990s further strengthened the authority and power of elected village councils. This trajectory of formal laws parallels developments in Mexico, which I discuss next. Nevertheless, villagization in Tanzania reinforced pre-existing social and political inequalities. Well-to-do descendants of hereditary chiefs often founded new planned villages, and rural residents voted overwhelmingly in favor of rich peasants in village council elections because of the belief that rich villagers would be more effective at negotiating with the ruling party and the government.[34] As part of building the infrastructure of the party, TANU also established the "ten-household cells," each led by an elder who reported to the village party chairman. The ten-household cells, which became the backbone of the party-state's rural political infrastructure, led to further stratification in rural Tanzania and reinforced local inequalities.[35] One scholar goes so far as to refer to the ten-cell system as an "unchecked ... system of petty neighborhood despots" that strengthened the Tanzanian state's capacity to coerce rural compliance.[36]

Second, the discourse of modernization shaped villagization deeply. Nyerere believed that "living scattered over a wide area" (a reference to people who lived outside of planned villages) was in the same league as being "haunted by the old superstitious fear of witchcraft."[37] Such discourses took hold among CCM's regional and local leaders.[38] Similarly, the Swahili-majority elite in Tanzania considered the Maasai, one of the prominent agro-pastoralist

30. Coulson 1982, 242.
31. Coulson 1982, 162.
32. Hyden 1980; Sundet 2004.
33. Ferguson 1990; Chhotray 2007; Li 2007.
34. Coulson 1982, 246; for similar "selection effects" in leadership chosen to lead forest rights committees in India, see Chapter 5.
35. Havnevik and Hårsmar 1999.
36. Lofchie 2013, 120.
37. Nyerere's presidential inaugural speech 1962, 183–4, cited in Sundet 2004, 13.
38. Mombeshora 2000, 40, quotes a district-level party functionary who referred to a traditional mud and thatch house as a "gruel house" and urged the villagers to build "European type houses."

groups, to be the "embarrassing relics of [Tanzania's] primitive past."[39] Groups involved in pastoralism and agro-pastoralism thus also suffered because of ethnic prejudices similar to the ones that India's Adivasis endured at the hands of agrarian communities. Forestland rights conflicts in the Mkomazi, Kiteto, Kilosa, and other regions of Tanzania are often intertwined with inter-ethnic rivalry between agro-pastoralists and the groups that practice settled and relatively large-scale commercial farming.[40] These rivalries lead to restrictions on pastoralism in areas conducive to commercial agriculture, while the anti-pastoralist views of forestry agencies and wildlife groups lead to the exclusion of pastoralist groups from forestry and wildlife reserves.[41]

The formal institutions of local governance and property rights thus failed to spur broad-based local development in Tanzania. Instead, the (perverse) incentives inherent in the political and economic systems, coupled with the dominant discourses about pursuing the development of a modern nation state, reinforced local inequalities while creating opportunities for external agencies and actors.

Peasant Mobilization and the Coerced Responsiveness of Political Elites in Mexico

Mexico's peasants came to enjoy greater land rights than peasants in other postcolonial environments, but only through a long history of political mobilization. The Mexican War of Independence (1810–21) brought to power elites who were "firmly committed to the maintenance of property rights and special privileges for officialdom, the Catholic Church, landed magnates, and the army."[42] Subsequently, the transitional administrations of Juan Álvarez and Ignacio Comonfort conceived and enacted the Ley Lerdo of 1857, a law that entailed privatization of the properties of the Church and the common lands of Indian communities, although it had little effect until the presidency of Porfirio Díaz, who served seven terms from 1876 to 1911.[43] Porfiriato, as the era of Díaz's rule is commonly known, was associated with "extreme concentration of wealth, land and political power."[44] However, even during this period, the government issued decrees to protect communal and smallholder peasantry against the misuse of liberal laws.[45] In practice, though, most Mexican

---

39. Hodgson and Schroeder 2002.
40. Benjaminsen et al. 2009; Askew et al. 2013.
41. Lane 1994; Turner et al. 2014.
42. Wolf 1969, 9.
43. Thomson 1991.
44. Madrid 1984, 63.
45. Mallon 1994, 74. All plots worth less than two hundred pesos would be "adjudicated for free, and, of necessity, to their de facto possessors, unless they clearly and specifically renounced their rights to such plots."

peasants could not obtain these legal protections and only secured land rights through political mobilizations. Emiliano Zapata led these mobilizations in the early 1910s, while simultaneously instituting extralegal land redistributions in the areas his forces controlled. He also organized a massive show of strength in Mexico City in late 1914, which compelled President Venustiano Carranza to enact a decree on land reform in 1915; this extended the purview of land reforms to include any group of landless peasants large enough to enjoy a "political status."[46] Subsequently, Article 27 of the Constitution of 1917 established the state as "the *sole creator of property*" and obliged it to grant land to landless *campesinos*—Latin-American smallholder farmer or farm laborer.[47]

Mexico's political elites supported the land reforms, but were extremely sluggish in implementing them until peasant mobilization forced them to respond. Beginning in the early twentieth century, Mexico's ruling Institutional Revolutionary Party (PRI) indulged in the politics of promise to maintain a "renewable lease on political legitimacy."[48] On many occasions, however, political elites created legal loopholes to allow property owners to avert or sabotage state-led land redistributions.[49] Widespread agrarian reforms did not materialize until the mid-1930s. A major impetus for reform was the Great Depression, which led to the U.S. government's expulsion of a million Mexicans from the United States.[50] The return of these landless campesinos led to rural unrest in many states, particularly in San Luis Potosí and Veracruz, which forced Mexican President Lázaro Cárdenas (1934–40) to implement widespread agrarian reforms. Cárdenas put in place a new social pact intended to secure "stability and peace in the countryside."[51] While it is difficult to ignore the context to which Cárdenas responded, some scholars suggest that his presidency was "devoted to the redemption of the worker, the peasant, and the underprivileged."[52] In any case, an inquiry into post-revolutionary Mexico would be incomplete if it did not account for Cárdenas's astute rehabilitation of "the figure of the peasant revolutionary Emiliano Zapata in the legitimating ideology of the ruling party" and making land reform politically important.[53] Cárdenas also instituted an intricately woven corporatist network comprised of PRI cadre members, government bureaucrats, and the *ejidatarios*—the male heads of the families who were beneficiaries of land redistributions to ejidos.

46. Hellman 1983, 4; Thiesenhusen 1995.
47. Gordillo 2009. For a fascinating account of the emergence of campesino as a political identity, see, Boyer 2003.
48. Sanderson 1981, 201.
49. Fox 1996; Thiesenhusen 1995.
50. Thiesenhusen 1995, 36–37.
51. Gordillo 2009, 3.
52. Boyer and Wakild 2012.
53. Klooster 2003, 98.

Over time, these PRI networks, funded by the state's social welfare and rural development programs, replaced the long-entrenched private networks led by large estate owners.

The Mexican state's support was not limited to political tutelage, but also included a "functional distribution" of basic social services including education, medical facilities, potable water, electricity, etcetera.[54] Moreover, in some cases the state also provided arms and military training so that ejidatarios could defend their newly won lands.[55] Notwithstanding the Mexican party-state's mainly instrumentalist motives, the country's agrarian reform must count among the twentieth century's most extensive state interventions in favor of peasants.

Politics of Local Development in Post-Independence India, Tanzania, and Mexico

As developmental studies scholars have long argued, development is not only about economic inputs and outputs, but also is negotiated within specific social, cultural, and political contexts. Departing from this book's focus on institutional and political dimensions, I demonstrated earlier that historically entrenched social and cultural relations shaped the models of local development that political elites in India and Tanzania thrust upon the poor peasants. Peasants in the hinterlands in these two countries exercised very little bargaining power within the mainstream policymaking processes. This is not to suggest that peasants did not mobilize (see Chapter 5), but their influence on their countries' immediate post-independence policy agendas was minimal. Moreover, overdeveloped bureaucratic machinery in India and Tanzania, especially India's powerful forestry agencies, meant that peasants' capacity to hold the state accountable was limited.[56]

On the other hand, while Mexico experienced a revolution at the beginning of the twentieth century, it also inherited extremely high rates of landlessness and inequality. Because of the centrality of peasant welfare to the legitimacy of the post-revolutionary state, Mexican peasants won land rights and secured state support for broad-based agrarian reforms. Additionally, the PRI and the state made extensive efforts to alter, in meaningful ways, the patron-client networks controlled by land owners and caciques (overseers, who also acted as local agents of big men). The next section shows how these differences in grassroots development affected debates about national development, and

54. Gordillo 2009.
55. Hellman 1983, 5.
56. Hyden 1980; Haque 1997, 1998; Baviskar 1995, 1997.

how the intersection of local and national development influenced the differences in these three countries' forestland regimes.

3.2 HINTERLANDS AND THE BURDEN OF NATIONAL DEVELOPMENT

India: Land Takings Under a Property-less Socialism

In India, the state was the most dominant political and economic force in the first four decades following the country's independence in 1947. Nehruvian socialism, a social democratic model of development, focused on building a modern and self-reliant nation through large-scale development projects, such as mega-dams, irrigation systems, and industrial projects. Nehru referred to these projects as the "temples of modern India," and party and government officials often equated their implementation with the national interest.[57] Most of these mega-projects were situated in the hinterlands, which supported more than 25 million Adivasis and millions of other forest-dependent peasants at the time of independence.[58]

During India's Constituent Assembly debates following independence, Nehru sought to keep forests under federal authority to facilitate "national planning."[59] While powerful provincial leaders had shot down Nehru's proposal, his administration amended the colonial-era 1927 Forest Act to make it even easier for the central government to declare any land as reserve forestland.[60] Moreover, during the integration of princely states into the Republic of India and the abolition of their systems of zamindari (landlordism) as part of the land reforms, the government designated all of the wooded areas of the newly acquired territories as state forests.[61] Consequently, peasant households lost access to the small parcels of land within forested areas that they used for farming, often through formal and informal tenancy arrangements with the princely states, landlords, or their appointees.[62] In the political context of nationalization, the government did not have to justify these actions.

The government's actions also preempted land rights that a "land to the tiller" framework of land reforms would have provided for forest-based

57. Wyatt 2005.
58. Anon 1954.
59. Austin 1966, cited in Ramakrishna 1984, 911.
60. Chhatrapati Singh 2000.
61. PUDR 1982; Sarin 2005; Springate-Baginski and Blaikie 2007.
62. Pati and Dash 2002.

peasant groups.[63] As a chronicler of forest rights struggles in India comments, "While *zamindari* abolition freed tenants in the plains from landlord oppression, in hilly forested areas it threw millions of forest dwellers into the clutches of a far more oppressive *zamindar*, the forest department . . ."[64] The government also preserved the colonial-era Land Acquisition Act of 1894 and used it to acquire land in the "national" interest. Moreover, in 1956 the government deleted the right to property from the list of fundamental rights guaranteed by India's Constitution and expanded the scope of eminent domain.[65] While the government excluded Adivasis from land reforms, as discussed earlier, its single-minded pursuit of national development reinforced their economic and political marginalization. Acknowledging such repercussions, Nehru appealed to an assembly of Adivasis on the occasion of the inauguration of India's first mega-dam in 1948: "If you have to suffer, you should suffer in the interests of the country."[66]

India's post-independence socialist governments thus did not indulge in populist land redistribution as the conservationists in the Global North had feared. Land "redistribution" took the form of the government taking land from poor rural peoples for national development, which led to the strange phenomenon of "development-induced displacements."[67] The estimated number of such development refugees in independent India range between 20 million and 40 million. Adivasis, who make up about 8 percent of India's population, constituted more than 40 percent of people displaced.[68] Furthermore, government statistics show that less than a quarter of the displaced people were ever resettled or rehabilitated, with Adivasis representing only a small portion of this resettled population.[69] In a number of cases, government agencies asked Adivasis who were displaced by official projects to settle into areas legally designated as state forests or other government lands, including lands already occupied by other forest-dependent people.[70] These "rehabilitated" households never received legal rights or land titles, thereby preserving the land's legal status as state forests.[71]

Forestry agencies also used a variety of other administrative and biophysical criteria to secure control over village lands. For instance, the Orissa state

63. For a review of land reforms in India's nonforested regions, see Herring 1983.
64. Sarin, 2005a, 2131.
65. Sundar 2010; Gupta and Sivaramakrishnan. 2011.
66. Chandhoke 1994, 2698.
67. McDowell 1996; Dwivedi 2002.
68. Drèze et al. 1997.
69. Louis 2006.
70. Kulkarni 1987; Baviskar 1994, 1995.
71. For a number of insightful case studies about Adivasi and other rural communities that have had to go through similar cycles of multiple displacements and rehabilitation, see Sainath 1996.

forest department issued an executive order designating all lands with a slope of more than 10 percent as state forestlands.[72] In the state of Madhya Pradesh, an "error" of accounting between the revenue and the forest departments relegated 12,274 square kilometers of land to an administrative limbo, which has affected hundreds of thousands of peasants.[73] In the Dangs district of the state of Gujarat, the forest department took control of 710 square kilometers of land, which had been under *raab,* a local version of swidden.[74] Similarly, forestry agencies leased village lands as part of social forestry and wasteland development programs in a number of states, but instead of returning the control of these lands to village councils, forestry agencies designated the leased village lands as state forests.[75] Because of India's long history of multiple changes in government land records, it is virtually impossible to do an accurate auditing of the changes in land area under different tenure types.[76] However, an examination of aggregate data offers some useful insights.

The net effect of various land tenure changes is evident in Table 3.1, which shows that the area classified as de jure state forestland increased from 54 million hectares in 1961 to 70 million hectares in 2010–2011, a nearly 30 percent *net* increase.[77] On the other hand, notice the steady decline in lands classified as "Other Uncultivated Land excluding Fallow Land," "which includes village common lands that are legally defined as "Permanent Pasture and Other Grazing Land" and "Culturable Wastelands" meant for land redistributions among landless and for putting up village infrastructure. The transfers of village land to the jurisdiction of forestry agencies, as discussed above, affected the poorest village residents the most because they relied heavily on what used to be the village commons. More importantly, the transfer of "culturable wastelands" (which were meant to be used for land grants to landless villagers) to the jurisdiction of forestry agencies deprived the state governments of opportunities for pursuing a modicum of land redistributions.[78]

The increase in area of land set aside as state forests in India is remarkable, especially considering the 168 percent increase in the country's population, as well as the expansion of agriculture, urbanization, and industrialization

---

72. Sarin 2005; Kumar et al. 2015.
73. Garg 2005.
74. WWF 2005, 14.
75. Saxena 1992, 2003; Iyengar and Shukla 1999; Sekhar and Jørgensen. 2003.
76. It takes experienced forestland rights activists several weeks of research in the archives to dig out documents needed for one village. Personal communication, forestland rights activist, New Delhi, July 24, 2013.
77. Note that this increase in the area of state forests is exclusive of the process of integration of princely states from 1947 to 1960 as discussed above. Source: *Agricultural Statistics at a Glance*, 2014, Ministry of Agriculture, Government of India. Last accessed on July 1, 2016 at http://eands.dacnet.nic.in/PDF/Agricultural-Statistics-At-Glance2014.pdf.
78. Jodha 1986; Brara 2006.

during the corresponding period.[79] While large areas of natural forests were cleared away to make way for dams, industrial facilities, and commercially valuable tree plantations managed by forestry agencies, government agencies compensated for the loss of standing forests by bringing large areas under the legal designation of state forests.[80] India's expansion of state forests is thus directly linked to the push for industrial development, which necessitated centralized control over the hinterlands.

The overwhelming dominance of the "development" agenda in the post-independence period posed a threat to ecological balance in the hinterlands during the first decade following the independence. However, as I show elsewhere in this chapter, "environmental conservation" gained political salience in India during the 1970s, which helped to avoid large-scale tradeoffs between ecology and economic development. But this has changed since the late 1980s after the Indian government formally launched its economic liberalization program and as maintaining economic growth has become the government's most important policy goal in the years since 2000. As a number of commentators have argued, the government's obsession with economic growth does not reflect a commitment to help India's teeming masses of poor people.[81] Recent forms of environmentally destructive economic growth are, therefore, also socially regressive, because they undermine the integrity of natural resources that are the main sources of subsistence and livelihoods for a large majority of India's population, especially the poorest.[82] As such, while India may be trading off environmental health for the sake of economic growth, such trade off has little to do with the goals of social justice.

Tanzania: African Socialism and the Machiavellian Politics of Land Laws

Following independence in 1961, Tanzania pursued intensive exploitation of its natural resources. With support from international agencies such as the World Bank, the government invested in agricultural expansion, which led to the removal of 50,000 hectares from forest reserves established by the German and British colonial governments. On the other hand, the openings created by large populations being moved out of forested areas under the villagization program led to the designation of an estimated 12,000 hectares of

---

79. Between 1980 and 2000, dams submerged 11.1 million acres or nearly 15 percent of land areas classified as state forests. See Agoramoorthy and Hsu 2008.
80. For a detailed discussion of budgetary provisions meant to incentivize land takings, see Haeuber 1993b.
81. Deaton and Drèze 2002; Drèze and Sen 2013.
82. Shrivastava and Kothari 2012.

forests as new forest reserves during the same period.[83] These forest reservations were part of the government's response to donor agencies, such as the Nordic Delegation of 1962, which encouraged Tanzania to export timber to meet the burgeoning demand for pulp and paper manufacturing in India and Indonesia.[84] The Arusha Declaration, a key policy document of Nyerere's government, outlined plans for developing natural resources of the hinterlands to produce export worthy plantations, e.g. sisal, cotton, coffee, tobacco, pyrethrum, and tea, that would help meet the country's foreign exchange needs.[85] The government set up para-statal corporations to develop large-scale agriculture and ranching operations, commercial plantations, and forestry development with the explicit goal of promoting export crops.[86] These initiatives saw some success; by 1968, plantation crops figured among four of the country's top five export-earning crops.[87] The plantation economy became even more salient in the 1980s in the wake of the government's failures to modernize agriculture through the villagization program discussed above.

Tanzania's 1983 National Agriculture Policy contained two major policy initiatives: granting private land tracts to commercial farmers and introducing village land titles.[88] While the agenda of issuing village land titles remains unfulfilled even today (see Chapter 6), the government swiftly executed the policy changes allowing land to be allocated to commercial farms financed by domestic and international investors.[89] Two land registries covering eight of the mainland's twenty regions showed that a total of 205,000 acres were granted to commercial farmers in the period from 1987 to 1992. More importantly, 86 percent of the land granted was in parcels of more than 500 acres, with an average of more than 3,000 acres per holding. These land allocations infringed on customary use of land by households and villages, which led to a large number of conflicts during the 1980s. The government attempted to address these conflicts in 1991 by instituting the Presidential Commission of Enquiry on Land Matters, known as the Shivji Commission. Following extensive nationwide consultations, the commission's chairperson warned, "Customary tenures . . . are under constant threat of alienation by government institutions, ostensibly for 'national projects' or in the 'public interest,'" and that rural lands often end up in the hands of bureaucrats or well-connected "outsiders."[90]

83. Hurst 2004, 61.
84. Hurst 2004, 91–98; Brockington and Igoe 2006.
85. Julius Nyerere, *Tanganyika African National Union*, 1967, http://www.marxists.org/subject/africa/nyerere/1967/arusha-declaration.htm.
86. Havnevik and Hårsmar 1999, 87.
87. Coulson 1982, 145.
88. Sundet 2004, 55.
89. Sundet 2004, 57.
90. Shivji 1998, 12.

Confronted with these conditions, the Shivji Commission recommended that land governance should be in the hands of autonomous boards of commissioners and local government bodies. The government rejected the commission's recommendations and argued that "land, being an important element for development, *has to be controlled* by the President. If land is vested in [the] Board of Land Commissioners and the Village Assemblies then the Government will be turned into a beggar for land when required for development . . ."[91] Next, the government recruited a foreign consultant to write the National Land Policy of 1995, which disregarded the Shivji Commission's most important recommendations. The new policy vested supreme powers regarding the allocation of land titles in the hands of the president and the land commissioner in the federal Ministry of Lands.[92]

This new land policy also informed the writing of twin land laws enacted in 1999—the Village Land Act and the Land Act. At first the government's simultaneous enactment of two land laws, instead of one unified law, seems puzzling. But an examination of such puzzling outcomes offers important insights into the political economy of institutional change. The government managed to retain control of future land allocations through these two land laws, which defined three categories of land in contradictory ways: village land, reserve land (protected areas and government forest reserves), and general land under the authority of the central government.[93] According to the Village Land Act, "general land" is a residual category, which includes all land that is not reserved land or village land. According to this definition, more than 70 percent of Tanzania's land would be considered village land, which contains nearly 70 percent of Tanzania's woodlands.[94] However, the definition of general land in the Land Act includes *"unoccupied or unused village land."* Village land, which government agencies deem as being unoccupied (such as pasture lands that are part of seasonal grazing grounds) or unused (such as the forestlands that rural communities use for subsistence activities without leaving visible signs of use) are thus subject to federal jurisdiction applicable to general lands. Such a definition of general land in the Land Act of 1999 greatly reduces the area of land under the jurisdiction of elected village councils and creates potential land conflicts due to the different legal provisions in the Village Land Act.[95] In the case of conflicts between the provisions of two land laws, however, the Land Act is supposed to prevail, which allows the president and land commissioner to maintain a tight hold over land allocations.

91. Sundet 2004, 91–92.
92. Ibid.
93. Wily 2001; Sundet 2004; Purdon 2013.
94. Purdon 2013.
95. Sundet 2004, 120, emphasis in the original.

These grey areas in the law also enable both the Forestry and Beekeeping Division (FBD) and Tanzania National Parks (TANAPA) to establish or expand forest reserves and game parks by staking claims to "unused" village lands. Despite some progressive community-based forestry and wildlife policies, forestry and wildlife agencies have found ways of appropriating a very significant share of income from wildlife and forestry enterprises, even though village groups were responsible for doing the work to raise the income.[96] This has led rural residents to refer to forestry officials as *chinja chinja*, or "people who eat your blood."[97] Overall, state and parastatal forestry and wildlife agencies today claim jurisdiction over 40 percent of the country's territory. While some of these lands have remained under state control since the colonial era, the Tanzanian state's "concern of freeing 'surplus' land from villages for external investors" has led to further centralization of control over land.[98] Such tendencies have resulted in allocation of "unused" village lands for biofuel crops (such as jatropha, sugar cane, and oil palm) as well as wildlife trophy hunting and tourism projects.[99]

The debate about local versus central control of forests and land resources continues even to this date, as do land-related conflicts. For instance, out of 1,825 general land disputes reported in Tanzania in the year 2011, more than a thousand involved powerful investors.[100] Despite the large number of land conflicts and very high levels of poverty among Tanzania's rural residents, the Tanzanian government's vision of development continues to prioritize national interest over local interest.[101] The minister for lands, housing and human settlements development recently said, "This exercise should also identify villages with extra land in which big plantations can be established, so that there would be a clear list that will be made available to investors ..."[102] As I discuss in Chapter 4, the introduction of multiparty democracy and other political reforms in Tanzania since 1996 have enabled citizens to be increasingly assertive about their rights and about holding the state accountable. Even so, the effects of these changes may not be apparent for many years.

96. Nelson and Agrawal 2008.
97. Sundet 2004, 129.
98. Sundet 2004, 120.
99. Sulle and Nelson 2009; Gardner 2012.
100. Orton Kiishweko, *The Guardian*, December 21, 2012, http://www.theguardian.com/global-development/2012/dec/21/tanzania-major-step-curbing-land-grabs.
101. For an unfortunate illustration of the confluence of these factors related to the ongoing conflict in Ngorongoro District, see "Wardens raze 114 bomas, thousands stranded," *Just Conservation*, http://www.justconservation.org/wardens-raze-114-bomas,-thousands-stranded.
102. Anna Tibaijuka, *The Guardian*, March 15, 2013, http://www.ippmedia.com/frontend/?l=52360.

Mexico: Insecure Political Elites Invest in Peasants

For the liberals in control of the Mexico's political and economic affairs, particularly in the last quarter of the nineteenth century, forests and large areas of land in the hands of indigenous groups were considered "vacant" lands—as these lands were not under public use or owned by corporations or individuals.[103] As in India and Tanzania, such lands were often subject to customary claims by Indians and campesinos, who enjoyed de facto rights to use the land. In many cases, indigenous communities had land titles from the colonial period.[104] Nevertheless, the Díaz administration (1877–80, 1884–1911) sought to exploit such lands with the aid of private corporations and government agencies. To attract developers, Díaz awarded the ownership of a third of the surveyed land to survey companies, fifty of which gained control of 21.2 million hectares of public land between the years 1878 and 1908.[105] This further reinforced the highly unequal distribution of land between the large landed estates, called the *latifundios*, and the peasantry.

Mexico's Porfirian political elites were not very concerned about inequalities in land distribution, and they cared even less about environmental conservation. They argued that a poor country such as Mexico could not afford to invest in forest conservation. The elites' anticonservation beliefs prevented the emergence of a strong forestry bureaucracy, and Mexico consequently avoided the path of exclusionary forestry that many equally poor, or even poorer, countries in Asia and sub-Saharan Africa followed. The state of affairs changed significantly in the post-revolutionary era. Similar to the colonial Indian Forest Act of 1927 discussed in Chapter 2, Mexico's 1926 Forest Law contained punitive forestry regulations and regional logging bans, and also created new national parks.[106] Even so, President Lázaro Cárdenas (1934–40) mandated the forestry service to integrate "the peasant timber sector into the government's greatly expanded land reform program," which led to the establishment of more than three hundred community producers' organizations.[107] However, Miguel Angel de Quevedo, "the father of Mexican forestry" and Cárdenas's choice to head the Department of Forestry, sought to exploit producer groups to monitor and regulate peasant logging practices and to enforce the restrictive provisions of the

103. Simonian 1995, 61–62; Kelly 1994, 549.
104. Bray 2013, 39.
105. Holden 1990, 579.
106. Klooster 2003, 100.
107. Boyer 2005, 29.

1926 law.[108] Instead of adapting the forestry agenda to the government's populist politics, Quevedo openly opposed land reforms and partnered with the national army to enforce forest laws.[109]

The tussle between foresters' politically retrogressive, technocratic methods and the ideals of the revolution eventually prompted Cárdenas to dismiss Quevedo, dissolve the autonomous Forestry Department, and move its functions over to the Agriculture Department.[110] This decision helped Cárdenas bolster his revolutionary credentials, and the elimination of the department also improved his government's fiscal situation at a time of economic crisis.[111] On the other hand, the president's decision set Mexico's forestry agencies and forestry professionals on a long and winding path toward "institutional fragility."[112] Mexican forestry thus lost the impetus for conservation and the early gains that the department made by engaging peasants in producer group forestry. These developments ushered in a long period of rent-seeking timber economics.[113]

Post-Cárdenas era forestry policies in Mexico reflected the elite bias of the politics of the time. During the period from 1940 to 1970, presidential decrees banned community timber harvesting, and the government brought 50 percent of the country's forests under logging concessions awarded to Mexican and international corporations.[114] In the 1960s, peasants in states of Durango, Guerrero, and Oaxaca began to mobilize against logging corporations' exploitative practices. More than a dozen communities organized a "timber suppliers' strike" against exploitative practices of the logging parastatal corporation Fábricas de Papel Tuxtepec (FAPTAUX).[115] The National Congress of Indigenous Organizations (CNI), PRI's indigenous peasant wing, and other autonomous indigenous advocacy groups increasingly took notice of their constituents' forest-related grievances and included forest and land rights in its list of demands to leaders in the government.[116]

As a result of this mobilization and the representation of agrarian communities' voices in the political system, the Mexican government enacted the 1971 Agrarian Reform Law. This new law enabled the formation of ejido unions, and gave them the right to engage in productive activities and obtain

---

108. For a related discussion of how such local regulatory mechanisms become a "technology" of government, see Agrawal 2005a.
109. In one instance, Quevedo reportedly called for the "death penalty for people who cut down trees." Wakild 2006, 12.
110. Klooster 2003, 99–101.
111. Vitz 2010; Mathews 2011.
112. Mathews 2011, 46–47.
113. Mathews 2002; Klooster 2003.
114. Garcia-Lopez 2012, 93–94.
115. Mathews 2011, 130.
116. Grammont et al. 2009.

state-sponsored access to credit for forestry operations, including collectively managed sawmills.[117] Despite this reform, peasants, including indigenous groups, continued to mobilize against the exploitative logging concessions. The 1986 Forestry Law fulfilled these peasant demands of ending the logging concessions issued to private and parastatal logging corporations. The 1986 law also gave agrarian communities the right to directly hire forest engineers to implement the management plans necessary to secure logging permits. These and other laws that the government introduced helped many agrarian forest communities become viable economic entities, often referred to as "community forest enterprises."[118] Additionally, as the Mexican government privatized parastatal logging corporations with the onset of economic liberalization during the presidency of Carlos Salinas de Gortari (1988–94), it transferred parastatal assets to producers' organizations or to ejidos.[119] Even though irregularities in the process reduced the policy's benefits, such transfers are unthinkable in either India or Tanzania, even today.

Mexico's community forest sector matured and consolidated during the 1990s. While the economic reforms of the 1990s and the withdrawal of state support for peasant agriculture since the inception of North Atlantic Free Trade Agreement (NAFTA) in 1994 has weakened the peasant sector, these changes have not affected agrarian communities' commercial community forestry operations.[120] In fact, agrarian communities in the forested regions have benefited from peasant mobilization against NAFTA and the policies of economic liberalization in general. For instance, a January 2003 demonstration by 100,000 campesinos in Mexico City prompted conservative President Vicente Fox to sign a pact with representatives of indigenous and campesino organizations known as the Agreement with the Countryside. The agreement led to the reform of the Payment for Ecosystem Services (PES)—Hydrological program, which greatly reduced the role of market players in communal forestry, enhanced the federal government's mediating role, and made poverty alleviation a major consideration.[121] Mexican governments have increasingly employed the system of payment for environmental services as an important source of funds for "rural development."[122] As I show in Chapters 4 and 7, concrete and active links between campesino and indigenous organizations and the state's policymaking institutions have meant that rural residents

117. Bray and Merino-Pérez 2002; Garcia-Lopez 2012.
118. Klooster and Masera 2000; Antinori and Bray 2005.
119. Foley 1995; de Janvry et al. 1997. Similarly, the privatization of government's coffee-buying organization INMECAFE benefitted the coffee producers' federations (Foley 1995).
120. Personal electronic communication, Mexican community forestry expert, March 20, 2015.
121. McAfee and Shapiro 2010, 589.
122. Haenn 2006.

in Mexico have been able to pressure the federal government to adapt environmental policymaking to the goals of local economic development in the Mexican hinterlands.

3.3 NATIONAL LEADERS AND THE POLITICAL ECONOMY OF NATURE CONSERVATION

Political elites in the case study countries devised forestland regimes to meet national development goals, which created conditions that could have led to the decimation of these countries' forests. However, as mentioned earlier, the forestland regimes have remained more or less intact since these countries' independence, and have even expanded in India and Tanzania. In this section, I examine the conditions that enabled political elites to maintain large areas of forests without sacrificing their core economic and political objectives.

India: Conservation as Geostrategic Bargain

During Jawaharlal Nehru's rule in India (1947–64), national and international conservationists such as Salim Ali and American ornithologist Dillon Ripley used their friendship with the prime minister to get his government to establish some of India's first sanctuaries and national parks, which deprived peasants of land rights.[123] However, India's environmental story truly belongs to Nehru's daughter, Prime Minister Indira Gandhi. She is best known among international environmental policy community for her widely acclaimed speech on poverty and the environment at the 1972 Stockholm Conference on Environment and Development. In the speech, Gandhi argued against Western attempts to force poor developing countries to limit their development in the name of preserving the environment. She argued, "We do not wish to impoverish the environment any further and yet we cannot for a moment forget the grim poverty of large numbers of people . . . Are not poverty and need the greatest polluters?"[124]

While Gandhi's domestic politics hinged around the rhetoric of poverty alleviation, she also sought to portray India under her leadership as a country with an "ecological vision."[125] In practice, Gandhi's ecological vision reinforced the protectionist history of Indian forestry, especially through her enactment of the Wildlife Protection Act of 1972 and her government's enthusiastic backing of Project Tiger in 1973–74. The World Wildlife Fund (WWF) chose the Indian subcontinent to launch global tiger conservation efforts in the form of

123. Lewis 2003.
124. Gandhi 1992.
125. Chhatre and Saberwal 2006, 698.

Project Tiger "because of the *assured personal interest and support* of the heads of state in India, Nepal, Bhutan and Bangladesh."[126] From a policy perspective, Gandhi's unequivocal support for the WWF brand of environmentalism is puzzling in light of her criticism of the Western countries' appeals for the protection of environment in the developing countries. But, as I demonstrate below, it is precisely this contradiction that made wildlife conservation a useful bargaining tool for Gandhi.

Environmentalism served multiple goals for the ambitious Indira Gandhi. First, she thought of the assembly of world leaders in Stockholm in 1972 as "a setting that would behoove a world leader who could use the stage to address a global audience."[127] Moreover, Gandhi's aspirations as a world leader were closely tied to her desire to secure authoritative control over one of the world's largest developing countries. Amid her indictment for electoral fraud and the rapidly growing popular support for opposition leader Jayprakash Narayan, Gandhi imposed a "state of emergency" between June 1975 and March 1977. The imposition of emergency entailed a nationwide suspension of civil and political rights, and it led to large-scale violations of human rights. Under these grim conditions, Gandhi deployed her support for environmental conservation to ward off criticism against her poor human rights record.[128] She also played India's wildlife resources to secure the support of Europeans royals, who led the WWF and gave her a million-dollar grant for Project Tiger.[129]

Gandhi's support for environmental conservation was not just instrumental, however, as evident from the laws she enacted while she had full control of policymaking during the emergency era. For example, in 1976 she enacted the 42nd Amendment to the Indian Constitution, which is often referred to as the "mini-constitution" because of its far-reaching implications for India's federal structure.[130] This amendment placed the subject of "forests" in the "concurrent list," which meant that the federal government would prevail over states in any conflict of interpretation between federal and state forest laws.[131] The enactment of the Forest Conservation Act (FCA) in 1980 (after Indira was voted back into power in the post-Emergency period) further centralized forestry decision-making. The FCA barred state governments from diverting forestland for nonforestry purposes without a prior approval from the federal Ministry of Environment and Forests (MoEF). It had the effect of removing the contested question of forest land rights from the arena of state-level electoral politics. Additionally, Gandhi also intervened personally to ask state chief ministers to address forest and

126. Mountfort 1983, 32, emphasis mine.
127. Rangarajan 2009, 300, citing Parthasarathi 2007, 250–251.
128. Rangarajan 2003.
129. Rangarajan 2009, 301.
130. Mirchandani 1977, 98.
131. See Ramakrishna 1984.

wildlife conservation issues.[132] Speaking to state forest ministers in October 1982, Gandhi argued that the country needed some really "hard measures" to halt the erosion of hill catchments.[133] This was clearly a reference to Adivasi practices of hill farming, which colonial conservationists had targeted as an environmentally destructive practice. The legacy of Indira Gandhi's vocal support for exclusionary conservation far outlasted her tenure as prime minister. By the turn of the millennium, Project Tiger alone had covered an expanse of 33,000 square kilometers, and 20 percent of India's state forestlands had been set aside for the goal of nature conservation.[134]

While the centralization of forest governance failed to stem the tide of deforestation that resulted with the onset of the era of economic liberalization,[135] Indira Gandhi's support for protectionist forms of nature conservation continues to influence policymaking in India even to this day. The role that this legacy played in the debates about forestland conflicts and the enactment of the Forest Rights Act (FRA) in 2006 is discussed in Chapter 5.

Tanzania: Conservation Means "Foreign Exchange"

If one were to select one document that embodied the various facets of international campaign for nature conservation, it would be the Arusha Manifesto that Tanzanian Prime Minister Julius Nyerere issued in 1961. In the manifesto, released at the Symposium on the Conservation of Nature and Natural Resources in Modern African States convened by influential Western environmental groups, Nyerere declared:

> The survival of our wildlife is a matter of grave concern to all of us in Africa . . . In accepting the trusteeship of our wildlife we solemnly declare that we will do everything in our power to make sure that our children's grandchildren will be able to enjoy this rich and precious inheritance.[136]

While conservationists often see the Arusha Manifesto as an epitome of developing countries' commitment to global goals of nature conservation, it was more of an inter-elite bargain between developed and developing countries. Debt-for-nature swaps—where resourceful developed countries support developing country politicians who deploy the environment as a

132. For a discussion of Gandhi's instructions to the Chief Minister of Uttar Pradesh, and the subsequent notification of Dudhwa National Park in 1977 amid the state of constitutional emergency, see Strahorn 2009.
133. Rangarajan 2009, 306.
134. Rangarajan 2001, 103.
135. See Shrivastava and Kothari 2012.
136. Julius Nyerere, September 7, 1961; quoted in MacKenzie 1997, 325.

bargaining chip in international political and economic affairs—constitute an important aspect of this kind of inter-elite bargain.[137] In this sense, it would be a mistake to think of international conservation as a mere imposition from conservation activists in the Global North. Developing country leaders, such as Indira Gandhi and Nyerere, also secured their priorities in the process. Nyerere reminded the delegates at the Arusha meeting that wildlife conservation requires "specialist knowledge, trained manpower and *money, and we look to other nations to cooperate in this important task* . . ."[138] He was even more honest when he commented privately later that year:

> I do not want to spend my holidays watching crocodiles. Nevertheless, I am entirely in favor of their survival. I believe that after diamonds and sisal, wild animals will provide Tanganyika with its greatest source of income. Thousands of Americans and Europeans have the strange urge to see these animals.[139]

According to this line of thinking, Tanzania's forests were meant for developing commercially attractive sisal plantations owned by European and Asian settlers and for "exporting" wildlife viewing.[140] One result was that Nyerere supported the evictions of agro-pastoralist Maasai from Serengeti National Park.[141] From the late 1970s onward, Tanzanian forestry shifted its focus entirely to wildlife and biodiversity conservation.[142] It has since become the country with largest conservation regime in all of Africa. According to the country's Ministry of Natural Resources and Tourism, Tanzania's wildlife protected area network covers 233,300 square kilometers, or 28 percent of the country's total territory.[143] Dan Brockington, a prominent scholar of nature conservation, with decades of field research in Tanzania, attributes the high percentage of land dedicated to wildlife conservation to an "environmental-conservation complex" with the following characteristics:[144] (1) a highly commercialized wildlife tourism sector, which contributed about 16 percent ($740 million) of the gross domestic product (GDP) in the year 2000; (2) readily available international assistance for nature conservation, which enables government officials and elected leaders to exploit

---

137. Burnett and Conover 1989; Amelung 1993; Dressler 2009.
138. Burnett and Conover 1989, emphasis added.
139. Neumann 1995, 365 citing Nash 1982.
140. See Neumann 1995; Levine 2002.
141. Sachedina 2008, citing Neumann 1998, 145.
142. Hurst 2004.
143. http://www.mnrt.go.tz/about/welcome-to-mnrt. According to the most recent World Development Indicators dataset of the World Bank, this percentage went up to 32 percent by 2014. http://data.worldbank.org/indicator/ER.LND.PTLD.ZS
144. Brockington 2006, 105.

international conservation for their own clientelistic gains; and (3) money available from nature conservation that helps finance politicians' electoral campaigns.

Economic liberalization in Tanzania since the mid-1980s has led to widespread corruption and rent-seeking in nearly every sector of the economy. Transparency International's Global Corruption Perception Index (CPI) consistently ranks Tanzania as one of the most corrupt countries in the world.[145] Corruption in trophy hunting and other tourism-related permits, which benefits leaders of the ruling party and park officials, is regarded as one of the key motivations for the government's refusal to decentralize control over the wildlife tourism sector, even though the country's forestry sector has witnessed substantial progress in developing models of community-based forest management.[146] The nature of forestland regimes is thus clearly linked to the distribution of costs and benefits associated with the competing policies and programs.

Mexico: International Conservation Placed in the Service of Local Economies

Mexico's agrarian revolution of 1910 did not sway forestry policymakers, who referred to campesinos "as an endless army of ants, driven by poverty and hunger, slowly but tirelessly finishing off Mexico's forests."[147] Moreover, similar to political elites in India and Tanzania, Mexico's President Lázaro Cárdenas (1934–40) and other Mexican presidents also pursued the goals of "national unity and federal resource control."[148] However, Mexico's political leaders could not pursue an exclusionary agenda for the management of natural resources in the hinterlands, because of the recurring episodes of militant peasant mobilizations. At the same time, large landholders preempted state policies for redistribution of the most fertile agricultural tracts covered by irrigation networks, which forced the government to redistribute the less productive and non-irrigated land in the forested regions.

Cárdenas also asked Mexico's forestry agencies and technical experts to design programs that would promote sustainable management of forests while also helping campesinos in the process.[149] He was sincere about pursuing a real balance between the goals of social justice and environmental conservation, as evident from the establishment of forty national parks during

---

145. Tanzania had dropped 15 places in the CPI from the 102nd position in 2008 to 117th in the 2015 rankings released recently. Transparency International. Corruption Perception Index 2015. http://www.transparency.org/cpi2015.
146. Nelson and Agrawal 2008.
147. Klooster 2003, 102.
148. Wakild 2007, 10.
149. Boyer and Wakild 2012, 76.

his presidency.[150] Even so, he did not hesitate to dismiss Miguel Angel de Quevedo, the head of the Mexican forest service, because of his "anti-revolutionary beliefs."[151] As discussed earlier in this chapter, Mexico's political leadership consistently thwarted valiant attempts by forestry technocrats to create an exclusionary forestry regime. In fact, the Mexican approach of balancing the concerns of social justice with the goals of environmental conservation led to a new model for international conservation—the Man and Biosphere Reserve Program administered by the United Nations Educational, Scientific, and Cultural Organization (UNESCO)—which is geared toward fostering conservation without violating the rights of forest-dependent people.[152]

Some of the earliest examples of these types of forest reserves in Mexico did justice to the new model, which is why this model of conservation is often referred to internationally as the "Mexican Model."[153] However, with the significant spike in the number of such reserves and other protected areas established in Mexico since the mid-1970s, the model has betrayed its core principles. For example, the national government declared three important biosphere reserves without consulting local communities: the Montes Azules Reserve (established in 1978), the Monarch Reserve (established in 1986), and Calakmul (established in 1988). The WWF successfully lobbied for the creation of the Monarch Butterfly Reserve without genuine consultation with the fifty-five ejidos and thirteen indigenous communities that owned 82 percent of the biosphere land.[154] Like India's Indira Gandhi, who utilized environmental policy to shore up her standing during a political controversy, President Carlos Salinas de Gortari (1988–94) used his support for the establishment of the Calakmul Reserve as a public relations ploy to deflect attention from charges of widespread voter fraud during the 1988 presidential elections that brought him to power.[155] Salinas also worked actively to position himself as an environmentalist in the run up to the United Nations Conference on Environment and Development (Rio Summit) in 1992.

Throughout the 1990s, Mexican administrations worked very closely with big international conservation NGOs to promote the park model of conservation. In a series of debt-for-nature swap deals executed throughout the 1990s, Conservation International purchased $4 million of Mexico's discounted national debt, which facilitated the establishment of a number of protected areas.[156] In addition, the Mexican portions of the Mesoamerican Biological

150. Wakild 2007.
151. Mathews 2002, 21.
152. Smardon and Faust 2006.
153. García-Frapolli et al. 2009.
154. Tucker 2004, 570.
155. Haenn 2003, 2010.
156. Zimmerer 2011.

Corridor (MBC), the conservation corridor running from Panama to southern Mexico, attracted more than $25 million in loans from the World Bank's Global Environmental Facility (GEF). Despite the internationally driven push for nature conservation, the Mexican conservation story looks remarkably different from what happened in India and Tanzania. For example, there have been few, if any, displacements or evictions due to the establishment of protected areas in Mexico. On the contrary, the Mexican national government has often gone out of its way to market nature conservation initiatives as a means to improve peasant welfare and promote rural development.

The Calakmul Biosphere Reserve, which is one of Mexico's largest and more controversial protected areas, offers an apt illustration of domestic bargaining related to forestland rights.[157] In Calakmul, campesinos entered into a "votes for development" deal with PRI's gubernatorial candidate who, following his electoral victory, invited President Salinas to address a large gathering of campesinos. The president announced the local expansion of the National Solidarity Program (PRONASOL), while requesting campesino support for the reserve.[158] Equally important, instead of putting a technocrat in charge of the reserve, PRI appointed one of its most experienced political operatives to "influence the politics in the area without being obvious ... [while maintaining] the 'facade' of being a Reserve Director."[159] Intriguing as these details may be, Calakmul is not unique on this account. In the case of Monarch Butterfly Reserve mentioned earlier, supporters of strict conservation policies are quite aware of both the legal and de facto powers that ejidatarios wield. Despite suggestions by the celebrity poet Homero Aridjis that the government should buy ejidatarios out of the reserve, conservation advocates concluded that ejidatarios cannot be stopped from using local resources unless the army was called in.[160]

The establishment of the reserves affect the ability of ejidatarios to realize their resource rights, particularly timber rights. Even so, a biosphere decree does not nullify land rights and ejido tenures, which are protected under the Constitution.[161] The presence of a specific rights regime, in conjunction with the local political context, makes a significant difference as to how international conservation agencies function on the ground. In the Monarch Butterfly Reserve, the WWF initiated conservation concession payments to compensate ejidatarios for their lost benefits. The WWF pays eijidatarios who own logging permits $18/cubic meter of unharvested timber, while landowners without logging permits receive $12/hectare.[162] WWF has not responded

157. Haenn 2005.
158. Haenn 2010, 412.
159. PRI leader and adviser to the state governor quoted by Haenn 2010, 418.
160. Alonso-Mejía and Alonso 1999, 188.
161. Durand and Vázquez 2011.
162. Zebich-Knos 2008, 195.

in the same way to peasant land rights in other countries. In both India and Tanzania, WWF interventions have been mired in forestland conflicts, but the national chapters of WWF in these countries have refused to yield to local rural residents' land rights.[163]

The disputes over biosphere reserves represent an example of the resilience of Mexican agrarian institutions, which also remained resilient in the face of government's subsequent, and more overt, attempts to weaken them (discussed in Chapter 6). Most importantly, nature conservation and economic development reinforced one another in ways that, contrary to the Indian and Tanzanian cases, benefited the peasant and indigenous residents of protected nature areas to some extent.

3.4 CONCLUSION

Forestry management scholars and practitioners argue that addressing the question of land rights in populist frontier environments entails "a clear trade-off between poverty reduction and environmental conservation."[164] Such concerns are understandable as most frontier settings do not have participatory institutions, which the common scholars associate with the successful management of local forests.[165] Yet, the concerns about tradeoffs between poverty alleviation and environmental protection are based on certain assumptions about the balance of power in the hinterlands. For poor people to secure land rights at the forest frontier, at least one of the following two conditions must hold true: either the state must be nonexistent or so weak that it cannot assert control over the frontier; or, the poor wield strong electoral clout, which creates incentives for elected politicians to promote land redistribution at the frontier. The evidence presented in this chapter shows that none of these assumptions was met in either India or Tanzania.

National-level leaders such as Nehru, Nyerere, and Cárdenas deeply shaped the contours of local and national development in India, Tanzania, and Mexico. Such a leader-dominated development model validates Partha Chatterjee's argument that in the hierarchical context of the developing countries, the political elite secure legitimacy "not by the participation of citizens in matters of state but by claiming to provide for the well-being of the population."[166] However, the mid-twentieth century experiences of Mexico, which was still a low-income country with strong hierarchies, challenges Chatterjee's argument. In that case, political elites not only made promises, but also invested

163. Colchester 1994; Beymer-Farris and Bassett 2012; Huismann 2014; Kashwan 2016b.
164. Kaimowitz 2002, 228–29; Pellegrini and Dasgupta 2011.
165. Ostrom 1990; Agrawal 2001a.
166. Chatterjee 2004, 34, emphasis added by this author; see also Williamson 1989.

significant political resources to bring the means of production under the control of agrarian communities.

The key theoretical insight that emerges from the analysis in this chapter is that techno-managerial, institutional, and policy interventions did not determine the nature and effects of forestland regimes in India, Tanzania, and Mexico. In each of these countries, forestland regimes and nature conservation are connected intimately to broader political and economic processes. Post-independence governments in India and Tanzania actively consolidated the state forestry regimes that they inherited from the colonial era. The main goals of such consolidation were related to the agendas of national development and foreign exchange earnings. On the other hand, Mexican leaders redistributed large areas of forestlands to peasants, which the peasants employed as an important base for agricultural and forest-based production.[167] Thus, the goals and politics of development shaped forestland regimes in the study countries and produced remarkably different results. Yet, instead of massive deforestation, each of these three countries has made significant strides in promoting forest protection.[168]

These outcomes generate some important questions. First, why did Mexico develop a more responsive political system in the latter half of the twentieth century, while India and Tanzania that were also known for their staunchly socialist leaders did not? Second, how did each of these countries deal with peasant mobilization? And third, what have been the implications for access to and control over the resources of the hinterlands in these three countries? I pursue these questions in the next chapter by analyzing differences in political elites' engagement with politically mobilized peasants who were demanding land rights in the hinterlands of India, Tanzania, and Mexico.

167. Bray 2013.
168. For an extensive bibliographical compilation of evidence about the success of these forest protection efforts, see Seymour et al. 2014.

CHAPTER 4

࿐

Political Mediation of Land Conflicts in the Hinterlands

A confidential U.S. State Department cable released via WikiLeaks in 2011 revealed details about debates within India's ruling Congress Party as it prepared to introduce the bill that would become the Forest Rights Act of 2006. The party's leaders argued that the bill would be a win-win situation because "if the bill gets through, tribals will align themselves with the ruling coalition. If the bill fails to pass, the UPA [United Progressive Alliance, the ruling coalition led by Congress Party] can still claim to be the champions of the tribal cause and win tribal votes."[1] Such a casual approach to the question of forest and land rights conflicts, widely considered to be one of root causes of the Naxalite rebellion in India's forested heartland, stands in marked contrast to the Mexican government's response to Zapatista insurgency in the state of Chiapas during the 1990s. Despite reforms in 1992 that formally ceased land redistributions, Mexican leaders worked overtime following the Zapatista rebellion to find legal loopholes to redistribute 300,000 hectares of land, an area larger than land redistributed at the height of agrarian reforms during the 1930s and 1940s.[2] India and Mexico's experiences lead to the following question: why do national elites take such different positions vis-à-vis the questions of land rights in the hinterlands?

In this chapter, I show that the differences in political mobilization over questions of land rights and the nature of engagement between peasant

---

1. Anon, "48157: UPA attempts at social engineering with Tribal Bill," *The Hindu*, March 24, 2011, http://www.thehindu.com/news/the-india-cables/the-cables/article1565619.ece.
2. Eisenstadt 2009.

groups and political elites (mainly via the structures of party-constituent links) are the two main causes of variation in forestland regimes in the study countries. This chapter focuses on the long-entrenched patterns of interactions between political parties and peasant organizations, while the politics of more recent institutional reforms is examined in Chapters 5 and 6. I focus on mobilization around the demands for forestland rights and overall policies and programs introduced by respective governments, not on the distribution of costs and benefits at the micro level.

4.1 DOMINANT PARTIES, ELECTORAL POLITICS, AND FORESTLAND REGIMES

In developing countries, the state is still by far the most important provider of social and civic services and owns most of the properties in the hinterlands. Elected representatives' preferences and government policies have a direct impact on rural constituents' everyday lives.[3] Sustained engagement between citizens and elected leaders is an important means of responsiveness to constituent demands. As discussed in Chapter 1, the avenues through which citizens engage with governments and government agencies, especially the well-established mechanisms of political intermediation led by a ruling party, are likely to influence the nature of political and economic institutions.

India's "Congress System" and the Politics of Status Quo

Even though India adopted a multiparty parliamentary system following independence in 1947, the Congress Party dominated politics during the country's first four decades.[4] Congress's success is attributed to Prime Minister Jawaharlal Nehru's politics of accommodation[5] and the "Congress system," which incorporated the leaders of competing regional, linguistic, or caste groups into the ruling coalition. Factions within the party competed for the allocation of resources and opportunities through vertical faction chains, many of which organized around "traditional institutions of kin and caste."[6] India's social structure thus facilitated inter-elite coalitions under the Congress

---

3. Véron et al. 2003; Corbridge et al. 2005.
4. An early shift to coalition politics happened at the state level in the second half of the 1960s (Brass 1968), even though coalition politics took roots at the center in the late 1980s and 1990s.
5. For an extensive analysis of Nehru's contribution to state-building, especially India's secular fabric, see Varshney 2014. This chapter focuses on political and economic effects of Nehruvian state-building for the majority of India's poor masses.
6. Kothari 1964, 1163; Chhibber and Petrocik 1989.

system in a country with underdeveloped institutions. The Congress system was most effective when responding to pressure from dominant groups of middle-caste agriculture communities, trading castes, and the industrial houses. It helped maintain the status quo in favor of the propertied classes, thereby ensuring "continuity and unity."[7]

The dominant models of post-independence economic development (discussed in Chapter 3) further reinforced the historically entrenched inequalities. Socially marginalized groups, such as Dalits (the so-called untouchables) and Adivasis (India's indigenous people), remained on the fringes of the Congress system. Even so, Adivasi leaders often think of themselves as unchallenged patrons and believe that they carry the votes of their co-ethnic constituents in their pockets.[8] India's political party elites in turn rely on regional and local satraps, most of whom belong to the families of traditional leaders.[9] The peculiar geography of distribution of Adivasi populations in small clusters prevented the emergence of supra-local organizations similar to the regional caste associations, which enabled the so-called higher caste groups to negotiate deals with Congress and other political parties.[10] The party and government machinery relied on local patron-client networks for the distribution of state welfare, which further reinforced Adivasi leaders' traditional advantages of relative wealth and power.[11] The patron-client networks at the bottom of the Congress system functioned as systems of local political and economic control. The social and economic differentiation within Adivasi groups thus helped political elites within and without Adivasi communities "manage" Adivasi vote-banks without bringing in radical reforms.

When the Congress Party based its electoral strategies on delivering pro-poor policies, they often fell prey to inter-elite squabbling after being elected into power, as in Gujarat during late 1970s and early 1980s, or faced all-out revolts by the middle classes, as in Madhya Pradesh during the 1990s.[12] In Gujarat during the mid-1970s, Gandhian social activists and Congress politicians stitched together a social coalition that went by the acronym of KHAM, which stands for Kshatriya (martial castes), Harijans/Dalits (the so-called untouchables), Adivasis (India's indigenous people), and Muslims. KHAM turned out to be a formidable social and political coalition, which at the time commanded more than 60 percent of the vote share in Gujarat. Moreover, the KHAM campaign marked a "massive infusion" of subaltern groups, whose representatives "captured" state power via electoral politics.[13] The first

---

7. Kothari 1970, 304; Kohli 1987; Rudolph and Rudolph 1987.
8. Tillin 2008.
9. See Chandra 2013b.
10. Rudolph and Rudolph 1960; de Haan 2008.
11. Hardiman 1987; Corbridge 1988, 2000.
12. Sheth 2002; Manor 2004; Sud 2007; Pai 2009; Kashwan 2014.
13. Sheth 2002, 20.

KHAM-backed and Congress Party–led state government in Gujarat (1980–85) resurrected land reforms, and Congress leaders announced their intentions to galvanize party cadres for effective implementation of land reforms on the ground.[14] Notwithstanding these stated intentions, the KHAM strategy was founded on individual leaders' strategic interests. But faction-ridden Congress leaders failed to counter the preemptive and reactionary mobilization engineered by landowning and other politically dominant groups.[15] As a result, the KHAM coalition unraveled within few years, not least because it failed to counter-mobilize its constituents.

The issue of forestland rights has long been entangled with electoral politics in a number of states with significant Adivasi populations and, thus, has been labeled a populist issue.[16] Dominant parties in the states with a sizeable Adivasi population acted under electoral pressure to promise land titles for peasants of the forested regions. However, once voted into power, state governments often neglected these promises and resorted to ad hoc executive orders authorizing usufruct rights (see the introduction to Part II). Moreover, the state governments entrusted forestry agencies with the task of implementing these executive orders, which created opportunities for rent-seeking and land grabs by local leaders acting in collusion with corrupt forestry officials.[17] A relationship of mutual aid developed between politicians and forestry officials, in which politicians benefited from forestry officials' discretionary powers.[18] These officials, in turn, relied on politicians to ward off the ever-present threat of being transferred to a new and undesired location.[19] This explains why, forestry and other government agencies got away with actively sabotaging reforms that were aimed to address the question of land rights in the hinterlands.[20] In an exceptional but telling illustration, the state government of Maharashtra issued a confidential circular asking its officers *not* to implement a law protecting Adivasis' land rights, which the state legislature had enacted unanimously.[21]

14. Sheth 2002; Sud 2007.
15. Patel 2001; Yagnik 2002; Sheth 2002. Readers must note that the counter-mobilization on the part of the dominant caste groups actually led to the emergence of multiple corporatist groups that connect market, society, and the state in intricate networks that India's Hindu nationalist groups and parties deploy for political gains (see Prakash 2003).
16. Saravanan 2009.
17. Baviskar 1995; Pathak 1994.
18. Corbridge and Kumar 2002; personal interview, former minister of tribal affairs, New Delhi, August 2015.
19. Fleischman 2012.
20. Drèze 2005; Kjosavik 2006.
21. Government Circular, Confidential, Revenue and Forest No Adivasi 1986/CR-251/T-9 dated July 31, 1986, cited in Kulkarni 1987.

The period from the late 1980s onward has witnessed economic liberal-ization in India, leading to increasing competition for the country's natural resources and attendant conflicts as the state has sought to expedite mining, industrial, or infrastructure projects in the hinterlands.[22] This recent push for economic growth has led to a decline in absolute poverty and an increase in inter-group and inter-regional inequalities.[23] Such differentiated effects have rendered economic liberalization politically more palatable, even though the large-scale dispossessions attributed to neoliberal policies is cited as the source of the resurgence in the recent years of the ultra-violent Naxalite movement, which dates back to late 1960s.[24] The threat of Naxalism was a key trigger for the Indian government's recent efforts to introduce forestland reforms, which are examined and analyzed in Chapter 5.

Tanzania: A Party-State and Its Subjects

Independent Tanzania witnessed the emergence of a very tightly managed party-state, so much so that the ruling TANU Party's National Executive Council "was explicitly tasked with developing national policy while the legisla-ture was viewed solely as its implementer."[25] Yet, neither the centralization of Tanzanian political institutions nor TANU's dominance was preordained. In the first post-independence District Council elections of 1963, TANU candidates lost to independent candidates who campaigned against the government's land policies, specifically, the Land Tenure Amendment (1962) Act, which abolished the individual freehold system and nationalized land ownership.[26]

The election results motivated Julius Nyerere, Tanzania's prime minster and the head of the TANU Party, to tighten control both at the national and local levels. First, Nyerere led Tanzania's transition from a multiparty politi-cal system to a "single party democracy" in 1965.[27] Second, he established an extensive network of ten-household cells in each of Tanzania's eight thousand villages, each led by a village party chairman who also doubled as a village council chairman. The stated goal was to leverage local governance for nation-building.[28] In practice, the network of ten-household cells functioned as a

22. See essays in Guha et al. 2012; Shrivastava and Kothari 2012.
23. Chamarbagwala 2006; Kijima 2006; Drèze and Sen 2013.
24. Nitin Sethi, "Pillai writes to green ministry on atrocities against MP tribals," *Times of India*, July 24, 2010, http://timesofindia.indiatimes.com/india/Pillai-writes-to-green-ministry-on-atrocities-against-MP-tribals/articleshow/6207032.cms Accessed March 11, 2013.
25. Morse 2014, 659.
26. Hyden 1980, 84.
27. Lofchie 2013, 120.
28. Samoff 1979; Havnevik and Hårsmar 1999.

system to incorporate peasants and other rural groups, which together consti-tuted an electoral majority.[29] Additionally, the government systematically un-dermined radical labor unions by disbanding them and isolating their leaders, or by coopting unions and their leaders into TANU-sponsored organizations. The government's efforts helped avert peasant political mobilization even in the face of a number of unpopular policy decisions, such as the abolition of district councils in 1972 and primary cooperative societies in 1975, as well as the quixotic policy of villagization examined in Chapter 3.[30]

Two events of 1977 further centralized political power in the hands of Tanzania's dominant political party: first, TANU's merger with the Afro-Shirazi Party of Zanzibar to create the Chama Cha Mapanduzi (CCM, or "Party of the Revolution") with a nationwide presence; second, the constitutional amend-ments that declared this new unified party as the "supreme organ of state," while giving the president (who was also the party president) the authority to dissolve the parliament "at will."[31] From that point onward, the party became the central organizing institution for all state and local government activi-ties, and it received another significant boost through the local government reforms of 1982. This seamless vertical integration of party hierarchy into the organs of the state created a "party-state" similar to the ones Marxist-Leninist parties led prior to 1990 in communist countries.[32] The party-state integration in Tanzania was so strong that when a multiparty system was reintroduced in 1994, village leaders were reportedly confused about whether the position of the leader of ten-household cells was primarily a party post or a position in the state hierarchy.[33] Ultimately, the party's main function was to provide an organized cadre capable of carrying the leader's message to the masses.

Tanzania's government structure differed from India's in one impor-tant way—Tanzania inherited a weaker bureaucracy. Nevertheless, Nyerere used his broad-based legitimacy to pursue an agenda very similar to that of Nehru—that is, to provide a baseline level of social protection in order to maintain social and political stability.[34] Rural constituents valued, and ex-pected to benefit from, their elected leaders' personalized access to govern-ment resources.[35] These personalized patronage links added to local leaders' authority, which was instrumental to the state's "cohesion and outreach" efforts.[36] The integration of actors and groups into the party structure mir-rored general societal expectations about status and hierarchy, creating a

29. Whitehead 2011; Morse 2014.
30. Kelsall 2000, 534.
31. Hyden 1980; Engel et al. 2000.
32. Hyden 1999; Hyden and Williams 1994.
33. O'Malley 2000.
34. Kelsall 2002.
35. Hyden 1999.
36. Havnevik and Hårsmar 1999, 116; Kelsall 2002.

sense of harmony and continuity. Over time, the general population came to value the centralization of authority in the CCM Party for its perceived contribution to the much-valued goal of social and political stability.[37] These factors help explain the very high levels of legitimacy that the CCM and Nyerere commanded until his resignation from the party and the government in 1985.

The changing of the guard within the party and the government brought about major changes in the government and the economy as well. While the motivations behind the political reforms following Nyerere's resignation were complex and multifaceted, the new party leadership eliminated the ethics code that made it illegal for party leaders to engage in commercial enterprises and business deals. The controversial Zanzibar Declaration of February 1991 formalized the widespread practice of political elites participating in business ventures, to such an extent that the "fiscal interests of government profiteers" drove some of the early changes in the economy and politics.[38] Even so, the ruling party's decision to relinquish its status as the only legal political party and to reintroduce multiparty democracy in 1993 boosted institutional political reforms in Tanzania. These reforms, however, failed to reduce the CCM's political dominance, although recent general elections have been increasingly competitive.[39] The parliament also has gained strength vis-à-vis the party and the government, as evident from its resolution calling on former President Jakaya Kikwete to remove four high-ranking party officials involved in the "escrow scandal," including the minister and permanent secretary of the Ministry of Energy and Minerals, the attorney general, and the minister of lands.[40]

Notwithstanding the genuine optimism surrounding the political changes currently under way, Tanzania's democratic institutions remain tenuous, as evident from the CCM's attempts to control the ongoing process of national constitutional review.[41] Part of this can be attributed to Tanzania's mixed

---

37. Booth et al. 1993, 42.
38. Lofchie 2014.
39. Nelson et al. 2012. The vote share secured by ruling CCM presidential candidates has been on a steady decline, from 89 percent in 2000 to 58.4 percent in the 2015 elections. The number of parliamentary seats secured by the opposition has seen an increase, with 68 seats in the 2015 elections, which is their best performance since the introduction of multiparty elections in 1995. Also see https://freedomhouse.org/report/countries-crossroads/2012/tanzania.
40. Michaela Collord, *Democracy in Africa*, December 5, 2014, http://democracyinafrica.org/parliament-pins-executive-corruption-scandal-tanzania/. The scandal came to light after the Public Accounts Committee released a report arguing that senior government officials had fraudulently authorized the disbursement of at least $122 million of public funds to a private company. Anon, "Tanzania probes banks over escrow scandal," World Bulletin/News Desk. January 1, 2015. http://www.worldbulletin.net/news/152029/tanzania-probes-banks-over-escrow-scandal
41. Ibid.

presidential and parliamentary system of governance. Direct elections for the presidency make the president the most popular political figure in the country, overshadowing the role of the cabinet members who are elected representatives also.[42] This institutional structure fosters the centralization of power, which militates against the rights of the population in hinterlands and reinforces the country's often problematic political and economic legacies.

Mexico's Corporatism: A case of "Regimented Empowerment"

The Mexican state invested in peasant development in the late twentieth century because it sought to prevent peasant revolts through some modicum of agrarian reforms and rural development. Hence, the Institutional Revolutionary Party (PRI)—which ruled Mexico from 1929 to 2000—established an extensive network of grassroots peasant organizations that worked as an extension of the state.[43] The *Cardenista* state (named for Mexico's 1930s President Lázaro Cárdenas) mobilized the peasantry into agrarian leagues at the regional and state level. Such grassroots mobilization created the foundations necessary for the emergence and consolidation of the National Peasant Confederation (CNC), which existed as a separate, party-affiliated organization. The CNC linked peasant groups to more than a dozen state agencies in charge of rural development and social welfare programs for campesinos. Such state agencies included the National Bank of Rural Credit (*Banrural*), the National Basic Foods Company (CONASUPO), and the National Ejidal Development Fund (FONAFE). PRI leaders, including many of the CNC leaders, acted as gatekeepers, and extracted economic and political gains from controlling the flow of state-sponsored programs, such as the provisions of credit for the peasant sector.[44] Local campesino leaders also utilized their access to regional organizations and their contacts with party bosses to launch political careers.[45]

The PRI's extensive control of the peasant sector has prompted many scholars to characterize agrarian-sector organizations such as the CNC as structures of political domination.[46] While political domination was certainly an important motivation for party leaders, an exclusive focus on party leaders' intentions fails to account for the structural imperatives and peasants' agency. The PRI's investments in building corporatist organizations varied according to levels of local economic development and electoral competitiveness.[47] The

42. Mallya 2009.
43. Hellman 1983; Harvey 1990; A. Knight 1994.
44. Wilshusen 2003.
45. García-López 2012; see also McDowell 1996.
46. Bartra 1975, 1982.
47. Magaloni et al. 2007.

PRI's corporatist machinery was thus not only a top-down channel of political control, but also a response to grassroots demands and political conditions. The failure of PRI-sponsored organizations to deliver also led to the emergence of rival organizations, which introduced vitality into the political process in Mexico.

Peasant groups looked for alternatives when CNC leaders failed to represent their concerns in the political arena, especially after President José López Portillo declared in 1976 that his government would cease land redistributions and focus instead on "creating wage employment and boosting productivity in rural areas."[48] In response, campesinos gave up their CNC membership and switched their loyalty to relatively more autonomous peasant confederations, which helped organize new land invasions on contested properties. Such "direct action" was meant to remind the state about its obligations to fulfill its revolutionary promise.[49] These mobilizations of grassroots organizations supported by regional and national confederations, coupled with the occasional windows of opportunities that the PRI offered to semi-autonomous peasant activism, contributed to the "thickening of civil society."[50] Mexican peasants and social activists refused to accept PRI corporatism as given and pushed the state to recognize alternative channels for peasant demands. The PRI domination of agrarian-sector organizations was thus far from complete. More broadly, the nature of party-constituent links is a product of the leverage that a group or a constituency can wield within a society.

The case study countries varied on this important question of how much leverage peasant groups had over the national government. I discussed this issue in Chapter 3, but it is worth a brief recap here. Peasants, especially those who live in and around forest areas, have long been marginalized in Indian society. While Tanzania experienced less social stratification than India, it also witnessed the emergence of neo-elites primarily focused on self-enrichment. Mexican society also is marked by very high levels of inequality.[51] However, since the Mexican Revolution, middle classes and elites have accepted the legitimacy of the revolutionary ideals as one of the driving forces of post-revolutionary nationalism.[52] Even before President Cárdenas instituted peasant corporatism in the 1930s, a prominent scholar of Mexican politics argued:

> There is now a wider sense of the political and social necessity for the program
> of land redistribution. The younger political elements take it as a fact, a matter

---

48. Harvey 1990, 185.
49. Grammont et al. 2009; Van Der Haar 2005; García-López 2013.
50. Fox 1994; see also Foweraker and Craig 1990; Grammont et al. 2009; Holzner 2010.
51. Levy and Walton 2009.
52. Malloy 1976.

of course. It seems possible to argue that even without any further impact the agrarian reform will continue for another generation at least.[53]

In all three case study countries, inter-class and inter-ethnic balance of power dynamics shaped various groups' competing claims to societal resources. The next section presents a comparative analysis of dominant parties' responses to peasant mobilizations regarding land rights in the hinterlands.

4.2 POLITICAL ARTICULATION OF PEASANT DEMANDS

The phrase "social mobilization" takes on a variety of meanings, especially in conjunction with debates about the role of civil society and nongovernmental organizations (NGOs). In this book, I use the term political mobilization to represent mass mobilization that is directed at making demands on the state. Such mobilizations also intersect, directly or indirectly, with the strategies and outcomes of voter mobilization by mainstream political parties.[54] This framing is in alignment with this book's focus on the links between peasants and the organs of the state and between peasants and the ruling party.

The Indian State: The Elephant That Did Not Move
(Until Very Recently)

This section considers two of India's most successful state-level sociopolitical mobilization regarding peasants' land rights (Jharkhand and Maharashtra). In the vocabulary of case study research, these are "most likely" cases that shed light on the fundamental limits that India's social and political contexts impose on political mobilization.[55]

Jharkhand Movement[56]

Jharkhand constitutes one of the "most likely" cases for three reasons. First, it has been home to a number of legendary rebellions: the Santhal insurrection of 1855–57 that involved a peasant army of more than thirty thousand; the Birsa Munda–led Adivasi rebellion from 1895 to 1900 against feudal lords and

---

53. Tannenbaum 1933, 205. Similar observations were made about the widespread popular support for the petroleum nationalization of 1938. See Knight 1994, 156.
54. For relevant discussions, see Lange 2008; Kashwan and Lobo 2014.
55. George and Bennett 2005.
56. This case draws significantly on Omvedt (1984) unless otherwise specified.

the British; and the Kol rebellion of 1931. "All land belongs to the tribals" was the battle cry of these rebellions against the Indian and British authorities.[57] Second, in response to this long history of insurgency, the British colonial government recognized customary forest and land rights in Jharkhand under the Chotanagpur Tenancy Act (CNTA) of 1908 and following India's independence, the Santhal Parganas Tenancy Act (SPTA) of 1949. These laws mandated the creation of a "record of rights" for each village, and gave Adivasis the right to reclaim farmland out of wastelands. Jharkhand residents saw these provisions as a victory that vindicated the struggles that their forefathers had waged against the intruders.[58] Even though CNTA and SPTA incorporate rights that are much stronger than the virtually nonexistent forestland rights in the rest of India, scholars have critiqued these laws for embodying a "rigid and over-simplified model of 'indigenous' social structure and customs."[59] Nevertheless, Jharkhand Adivasis have often deployed the colonial-era land laws as a strategic tool to aid struggles for forest and land rights in independent India.

The Jharkhand Party led by Adivasi leader Jaipal Singh, a Columbia University graduate who participated actively in the Constituent Assembly debates discussed in Chapter 2, mobilized Adivasis to demand a separate Jharkhand state within India. The merger of the Jharkhand Party with the Congress Party in 1963 dealt a setback to this movement. The Jharkhand Mukti Morcha (JMM, Jharkhand Liberation Front) was founded in 1973 to pursue the demand of a separate province.[60] Backed by the long history of Adivasi rebellions in the region, the JMM was born as a radical movement that placed demands for land and forest rights at its center. The JMM organized militant rallies and direct action to protest against dams and other development projects that threatened to take away large areas of land and forests crucial to the livelihoods of Jharkhand Adivasis. The tone and tenor of JMM's campaign reflected its origins with a "green and red flag," which signified an assertion of control over local natural resources while opposing the exploitative practices of traders, contractors, and government officials.

The JMM successfully forced the abandonment of a World Bank–sponsored "social forestry" project during 1978 and 1979. In their opposition to the project, Adivasis cut down the teak trees that the World Bank project had planted as a replacement for native sal trees that were important to Adivasis for cultural and economic reasons. For a short while, the JMM also fostered alliances between the mine workers, lower-caste peasants,

---

57. Sharma 1976, 38.
58. Sundar 2009, 5.
59. Upadhya 2009, 36.
60. The JMM was by no means the singular representative of the demands for a separate state, but certainly the most visible and most influential in the long run. See Prakash 2011.

and Adivasis. The state dealt with these militant campaigns through *"goondaism* [hooliganism] and police firing."[61] Surprisingly, the Communist Party of India–Maoist (CPM), which was quite influential in the region, opposed the JMM campaigns. The CPM labeled the JMM as a "splittist" and "separatist" force detrimental to the success of "pure" class struggle. The models of Marxism that the CPM supported prioritized "struggle for wages and expansion of the party" over the questions of peasant land rights.[62] The JMM's autonomous growth also threatened the Congress Party and its nationalist project. Congress launched a campaign to stigmatize the "red" elements within the JMM as antinational radicals and to mobilize the Adivasi "middle classes" in favor of an exclusively "green" JMM.[63] Congress eventually managed to co-opt some of the main JMM leaders, which resulted in the JMM formally adopting an exclusively green flag in 1983. In practice, the green flag signified less a prioritization of the "green" agenda items and more the exclusion of the "red" ones.

From the vantage point of formal institutional politics, the de-radicalization of the JMM helped the cause of statehood, which Jharkhand won in November 2000. In the process, the JMM deployed the politics of ethnicity and cultural nationalism, which was popular among Adivasi elites.[64] As the JMM transformed "from a party of workers and peasants demanding a . . . Lalkhand (literally, a red zone) to a champion of ethnoregionalism," forest and land rights ceased to be the main demands.[65] Meanwhile, displacements and dispossessions continued throughout the years leading up to the birth of Jharkhand. An estimated ninety thousand people were displaced in the 1990s alone by the Damodar Valley Corporation, which was modeled after the Tennessee Valley Authority Project (TVA) in the United States.[66] This does not mean that questions of forest and land rights are excluded entirely from contemporary political discourses in Jharkhand. Citing fears that non-Adivasi men might marry Adivasi women to capture Adivasi land, the JMM opposes women's land rights even though Adivasi customs and the provisions of the 1949 SPTA law recognize women's land rights in exceptional cases.[67] Similarly,

---

61. Omvedt 1984, 1865.
62. Omvedt 1984, 1866.
63. Similar findings are reported from the state of Gujarat, in which an Adivasi worker under Gandhian influence commented to a scholar, "Communism is bad for the country. It will destroy culture and religion" (G. Shah 1972, 440).
64. I. Basu 2012; Corbridge 2002.
65. Chandra 2013b, 274.
66. Jewitt 2008.
67. Rao 2007. The JMM's use of ethnoregionalism has taken roots, as evident in the efforts by a section of Jharkhand activists to counter the increasing influence of the Hindu nationalist BJP, by "reviving tribal customs around nature worship and local governance, and by policing negatively-perceived behaviours around drinking and sexuality" (I. Basu 2012, 1305).

the present system of communitarian land rights does not prevent Adivasi elites from accumulating landholdings, misappropriating village "wastelands," and exploiting forests for timber and minerals by colluding with government officials.[68]

The ultimate failure of the JMM movement should be understood on two different levels. First, even though the nascent JMM showed all the signs of becoming a genuine mass movement and a democratizing force, dominant political players such as Congress and the Communist Party of India (Marxist) (CPI (M)) undermined such potential. Second, to the extent that the JMM served the interests of local elites, it was more than willing to negotiate with Congress and later with the ruling Hindu nationalist Bharatiya Janata Party (BJP) to secure the politically populist goal of a separate Jharkhand state. Research shows that the creation of the new state has further reinforced the entrenched power differences between the leaders and constituents, especially because of the ongoing withdrawal of state support for the social sector catering to marginalized groups, including Adivasis.[69] As mentioned earlier, similar to the effects of a cultural framing of Adivasi development in the rest of India, the ascendance of a politics of ethnoregionalism in Jharkhand has serious consequences for poor Adivasis. For example, Jharkhand has lagged behind in the implementation of the Forest Rights Act of 2006.[70] In a validation of the key argument made in this chapter, scholars of the Jharkhand movement have attributed the absence of distributive justice in the new state of Jharkhand to the nature of "political structures and the power relations that constitute them."[71] Notwithstanding a long history of active rebellion in the region, distributive justice is likely to remain impossible in the absence of contemporary spaces for popular contention of government's policies and programs.

Adivasi Peasant Movements in Maharashtra

The second case of forestland rights mobilization in India is related to a number of prominent Adivasi peasant mobilizations in the state of Maharashtra, including the Shramik Sangathana (Laborers and Peasants' Front) and the Kasthakari Sangathana (the Peasants' Front). Shramik Sangathana (or "Sangathana") was established in the state of Maharashtra in 1972.[72] The

---

68. Chandra 2013b, 259–60.
69. See essays in Sundar 2009; Corbridge and Srivastava 2013; Higham and Shah 2013.
70. MoTA 2014; Amit Gupta, *The Telegraph*, May 30, 2014, http://www.telegraphindia.com/1140530/jsp/frontpage/story_18425991.jsp.
71. I. Basu 2012, 1291.
72. This case draws upon Basu (1987) unless otherwise specified.

Sangathana's main demands included respectable wages for agricultural and annual contract laborers, restoring tribal land grabbed by landlords and rich settlers in the past, tribals' rights to cultivate forest land, and for public investment in creating local employment during periods of scarcity. From 1972 to 1974, the Sangathana successfully restored to peasants 4,000 acres of land that had been illegally occupied by settlers, forced the government to issue legal land rights, and successfully asserted the rights of Adivasi peasants who farmed parcels in state forestlands.[73]

The imposition of a state of constitutional emergency from 1975 to 1977 further constrained the already limited opportunities for autonomous political mobilization. This prompted Sangathana activists to think of long-term strategies to leverage grassroots mobilization for gaining greater influence in the political and policy arenas. As a first step, the Sangathana dabbled in electoral politics from 1977 to 1980, with very disappointing results.[74] Ultimately, the activists who were still convinced about the need to engage in electoral politics joined the CPM. Radical activists who chose to continue to work autonomously, meanwhile, faced repression at the hands of the state agencies.[75] As the Sangathana was gradually weakened, its members voted for Congress, which its supporters saw as the most viable political option. All was not lost though; Adivasi activists from the region filed a writ petition on the question of forestland rights in the Supreme Court of India in 1982.[76]

In addition, the decline of Shramik Sangathana coincided with the emergence of Kasthakari Sangathana founded by Jesuit activists. Kasthakari Sangathana was a professionally run advocacy group with strengths in legal and policy advocacy, which joined the ongoing legal battle regarding forestland rights at the Supreme Court in 1986. The Supreme Court ruled in 1995 in favor of protecting peasants' rights over the lands they farmed within areas set aside as state forests.[77] The Supreme Court also asked the state government to recognize land rights according to the "Maharashtra model" that these two Sangathanas had developed for the adjudication of forestland claims. The Sangathanas cited a long litany of rent-seeking practices and multiple conflicts of interest to question both the forestry officials' neutrality regarding land conflicts in forested areas and the legitimacy of documents

73. Joseph 2006.
74. As a matter of rule, social activists rarely do well in the electoral arena, irrespective of the length and strength of their association with prospective voters. Multiple instances from the states of Gujarat, Rajasthan, and Madhya Pradesh validate this conclusion. The results of the 2014 general elections also supported this rule as very senior activists who fought on the ticket of the Aam Admi Party (AAP) lost their elections by large margins.
75. Also see Baviskar 2001.
76. Lobo 2011; Asher and Agarwal 2007.
77. Lobo 2011.

the department used as "evidence" of de facto land occupation. Instead, the Supreme Court recognized the validity of elders' testimony as legal evidence of de facto land occupations. The Maharashtra model of adjudicating land rights informed the writing of the Forest Rights Act of 2006, discussed in Chapter 5.

Sociopolitical mobilization organized by the Sangathana, coupled with judicial and policy interventions by the Supreme Court, helped make a dent into forestry agencies' long-held monopoly over forestland policymaking. Despite repeated pleas by forestland rights activists, India's political leadership remained indifferent to concerns about conflicts of interest on the part of forestry agencies, which undermined the resolution of forestland conflicts. The two cases examined in this section show how the political and institutional contexts shaped the political mediation of forestland conflicts. While electoral competition is often recognized as an important force for pro-constituent policymaking, political rivalry between the JMM, the Congress Party, and the CPI (M) had the opposite effect in Jharkhand and Maharashtra. In the absence of well-organized mass organizations with sustained access to structures of political intermediation, electoral competition may undermine the interests of marginalized groups.

Tanzania: The Muzzling and Fragmentation of Peasant Dissent

The opening up of the civil and political space in Tanzania during the 1980s led to a surge in social and political mobilization. Many of the newly formed associations built on the remnants of earlier mobilization against the state's appropriation of customary land and forests. This included the 1989 grassroots mobilization in northern Tanzania against the leasing of 100,000 acres of land to a European company, Cattle Ranching Inc. In that case, community elders worked with a Maasai member of parliament, Edward Mollel, to have the lease canceled.[78] Such successes were few and far between, however. The period from 1985 to 1995 witnessed the appropriation of customary land fueled by party leaders and government officials' corrupt practices. Individuals in the positions of power resorted to overt and covert oppression of civil society actors, a process which was made easy by the involvement of some of the NGOs in neo-patrimonial activities.[79] In the wake of a sharp increase in the cases of land appropriations and land conflicts, the government set up the Shivji Commission, which fostered a lively engagement with civil society organizations in brainstorming land policy (see Chapter 3).[80] The government

78. Igoe 2003.
79. Ibid.; see also Tripp 2000.
80. The Shivji Commission was successful at starting a wide-ranging debate on land policy issues. Women's advocacy groups also took the commission to task for

promptly rejected the commission's recommendations, however, and came up with a National Land Policy in 1995 without a proper debate.[81]

The failure of political institutions to respond to local grievances related to land conflicts pushed these conflicts into the judicial arena.[82] Peasants approached the courts to redress various cases of land dispossession, including ones that resulted from Tanzania's villagization project. The government made an unsuccessful attempt to use legislation to negate judicial challenges to the government's absolute monopoly of land governance.[83] State attorneys argued in the Court of Appeals that "persons who held their land by customary law . . . did not have a property right in the land and so were not protected by the constitutional provisions against deprivation of property without compensation."[84] The Court of Appeals rejected these arguments and forced the government to amend land laws to recognize an individual citizen's right to be compensated for state-led land acquisitions, including the possibility of compensation for hardships and losses suffered during villagization. This success in the judicial arena attracted the interest of international human rights groups who collaborated with Tanzanian "indigenous" rights groups to bring more land conflicts to the courts.

This surge in legal interventions, which the international NGOs had hoped would herald protection of land rights for pastoral and other indigenous groups, produced two major unanticipated (and negative) effects. First, the publicity that high-profile international groups brought to the land cases transformed these legal contests into "politically difficult" affairs that judges did not want to handle.[85] Second, engaging with the legal system distracted Tanzanian NGOs from their core agenda of sociopolitical mobilization. Instead of alerting international organizations to these and other domestic political realities, Tanzanian indigenous advocacy groups became an instrumental link between local populations and a "global system of institutions, ideas, and money."[86] Overall, these legal interventions undermined the prospects of greater engagement between social movements, political actors, and state institutions. Such engagement is extremely important because unlike other African countries, the issue of land rights in Tanzania does not engender political mobilization along ethnic lines.[87] While it is desirable to avoid

endorsing customary land inheritance laws without first addressing the discriminatory effects of customary law on women's land rights (Mallya 1999).

81. Kamata 1998, cited in Mallya 1999.
82. Cf. Boone and Nyeme 2015.
83. Fratkin and Sher-Mei-Wu 1997.
84. McAuslan 1998, 528.
85. Igo 2003.
86. Igoe 2003, 868.
87. Boone and Nyeme 2015.

mobilization that threatens to create, or reinforce, ethnic divisions, there is a need for mobilizing to promote political and economic interests of peasants.

Recent developments in the case of the Loliondo wildlife corridor further validate the argument in favor of such a mobilization. The Loliondo region has been home to recurring forestland conflicts since 1992, when the Tanzanian government leased a large area of land to the Ortello Business Corporation (OBC), which is owned by a senior official in the United Arab Emirates (UAE) military. OBC's business model is to fly wealthy clients into Tanzania to indulge in trophy hunting of lions and leopards. OBC did not bring in any visitors for first few years, so it did not enforce its control over the leased land, which kept the conflicts to a minimum. In 2009, however, the paramilitary Tanzanian Field Force unit forcefully relocated nearly three hundred Maasai households in the Loliondo region, with the intention of creating a 1,500-square kilometer (579-square mile) livestock-free wildlife corridor under exclusive OBC control.[88] This attempt to create the new wildlife corridor under the provisions of the 2009 Wildlife Conservation Act would have displaced twenty thousand to thirty thousand people and affect tens of thousands more that used the land for cattle grazing during the dry season.[89] In the run-up to Tanzania's 2010 election, Maasai women in Loliondo decided to organize protests against the government's predatory land policies. The following account from activist and blogger Susanna Nordlund offers a vivid account of the events:

> On 6 April 2010 women had started gathering to go to Loliondo town to hand in their CCM member cards . . . In Ololosokwan 400 women had gathered but were warned by the police that they would be fired at if they moved to Loliondo. They neglected the warning and set off, only to be intercepted in Oloipiri where they . . . were put on a truck back to Ololosokwan. Another 60 women coming from Enguserosambu were arrested and interrogated for hours, but 500 women, who had spent the night in the bush near Wasso, reached the CCM office in Loliondo and handed in 1,883 party cards . . . If their demands were not met by 16 April, the women said they would return . . . [in] thousands. In response the DC [District Commissioner] went after NGOs [he blamed for instigating] the protest. On 12 April three male civil society organisation representatives . . . were arrested, interrogated and locked up for the night by the Officer Commanding District.[90]

88. Blomley et al. 2013.
89. The BBC put the number at thirty thousand. See Jason Patinkin, "Tanzania's Maasai battle game hunters for grazing land" BBC News, Loliondo, Tanzania, April 18, 2013. http://www.bbc.com/news/world-africa-22155538. *The Guardian* put it at twenty thousand. See Maanda Ngoitiko and Fred Nelson, "What Africa can learn from Tanzania's remarkable Masai lands rights victory," *The Guardian*, October 8, 2013. http://www.theguardian.com/global-development/poverty-matters/2013/oct/08/africa-tanzania-masai-land-rights-victory.
90. Susanna Nordlund, "OBC—Hunters from Dubai and the Threat against 1,500 km² of Maasai Land in Loliondo," December 30, 2015. Last accessed March 18, 2016.

The importance of these women's mobilization is corroborated by other scholars, who suggest that these events likely dented the support in Loliondo for the ruling CCM during the 2010 elections, thereby allowing the opposition CHADEMA Party (Chama cha Demokrasia) to make significant inroads.[91] The Maasais also collaborated with a number of Tanzanian and international NGOs that made effective use of a range of advocacy tools, including the online petition site Avaaz.[92] These efforts seemed to have prompted Tanzania's President Jakaya Kikwete to personally tweet a denial of claims that his government was planning to evict the Maasais.[93] However, barely four months after the president's tweet, wildlife rangers burned and destroyed 114 Maasai households, which rendered thousands of people homeless in the middle of winter.[94] Despite all these conflicts, the ruling party managed to secure the Ngorongoro parliamentary constituency in the general elections held in October 2015 by nominating William Ole Nasha, who is an activist for the pastoralist communities.[95]

The disconnect between popular interests and policies and politics in Tanzania is explained by the phenomenon of electoral authoritarianism, as the ruling party enjoys "competitive hegemony" and is able to dominate elections without having to resort to electoral fraud or coercion.[96] As opposed to the Indian case discussed earlier, the Maasais and other forest-dependent groups in Tanzania have been unable to make the country's institutions work in their favor.

Peasant Mobilizations and Political Articulation in Mexico

Most discussions of Mexico's social movements concentrate on the neo-Zapatistas who took to arms in the state of Chiapas during January 1994. Even so, myriad other peasant groups that do not see confrontation with the

http://termitemoundview.blogspot.com/2015/12/obc-hunters-from-dubai-and-threat.html.

91. Nelson et al. 2012.
92. Avaaz, "Stand with the Maasai." https://secure.avaaz.org/en/save_the_maasai_sam/.
93. Jakaya Kikwete, Twitter status. November 23, 2014 https://twitter.com/jmkikwete/status/536439161927266305. For an updated report from the field, see Susanna Nordlund, "Reply to the Ministry for Natural Resources and Tourism's press release about Loliondo." November 28, 2014 http://termitemoundview.blogspot.se/2014/11/reply-to-ministry-for-natural-resources.html.
94. Charles Ngereza, "Wardens raze 114 bomas, thousands stranded," *Just Conservation*, February 15, 2015, http://www.justconservation.org/wardens-raze-114-bomas,-thousands-stranded.
95. Zephania Ubwani. "Chadema retains northern stronghold." *The Citizen*, October 28, 2015. http://www.thecitizen.co.tz/tanzaniadecides/-/2926962/2933554/-/cawqkqz/-/ index.html.
96. Morse 2014.

state as their main goal have contributed as much, if not more, to the resilience of peasant politics in the country. These groups mobilized to hold the state accountable for its constitutional mandate of fulfilling the revolutionary dream. For most of the twentieth century in Mexico, party-controlled peasant federations held the most sway over rural areas. But in the 1970s, a new breed of peasant organizations and federations emerged to tap into state-led programs designed specifically for peasants and indigenous groups.

An overview of the Union de Ejidos Lázaro Cárdenas (UELC) offers some insights into this kind of mobilization. A group of community organizers working with PIDER (Integrated Investment Program for Rural Development) founded the UELC in 1975.[97] Like many other regional peasant organizations founded in the 1970s, the UELC built on the accumulated political energy of the previous rounds of peasant mobilizations.[98] With the intention of preventing these new peasant organizations from becoming autonomous, Mexico's PRI ruling party leaders sought to coopt them. Additionally, the UELC also encountered state repression. Even so, the UELC reorganized in 1980 as part of another federal food distribution program. Under that program, the UELC administered a new region-wide community food supply council and subsequently implemented a self-managed housing project, led campaigns for higher crop prices, and fostered a women's network. Each of these activities created new opportunities for local economic development and fostered political participation.[99] The UELC is not an exception, however. State-sponsored social welfare programs led to the emergence of a large number of peasant mobilizations and a new wave of contentious politics.[100] Neil Harvey lists fourteen "principal peasant movements" active in Mexico at different times during the fifty years from 1938 to 1988.[101] Especially insightful is Harvey's discussion of the dense set of associational activities that led to the evolution of the National "Plan of Ayala" Coordinator (CNPA), a semi-autonomous confederation of peasant groups, which in the 1980s assisted many ejidos entangled in political and legal battles against logging corporations.

Many autonomous regional peasant organizations came together in 1985 to form the National Union of Autonomous Regional Peasant Organizations (UNORCA), which adapted rapidly to the changing political and economic context of the second half of the 1980s. A month before the inauguration of Salinas's presidency in 1988, ten national peasant and indigenous organizations signed the Unitary Action Agreement *(Convenio de Acción Unitaria,* CAU), which articulated demands for land redistributions, state support for

---

97. PIDER stands for *Programa de Inversiones en el Desarrollo Rural.*
98. Stephen 2010.
99. Fox and Hernández 1989.
100. Fox and Hernández 1989; Fox 2007.
101. Harvey 1990.

the peasantry, and respecting the territorial rights of indigenous peoples. This mobilization forced the new president, who was fully committed to getting the state out of the rural sectors, to announce "Ten Items for Freedom and Justice in the Countryside," which included the allocation of resources for land redistributions.[102] Even though this chapter focuses on land rights, it is worth pointing out that many of these peasant organizations went on to play an important role in the Mexican model of community forestry that evolved in the late 1980s and the 1990s. Thus, well before the new-age environmental services program became fashionable, these peasant organizations realized that rural poverty could not be conquered without the rejuvenation and productive use of the natural resource bases, including through the "niche" markets and alternative production techniques.[103]

Despite the strongly Marxist ideological background of many of the leaders of these organizations, they worked to build parallel pathways of multipronged engagement with the new economy and politics. Many campesino organizations actively participated in the debates in the run-up to and aftermath of the agrarian reforms the government pushed through in 1992. More importantly, as I discuss in Chapter 6, the government has been forced to recast wildlife and forestry conservation interventions into rural development programs because of the strong engagement of peasant organizations on the ground and continued volatility of rural voters.[104] Several peasant organizations, such as UNORCA, successfully straddle domestic and international policymaking arenas. UNORCA worked with the Salinas administration and participated in community forestry development; it also became part of the International Peasant and Indigenous Forum, which was organized in opposition to the fifth World Trade Organization (WTO) Ministerial Conference held in September 2003 in Cancún, Mexico.[105]

None of these strategies have produced perfectly happy outcomes for all parties involved, especially as economic liberalization continues to undermine peasant organizations in a variety of ways.[106] Even so, as this section showed, the multipronged, cross-scale engagements between campesino federations and the ruling party have yielded important gains in forest and land rights, economic development, and social organization.[107] Further evidence to this effect is presented in Chapters 6 and 7, which analyze contemporary policy processes and outcomes of institutional reforms.

102. Bartra and Otero 2005.
103. Bray 1995, 189.
104. Haenn 2003, 2006; Shapiro 2013.
105. Bartra and Otero 2005; Jung 2008.
106. Rosset et al. 2006.
107. Fox 1994, 1996, 2007. For a contrary perspective, see Grammont et al. 2009.

4.3 CONCLUSION

References to colonial-era policies or the neo-colonial attitude of political elites are commonplace in the discussion of forestland rights, especially in the context of indigenous land rights.[108] This chapter analyzed the variation in political mediation of land rights conflicts in the case study countries. Even though the imprint of historical legacies—both detrimental (as in the case of India and Tanzania) and supportive (as in the case of Mexico)—are evident in this chapter, political structures played an important role in the post-independence and post-revolutionary mediation of land rights conflicts. While the dominant parties in both India and Tanzania instituted a corporatist party structure to integrate the party states with strategies of voter mobilization, it led to creation of local despots, whose main role was to contain the peasantry. These strategies served the interests of the country's political elites and the middle classes, while successfully preventing large-scale civil disturbances.

This chapter demonstrates that sociopolitical mobilizations, and forestland advocates' access to institutions of judiciary, have been much stronger in India than in Tanzania. Yet, for the large part, these disparities did not make a proportionate difference to the security of forest and land rights in the two countries. Both of these cases differed from Mexico, where forest and land rights were facilitated by the emergence of party-constituent links and mechanisms of political intermediation. One must be cautioned against reading these differences through a design-oriented perspective—the notion that mechanisms of political intermediation can be designed into effectiveness. Instead, as scholars of development studies have argued in the context of poverty alleviation, opportunities for political engagement emerge as a result of a configuration of actors, agencies, and institutions within a political context, thereby offering a meaningful space to marginalized groups.[109] Even so, as comparative politics scholars would argue, political parties will not bear the cost of putting up well-organized corporatist structures unless they are forced to.

Mexican peasant corporatism did indeed serve the ruling PRI well, allowing it to retain power for the most part since the introduction of multiparty elections in 1994. It also helped peasant groups retain a foothold in the policy process, although the implications of such engagement are contested by scholars from different perspectives.[110] Some scholars may question the inferences drawn either because of the qualitative nature of the evidence, or because of the positive institutionalist approaches to questions that are normatively contested. The conclusions drawn up to this point have been based on snapshots

---

108. Philip 2001; Saldaña-Portillo 2003.
109. Webster and Engberg-Pedersen 2002; Bebbington 2008.
110. Bartra and Otero 2005; Jung 2008; Grammont et al. 2009.

of the colonial and post-colonial era processes and outcomes related to contestations over forestland regimes. In later chapters, these conclusions will be subjected to further scrutiny via an analysis of contemporary institutional reforms and policy processes.

What if the political context changes in ways that improve forestland advocacy groups' ability to engage more directly with the political and policy processes? The political economy of institutions framework would suggest that when these conditions exist (as they did in India beginning around 2000), political parties and elected governments demonstrate perceptible improvement on the question of forestland rights (see Chapter 5). On the other hand, working with the support of donor agencies, the Tanzanian government also decided to afford greater security of land rights to the country's forest-dependent people, while Mexico's leaders decided to weaken the level of protection afforded to peasant groups and forestland rights. In each of these cases, the framework outlined in this book would suggest that the status of land rights, in the either direction, would be tempered according to the structures of political intermediation accessible to forest-dependent peasants. Testing these claims is the main analytical goal of the two chapters in Part II. Chapters 5 analyzes the issue in the Indian context, while Chapter 6 examines the politics of recent institutional reforms in Tanzania and Mexico, and concludes with a comparative analysis of the responses in all three countries.

PART II

Politics of Institutional Change

It is notoriously difficult to enact institutional reforms that constrain the executive and even more difficult to implement them. A majority of developing countries' policies, especially regarding the hinterlands, far too often fall prey to "implementation failures." The emphasis on explaining these implementation "failures," however, detracts from an acknowledgment that these reforms are often actually "designed to fail."[1] Two chapters in this part examine the politics of institutional reforms, by situating reforms within the political contexts of the national forestland regimes examined in Part I. This contextualization of policy formulation and implementation sheds light on various parties' motivations in the run-up to reforms and in the course of their implementation. The comparative analysis of institutional reforms in this part is divided between Chapters 5 and 6, and this part summary introduces ideas and concepts that inform the analysis in each of those two chapters.

The main goals of the reforms in each of the three case study countries was to bring about a greater formalization of both household land rights and community forest rights. Household land rights pertain to de facto land use practices (mainly related to farming) and collective rights to pastoral and forest-based land use. But in none of these countries were the reforms designed to redistribute land or to impose a predetermined choice of property rights (see Table 5.1).

In India, reforms recognized land tenure rights for the parcels of land that peasant households had been farming before the cutoff date of December 2005. Wildlife activists cried foul, arguing that it would cause a scramble for land in areas that house India's "last remaining forests."[2] On the other

1. R. Mitchell 2001, 222; See also Ascher 1999; Wagemans and Boerma 2000.
2. Ashish Kothari, "Saving conservation laws from the conservationists!" *InfoChange News & Features*, April 2008. http://infochangeindia.org/environment/politics-of-biodiversity/saving-conservation-laws-from-the-conservationists.html.

Table 5.1 INSTITUTIONAL REFORMS FOR ADDRESSING LAND RIGHTS CONFLICTS

Country	Key legislations	Relevant local authority	Final decision-making authority	Pre-reform constraints	De facto status (pre-reform)	Post-reform status (de jure)
India	Forest Rights Act of 2006	Forest Rights Committee/ Village General Assembly	District Forest Rights Committee led by government officials	Landholding illegal. Threats of dispossession significant.	Farming continues if forest officials are suitably bribed.	Land rights recognized in the statute; "title" with restrictions on sale/lease.
Mexico	Article 27 of the Constitution/1992 Reforms	Ejido Commissioners/ ejido general assembly	Ejido general assembly	Formal restrictions on land and labor markets; lease or sale not allowed.	Informal/"black" labor and land markets common	Legal to hire labor for working ejido land. Depending on the level of "privatization" approved by an ejido, parcel land could be leased/sold to other ejidatarios/outsiders.
Tanzania	Land Act (LA) 1999; Village Land Act (VLA) 1999 plus the ongoing processes of land registration according to the provisions of the acts.	Village General Assembly	District Government/ National Land Commissioner	Landholding is legal, but without a title. Threats of dispossession significant in forested regions.	Landholding safe, until government decides to take over the land for some "public purposes."	Mortgage and sale of the household land allowed; village councils/assemblies gain authority to issue certificates of customary land ownership (CCLOs) to households. Government must compensate a registered landowner if it acquires land.

hand, some Adivasi activists argued, quite erroneously, that peasants were not actually interested in claiming household land rights, which these activists considered to be part of a neoliberal agenda.[3] The reforms in Tanzania followed the model of land registration popularized by Peruvian economist Hernando de Soto.[4] In Mexico, meanwhile, the debates about land reform were particularly intense; opponents accused the government of privatizing the ejido sector, while reform supporters argued that peasants needed to be freed from the political and economic shackles put in place by the PRI regime. Scholars in Mexico who were critical of the 1992 reforms often refer to them as "counter-reforms."[5]

Ultimately, these land reforms in India, Tanzania, and Mexico did not lead to the dramatic changes that either the proponents or the detractors had anticipated. Taking such counterintuitive outcomes as a point of departure, I argue that existing property rights theories as well as popular ideas about indigenous and customary land rights are inadequately nuanced to predict how peasants think of land rights within the context of forestland regimes in each of these countries. The arguments presented here differ significantly from one important body of property rights scholarship that emphasizes ambiguity.[6] While responses to property rights reforms may appear ambiguous compared with the expectations that are attached normally to the promises of private property rights, I argue that such ambiguity reflects peasants' purposive actions and strategies that are based on their understanding of their political, economic, and institutional contexts. Chapter 5 offers a detailed analysis of the politics surrounding the enactment and implementation of India's Forest Rights Act (FRA) in 2006. By employing the tools of political ethnography, I also show how practices of claim-making are deeply intertwined with the political economy of state-society relations, especially with the mediating role of elected representatives. Chapter 6 offers a similar examination of the politics of institutional reforms introduced in Tanzania and Mexico.

At the center of this analysis are the claims to land rights associated with de facto land use practices of farming, agro-pastoralism, and pastoralism. In many cases, however, and particularly in forested regions, these practices, including farming, are not recorded in the formal law. Researchers and policymakers often refer to these de facto land use practices as "traditional" or "customary" practices of land access and control.[7] The de facto land rights and

---

3. Group discussion, Adivasi Academy, Tejgarh, March 6, 2009. Personal interview, Adivasi political activist, summer 2009.
4. de Soto 1989, 2000.
5. Navarro Olmedo et al. 2015.
6. von Benda-Beckmann et al. 2009. For a critical engagement with this scholarship, see Sturgeon and Sikor 2004.
7. Catherine Boone's work shows that many of the "customary" land tenure regimes are a result of state interventions in the twentieth century. See Boone 2013.

land use claims discussed here are similar to the de facto asset "ownership" that economist Hernando de Soto refers to as "extra-legal."[8] Even though de Soto's work pertains to informal urban squatter settlements, his ideas have been influential in the formalization of land rights more generally.[9]

While de Soto's emphasis on the security of land rights overlaps with the core concerns of this research, his emphasis on marketization and financialization of "dead capital"—land and other assets owned without formal legal recognition—does not. The notion of dead capital is misplaced on at least two counts. First, de facto forest and land use practices are often integral to local livelihoods in developing countries, particularly for a large number of rural residents' subsistence activities. Consequently, the so-called extra-legal land and forest uses are "productive" in ways that matter significantly to the de facto landowners. Second, government officials and agencies often use the extra-legality of land claims as a way to extract rents from de facto land users. The extra-legal use and ownership is thus also "productive," because it serves important political and economic goals for powerful local actors. Accordingly, the extra-legal assets are not dead capital, nor is the financialization of assets a priority for a large number of forest-dependent peasants. However, security of land rights is still an important issue because residents in the forested regions would prefer not to be subjected to diktats from local elites or be held hostage by the vagaries of colonial-era forest laws.

The ability of individuals or groups of individuals to secure effective access to forest and land rights is often tied to a variety of other means of access.[10] The design of forestry and wildlife laws forces forest-dependent people in developing countries to enter into clientelistic relationships with forestry officials.[11] In the absence of formal state-backed protection and enforcement of forest and land rights, forest-dependent individuals and groups must depend on influential actors and agencies that can provide locally effective enforcement.[12] Enforcement in this context means an assurance that if a government official or agency instructs a de facto landholder to give up his occupation of land, a local chief or leader would argue on his or her behalf. As discussed earlier, one must not equate the absence of state-backed *enforcement* to the absence of the state or state agents. State officials—whether elected or appointed—are often the first beneficiaries of the discretionary and uncertain

8. de Soto 1989, 2000.

9. In fact, in many of the countries that are part of de Soto's studies, including Indonesia and his native Peru, the questions of forestland rights are mired in ongoing conflicts. In this sense, the core problem is not necessarily about informal land rights, but about *contested* land rights.

10. For an extensive discussion of "access," as a critique of property rights theory, see Ribot and Peluso 2003.

11. For a related discussion, see Kashwan and Lobo 2014.

12. Joireman 2011; Peters and Daimon 2007; Boone 2013.

enforcement of laws related to the regulation of natural resources.[13] These officials also recruit influential local leaders and elites to establish and maintain effective networks of discretionary enforcement.

Laws constitute one important element within a broader configuration of enabling conditions that contribute to an effective social and political order. Accordingly, law is necessary—but by itself insufficient—to help peasants achieve security of land rights. Yet, the weaknesses of poorly enforced laws in the Global South has led some to question the value of enacting laws that offer legal and statutory protection of land rights. Such ambiguity about laws seems to have preempted an examination of the comparative differences in how laws perform in different political contexts. The debates about the necessity of land rights laws gain new salience in the context of several developing countries' recent large-scale land acquisitions for economic development and environmental conservation projects.[14] Government's ability to realign local property relations is integral to the pursuit of the lofty goals of "national" development or nature conservation as a global public good, each of which requires control over and regulation of the resources of the hinterlands. For the sake of political and economic advancement, local and regional leaders are often willing to facilitate the transfer of resource control from informal local economies to regimes of national and transnational resource use. Because household land rights and community forest rights remain unrecognized or are subject to competing interpretations by different government agencies, national governments often find it easy to justify the allocation of these lands for large-scale development or conservation projects.

The effects of contested land rights are not restricted to land takeovers; their effect on the recognition of forest-dependent people's role in environmental conservation deserves greater attention. First, let us consider the role of government forestry agencies in Mexico, which is an example of environmental regulation, as it is commonly understood in the environmental policy literature.

Mexico's forestry sector is characterized by relatively secured formal rights for peasants and regulatory laws that place restrictions on specific activities that are likely to undermine the outcomes that the country's forestry regulations are intended to protect. As discussed earlier, campesinos and indigenous groups that are organized into agrarian communities own nearly 70 percent of the country's forests. More specifically, Mexican agrarian communities hold proprietary rights in these lands, which is not same as private ownership though that is how proprietary rights are understood in common parlance.[15]

---

13. Onoma 2010.
14. De Schutter 2011; German et al. 2013.
15. For a theoretical explanation, see Schlager and Ostrom 1992.

It means instead that proprietary right holders control all aspects of land use and management, except alienation (the ability to sell these properties).[16] Mexico's federal forestry agencies have the power to restrict activities that damage the forests that stand on the lands controlled by agrarian communities. More importantly, communities have a right to make sustainable use of forest resources, including timber logging organized according to a pre-approved management plan. In other words, agrarian communities in Mexico are free to use their lands in the way they please, with the exception of activities that are prohibited explicitly under specific laws.

But the Mexican forestry sector is something of an exception in the developing world. According to forestry laws operational in most countries in Asia and sub-Saharan Africa, forest-dependent people who live within areas that have been designated as state forests may only undertake activities specifically permitted under the law; everything else is prohibited.[17] For example, according to the 1927 Indian Forest Act (IFA) covering reserve forests (one of the two categories of territorial forests), "all activities are prohibited unless permitted."[18] In these cases, forestry laws' wide-ranging restrictions essentially criminalize the life and livelihood of forest-dependent people. As one British colonial forest officer once said to anthropologist Verrier Elwin, "Our laws are of such a kind that every villager breaks one forest law every day of his life."[19] The IFA, which remains in effect even to this day, enables forestry officials to arrest suspected offenders without a warrant.[20] Similarly, the forest-dependent Maasai population in Tanzania does not hold effective jurisdiction over fixed areas of land where they practice pastoralism. They have been threatened repeatedly, and as mentioned earlier in Chapters 3 and 4, subjected to gross human rights violations at the hands of Serengeti park rangers.

The high-handed approach of forestry agencies in India and Tanzania is neither a coincidence nor exceptional. Forestlands in these countries are governed with an approach that political ecologists recognize as "territoriality," which is the attempt, mainly by governments, to "affect, influence, or control people, phenomena, and relationships by delimiting and asserting control over a geographic area."[21] It entails controls over human behavior as if human presence, even if well-established and continuous, is an anomaly to

16. Some scholars suggest that the 1992 reforms "privatized" Mexican community lands. As I explain in Chapter 6, this is an erroneous representation of the reforms' statutory and practical outcomes. For a careful analysis of how the 1992 reforms further strengthened community control over commons, see Bray 2013.
17. Neumann 1997.
18. Macura et al. 2011, 10.
19. Guha 2001, 219.
20. Haeuber 1993a, 57.
21. Sack 1986, 19.

be kept under constant surveillance.[22] This is the most important aspect of territoriality, which cannot be altered simply by granting household land rights or collective customary rights. Instead, it requires changes in super rules—the "rules that govern how other rules are made."[23] They determine what questions are debated within political and policy arenas, who participate in these discussions, how priorities are determined, and which among a variety of possible operational rules become part of a policy or a program. These questions are yet to be revisited in the context of developing country forestry policies because a narrowly defined agenda informs forestry laws and their strict enforcement by forestry agencies and wildlife rangers. This narrow approach vis-à-vis forestry enjoys broad-based national and international legitimacy and support, which enables them to disregard other laws meant to protect peasant land rights.[24]

Forestland rights conflicts are therefore not just about the insecurity of household land rights, but also about the powers and authority that government agencies enjoy in the forested regions.[25] The next two chapters analyze institutional reforms related to forest and land rights formalization within the context of the competing layers of institutions described above.

22. This discussion builds on, but adds to, the explanations by Véron and Fehr 2011, 285 citing Vandergeest and Peluso 1995.
23. Steinberg 2015, 178. Scholars of institutional analysis and development theories refer to them as "constitutional choice rules." See Ostrom 2011
24. Ribot and Larson 2011; Kashwan 2013.
25. Neumann 1997.

CHAPTER 5

✂

Politics of Institutional Change in India's Forestland Regimes

Nearly sixty years after independence, India's parliament finally managed to make a dent in the well-entrenched status quo in India's forestland regimes with the Forest Rights Act (FRA) of 2006. The FRA prompted a wide range of responses. While a local forest rights activist from northern India called it the moment of true freedom for hundreds of millions of India's forest-dependent people, the editor of a prominent nature conservation magazine described it as the Indian democracy's "lowest hour."[1] This chapter examines the contested politics of the FRA, which constitutes a case of over-time variation in India's forestland regimes. While the political mobilization of constituents is a necessary condition for reform, in most cases it is not sufficient to produce transformational institutional change.[2] In this chapter, I argue that the FRA's enactment can be attributed to the emergence of a number of interrelated political intermediation mechanisms. Furthermore, I show that the FRA's implementation failures can be attributed to the absence of state-society networks and the robustness of power relations within specific institutional niches, which benefit from the pragmatic legitimacy that the state enjoys among many forest-dependent people and local leaders.

In the next section, I show how the status quo regarding forestland rights in India at the onset of the twenty-first century was itself a product of the past struggles geared to prompt the state into taking action. The institutional

---

1. Roma and Chowdhury 2010; *The Hindu,* "A nation's progress." New Delhi, April 14, 2010.
2. Agrawal and Ostrom 2001; Fox 2007.

and individual legacies of those struggles shaped the contemporary political contestation related to forestland questions, which led to the enactment of the FRA. Despite the emergence of a uniquely conducive political opportunity structure, the forestland rights movements and their supporters had to mobilize elite policymakers in the nation's capital and their constituents on the street to push the policymakers to enact the FRA (Section 5.2). The access that some members of the forestland movements had to the mechanisms of political intermediation via formal institutions was crucial, but proved insufficient in the end. The forestland movements overcame their limitations by relying on other mechanisms that were peripheral to the policymaking process, but were tied more closely to popular politics in the hinterlands (Section 5.3). Lastly, this chapter examines how elected representatives' involvement at each of the three stages of FRA implementation did not guarantee effective implementation of the law. The law encountered two major barriers: first, the subjective understanding of political representation, which guided elected representatives at district and subdistrict levels, and second, the entrenched power of political brokers in local enclaves.

5.1 BACKGROUND: INSTITUTIONAL LEGACIES

In 1976, the Indian central government passed an ordinance that allowed it to deprive state governments of the powers to alter land use in large tracts of land designated as state forests. This ordinance, along with the Forest Conservation Act of 1980, took away state governments' ability to resolve longstanding forestland conflicts, as discussed in Chapter 3. As such, India's forestland regime witnessed a recentralization of decision-making powers related to questions of social justice in forestry.

On the other hand, India's forestland regime was poised for de-concentration of authority required for forest management via the Draft Forest Bill of 1980. This bill proposed to authorize state governments to enclose a forest for thirty years and to suspend individuals' land rights. It also proposed to empower a forest officer or a police officer to arrest an individual, without a warrant, on a *reasonable suspicion* of a person's involvement in a forest offense.[3] The centralization of decision-making powers vis-à-vis questions of land use governance, and the de-concentration of local regulatory authority contradicts the assumptions, common in the forestry policy literature, that Indian forestry has witnessed progressive decentralization since the 1980s.[4]

---

3. Kulkarni 1982, 57; Guha 1983.
4. Cf. Hobley 1996; Saxena 1997; for creation of community-based regulatory authority, see Agrawal 2001b.

The draft forest bill became a rallying point for civil and political liberties activists and forestland rights movements. While this mobilization centered on questions of forest rights and had as its main demand the increased decentralization of forest management, the People's Union for Democratic Reforms (PUDR) and other civil liberties groups invoked the longstanding questions of forestland conflicts.[5] Concerted social and political mobilizations led by forest and land rights groups forced the government to shelve the draft bill, but it did not lead to much progress on resolving the question of forestland conflicts. Even so, these questions drew the interest of other constitutional authorities, such as the Commissioner for Scheduled Castes and Scheduled Tribes. In a 1988 report to the president of India, Commissioner B.D. Sharma appealed for justice and proposed a comprehensive framework for ending the chronic conflict between Adivasis and the forest officials.[6] This report formed the basis of yet another report authored by Sharma, in his capacity as the secretary of a committee of parliamentarians. This committee, named after its chairman and popularly known as the Bhuria Committee, asked the government to grant greater autonomy to Adivasi communities in the governance of local affairs, including the management of natural resources.

The federal government failed to pay heed to the commissioner's report or implement the Bhuria Committee's recommendations in a timely fashion.[7] Activists groups, including Sharma's Bharat Jan Andolan (lit., Peoples' Movement of India), organized mass protests and marches, which combined with the presence of supportive political actors in key positions, led to the enactment of the Panchayat (Extension to the Scheduled Areas) Act 1996 (PESA).[8] PESA is the local governance law that applies exclusively to Adivasi-dominated forested regions and gives village assemblies the right to determine the appropriate use of forests, land, minerals, and other natural resources.[9] The persuasive efforts of Purno Sangma, an Adivasi leader from northeast of India who was speaker of the lower house of Parliament, led to a unanimous enactment of PESA "without any discussion" in Parliament.[10] For a variety of reasons, the discussion of which is beyond the scope of this text, the PESA failed to transform local governance and resource management.[11] Even so,

5. The PUDR brought out a comprehensive report about the political economy of forestland conflict with an evocative title—*Undeclared Civil War*. See PUDR 1982.
6. Sharma 1989; Kalpavriksh 2002, 7.
7. While the Ministry of Environment and Forests issued a set of six executive orders in 1990 outlining a framework for resolving forestland conflicts, it is widely recognized that no sincere efforts were made to implement them. See MoEF 2004; Drèze 2005.
8. Kalpavriksh 2000.
9. PESA shares a number of important features with Tanzania's Village Land Act, discussed in Chapters 4 and 6 though, to the best of my knowledge, no comparative analyses exist.
10. Singh 2005.
11. Kurup 2008.

PESA constitutes an important legal and symbolic anchor for the advocates of Adivasi forest and land rights.[12] PESA's jurisdiction extends to the governance of natural resources in large tracts of hinterlands, which the central and state governments consider crucial for industrialization and infrastructure development in contemporary India.[13]

The PESA also has produced a number of highly salient institutional effects. Based on a reading of the PESA and a local government law in the state of Andhra Pradesh, the Supreme Court of India barred the central and the state governments from granting private corporations any mining permits in areas under PESA jurisdiction.[14] In this judgment, widely known as the Samata judgment, the court argued that neither government agencies nor private industries may make unilateral decisions about the use and management of resources without prior and informed consent of the affected communities.[15] The PESA and the Samata judgment stand as important legal precedents, though in practice they do not deter governments from making unilateral decisions regarding the exploitation of natural resources.

Despite the "liberalization" of India's economy in late 1980s, the Indian state remains at the center of the contemporary landscape of economic development.[16] The situation is especially precarious in the hinterlands, where the state has authorized the acquisition of lands designated as village commons and state forests for mining and industrial development.[17]

Of the 921,760 hectares of state forestland officially diverted for non-forestry activities between 1980 and 2003, more than 94 percent were allocated to large-scale development projects, including dams, mines, industrial enterprises, and roads.[18] A recent analysis by the Center for Science and Environment revealed that between the years, 2007 and 2011, the Ministry of Environment and Forests (MoEF) reallocated an additional 204,425 hectares of forestland for non-forestry purposes mentioned above.[19] The Ministry of Mines in New Delhi has made concerted efforts to convince various central

12. Sundar 2005; Menon 2007; Noronha et al. 2009.
13. Dandekar and Choudhury 2010.
14. Menon 2007.
15. The lands in question also were farmed by Adivasis who had been demanding land rights, although most discussions of Samata judgment emphasize its implications for lands that have been designated as village commons. See Samata, "The Fifth Schedule of the Constitution and the Samatha Judgment," November 15, 2001. http://www.samataindia.org.in/documents/SAMATA_EDIT1.PDF.
16. Gupta and Sivaramakrishnan 2011; Oskarsson 2013; Chandra 2015.
17. See essays in Rights and Resources Initiative 2012.
18. Rajya Sabha (Upper house of the Parliament) Unstarred Question No. 395, dated December 5, 2003, cited in Bijoy 2008, 1767.
19. Center for Science and Environment (CSE), *Public Watch: Overview (Forest and Environmental Clearances)*. Last accessed November 22, 2015 at www.cseindia.org/userfiles/Overview.pdf.

and state ministries to counter and nullify the effects of PESA and the Samata judgment, as a secret office memo now available in the public domain reveals.[20] The federal government and state governments also appealed formally to the Supreme Court in early 2000 to review the Samata judgment.[21] While the court ruled out such a revision, governments have not abandoned the agenda.[22] The illegal allocation of resources continues nevertheless, as evident from the coal block allocation scandal, in which between 1993 and 2011, Indian governments gave away, to government and private companies the rights to mine more than 60 billion tons of coal for free and without following transparent procedures.[23] Because of the devastating environmental consequences of such large scale mining and the potential for utilizing the income the government could have earned through transparent auctions, the coal block scam is closely intertwined with questions of social justice and environmental protections.[24]

As discussed in Chapter 4, because forested landscapes contain large areas of lands and valuable natural resources, they are at the center of a variety of resource transfers. Lest the reader thinks of these conflicts as a result of the "trade-off" that the state must make in an effort to pursue economic growth, consider the following assessment by Raghuram Rajan, the University of Chicago economist and the former governor of the Reserve Bank of India:

> Unfortunately, powerful interests who thrive on … murkiness of land rights never want any reforms to see the light of day. This group of powerful "insiders" includes corrupt politicians, well-connected industrialists, developers and the mafia. They control much of the lucrative land market and make enormous monopolistic gains.[25]

The centralization of regulatory powers over corporate and state-sponsored projects in forested regions creates opportunities for rent-seeking. Similarly, a former minister of tribal affairs who I interviewed implied that large-scale collusion occurs between corporations, forest bureaucrats, and politicians.[26] This

20. Anon, "Secret: Government of India, Ministry of Mines, No.16/48/97-M.VI, Dated the 10th July, 2000" publicly available via http://mmpindia.in/Mining%20 secret%20note.htm.
21. See Mathur 2009.
22. Behar 2002; Sundar 2006; Menon 2007.
23. Author's computation based on the data available from media reports. See Vivek Kaul. "All you wanted to know about the coal scam." *DNA India*, March 11, 2015. http://www.dna-india.com/money/report-all-you- wanted-to-know-about-the-coal-scam-1735936.
24. M. Rajshekhar, "How weak checks and balances in mining are destroying forests and livelihoods in India," January 10, 2013, http://articles.economictimes.indiatimes. com/2013-01-10/news/36258334_1_hasdeo-arand-coal-ministry-coal-blocks;
25. Raghuram Rajan cited in Sahoo (2011, 18).
26. Personal interview, former minister of tribal affairs, New Delhi, July 2015.

explains why powerful regional parties have sought environment and forest portfolios when they are part of national coalition governments.[27]

The data and cases cited above demonstrate that in addition to the colonial legacies (Chapter 2) and the institutional effects of a post-independence developmentalist state (Chapter 3), the contemporary pursuit of economic growth also undermines Adivasi resource rights.[28] The push for economic growth since the late 1980s has not led to a complete abandonment of the Indian state's pursuit of environmental conservation. The intersection of economic liberalization, political competition, and environmental conservation created an unintended political opportunity structure, which eventually led to the enactment of the FRA.

5.2 EMERGENCE OF A POLITICAL OPPORTUNITY STRUCTURE

Institutional Context: State-led Environmentalism and Its Social Consequences

One strand of social science scholarship about environmentalism makes an important distinction between "environmentalism of the poor," which reflects the subsistence needs of the poor people who rely on environmental resources, and the "environmentalism of the rich," which seeks to preserve environmental resources as a source of aesthetic and recreational values.[29] Developing countries, including India, have witnessed the emergence of a sizeable middle-class constituency that identifies passionately with the aesthetic and recreational value of environmental resources.[30] However, as a great deal of research by political ecologists suggests, any analyses of competing notions of environmetalisms must account for the nature of material interests and the practices of state-making linked to environmental resources.[31] Equally important, middle-class anxieties about environmental destruction may become a convenient vehicle for state and nonstate actors seeking to maintain their gatekeeping of environmental resources.[32] An important site for these contestations over competing notions of environmentalism in contemporary India is the Supreme Court, which has significantly influenced the contestation between environmental conservation and social justice.[33]

27. Gopal Krishna, "At play in the fields of the lord" (Web Special, Environment), *Tehelka*, November 24, 2010. http://archive.tehelka.com/story_main47.asp?filen ame=Ws241110ENVIRONMENT.asp.
28. Drèze and Sen 2013; Krishna 2015.
29. Guha 2002.
30. On bourgeois environmentalism, see Baviskar et al. 2006; Mawdsley et al. 2009.
31. Agarwal 1992; Baviskar 2003.
32. Cf. Baviskar 2003.
33. For a recent analysis of judicial environmentalism in India, see Sivaramakrishnan 2011.

India's forestland regime is best described as a case of fragmented centralization, such that the centralized monopoly of government forestry agencies has been challenged by the even stronger centralizing tendencies of the judiciary. The origins of this most recent round of judicial activism with respect to India's forestry sector are linked to the abolition of feudal estates in the 1950s, which led to the government of India taking control of forested lands owned by former feudal lords. A descendant of former feudal landowners named Godavarman sent a letter to the Supreme Court in 1996, arguing that because forestry agencies had failed to protect the forests formerly owned by his ancestors, he had right to reclaim his family land. Taking *suo moto* action, the court converted Godavarman's letter into a public interest litigation about government agencies' failure to protect the country's forests.[34] Moreover, the Supreme Court barred lower courts from intervening in the forest-related cases, all of which were brought together under "continuing mandamus" directly overseen by the Supreme Court. To deal with the deluge of cases, the court appointed a central empowered committee (CEC), which reports directly to the highest court and is beyond the interventions of the other branches of state.[35] Scholars have questioned the ability of CEC members—three forest officers and two wildlife activists, all of whom come from the elite—to adjudicate the conflict-ridden negotiations over forests and forestlands.[36] In this case, the Supreme Court stretched itself well "beyond its traditional role as the interpreter of law, and assumed the roles of policymaker, lawmaker and administrator."[37]

The courtroom contestations between distinct visions of environmentalism have led to socially discriminatory consequences. As a noted public interest lawyer argues, "When environmental protection comes into conflict with socioeconomic rights of the poor and the marginalized, the poor usually get the short shrift ... [but] when environmental protection comes into conflict with powerful vested commercial and corporate interests or what is perceived by the court to be 'development,' environmental protection is given the short shrift."[38] The clearest indication of such effects have been witnessed in the context of forestland rights examined in this book. During the hearing of the forest case in November 2001, the Supreme Court issued an order *"restraining the Union of India"* from legalizing any forestland encroachments without the Court's permission.[39] The inspector general of forests, the top ranking forest

34. S. Joshi 2003; Rosencranz and Lélé 2008; Upadhyay 2009.
35. The Supreme Court soon found itself entangled in contentions around "timber pricing, licensing of timber industries, felling of shade trees, budgetary provision for wildlife protection, disposal of infected trees ... confidential reports of forest officers, and even painting of rocks in forests." See Rosencranz and Lélé 2008.
36. S. Joshi 2003.
37. Rosencranz and Lélé 2008, 11.
38. Bhushan 2009, 35; see also Ramanathan 2002.
39. CSD 2004, emphasis added.

bureaucrat in the country, used the November 2001 court directive to instruct state forestry agencies to evict anyone who had occupied forestland in the post-1980 period.[40] These instructions, issued in May 2002, triggered a nationwide "eviction campaign" in which government forestry agencies claimed to have cleared forestland encroachments spread over 152,400 hectares that comprised micro-farm parcels of an estimated 150,000 to 165,000 families.[41] This official data is likely to be a gross underestimation, because local forest officials have incentives to underreport the actual area of forestland farmed within their jurisdiction.[42] Obviously, the forestland cultivations not recorded in the first place could not be officially evicted.

This nationwide eviction campaign entailed numerous cases of violence, including the deployment of intoxicated elephants to dismantle Adivasi huts and incidents of police firing on protestors.[43] The evictions led to serious human rights violations, duly noted by Amnesty International.[44] Social activists and organizations led concerted grassroots mobilization in different parts of the country to protest against the events. Simultaneously, a large number of national and regional social movements joined together to form the Campaign for Survival and Dignity (CSD), which focused specifically on the question of forestland rights.[45] At its peak, the CSD claimed membership of fourteen state level federations, comprising more than 150 mass organizations.[46] Shankar Gopalakrishnan, the convener of the CSD, stated, "It was the brutality of this eviction drive that . . . *made it possible* for mass organizations across the country to come together in the struggle for forest rights."[47] At a

---

40. This directive was issued in May 2002, and the department was expected to use its faulty records to decide whom to evict. See Drèze 2005.
41. For a copy of the official press release, see MoEF 2004. For journalists' estimate of the number of families dispossessed during these campaigns, see T. K. Rajalakshmi, "Fatwa raj is over." *Frontline*, volume 23, issue 26, Dec. 30, 2006–Jan. 12, 2007. http://www.frontline.in/static/html/fl2326/stories/20070112003201100.htm; "Forced evictions target Adivasi," *Amnesty International Australia*, April 27, 2007, http://www.amnesty.org.au/news/comments/1160/.
42. Other estimates suggest that 750,000 people were affected during the eviction drive. See Bose 2010, 24. For ethnographic discussions about relationships between peasants and local forest officials, which sustain farming of micro-plots within lands designated as state forests, see Pathak 1994; Baviskar 1995; Kashwan 2011.
43. Janu 2003; CSD 2004.
44. "Forced evictions target Adivasi," *Amnesty International Australia*, April 27, 2007, http://www.amnesty.org.au/news/comments/1160/. See also Anon, "Eviction of tribals by force in Kerala to be taken up with NHRC," February 26, 2003. http://www.thehindu.com/thehindu/2003/02/26/stories/2003022604820700.htm.
45. This assessment is relative. While the forestland rights movements stayed united for the most part, as I discuss in the next section, serious differences in approach emerged in due course. See Chowdhury and Roma 2009.
46. See Campaign for Survival and Dignity, "About us," https://forestrightsact.com/about/.
47. Gopalakrishnan 2010, 13, italics added for emphasis.

public hearing that the CSD organized in the national capital, it presented evidence that the eviction drive contravened the Ministry of Environment and Forests' guidelines of 1991 for resolving forestland conflicts.[48] The public hearing, especially the in-person testimonies of the people affected directly by the evictions, combined with the CSD's active engagement with print and electronic media, drew attention to a large number of human rights violations that occurred during the eviction campaign and highlighted the level of resentment it caused among sections of rural populations in forested regions.

Electoral Politics and the Emergence of a Political Opportunity

The struggles over forests and forestlands discussed in the previous section unfolded within a political and economic context infused with debates about the direction and effects of economic reform India pursued since the late 1980s. Noted economists, including the 2015 Economics Nobel Laureate Angus Deaton, show that economic liberalization divided India between the winners—mainly the urban sectors in the more successful states in the south and west—and the losers, especially the rural communities in central and eastern India, which exacerbated preexisting economic inequalities.[49] The discriminatory effects of economic liberalization also reinforced the interregional development deficit, which has characterized the hinterlands since India's independence (Chapter 3).[50] The acquisition of forestland for both "environmental" and "developmental" projects led to new enclosures and dispossessions, which in turn produced serious social and economic consequences for forest-dependent people.[51]

The context of increasing dissatisfaction with the direction of the country's economic policies added to the salience of the issue of forestland conflicts to key political players, and it opened up a new political opportunity structure.[52] Responding to the nationwide eviction campaign in the second half of 2002, the CSD worked closely with its constituent groups to create grassroots pressure on political parties.[53] Activist groups active in specific regions invited major political party candidates to public hearings, and mass rallies focused on forestland conflicts. Nearly 70,000 Adivasis from some of the poorest districts in the state of Orissa threatened to boycott the parliamentary elections if the state government did not work to resolve forestland conflicts.[54] Several state legislative elections scheduled for 2003 propelled a group of state chief

48. CSD 2004.
49. Deaton and Drèze 2002; Deaton 2003.
50. Shah et al. 1998; Haan 2008; Dandekar and Choudhury 2010.
51. Prasant and Kapoor 2010.
52. On political opportunity structure, see Tarrow 2003.
53. Asher and Agarwal 2007.
54. Bijoy 2008.

ministers to ask for amendments to forest laws to resolve forestland conflicts.[55] Both of India's two major national political parties—the Bharatiya
Janata Party (BJP) and the Congress Party—were concerned about their performance in the crucial general election to be held in 2004. A senior Congress
leader published a frank assessment of his party's failure to address Adivasi
grievances born out of government control over forests and forestlands. He
argued, "A Congress which imaginatively examines the problem and provides
a constructive, detailed solution in time to reach it to far-flung tribal communities would snatch back the tribal vote."[56] In the state of Gujarat, NGOs—including the ones led by Congress Member of Parliament (MP) Madhusudan
Mistry, whose political career was a spinoff from his first career as an activist
fighting for the rights of forest people and informal laborers—organized a
number of well-attended rallies within the span of a month.[57] BJP cadres also
mobilized in the southern Indian state of Karnataka to demand that the state
government provide alternative land to resolve forestland conflicts.[58]

Notwithstanding leaders and cadres' mobilization, the two national parties
displayed "complete cynicism" in how they exploited the issue of forestland conflicts.[59] The states of Assam and Kerala, ruled by Congress Party governments,
witnessed some of the most violent scenes during the nationwide eviction drive
discussed in the previous section, including violent clashes and paramilitary
forces killing a woman.[60] The government in Kerala justified violent police action
by accusing the agitating Adivasis of joining hands with ultra-violent insurgent
groups, such as the Marxist-Leninist People's War Group, and the Sri Lankan ex-
tremist group, the Liberation Tigers of Tamil Eelam.[61] Most scholars attribute the
lack of national political attention to Adivasis' issues to the peculiar geography
of Adivasi votes—which are thinly spread out in small pockets of population—
and the dominant economic interests attached to the status quo in forestland regimes.[62] However, as political theorists and comparative politics scholars argue,
electoral democracy often creates transient electoral and political opportunities,
which enable political actors to push forward a specific agenda.

The mass mobilization organized by forestland rights movements, coupled
with some state-level mobilization by the political party cadres, prompted

55. S. Joshi 2003.
56. Aiyar 2003.
57. Times News Network, *Tribals up in arms against eviction drive.* Ahmedabad, Jul 31,
    2003.   http://timesofindia.indiatimes.com/city/ahmedabad/Tribals-up-in-arms-
    against-eviction-drive/articleshow/103984.cms.
58. Anon, "BJP takes out protest rally," March 2004, 2003. http://www.thehindu.
    com/2003/03/24/stories/2003032402090300.htm.
59. Sundar 2004, 213.
60. S. Joshi 2003.
61. Bijoy 2003.
62. Lélé and Rao 1996a, 1996b; Aiyar 2003.

the BJP-led National Democratic Alliance (NDA) government in New Delhi to issue an executive order in February 2004, which promised certificates of legal occupancy to forest-dependent people. The Supreme Court, as part of the proceedings of the forest case discussed earlier, quashed the circular by declaring it an election-time ploy. All of these events ensured that the question of forestland conflicts became part of a broader debate about the social impact of policies and programs of the NDA government (1999–2004). Opposition parties and social movements blamed the NDA regime for exacerbating inequalities, the agrarian crisis responsible for a large number of farmers' suicides, and the resurgence of ultra-left Naxal radicalism, which had claimed nearly five thousand lives between 1990 and 2004.[63] Amid such a gloomy scenario during the 2004 general election campaign, the incumbent NDA government launched a massive media blitz with the catchy moniker of "India Shining."[64] The Congress Party responded with a campaign focused on *Aam aadmi*—the "common people"—which included promises to resolve the forest question. Even so, instead of addressing the question of forestland conflicts directly, Congress's election manifesto made vague references to "sustainable livelihoods."[65] Evidently, the specific details of the party platform mattered less than the strategic leverage that the opposition gained from drawing attention to a range of issues linked to economic inequality.

This chapter's focus on political and economic inequalities may make it seem as if the incumbent NDA was in trouble; however, readers should note that Adivasis constitute a mere 8 percent of India's population, and not all of them were affected equally. Moreover, there are few efforts to coordinate political mobilization among different groups of Indian society that are affected by poverty and marginalization, such as the so-called lower castes and other backward classes. Considering the media blitz unleashed by the NDA government's India Shining campaign and generally favorable opinion toward the NDA in the electronic media, opinion polls and pundits predicted a comfortable victory for the NDA in the 2004 general elections. Yet the left-of-the-center United Progressive Alliance (UPA), led by the Congress Party, earned a surprise victory.[66] Analysis of the National Election Study 2004 data indicated the relevance of economic voting: "The Congress and its allies gained more votes from those who felt that economic reforms either benefited the rich or none ... NDA parties got more votes among those who felt that the country

---

63. Anon, "Naxal insurgency in India," not dated, last accessed April 30, 2016, via http://carnegieendowment.org/files/RS.pdf. For yearly data on Naxal-related fatalities, see Anon, "Annual fatalities in left wing extremism," http://www.satp.org/satporgtp/countries/india/maoist/data_sheets/lwe2016.htm.
64. Thachil and Herring 2008.
65. Manifesto 2004, at http://allindiacongress.com/admin/upload/pdf/Manifesto%20 2004. pdf, last accessed on November 6, 2015.
66. "India's election; The voters' big surprise: A stunning defeat for the ruling party," *The Economist*, May 13, 2004.

as a whole benefited."[67] Lastly, the 2004 elections also witnessed the peak of electoral competition as measured by "effective number of parties," a political science measurement of the inter-party competition for votes, which had been on the rise since the late 1980s.[68] The 2004 elections presented a unique political opportunity structure, which the CSD and other forestland rights movements utilized very effectively.

Despite the importance of a conducive political context that catapulted the forestland question to national political prominence, political actors' agency both within and outside of the state was critical for the enactment of the FRA.

5.3 INSTITUTIONAL CHANGE IN LAW: THE WRITING AND ENACTMENT OF THE FRA

The post-2002 national forestland rights movement built on previous mobilizations at the national and subnational levels discussed above, but it differed in two important ways. For the first time, the activists fighting for forestland rights came together at the national level to systematically lobby political parties and national leaders. Second, and perhaps as a result of the strong pre-election mobilizations, social activists secured direct access to the policymaking process in the national capital. While these two factors enabled forestland rights activists to make inroads into the policy process, it was far from certain that this opening would lead to meaningful policy change. The mobilization of various actors, including a variety of political institutions, was critical to the eventual success of forestland policy change. The FRA policy process offers insights into the interface between political parties and their leaders on the one hand and the representatives of forestland movements on the other. My analysis builds on the scholarship that challenges state/society and civil society/political society distinctions and demonstrates how divisions within and the links between these camps played an important role in shaping the eventual institutional outcomes.[69]

Many Faces of "Civil Society": The NAC, Wildlife Groups, and Forestland Rights Activists

The results of 2004 parliamentary elections greatly influenced the Congress Party's strategy toward the UPA government. The left front—especially the

---

67. Suri 2004, 5410.
68. See Milan Vaishnav and Danielle Smogard, "A New Era in Indian Politics?" June 10, 2014, http://carnegieendowment.org/2014/06/10/new-era-in-indian-politics.
69. For an extensive recent review, see Gudavarthy 2012.

Communist Party of India–Marxist, which secured 43 seats of the 58 parliamentary seats secured by the left—produced one of its best electoral performances in recent times. Consequently, the communist parties became an indispensable part of the UPA government.[70] The Congress Party's history of introducing India's post-1980 economic reforms juxtaposed somewhat uncomfortably with the backdrop of debates about the unequal effects of the NDA's economic liberalization. As a result, Congress had to agree to a National Common Minimum Program (NCMP), which one scholar referred to as "an instrument for the Left to bend the government to its preferences."[71] The NCMP stated unambiguously, "Eviction of tribal communities and other forest-dwelling communities from forest areas will be discontinued . . . The rights of tribal communities over mineral resources, water sources, etc. as laid down by law will be fully safeguarded."[72]

Attempts to maintain a balance of power between the Congress Party and its governing coalition partners led to the establishment of the National Advisory Council (NAC) under the leadership of the powerful Congress Party President Sonia Gandhi. The NAC was a semigovernment body comprising eminent academics, professionals, and social activists, which functioned as a platform for collaboration between the UPA government and selected sections of civil society and activists. The NAC's main mandate was to advise the government regarding the implementation of the National Common Minimum Program. Soon after the NAC was established, two of its core members consulted CSD representatives about the question of forestland conflicts and connected them to the Prime Minister's Office (PMO). Prime Minister Manmohan Singh, who believed that the proposed forestland legislation was the best way to fight the resurgent ultra-violent Naxal rebellion, asked the Ministry of Tribal Affairs (MoTA) to draft comprehensive legislation to resolve forestland conflicts. As the MoTA worked with the PMO and the NAC, it tapped into the expertise of prominent CSD activist Pradip Prabhu, who had helped develop the Maharashtra model for the adjudication of forestland conflicts discussed in Chapter 4.[73]

Prime Minister Singh, quite possibly following advice from Gopalakrishnan, cited conflict of interest as the reason for his decision to not ask the Ministry of Environment and Forests (MoEF) to lead the UPA's efforts to write and enact the Forest Rights Act (FRA). The MoEF fought very hard to protect its turf; it promised to implement the executive orders from the past and

70. Swamy 2004.
71. Nayar 2005, 77.
72. National Common Minimum Programme of United Progressive Alliance Government http://nceuis.nic.in/NCMP.htm, last accessed November 6, 2015.
73. Vaidya 2016.

even wrote an alternative law that would allow easier access to nontimber forest products.[74] The National Forestry Commission, a MoEF-appointed panel, argued that the FRA represented an attempt to compensate for the failures on the economic development front by "gifting away the country's forest heritage."[75]

These arguments also found support among India's wildlife conservation groups. Some of India's most influential conservation groups—including the Wildlife Protection Society of India, the Bombay Natural History Society (BNHS), and the Center for Environmental Law, among others—labeled the FRA as a "land distribution" program.[76] One should note that throughout the policymaking process, the FRA was never meant to distribute any land, but to grant legal rights for the farm parcels that already existed within the boundaries of de jure forests. In addition to relying on factually inaccurate representations of the bill, FRA opponents also repeated clichéd and unsubstantiated exaggerations about the impact of Adivasi livelihoods on forestland and wildlife conservation.[77] This includes the often-heard claim that the formal recognition of land rights would spell doom for the tiger, India's national animal and a keystone conservation species.[78] The anti-FRA campaigns subscribed to a problematic view of forested regions as pristine landscapes filled with wild flora and fauna, images based on an elite and exclusionary view of the nature-society interface.[79]

This elite perspective regarding the environment was most evident in a series of YouTube videos, which a Mumbai-based citizens group called Vanashakti (literally, "forest power") sponsored and promoted. Vanashakti ran a highly professional electronic media campaign, the first of its kind in India's policymaking history, to paint the FRA as a political gimmick perpetrated by vote-hungry politicians. Each of the Vanashakti YouTube videos concluded with an appeal: "Forest Rights Act—Stop it Before It's Too Late for Our Forests and Our Children."[80]

These videos and press reportage sought to appeal to middle class anxieties about popular politics and its destructive consequences for India's natural patrimony (see also Chapter 4). The wildlife advocates successfully provoked the middle class sensitivities among members of the Tiger and Wilderness Watch, a forum of parliamentarians who were concerned by reports about

74. Rajshekhar 2012, 13.
75. Ganapathy 2005.
76. Nitin Sethi, "Land unsettled," *Down to Earth*, May 31, 2005.
77. Bose 2010; Ashish Kothari, "For Lasting Rights," *Frontline* 23 (26), December 30, 2006.
78. *The Hindu*, "In Tiger Territory," March 4, 2006, http://www.thehindu.com/todays-paper/tp-features/tp-metroplus/in-tiger-territory/article3188292.ece.
79. Brockington 2002.
80. Down to Earth, "Vanashakti against forest rights act," November 30, 2007.

declining numbers of tigers."[81] Tiger and Wilderness Watch included Congress Party heir apparent Rahul Gandhi, who raised the issue with his mother, UPA chair Sonia Gandhi—arguing that the proposed bill posed a "danger to wildlife."[82] Responding to these concerns, Sonia Gandhi asked the Ministry of Tribal Affairs (MoTA) to exclude wildlife reserves from the FRA and to recognize land rights only for the parcels of land farmed prior to October 1980.[83]

Deeply concerned about these objections and the resulting delays, social movements led by the CSD promptly mobilized a grassroots show of strength to reiterate their demand for a permanent solution to forestland rights conflicts. As the nation celebrated its Independence Day on August 15, 2005, the forestland rights movements launched a nationwide protest. CSD claimed that more than a hundred thousand forest-dependent people participated in these protests held in various states to register their opposition to the government's dilly-dallying on the issue.[84] At the same time, the CSD also sought to mobilize Adivasi MPs from all major parties, many of whom were reluctant to diverge from their respective party lines.[85] Eventually a delegation of Adivasi MPs met the UPA chairperson and secured a commitment that the forest rights bill, duly approved by the National Advisory Council (NAC), would not be stalled.[86]

Under the UPA government, the PMO and the NAC functioned as two distinct but unequal power centers—with the NAC headed by the UPA chairperson, who wielded so much power that the NAC was sometimes referred to as the "shadow cabinet."[87] However, because of the influence of wildlife advocates, including the members of Tiger and Wilderness Watch, the top government leaders and the NAC were broadly in agreement that the FRA could not be allowed to threaten India's precious wildlife. Their positions may have been motivated partially by genuine concerns that the proposed FRA might unleash a wave of new forestland claims. However, a more important reason had to do with the fear that the FRA might make a big dent in the Congress Party's legacy of important conservation policies, such as the Wildlife Protection Act, Project Tiger, and the Forest Conservation Act—all

81. Express News Service, "MPs form tiger caucus, to meet PM by weekend," *Indian Express,* April 28, 2005.
82. Prerna Singh Bindra, "Task Force discusses everything, but tiger," *Pioneer,* June 15, 2005, New Delhi. "48157: UPA attempts at social engineering with Tribal Bill," *The Hindu,* March 24, 2011, http://www.thehindu.com/news/the-india-cables/the-cables/article1565619.ece.
83. This cut-off date is based on the premise that the provisions of the FCA, which forbid use of "forest" land for nonforestry activities, must be respected. Rajshekhar 2012, 10.
84. Bijoy 2008.
85. Personal interview, BJP MP and former tribal affairs minister, summer 2007.
86. Aasha Khosa, "Tribal MPs claim Sonia to protect Forest Rights Bill," *Indian Express,* New Delhi, May 6, 2005.
87. Baru 2014.

of which were enacted under former Prime Minister Indira Gandhi.[88] While a more detailed discussion is beyond the scope of this book, it should be noted that in the latter stages of policy process, the NAC ultimately let FRA's wildlife conservation–minded opponents drive the process of writing the executive rules that would govern the FRA implementation.

The first draft of the FRA narrowed the act's scope in several ways. The bill introduced in Parliament provided land rights *only* to the households that had already been farming parcels in state forestlands prior to 1980, the year enactment of the Forest Conservation Act (FCA) restricted state governments from addressing forestland conflicts. Additionally, this draft of the law offered vaguely formulated protections of land rights to the four million people living inside protected national parks and wildlife sanctuaries, which cover more than 5 percent of the country's landmass.[89] Moreover, establishing October 1980 as the cutoff date was designed to grant significant power to forestry agencies, which maintain the "official" records that were far from impartial, exhaustive, or accurate. Most significantly, the first draft of the bill excluded non-Adivasi forest-dependent people from securing rights under the FRA, even though many of them live under conditions very similar to those faced by Adivasis. The FRA opponents' attempts to make a distinction between Adivasis and non-Adivasi forest-dependent people created a politically salient identity trap. It opened up an entirely new set of arguments and political negotiations, which I discuss in the next section.

Parliamentary Politics Meets Subaltern Mobilization

The policy process that preceded the FRA enactment forced a meeting of three different types of politics: first, the political mobilization of peasant groups demanding resource rights; second, the metro-based political lobbying by wildlife activists; and, third, the high politics of parliamentary proceedings. In their battle of nerves with FRA opponents, the CSD representatives who were most involved in the writing of the FRA acted pragmatically; they sought to secure a reasonably progressive bill, even if it did not meet all their demands.[90] Other forestland rights groups, such as the National Forum for Forest People and Forest Workers (NFFPFW), supported the CSD but disagreed about the strategy of compromise. The NFFPFW was founded by forestland rights activists with the goal of helping forest-based workers and communities secure their "citizenship rights and their right to livelihood."[91] While NFFPFW and

88. Rangarajan 2009; Bose 2010, 21.
89. Kumar and Kerr 2012; Sekhsaria and Vagholikar 2004.
90. Bose 2010, 22.
91. Chowdhury and Roma 2009.

other similar groups partnered with the communist parties to influence the FRA policy process, they had limited success in influencing the PMO and the NAC. They had better success after December 2005 when the bill had been introduced in Parliament—a forum more amenable to political pressure from the left parties.

The benefits of the FRA bill first introduced in Parliament would have been limited to "scheduled tribes" (STs)—an administrative category meant to represent Adivasis. However, the official designation of STs leaves out a large number of Adivasi groups, estimated to be nearly equal in population to that of officially recognized STs.[92] Critics of the bill argued that while the identity of STs remains a deeply contested topic, a large number of non-Adivasi forest-dependent groups have also been subject to the historical injustices that the bill was meant to address.[93] The two competing proposals—about whether to apply FRA provisions to a narrowly defined group (Adivasi groups officially recognized as STs) or a more expansive one (forest dwellers, including non-Adivasi forest-dependent people)—had important political implications. Non-Adivasi forest-dependent people are important political constituencies for the left parties and for backward caste parties, which held nearly a hundred parliamentary seats and wielded significant influence in the UPA.[94] The proposal for a more expansive FRA found support among these parties.

The political salience of non-Adivasi constituencies, coupled with the ideological commitments of communist parties, led to strong protests against the bill in Parliament and on the street, which forced the government to refer the bill to a joint parliamentary committee (JPC). The JPC's proceedings attracted significant public input, including 109 written and 44 oral testimonies by academics, experts, and social activists. Based on this input, the JPC proposed some crucial changes in the bill: expanding the bill's purview to include "other traditional forest dwellers" among the FRA beneficiaries; recognizing land rights for parcels of land farmed any time before December 2005 (instead of the original 1980 cutoff date); and instituting a democratic and scientific processes of designating protected areas for biodiversity and wildlife conservation.[95] While the JPC report was praised by social activists and academics, it was criticized by FRA opponents for its potentially disastrous effects on ecology and conservation. These opponents lobbied successfully to get the government to constitute a group of ministers (GOM) to re-evaluate the question about whether the forest and land rights of non-Adivasi forest-dependent people should be brought within the purview of the

92. See Sau 2006.
93. Bhullar 2008.
94. Rajshekhar 2012.
95. For a detailed examination of the collective forest rights and democratization of forest and wildlife conservation that the FRA established, see Kumar and Kerr 2012; Kashwan 2013, 2016b.

law. Meanwhile, the MoEF introduced the Wildlife Protection (Amendment) Act 2006—often referred to as the "Tiger Amendment"—with the intention of preempting the implementation of the FRA in forest areas set aside for wildlife conservation.[96]

Even as the FRA tug-of-war was in its last round, a number of states were scheduled for state legislative elections in 2009. While the Congress Party leaders from the states where elections were taking place were keen on early implementation of the FRA, the Congress Party-led national government did not prioritize the issue. On the contrary, the government in New Delhi was so reluctant to finalize the FRA executive rules despite the parliamentary mandate that Brinda Karat, a senior communist leader, argued that the government was "subverting the will of Parliament."[97] In some states, forestry agencies also sought to remove people from protected areas before the FRA came into effect. Communist party leaders also argued that the government was delaying the enactment of the law due to "opposition from a powerful section of the Congress led by the arguments of the wildlife lobby."[98]

By the time the FRA's accompanying rules came into force in January 2008, the bill's opponents had successfully transformed it without working formally with the NAC or without being part of the expert group that was charged with the task of writing the bill.[99] In the end, the FRA and its accompanying rules turned out to be a hodgepodge of conflicting interests and perspectives.[100] After the FRA had been enacted and the executive rules required for its implementation had been finalized, the association of retired foresters, national wildlife conservation groups, and a family of erstwhile feudal lords filed lawsuits against the FRA in nine different courts, including state high courts and the country's Supreme Court.[101] They argued that the FRA was "repugnant to all other laws aimed at protecting forests and preserving wildlife and hence *ultra vires* the Constitution."[102] While some of these wildlife and forestry actors and agencies had also engaged with the policy process, they approached the courts because in the words of one very prominent conservationist, "we knew we could get what we wanted."[103]

96. Bijoy 2011, 37.
97. Times News Network, "Oppn takes on govt over Forests Rights Act logjam," November 28, 2007. See also "Central Party Communique" 6, http://www.cpim. org/content/central-committee-communiqu%C3%A9-6.
98. Times News Network, "Oppn takes on govt over Forests Rights Act logjam," November 28, 2007.
99. Bijoy 2008; Vaidya 2016.
100. Rajshekhar 2012; Springate-Baginski and Blaikie 2007.
101. Campaign for Survival and Dignity, "Court cases," http://www.forestrightsact. com/court-cases.
102. Ramakrishnan 2008.
103. Personal communication, a public interest lawyer from India, New Haven, Connecticut, April 28, 2012.

Ultimately, social forces and actors outside the formal political structure in India influenced the judiciary and political institutions' actions regarding forestry and land rights, in ways that is difficult to capture via formal institutional analysis or empirical analysis of electoral politics. The FRA policy process discussed above also questions the stereotypical view of party politics as being synonymous with popular politics. The next section examines the ways in which the micro- and meso-level politics shaped the actual implementation of the FRA.

5.4 INSTITUTIONAL CHANGE IN FORM: THE PARTIAL IMPLEMENTATION OF THE FRA

Institutional change is a multilevel affair. The statutes enacted by parliaments and governments must actually be implemented in order to change the status quo. The conventional wisdom in political science and economics would have us expect that India's FRA would trigger high-decibel grassroots activities. Moreover, conventional theories would predict that the procedural rights the FRA granted to village assemblies and local elected leaders made the FRA implementation even more susceptible to patron-client relations and opportunistic claim-making.

Figure 5.1 summarizes the main steps involved in the FRA's adjudication of household land rights. First, the law placed the adjudication of forestland claims at the village level under the control of locally elected FRA committees. Second, the members of these village-level committees had a variety of incentives to validate as many land claims as possible. Third, elected leaders constituted half of the voting members on the subdistrict and district-level FRA committees, responsible for final adjudication of land claims.[104] Regional or local political leaders are often expected to exploit such appointments as opportunities to provide selective favors and benefits to electorally salient constituencies. Surprisingly, none of these fears materialized in practice. A large majority of the FRA's beneficiaries did not indulge in opportunistic land claims, most politicians did not exploit the act as a populist policy measure, and the FRA did not contribute to the decimation of India's forests. Contrary to the doomsday predictions that the FRA would destroy more than 10 percent of India's remaining forests, Table 5.2 show that the total area of land claimed under individual ownership in fifteen major FRA states stands at a mere 4 percent, even after multiple state and national elections.[105] As a result,

104. Each of these committees has six members, out of which three are government officials from the district administration, forest department, and the tribal welfare department.
105. Sahgal and Scarlott 2010.

The district collector issues a "title for forestland under occupation" contingent on the following steps:

1. The subdistrict level FRA committee calls a meeting of the village assembly to constitute the forest rights committee (FRC).
2. The FRC calls for, compiles, and validates land claims, and makes a recommendation to the village assembly.
3. The assembly makes a decision about the validity of land claims in a public meeting in the village.
4. The FRC forwards the land claims to the subdivisional FRA committee (SDC).
5. SDC compiles a jurisdiction-wide record of land rights approved by village assemblies and sends it to the district-level FRA committee (DLC).
6. DLC is responsible for the final vetting and approval of the land claims and resolution of outstanding conflicts.
7. The district collector, who is the head of the DLC, issues titles for the land claims, and ensures that government's land records are updated.

Figure 5.1 Land Rights Formalization under India's FRA.

forest officials have privately expressed pleasant surprise at seeing the low number of land claims under the FRA.[106] A compilation of land claims data at national, regional, and district levels is presented in Table 5.2.

The perplexingly low area of FRA land claims is not an artifact of national-level data aggregation. Micro-level data from the major forested states in the country show that the typical land claims are in the range of 1.5 to 2 hectares, which is less than half of the 4 hectares forest peasants could have claimed had they resorted to opportunistic claim-making.[107] Social science scholars studying the FRA have attributed these outcomes to bureaucratic sabotage and legal complications,[108] and there is now extensive evidence to suggest that the forestry agencies have actively undermined the implementation of the FRA.[109] Recent research shows that civil society actors' inability to create meaningful and effective coalitions geared toward coordinating grassroots strategies also undermined their efforts to facilitate effective implementation.[110] Even so, little scholarly attention has gone into examining why political actors— parties, party leaders, and local elected leaders—did not respond to the FRA's inherent incentives and procedural rights, as the act's opponents of FRA had expected.

106. Personal communication from a graduate researcher (based on his interviews with forest officials in the state of Madhya Pradesh), Anand, July 26, 2009; Personal e-mail communication, NGO professional, August 31, 2010.
107. NCFRA 2010.
108. Kumar and Kerr 2012; Kashwan 2013.
109. Lélé and Menon 2014; Kumar et al. 2015; Kashwan 2016b.
110. Barnes et al. 2016.

Table 5.2 HOUSEHOLD LAND CLAIMS UNDER THE FRA[A]

State/s	Details	Total Number of Claims	Per-household Area of Forestland Claimed/ Approved (in hectares)	Source
		Village-level data		
Gujarat	Primary data collected from 60 randomly selected villages	3,156	1.63[b]	Kashwan (2011)
Andhra Pradesh	Primary data from 439 households from 5 villages	275	1.67[b]	Reddy et al. (2010, 26)
		District-level data		
Andhra Pradesh	Adilabad district as of May 2010	36,319	1.45[b,c,d]	Reddy et al. (2010, 36)
Orissa	Kandhamal district as of 15.02.2012	54,216	0.64[b,d,e]	Data from the district administration portal
		State-level data		
Maharashtra	State level data as of April 30, 2012	97,176	0.87[c,d]	MoTA (2012)
Kerala	Citing starred question number 428 (23-3-2010) posed in the state legislative assembly	6,004	1.00[c]	Sathyapalan and Reddy (2010)
Andhra Pradesh	Status of claims made throughout the state as of April 2010	3,22,955	1.17[c,d]	Reddy et al. (2010, 39)
Chhattisgarh	State-level data as of April 30, 2012	2,14,668	1.00[c,d]	MoTA (2012)
Orissa	State-level data as of December 31, 2014	340,594	0.64[c,d]	MoTA (2014)
Karnataka	State-level data as of December 31, 2014	7,604	1.91[c,d]	MoTA (2014)
Rajasthan	State-level data as of December 31, 2014	34,082	0.60[c,d]	MoTA (2014)
Tripura	State-level data as of December 31, 2014	1,20,418	1.38[c,d]	MoTA (2014)

(continued)

Table 5.2 CONTINUED

State/s	Details	Total Number of Claims	Per-household Area of Forestland Claimed/ Approved (in hectares)	Source
Gujarat	State-level data as of December 31, 2014	68,562	0.57[d]	MoTA (2014)
Total of 5 States (Chhattisgarh, Maharashtra, Orissa, Rajasthan, and West Bengal)	State-level data as of December 31, 2014	8,91,183	1.07[d]	MoTA (2014)
Total of 15 major FRA States[f]	State-level data as of April 30, 2016	2,756,544.4	1.62[d]	MoTA (2016)

[a]   The Ministry of Tribal Affairs releases monthly updates through http://www.fra.org.in. However, most of the data made available in these updates does not clearly distinguish between the private/household claims and the various types of collective claims. Therefore, the choice of states represented in this table is determined solely by availability of unambiguous data on the area of forestland claimed or approved per household, aggregated at different levels. The table covers all of the important forested states in India with significant Adivasi populations.

[b]   The data reflect the area of forestland *claimed* at the village level.

[c]   The data reflect the area of forestland approved by the district-level FRA committee. In the Adilabad district of Andhra Pradesh, that committee did not reject any claims. Therefore, in this case, the average area of forestland approved for private titles is the same as the average area of forestland claimed.

[d]   Original data in units of acres, converted to hectares for this table (1 ha = 2.5 acres)

[e]   kandhamal.nic.in/main/results/itda.pdf

[f]   These major FRA states, according to the MoTA, are Andhra Pradesh, Assam, Chhattisgarh, Gujarat, Jharkhand, Karnataka, Kerala, Madhya Pradesh, Maharashtra, Odisha, Rajasthan, Telangana, Tripura, Uttar Pradesh, and West Bengal.

The fragmentation of Adivasi votes across large number of constituencies spread over a dozen states makes them politically less salient.[111] By the time the UPA had completed its second term (2009–14), the coalition had pushed the forest and land rights issue onto the backburner.[112] One reason for this was that the second UPA coalition did not need the support of the communist parties, due to the fact that the Congress Party faced weaker competition in the 2009 general election. While no systematic comparative analyses of the link between electoral salience and effective implementation of the FRA exist, an extensive survey of media reports suggests very few of the

111.   Shah et al. 1998; Xaxa 1999, 2001.

112.   A booklet that the UPA-II government published to showcase its achievements did not include words such as Adivasi, Dalit, or, their English/official translations. The booklet is now archived at http://archivepmo.nic.in/drmanmohansingh/getdoc.php?id=YSVWBM387.pdf.

UPA-II's constituent parties, which did not include the communist parties, made the enactment of the FRA a major election issue. One exception was the Y.S.R. Reddy–led Congress government in the state of Andhra Pradesh.[113] The Andhra government promised to grant titles for a "whopping [1.4 million] hectares."[114] Only a very small fraction of those lofty aspirational figures actually translated into titles, however. As of July 2015, the state had titled a meager 0.18 million hectares.[115] Moreover, even as Reddy proactively sought to implement the FRA, he also approved the Polavarman Dam project, which threatens to displace an estimated 188,000 to 300,000 Adivasis and is clearly a violation of the FRA provisions related to collective forest and land rights.[116]

Few state-level party leaders and parties have taken a cogent and well-considered view of the resource rights of Adivasis and other forest-dependent people. To gain further insights into the political context regarding these issues, the next section presents evidence about local and regional dynamics that influenced the implementation of the FRA.

What Do Elected Representatives Do? The Local Political Economy of FRA Implementation

The a priori predictions about the incentives that the FRA would create for local leaders required assuming a certain type of interest on the part of the elected representatives involved in the implementation of the FRA at district, subdistrict, and village levels. However, those theories do not account for the possibility of these leaders recognizing other competing interests that might influence their actions related to the FRA. During my interviews and participant

113. Fleischman 2012; Anon, "YSR distributes land pattas to tribals," July 20, 2009. http://www.newindianexpress.com/states/andhra_pradesh/article97060.ece.
114. Sudipta Sengupta, "Animals desert sanctuaries in Andhra Pradesh," March 20, 2012. http://timesofindia.indiatimes.com/city/hyderabad/Animals-desert-sanctuaries-in-Andhra-Pradesh/articleshow/12335892.cms.
115. The data reflect my computations and conversions of units to make them comparable across time. The July 2015 data correspond to the total area of forestland titled in the two states of Andhra Pradesh and Telangana, which were carved out of the unified Andhra Pradesh in 2013. Anon, "Forest dept foils pattas to tribals," July 27, 2015. http://www.thehansindia.com/posts/index/2015-07-27/Forest-dept-foils-pattas-to-tribals-166100.
116. The lower figure is based on the government's official statistics. See Anon, "Polavaram may displace 1.88 lakh people: Govt," May 7, 2015. http://www.thehindubusinessline.com/news/national/polavaram-may-displace-188-lakh-people-govt/article7180977.ece. Other reports suggest figures between two hundred thousand and thee hundred thousand. See S. Rama Krishna, "Andhra Pradesh, Telangana spar over Parliament's Polavaram dam move," July 12, 2014. http://www.sunday-guardian.com/news/andhra-pradesh-telangana-spar-over-parliaments-polavaram-dam-move.

observations, I investigated how elected representatives viewed their own role in implementing the FRA. A small slice of the evidence from political ethnography I conducted during my field research in India is presented below.

As discussed earlier, forestry agencies and officials do have a real conflict of interest vis-à-vis forestland rights. The forestland rights movements, which are active in the field sites in the Vadodara and Narmada districts of the state of Gujarat, invested a significant amount of time and energy to disseminate information about the FRA's key provision. Time and time again, they stated clearly that it was not necessary to secure official Forest Department records to register land rights claims under the FRA. These social movements also engaged actively with the elected leaders who were part of the district-, subdistrict-, and village-level FRA committees, and requested that they not support the forest officials' biased interpretation of the FRA and its provisions.

In many cases, these efforts proved in vain, as in the case of Shannu Bhai, a Congress Party leader and elected subdistrict representative who was also a member of the subdivisonal FRA committee that vetted the forestland claims. Responding to my query about the committee's vetting process, Shannu Bhai expressed his disappointment that most of the applicants had not attached the official forest department documents, which he believed were crucial for proving the validity of their land claims.[117] He accused the NGOs active in his constituency of opportunism and of deliberately creating a situation of confrontation with forestry agencies so that they could gain public support. As he went on a long tirade against the NGOs, the statements that he had made at a public meeting a few days earlier began to make sense. Referring to contested forestlands, he rhetorically asked those present in the public meeting, "Do you realize who owns this land? . . . Do not forget that Forest Department is the owner of this land." Cautioning those present at the meeting against following the FRA activists' confrontational position against the Forest Department, Shannu Bhai sought to distance himself from the NGO that had organized the meeting. On the other hand, he aligned himself more closely with the state agencies and promised his constituents that he would work with forest officials to ensure that they approved of forestland claims.

Elected leaders' inclination to work with forestry agencies came to the fore again as leaders from Motapahada, a politically important village with more than a dozen hamlets, sought the assistance of a very senior leader who had been a minister in the Congress-led UPA government. Instead of referring their case to the party leaders, who were members of the district forest rights committee (FRC), or to the district collector who acted as the committee's chairperson, the former minister directed Motapahada leaders' application

117. Personal interview, Netranpura, October 15, 2009.

to forest department officials, who had no formal powers to intervene in the process.[118] The former minister's actions could not have been out of ignorance, because his active participation in social mobilization over questions of forestland rights had been instrumental for launching his political career.[119] Moreover, as a minister in the federal government, he had participated in the debates about the framing of the FRA.[120]

The forestry-related positions of politicians from the Congress Party, which had long been out of the power in the state, could perhaps be explained as a defensive strategy to ensure that they retained their leverage with the forestry officials. However, several interviews I conducted with the ruling BJP's party leaders also brought up similar evidence. A subdistrict-level BJP leader explained how he dealt with his constituents' complaints about the failure of forest officials to abide by the FRA rules: "I talk to the forest officials, who *oblige* me if there is something they can do within the rules of the forest department."[121] Another senior BJP leader from the neighboring district, who was also a member of Parliament, warned people not to confront forest officials under the "misguided influence" of social activists (the NGOs).[122]

All of these leaders—Shannu Bhai, the former Congress minister, and several BJP leaders—took upon themselves the task of defending the government agencies, and the state in general, because they derive power and influence through their links to the state machinery. This evidence is in line with scholarship that suggests that the main goal in Indian politics is to capture and distribute scarce state resources to secure influence, wealth, and political power.[123] The elected leaders' ability to influence the state bureaucracy is thus at the heart of their role as a leader, and confrontation with any of the state agencies goes against the very core of their modus operandi. Social movements and NGOs not only challenge the monopoly that politicians exercise in representing society at large, but they also question the essence of what it means to be a leader. This explains why, despite there being a natural affinity between the agenda of NGOs and the political program of the Congress Party, there were very few local coalitions between the two. In fact, when an important forestland rights activists offered to assist the Congress Party in a state during the 2009 general election if the party actively mobilized its cadre to implement the FRA, a top Congress leader remained noncommittal.[124] Later interviews revealed that most Congress leaders were hesitant to support the FRA because

118. Group discussion, Motapahada, March 26, 2009.
119. See Anon. 1995.
120. Personal interview, Gandhian social activist, Jambuwas, August 8, 2009.
121. Personal interview, BJP subdistrict head, Sheeshpura, July 28, 2009.
122. Personal observation, Patansar, November 11, 2009.
123. Chatterjee 2004; Corbridge et al. 2013.
124. Personal interview, social activist, August 13, 2009.

the agenda of forestland rights in this state was associated with one particular party leader that other leaders did not want to see rise in the party ranks.[125]

These Congress Party leaders were also able to sideline forestland rights because the issue is shrouded in complex institutional memories. The deeply contested terrain of state-society relations and the recursive effects of past failures of NGO mobilization on this issue influence the voters' beliefs and expectations. Until as late as 2004, when the debates over what would become the FRA were in the incipient stages, forestland rights movements demanded that forestry agencies regularize the occupation of farmlands within the boundaries of de jure state forestland. In other words, instead of questioning the territorial authority exerted by forestry agencies, the land rights groups appealed to forestry agencies' authority to regularize the otherwise "irregular" peasant land claims. Thomas Sikor and Christian Lund argue that by demanding recognition of rights, citizens and social activists legitimize, and even reinforce, the authority toward which such demands are directed.[126] In that sense, the three-decade-long forestland rights movement (1970–2000) contributed to the legitimization of forest department officials' authority through their vociferous demands that the department recognize forestland rights. Additionally, there have been more visible recursive effects from the series of failed interventions designed to bring about institutional change in India's forest areas.

State governments, even when not sincere about resolving land rights questions, issued executive orders asking and authorizing forestry agencies to process these land claims. In every such case, NGOs and land rights movements popularized these ad hoc circulars as an important opportunity for peasants to claim their land rights. The activists motivated landholders to prepare applications for land claims in the formats prescribed by forestry agencies. The main piece of evidence needed as part of these land claims was the penalty receipts that forest officials issued to certify the existence and area of "illegally" farmed parcels. Forest officials, for their part, often used these proceedings to extract rents.[127] These earlier rounds of forestland claims had three main effects. First, because forest officials needed to be paid off in most cases, comparatively well-off people within forest-dependent groups benefited from successive rounds of legalization, leaving a majority of the poorest peasants without land titles. Second, as the most vocal community leaders secured land rights in the successive waves of regularization, they lost interest in supporting the grassroots land rights movements.[128] As such, the land rights

---

125. Interview by research assistant, Congress leaders, April 27, 2011; May 1, 2011.
126. Sikor and Lund 2009.
127. Baviskar 1994; Pathak 1994.
128. Meeting of the community leaders, Paramgarh, July 31, 2009; Focus group discussions, trainee social activists, Jambuwas, October 5, 2009. For a similar illustration from South India, see Poorna Balaji and Siddhartha Krishnan,

movements suffered attrition at the top end of local mobilization. Third, and perhaps most important, the first two effects led to disenchantment among the poorest forest-dependent people, who had invested in multiple rounds of land rights applications without necessarily benefiting personally from such investments. This history of land rights created a formidable cognitive barrier among potential FRA claimants, which the activists working on FRA implementation needed to overcome.

Despite the FRA, local leaders who worked closely with forest officials had a variety of incentives to reinforce the authority of government agencies and officials. These local leaders, including many elected to the village-level FRA committees, continued to block the implementation of FRA provisions within their zones of influence. Many potential FRA beneficiaries found it difficult to question the legitimacy of state forestry agencies, which have long exercised de facto authority in shaping the outcomes of forestland conflicts. As a result, my interviewees often reported having bribed forest officials to "double safeguard" their land claims.[129] Instances of locally elected village leaders demanding bribes and the FRA beneficiaries bribing forest officials have also been reported in other states.[130]

Despite these reports of clientelistic and rent-seeking practices, there is little quantitative research to examine what factors have a significant effect on the implementation of progressive reforms, such as the FRA. Based on the aggregate village-level forestland claims data that I collected from sixty villages, selected through a controlled comparative sample design, I tested the influence of leadership profile of FRA committees in explaining variation in total area of forestland claimed at the village level.[131] Statistical evidence presented in Appendix V shows that the profile of individuals elected to village FRA committees has a statistically significant influence on the level of claim-making. All else held constant, villages where the key FRA committee positions (the chairperson and the secretary) were held by leaders with previous engagement with forest-department projects recorded a significantly lower area of forestland claims.

What shapes the ideas, interests, and actions of local leaders elected to village FRA committees that in turn influence the local claim-making processes?

"History matters," May 15, 2011. http://www.downtoearth.org.in/blog/history-matters-33428.

129. I owe this phrase to Odgaard 2002; personal interview, Adivasi rights activist, August 23, 2009.
130. Sarkar 2011 cites several instances from the states of Orissa and Jharkhand, including those reported by other researchers and practitioners.
131. Village-level data was aggregated from a roster of household land claims available at the village level. The sensitive nature of contested forestland claims made it difficult to collect the household-level socioeconomic data needed for analysis of claims at the household level.

Building on the existing literature and additional evidence from my field research, I argue that these outcomes are attributable to three processes.

First, forest officials launched a systematic propaganda campaign, by organizing meetings of the FRC leaders associated with forestry agencies in the past, and in some cases, by creating new village-level committees to divide villagers and create an additional basis of local support.[132] At these committee meetings, forestry officials used a variety of pro-forestry discourses and arguments, and the promises of future benefits, to encourage forest leaders to minimize the type and the area of forestland claims they could accept at the village level.[133] Second, in some cases, leaders seemed to genuinely believe that forestland claims were detrimental to local forest conservation efforts. Such a position might have been a result of the environmentality effect that Arun Agrawal examines in his work: namely, a sustained engagement with local institutional practices of forest conservation might have converted many of these leaders into environmental subjects.[134] And third, these leaders, knowing that the agenda of environmental conservation resonates quite well with external government and nongovernment agencies, may have acted strategically to articulate concerns for the environment, even though they themselves were not genuinely committed to the goals of environmental conservation. In these cases, pro-conservation arguments in favor of not accepting forestland claims may be an alibi that these leaders used to reinforce the power and authority they derive from collaborating with forestry officials and NGOs on projects of forest conservation.[135] Clearly, more empirical research is needed to shed light on the complex micro-political economy of local environmental and social movement leadership.

5.5 CONCLUSION

This chapter's analysis of the social and political mobilization that led to the enactment of the FRA adds to contemporary scholarship, which demonstrates the importance of paying careful attention to state-society interactions. Popular politics played a large part in shaping the political struggle over the debates related to the question of forestland rights, the framing of the FRA, and the FRA's eventual enactment and implementation. In fact, popular politics was intertwined with social mobilization—both of which then shaped the emergence of formal political institutions, including the local government

132. Kumar Sambhav Shrivastava, "Forest title claims of over 50% tribals, forest dwellers rejected: report." *Down to Earth*, New Delhi, June 15, 2012.
133. Personal interview, local NGO leader, Mevapada, June 2, 2009.
134. Agrawal 2005a; see also Singh 2013.
135. Sivaramakrishnan 1996; Agrawal 2001b; Sundar 2001; Sanjay Kumar 2002.

statute—PESA, the national advisory council (NAC), the Congress-led coalition's common minimum program (CMP), and the joint parliamentary committee (JPC), without which the FRA would not have happened.

While the political and policy process was characterized by a variety of confrontations, each moment of confrontation also gave birth to engagements between the representatives of the state and society.[136] In the process, elite actors at the center of modern institutions, such as the members of the Tiger and Wilderness Watch, used informal ties related to familial and social networks to pursue their agenda. On the other hand, some of the most radical grassroots groups, quite comfortable with the rough-and-tumble of informal politics, capitalized on the sophisticated proceedings of parliamentary institutions, such as the JPC, to pursue progressive institutional change. Such reversals of roles between informal and formal politics do not mean that efforts to transform institutions were a battle of equals. In the end, however, entrenched national and local actors influenced the policy process, which weakened the FRA's legal provisions and greatly limited its implementation.

In an impressive chronicle of the policy process leading to the FRA's enactment, M. Rajshekhar argues that the CSD asked for "nothing more than the implementation of existing law . . . [an approach, which] *subtly* challenges the legitimacy of the state, for a government that doesn't implement its own laws loses legitimacy."[137] Yet, as this chapter's examination of the FRA implementation process demonstrated, state legitimacy cannot always be used as a tool to speak truth to the sovereign. Within the context of local contestations over the FRA's implementation, politicians' ability to claim legitimacy as representatives of the state, in opposition to the activist strategies of holding the state to account, ultimately undermined the FRA.

Even though change may seem quite beyond the reach of a humble citizen or even the better equipped social activists and movements, these multifaceted state-society engagements have in them the seeds of transformational change. This will be especially evident in the Mexican case discussed in the next chapter.

136. Hertel 2015; Barnes et al. 2016.
137. Rajshekhar 2012, citing Calman 1985, italics added for emphasis.

CHAPTER 6

ᴄᴠᴐ

Politics of Institutional Change
in Tanzania and Mexico

The problem of conflict-ridden land claims and land rights examined in the context of India's hinterlands (see Chapter 5) also exists in Tanzania and Mexico, albeit in different forms. Unlike India, in which the 2006 Forest Rights Act (FRA) was the first nationwide formal attempt to reform forestland conflicts, both Tanzania and Mexico have had a longer history of statutory recognition of land rights in the hinterlands. This chapter examines the outcomes of the property rights reforms that Mexico (beginning in 1992) and Tanzania (beginning in 1999) pursued in the 1990s and the first few years of the twenty-first century. The reforms and the response they evoked at the regional and local levels offer useful insights into the political and economic determinants of land rights in the hinterlands.

Peasant land rights enshrined in Mexico's Constitution of 1917 became "real," to borrow Ben Cousins' formulation, after President Lázaro Cárdenas implemented land redistributions in the 1930s, along with extensive state-led agrarian and rural development programs.[1] Even so, as scholars of Mexican agrarian reforms have shown, the long history of corporatism by the ruling Institutional Revolutionary Party (PRI) had constrained the autonomy that the Constitution provided for agrarian communities. These distortions, along with the political and economic liberalization of the 1980s and 1990s, shaped the 1992 agrarian reforms examined in this chapter.

In the case of Tanzania, the competing provisions of the Village Land Act of 1999 (VLA) and the Land Act of 1999 sowed the seeds of contemporary

---

1. Cousins 1997.

land politics, which is dominated by large-scale land allocations for biofuel and other commercial crops, hunting reserves, ecotourism, wildlife conservation, and more recently, carbon forestry.[2] Responding to the government's campaign of making productive use of the supposedly unused lands, national and international investors applied to lease nearly 4 million hectares of land for biofuel production from 2005 to 2008. In the words of a senior policy analyst with the charity group Action Aid USA, "To state it bluntly, most of the lands that the government wishes to see developed will need to be taken away from the villagers and leased to investors."[3] The formalization of rural property in both Mexico and Tanzania have important implications for social justice and nature conservation amid a significant push for large-scale investments in the hinterlands.

The next section (6.1) provides essential information about the context within which the reforms unfolded in Mexico and Tanzania. In Section 6.2, I introduce the provisions and mechanisms of the reform process, which is followed in Section 6.3 by a discussion of the overall patterns of reform outcomes on the ground. Section 6.4 analyzes the negotiations that shaped these reform outcomes. The chapter concludes in Section 6.5 with a short comparative analysis of the insights drawn from this investigation of institutional change in forestland regimes. Notably, even though the evidence in this chapter relates to Tanzania and Mexico, the comparative analysis in the concluding section also brings in the findings from the analysis of India's forestland reforms in Chapter 5.

6.1 INSTITUTIONAL REFORMS: BACKGROUND AND MOTIVATIONS

Both Tanzania and Mexico pursued reforms of rural property, but the context that shaped these reforms and their implementation varied significantly. This section offers a brief overview of the context of property reforms in these two countries.

Security of Customary Forestland Rights in Tanzania

The Shivji Commission's nationwide consultations, discussed in Chapter 3, spawned a generation of land rights activism in Tanzania, which led to the

2. Sulle and Nelson 2009; Beymer-Farris and Bassett 2012; Gardner 2012; Nelson et al. 2012.
3. Kizito Makoye, "Complex land rights feed 'grabbing' complaints in Tanzania," Thomson Reuters Foundation, April 17, 2014, accessed online at http://news.trust.org//item/20140417110316-z13bv/.

formation of the National Land Forum in 1997. The forum issued a "Land Declaration," which came to be seen as a counter to the provisions of the proposed 1996 Land Bill. The government responded to increasing civil society protests regarding land reform by adding new rules without having to either remove old rules or significantly modifying the impact of old rules. This strategy that scholars of institutional change appropriately label as "layering," prompted the government to enact a set of two land laws in 1999: the Land Act and the Village Land Act.[4] The Village Land Act recognized the security of customary rural land rights on par with those that existed for urban land. However, these rights have not been guaranteed in practice, because of the overriding provisions of the Land Act of 1999 and a lack of political commitment from the Tanzanian government, as discussed in Chapters 3 and 4.

Under the influence of Peruvian economist Hernando de Soto, who is known for his advocacy of formalization of property rights, Tanzania's government launched a program for the formalization and financialization of rural property. Professor Anna Tibaijuka, the former minister for Lands, Housing, and Human Settlements Development, articulated the following two key objectives of Tanzania's land titling efforts: first, to unleash the "dead capital" that rural residents cannot capitalize because of the lack of titles to the land they own; and second, to create a list of villages with extra land that will be made available to investors for growing commercial plantations.[5] The government is pursuing these goals via a number of programs for property formalization currently being implemented with the support of international agencies.

The international donor–supported projects promoting these goals include the Property and Business Formalization Programme (MKURABITA) and the Strategic Plan for the Implementation of the Land Laws (SPILL). These projects aim to formalize and register land rights, with the main goal of promoting business investments and the development of commercial agriculture.[6] As a MKURABITA document suggests, this program aims to "empower groups and individuals, especially in the informal sector, so that they can participate effectively in the market economy."[7] Such documents do not, however, provide criteria that relevant agencies would use to prioritize among the diverse goals of land formalization—such as business promotion, poverty alleviation, etc.[8] Such prioritization is important because the government leaders say they can only

---

4. Mahoney and Thelen 2010.
5. Anon, "Govt surveying country's 12,000 villages- Prof Tibaijuka," *The Guardian* (Tanzania), March 15, 2013, http://www.ippmedia.com/frontend/?l=52360. See also Sundet 2004,120; Stein 2014.
6. Pedersen 2014.
7. Clark et al. 2007.
8. For a similar critique of the property formalization approaches adopted in the Southern Agricultural Growth Corridor of Tanzania (SAGCOT), see Bergius 2014.

afford to provide 3 billion Tanzanian shilling (TSh) out of 300 billion TSh needed for the nationwide registration of properties.[9] Besides, any such program must also address inter-regional differences of geography and the socioeconomic profiles of local residents. Instead, the program promoters seem to imply that these issues either do not matter or would be addressed in due course.

Liberalization of Mexico's Agrarian and Forest Sectors

The international macroeconomic context of liberalization—namely, the North American Free Trade Agreement (NAFTA)—shaped the 1992 land reforms in Mexico. Unlike India and Tanzania, the constitutional protections accorded to Mexican rural property were not weakened, even though the campesino control over agrarian property had always been subject to the interference of the party-state. The 1992 agrarian laws recognized ejidos as legal entities (*personalidad juridica*) with proprietary rights (*propietarios*) of *all* land within ejido boundaries.[10] Between 1920 and 1992, Mexico's agrarian reforms led to the redistribution of 106 million hectares of land to 29,162 agrarian communities (estimated 5.6 million rural households). Out of the land redistributed, nearly 70 million hectares were registered as common property (forests, rangelands, and pastures), while 34 million hectares were registered as agriculture parcels.[11] Mexico's agrarian communities thus held proprietary rights over 56 percent of the country's agricultural land and 70 percent of its forests.[12]

The early twentieth century agrarian law permitted a household with registered ejidatario (the right holder) to use agricultural parcels exclusively for self-cultivation. The law prohibited the use of hired labor for working agricultural parcels and prevented ejidatarios from leasing or selling these parcels. Under the law, the ejido general assembly made up of all male household heads has the authority to dismiss erring ejidataios, as well as to take over parcels and to reassign them to another member or to put them to a collective use. In practice, ejidatarios have participated in a variety of informal, local land transactions—including leasing, renting, and sales—leading to the development of an extra-legal market in ejido land.[13] While quite effective in many ways, the transactions in the extra-legal domain affected the ability of ejidatarios to pursue the course of action best suited to their specific situation.

9. Pedersen 2014, 256.
10. Barnes 2009, 395.
11. Nuijten 2004.
12. Deininger and Bresciani 2001. By 2007, there were 31,514 ejidos and comunidades with 4,210,830 beneficiaries (IX Censo Ejidal, INEGI, 2007, cited in Torres-Mazuera 2013).
13. Nuijten 2003; Gordillo 2009.

Despite widespread agreements about the need for reforms in the agrarian sector in the years preceding the 1992 reforms, experts and activists were divided in their opinions about the type of reforms that would strengthen the sector. Surveys conducted by both government and independent research organizations showed that more than half of the surveyed constituents and 62 percent of rural constituents in the sample supported reform of Article 27 of the Constitution, which outlined the state's obligation toward and control over the agrarian sector.[14] Such a demand, along with the changing macroeconomic environment of the late 1980s and the imminent passage of NAFTA, prompted the government to pursue reforms.

Unlike Tanzania's opaque policymaking process, Mexico's reforms were hotly debated within the government. At least two different groups within President Carlos Salinas de Gortari's administration (1988–1994) sought to shape the contours of the proposed reform: First, *"campesinistas"* who believed in the utility of ejidos as an important social and economic institution, if only they could be freed from government interference and party control; Second, "modernizing technocrats" who were in favor of a complete or near complete privatization of ejido properties.[15] While the intent of the campesinistas was to introduce dynamism into the ejido sector, the "modernizing technocrats" wanted to bring ejido lands under market rules and commercialize ejido operations. These goals bear significant resemblance to the motivations behind Tanzania's programs of property formalization. The eventual reforms, and their outcomes in practice, were a result of a compromise between these two groups with significantly different intentions.[16]

6.2 THE PROVISIONS AND MECHANISMS OF REFORMS

While property rights reforms in Mexico and Tanzania had similar motivations and objectives, differences in the countries' domestic political contexts led to significant differences in how these two countries addressed the interests and concerns of forest-dependent people. These differences also led to variation in the reforms' design and key provisions, which are the subject of this section.

Key Aspects of Property Formalization in Tanzania

Drawing on the provisions of the Village Land Act, Tanzania's property formalization programs are structured to survey and register boundaries of the

14. Cornelius and Myhre 1998, 10.
15. Ibid., 4–5.
16. See also Assies 2008; Gordillo 2009.

Tanzania's national land commissioner issues a certificate of village land (CVL) contingent on the following steps:
1. Preparation of a village land use plan.
2. Clarification of village boundaries and resolution of boundary conflicts between neighboring villages.
3. Survey of village boundaries by official surveyors.
4. Establishment of a village land council to resolve conflicts.
5. Securing a CVL.

To secure a certificates of customary rights of ownership (CCRO), households or groups of households must secure the following approvals on a case-by-case basis:
1. Approval from the village council and village assembly.
2. Parcel survey and registration with the district council.
3. Registration with the Ministry of Lands in Dar es Salaam.

Figure 6.1 Land Rights Formalization in Tanzania.

country's twelve thousand villages, and issue land titles to households and groups of households for privately or collectively used agricultural and pasture lands. The national land commissioner issues a certificate of village land (CVL) for the entire village territory after a village council has taken steps outlined in Figure 6.1. One of the first steps in the formalization process is the preparation of village land-use planning (VLUP). The core tenets of VLUP draw upon the authority that the Local Government Act of 1982 grants to village councils to create by-laws about the management of village's natural resources. If the village land use by-laws are approved by both the village assembly and the district council, and they do not conflict with any existing national or district by-laws, they become part of the legal code enforceable in a court of law.[17]

After a village has secured a CVL, the village council is authorized to grant certificates of customary rights of ownership (CCROs) to individuals, households, or groups of households that are engaged in collective use of land for, say, pastoralism. Individuals or groups interested in seeking CCROs must also follow the sequence of steps outlined in the second half of Figure 6.1. Households must also pay for the surveys and land registration costs, which one scholar estimates to be upward of TSH 300,000 (US$ 165).[18] The burdensome cost is alleviated if one happens to live in a village covered by a donor project, but for a majority of villages, the costly process of registration has acted as a significant barrier to land registration. Such an individualized approach

17. Nelson 2004, 14.
18. Others estimate the cost to be U.S. $10 per CCRO followed by a land tax of U.S. $0.90 per hectare after a CCRO is issued (Fairley 2013, 67). Perhaps the difference is related to whether some parts of the costs associated with the entire process are covered under a state-sponsored pilot project.

Process of implementing Mexico's 1992 agrarian (counter) reforms:
1. PROCEDE staff visits an ejido to disseminate program information.
2. Two-thirds of ejidatarios must agree to participate in PROCEDE.
3. The staff measures and registers ejido boundaries, and updates in government records the list of right holders provided by the ejido management.
4. Ejidatarios receive a certificate of share in the ejido common property.
5. If the ejido assembly approves, Procuraduria Agraria (PA) staff measures the boundaries of agricultural parcels.
6. Individual ejidatarios/households get certificates of land rights for the agriculture parcels and household plots.

Figure 6.2 Land Rights Formalization in Mexico.

imposes steep costs on those interested in securing titles, as compared with the case of India's Forest Rights Act analyzed in Chapter 5, in which locally elected village FRCs adjudicated land rights claims at the village level, followed by verification of the claim documents by a subdistrict level committee. In the Indian case, making land claims required households to put together a set of official documents, including caste certificates, which often created opportunities for bureaucratic rent-seeking. Because effective institutions are a public good that provide society-wide benefits, there appears to be a sound logic for the state to bear most of the costs of implementing institutional change.

Main Provisions of Agrarian Reforms in Mexico

The 1992 reforms in Mexico formally ceased the state's constitutional obligation, enshrined in Article 27, to redistribute land. At the same time, these reforms led to the creation of conflict resolution mechanisms. The state set up agrarian tribunals for expedited resolution of property-related conflicts among ejidatarios, or between ejidos and their neighbors. The Mexican government set up the Program for Certification of Ejido Land Rights and the Titling of Urban Housing Plots (PROCEDE) to organize the process of surveying agrarian property and to issue collective and household certificates. Implemented by personnel from the federal agency Procuraduria Agraria (PA), the 1992 reforms progressed in the sequence of steps shown in Figure 6.2.[19]

Following the completion of PROCEDE, ejidatarios have the right to legally sell, rent, sharecrop, or mortgage their individual land to other members within the ejido. An ejido assembly also can, with a two-thirds majority vote, grant to ejidatarios the right of *"dominio pleno,"* or complete private ownership of the parcels, which may then be legally sold, rented, or

19. Cornelius and Myhre 1998; Assies 2008.

mortgaged to nonmembers, including corporations. Finally, ejidatarios can also decide to liquidate the entire ejido—in which case ejidatarios get equal shares of the ejido property, excluding the forests (*bosques*) or tropical forests (*selvas tropicales*).[20]

The 1992 reform thus created an extensive and multilayered framework that allowed ejidatarios to acquire stronger property rights. Notwithstanding the common refrain about the government's intentions to privatize social property, as Peter Wilshusen put it, the "reforms strongly *encouraged but did not mandate* resource privatization."[21] The Mexican reforms differ from reforms in India and Tanzania in at least three important ways: first, the reform process granted multiple vetoes to agrarian communities—it would proceed only as far as ejido assemblies approved by a series of two-thirds majority votes; second, at no stage do individual households need to either spend their own resources or run over to government offices in distant towns, except in the case of conflicts that ejido leaders fail to resolve. In India and Tanzania, meanwhile, bureaucrats hold vetoes over community decisions. Moreover, reforms in these two countries imposed higher costs on individual households interested in securing land titles, especially in Tanzania. Third, instead of entirely undermining collective rights, Mexican reforms afforded significant space for the autonomy of ejidos and comunidades (See also, Chapter 7).

6.3 PATTERNS OF RESPONSE TO FORESTLAND REFORMS

A power-centric view of institutions cautions us against taking formal rules at their face value or relying on them exclusively to draw quick conclusions about reforms outcomes. In the context of present discussion, the Mexican reforms entailed very few transaction costs for the ejidatarios, and facilitated the potential for significant transformation of property rights. Economic theory in general, and the theories of property rights in particular, would predict that the 1992 reforms would lead to a high level of privatization of ejido properties. The costly process of securing land titles in the Tanzanian case, meanwhile, would be expected to deter formalization of land rights. Even so, promoters of land formalization often ignore these costs, including transaction costs, as do some of the critics of these programs who blame the failures on the misfit between "customary law" and the intent of privatization implied in land titling programs. As mentioned earlier, however, the actual outcomes of reforms in

20. Article 29 of the 1992 Law of Agrarian Reform, cited in Barnes (2009, 397). According to the law, "*ejidatarios* are restricted from cutting forest growth of more than 20 years, even if it exists on their land" (Geoghegan et al. 2001, 29).
21. Wilshusen 2010, 770. Italics added for emphasis.

these two countries varied from these expectations. In this section, I offer a summary of the outcomes of reform implementation.

The Outcomes of Property Reforms in Tanzania

The government of Tanzania has pursued the formalization of land rights rapidly over the past decade. According to one estimate, since the passage of the Village Land Act in 1999, more than eleven thousand of Tanzania's twelve thousand villages have been surveyed, and seven thousand had been registered by early 2012.[22] The most recent pilot project in the country's Babati and Bariadi districts produced more than thirty thousand CCROs, almost 90 percent of the target. However, contrary to the government's assessments, research in a Bariadi district village revealed that by October 2012 "no villagers had received a customary certificate."[23] The implementation of the pilot project was rushed to such an extent that the project staff "mixed up people's identities, photos and plots."[24] The implementation of the property formalization has been hampered for two important reasons: first, the requirement that every village must prepare a VLUP; and, second, the laborious process that households or groups of households must go through to secure CCROs. Let us consider each of these factors.

Tanzania's land laws provide for the creation of VLUPs, and these plans are enforceable through local laws. Accordingly, if the VLUPs are developed through a participatory process, the preparation of VLUPs could serve as a means for resolving local land use conflicts related to competing uses of land for agriculture, pastoralism, and wildlife conservation. In practice, however, the development of VLUPs has been reduced to a technocratic exercise dominated by government experts, which has undermined VLUP's potential to contribute to conflict resolution and has added to the unwieldiness of the process of formalizing rural property.[25] These outcomes are not merely a "failure"—they also serve to redistribute forest and land rights in specific ways.

Elizabeth Fairley's ethnographic research regarding the preparation of VLUPs in the Bariadi district reveals that the outside experts charged with facilitating the process behaved as teachers disciplining "children who knew very little and who had to be chastised if they didn't perform to expectation."[26]

22. Byamugisha 2014, 57
23. Pedersen 2014, 257.
24. Ibid.
25. Chatterjee 2004, 34–35, argues that citizens of developing societies have been turned into a "multiplicity of population groups that were the objects of governmentality—multiple targets with multiple characteristics, requiring multiple techniques of administration."
26. Fairley 2013, 151–52.

Fairley also reports the case of a village in the Mbozi district where the VLUPs depicted forest reserves even though there were none (nor any plans to create them). Fairley attributed such anomalous outcomes to the village councils' attempts to avoid breaking "the illusion of compliance."[27] Importantly, unless a village council authorizes a government agency to assist in resource management, government agencies cannot impose any stipulations vis-à-vis the management of village lands and forests. Even so, government and non-government agencies and actors often collaborate with village leaders to design VLUPs according to the interests and priorities that a majority of villagers do not share. For example, an evaluation of the U.S. Agency for International Development (USAID)–sponsored community-centered ecosystem conservation project in Tanzania's Greater Masito–Ugalla landscape concluded that while most villagers did not care about the VLUPs, village leaders viewed VLUPs as a means to secure management rights to resources.[28]

This conclusion requires a careful interpretation. Village councils have rights to manage and control "village lands," but, as discussed previously, Tanzania's forestry agencies consider large areas of unused village lands to be part of the category of government land called "general lands." When the country's forestry agencies and international conservation groups promise new management rights to village leaders, they are basing these rights on the forestry agencies' interpretation of the unused village lands. Such interpretations stand in contradiction to the VLA, which grants village councils and village assemblies management rights over all village lands. In many cases, VLUPs are used also to override the prior claims of villagers who have farmed parcels of land that are subsequently set aside as "village forest reserves." Village councils are authorized to resolve these land use conflicts in favor of peasants, especially if the village council had approved household land rights prior to the proposals for the creation of village forest reserves.[29] In other words, the expert-driven development of VLUPs leads to prioritization of specific types of land use plans, which often violate competing claims of rural residents recognized as legitimate in Tanzania's VLA. The USAID report cited above thus concludes that " . . . village and district leaders [exploit VLUPs] as a strategic tool for managing conflict."[30] This observation must be read in the context of Tanzania's villages lacking the means of holding local leaders and party bosses accountable, as these leaders are often part of patron-client networks within the country's informal economy of rent-seeking linked to tourism permits and trophy hunting licenses.[31]

27. Ibid, 149.
28. Turner et al. 2014.
29. Rantala and German 2013.
30. Turner et al. 2014, v.
31. Nelson and Agrawal 2008.

Elsewhere, the proponents of Reducing Emissions from Deforestation and Forest Degradation (REDD+) or wildlife projects in Tanzania have financed the preparation and implementation of VLUPs. Consider the case of the Jane Goodall Foundation's interventions related to the preparation of VLUPs, which also were evaluated in the USAID report cited above. A foundation staff member involved in assisting villagers with the preparation of VLUP commented, "Without land use plans, there is no law you can use to keep agro-pastoralists from bringing their herds into the villages ... It is a national problem."[32] Another staff member sought to link land use to the supposed "carrying capacity," even though the project team did not provide a systematic synthesis of local and expert knowledge needed for making judgments about carrying capacity.[33] Such expert opinions, couched in the form of scientific-sounding judgments about carrying capacity, influence the contents of VLUPs, which then become exclusionary and discriminate against socially marginalized groups, such as pastoralists.

Tanzanian government officials often rely on an uncritical acceptance of the "tragedy of the commons" thesis, often attributed quite mistakenly to rural uses of forests that include open-range grazing.[34] The undue influence of forestry and wildlife officials, conservation groups, and local leaders that have a vested interested in promoting exclusionary conservation has led to the negation of peasant land rights. While conflicts related to the claims of agro-pastoralist Maasai are well known among indigenous rights advocacy groups around the world, this chapter shows that the writing of VLUPs triggered myriad micro-level disputes and conflicts related to the claims of other smaller agro-pastoralists groups.[35] Additionally, local conservation projects and the VLUPs developed as part of these projects also run into conflicts with competing claims for household farming parcels. Detailed ethnographic research in the East Usambara Mountains show that in many villages, the creation of village forest reserves led to peasants' uncompensated loss of farmlands.[36] Researchers in other regions of the country have reported similar findings, which show that land formalization has "created new landlords and formalized landlessness."[37]

The expensive and cumbersome process of securing CCROs is another major hindrance to formalizing household land rights. Individual households must go through an extremely tedious and lengthy process to secure CCROs.

32. Turner et al. 2014, 9.
33. Ibid.
34. Mbozi's district land officer remarked, "Africans have a difficult relationship to trees" and argued for a need to spread a "different mentality regarding sustainable land-management" (Bergius 2014, 53–54).
35. Nelson and Ole Makko 2005.
36. Rantala and German 2013, 362.
37. Sundet 2008, 6. See also Nelson and Makko 2005; Kangalawe and Noe 2012; Beyene et al. 2013.

Even donor agencies have struggled to comply with the process. For instance, the donor agency Concern Worldwide could only afford to support a limited number of applicants from each village in its project.[38] The rationing of program support creates new inequalities of access to land titles without contributing to greater land security.[39] This result could have been avoided if the government had adopted the model developed as part of the World Bank–funded pilot project in Mbozi district, which is quite similar to Mexico's PROCEDE model. During the village surveys in the Mbozi project, every agricultural and household parcel is "adjudicated," mapped, and recorded in a district-level dataset.[40] Once household plots are recorded in the dataset, issuing CCROs for a small administrative fee should, in principle, be much easier and cost-effective. However, contrary to the rhetoric of land formalization programs, the Tanzanian government has not introduced instruments that would ease the burden of institutional change for the rural residents who make up the majority of the country's population. Instead, as scholars of Tanzania's land reforms have noted repeatedly, the government's land formalization program has focused on fixing village boundaries and freeing up land that it could lease to investors.[41]

It is clear that the aspects of land formalization that would have provided greater security to peasants or agro-pastoralists have been the least implemented aspect of the land formalization program. Meanwhile, a large number of VLUPs have systematically supported the interests and goals of national and international conservation groups, forestry and wildlife agencies, and village leaders. Thus, the land formalization program's highly ineffective implementation process has produced discriminatory effects, which tend to benefit relatively powerful actors at every level.[42] Equally important, none of these outcomes are driven by conflicts between wildlife conservation and peasant resource use. On the contrary, studies show that larger private landowners responding to market opportunities for mechanized agriculture (and not agro-pastoral, smallholder land use) are the main driver of resource degradation that affect, say, the spectacular wildebeest migration in Tanzania's Serengeti-Mara.[43] As such, weak implementation of legally enshrined peasant land rights helps at least one of the following two enterprises: elite interests in continued control over local natural resources and the benefits of wildlife

---

38. The district of Mbozi, the site of the first pilot project, funded by the World Bank, has issued more than twelve thousand CCROs (Fairley 2012).
39. Stein and Askew 2009.
40. Fairley 2012.
41. Shivji 1991; Sundet 2004.
42. Such effects of donor-supported projects are in tune with arguments by Ferguson 1990 and Li 2005, among others.
43. Homewood et al. 2001.

conservation, or the plans to set aside significant parts of hinterlands for commercial investors.[44]

These findings have important implications for contemporary debates.
Advocates of community rights often juxtapose egalitarian communities
against predatory governments and corporations. However, reification of
"local" leaders and institutions with egalitarian values blinds us to some of
local leaders' cross-scale collaborations with corporations and governments
on programs of land formalization. Under conditions of entrenched power
inequalities of various types, "community-based" projects often constitute an
important node around which elite interests tend to converge. The intent of
this chapter is not to question the desirability or efficacy of local institutional
development, but to shine a light on power asymmetries that undermine
these efforts. The outcomes of similar reforms in Mexico offer positive coun-
ter-examples, which is the topic of the next sub-section.

Peasants Make the Most of Mexico's (Counter) Reforms

Both supporters and critics of Mexico's 1992 "counter-reforms" "expected an
increase in land sales and the concentration of land in a few hands," although
for different reasons.[45] On the ground, the reforms' signature rural land formalization program, PROCEDE, took off very slowly, though it picked up
pace in the later stages. As the program neared completion in October 2006,
PROCEDE had been implemented in 95 percent of Mexico's ejidos and indigenous communities, with significant variation regarding which aspects of this
program individual ejidos chose to engage in.[46] While participation rates have
been low among the states with large indigenous populations (such as Oaxaca,
Chiapas, and Morelos), participation rates of 50, 60, and 69 percent in these
three states are still far greater than participation rates in similar formalization interventions launched by the government in Tanzania.[47]

Notwithstanding relatively high rates of participation, PROCEDE did not
lead to the outcomes that the proponents of privatization of ejido property
had desired. Post-reform ejidos mirror the continuum between private and
collective ownership, with a new combination of de facto and de jure arrangements for forestland rights.[48] Agrarian communities decided to privatize only
1.4 percent of the land already under de facto household control through

---

44. Nelson et al. 2012.
45. Nuijten 2003, 493.
46. Procuraduría Agraria 2007 cited in Barsimantov et al. 2009, 297; Perramond
    2008, 364.
47. Perramond 2008.
48. Haenn 2006; Perramond 2008.

provisions for dominio pleno.[49] Additionally, according to one estimate, only 0.33 percent of the country's ejido commons were privatized.[50] Most agrarian communities opted to have the ejido boundaries surveyed and delineated, and established common property rights in a manner where individual households received a certificate stating the household's share in the common property. By 1997, 2,579 nuclei (ejidos or comunidades) had rejected the privatization program because of conflicts related to land boundaries or other issues.[51]

Scholars and practitioners often read these outcomes in two different ways. Some scholars interpret the reform outcomes as a rejection of private land titles and market economics and the reassertion of a communitarian ethos.[52] However, most scholars of these agrarian institutional reforms offer a significantly more nuanced reading of reform outcomes. A careful review of both qualitative and quantitative research shows that these outcomes exemplify the phenomenon of equifinality—that is, multiple causal factors in different contexts lead to the same outcome, but with different implications. Ejido members from Baviácora to Sonora to Quintana Roo to Campache preferred greater household control over farm parcels, but did not believe that securing a full private title via dominio pleno was necessary.[53] In some cases, ejidatarios feared an increased tax burden and government intervention. In other instances, ejidatarios characterized the land certificates as a sign of freedom from the government's guardianship.[54] Ejidos located near major urban centers often chose full privatization, especially if the ejidatarios were mainly dependent on the production of cash crops.[55] In many cases, ejidatarios decided to join the program after they came to know about the successful implementation of the program in neighboring ejidos.

Each of the above responses reflects the ejidatarios' keen understanding of the complex interaction between broader political economic contexts and the institutional changes introduced by the law. Despite the careful vetting of the reform proposal and the general confidence the ejidatarios demonstrated in how they dealt with PROCEDE, it would be unhelpful to romanticize the collective decision-making process. Significant power differences existed between ejido members, and leaders strongly influenced these decisions.[56] Even though ejidos were founded in the decades following the 1910 revolution on the principle of absolute equality among members, it is best described as an

49. Assies 2008, 53; Wilshusen 2010, 781.
50. Corbera et al. 2011.
51. Appendini 2001, 34.
52. de Ita 2006.
53. Haenn 2006; Perramond 2008; Digiano 2011.
54. Appendini 2001.
55. Note that inequalities are likely to be substantial in ejidos close to urban centers and in ejidos that rely on cash crops, such as avocados (see Gledhill 1997).
56. Wilshusen 2003.

equality of opportunity, as households had to undertake land clearing and other land development measures at their own expense. As Jennifer Alix-Garcia shows, inequality of landholding occurred in the very early stages of ejido establishment.[57] Additionally, because of their role as intermediaries between ejidatarios and PRI leaders, ejido leaders and other influential individuals accumulated both economic and political power.[58] The debates that the 1992 land reforms triggered within the ejidos showed that some of these inequalities may have been disguised or at least not openly discussed in the past.[59]

The formal institutional structures of ejido rights created another set of inequalities. Only the head of the household enjoyed full rights as an ejidatario, and these rights could be transferred to only one member of the family, often the oldest son. Even though some non-ejido members and family members secured access to private parcels of land through a variety of informal arrangements with individual ejidatarios, or ejido assemblies, ejidos populations often included two groups of non–right holder residents: (1) *avecindados*, the residents who have lived in an ejido for at least one year but do not have their own land parcels or a right to vote at ejido assembly meetings; and (2) the *posesionarios*, who are individuals in possession of portions of ejido lands but who have not been recognized as ejidatarios.

The population of posesionarios and avecindados has been on an increase—in some cases, they exceed the number of ejidatarios. A study in central Mexico showed that the number of non–right holders was two to four times the number of ejidatarios.[60] Before 1992, the non–right holding ejido residents often worked ejido plots on "stony, steep slopes" of the common lands that ejidos "loaned" to landless families in return for labor contributions.[61] The 1992 agrarian law allowed ejido assemblies to create a formal list of posesionarios and avecindados, even though they would still not enjoy full rights as ejidatarios. A World Bank study, which compared data related to the number of formal right holders pre-, and post-1992 reforms, shows that PROCEDE led to the formal recognition of land rights for more than one million avecindados and posesionarios households that previously did not have property rights.[62] Others show that depending on whether the ejidos decided to incorporate new members and if they divided the commons, PROCEDE reduced both poverty and inequality of landholding.[63] However, scholars of

57. Alix-Garcia 2008.
58. de Janvry et al. 2001; Gordillo 2009.
59. Muñoz-Piña et al. 2003.
60. Torres-Mazuera 2013, 404. Similarly, a study conducted in Tijuana River Watershed showed that in the ejido that was not considered to be exceptional by the authors, the composition of the population was as follows: 28 percent ejidatarios, 4 percent posesionarios and 67 percent avecindados (Farley et al. 2012).
61. Nuijten 2004, 191.
62. World Bank 2001.
63. Munoz-Pina et al. 2003, 154.

agrarian studies challenge these findings and show that if non–right holders achieved any new rights at all, such outcomes were contingent and subject to intense negotiations—a topic I discuss in the next section.

Lastly, it is useful to explore PROCEDE's performance in areas set aside as nature protected areas (NPAs), in which conservation agencies tend to exert relatively greater regulatory controls. More than 95 percent of the NPA lands are subject to the proprietary rights of agrarian communities—ejidos and co-munidades. While Mexico's forestry and wildlife agencies do not hold authori-tative powers in the areas under the control of agrarian communities, they leverage stronger powers in the NPAs, which are comparable to the generally more powerful forest policy regimes in India and Tanzania. The NPAs staff sought to impose limitations on PROCEDE implementation. A daunting con-dition that NPA staff members imposed was that state environmental officers needed to study, map, and exclude from household parcelization any area with standing forests. If ejidatarios opted to receive parcel certificates, they would have lost parts of agricultural parcels with standing forests or tree cover. Partially wooded agriculture parcels are a common occurrence in the area be-cause of the high incidence of milpa, the local variant of swidden.[64] As such, the NPA staff members responsible for overseeing areas within the Calakmul Biosphere Reserve made household title claims unattractive for campesinos. Similar findings are reported from research about other sites in the Yucatan Peninsula and Quintana Roo.[65] Despite these difficulties, Mexican campesinos dealt with the incursion of conservation-related restrictions far more effec-tively than did their counterparts in India and Tanzania.

6.4 NEGOTIATIONS OVER LAND RIGHTS AMID POWER ASYMMETRIES

Tanzania: The government is everywhere!

The discussion of forestland conflicts may seem out of place in the Tanzanian con-text. The country has large areas of wildlife and forest reserves, with a relatively low population density (Table 1.1). Moreover, pastoralism—practiced widely in north and northeast Tanzania—entails low intensity land use, which does not undermine the land's ecological functions or its biodiversity.[66] However, land

---

64. Chowdhury, 2014.
65. García-Frapolli et al. 2009; Digiano 2011; Digiano et al. 2013.
66. For a discussion of pastoral-biodiversity links in the Himalayas, see Saberwal 1999; for African savanna, see Du Toit and Cumming 1999; and, for an examina-tion of livelihoods of northern India's forest pastoralist group called Gujjars, in a region with much higher population densities, see Gooch 2009.

use conflicts related to pastoralism, including the land rights of agro-pastoralist groups, result from the adversarial relationships that exist between rural residents and the government agencies responsible for forestry and wildlife management.

The Maasai of the Loliondo tract in Tanzania have lost much of the area they have used traditionally for seasonal grazing. As recently as 2001, the Maasai faced a real food security threat when the government imposed a complete ban on the group's farming activities instead of assisting them in registering their land rights.[67] National and international outcry forced the government to remove the ban, but the government was only willing to permit women to cultivate 1 acre of land per household by hand, without even the use of a hoe. This was despite the fact that most of the villages in the Loliondo tract possessed government papers to show registration of village land rights in the 1950s and 1960s, when the post-independence government acted to address historical injustices that Maasais suffered under colonialism. Nearly half a century after independence, however, the government cited the provisions of the Wildlife Conservation Act of 2009 to classify the entire Loliondo region as a game-controlled area. For their part, Maasais cited the provisions of the Village Land Act 1999 and the government-issued certificates of customary land rights to claim the entire area of 6,000 square kilometers as pastoral grounds for the forty thousand Maasais who live in the region.[68]

In 2010, the government proposed a draft district land use plan that would leave 2,500 square kilometers for the community, while setting aside the remaining 1,500 square kilometers for a wildlife corridor that was reserved exclusively for the annual wildebeest migration.[69] The Ngorongoro District Council that holds statutory jurisdiction over the Loliondo tract under the Local Government (District) Authorities Act of 1982 rejected the draft district land use plan prepared by government agencies. On one hand, the government insisted on imposing the VLUP it prepared. Yet on the other hand, Tanzania's president took to Twitter to dismiss reports that his government was considering evicting the Maasai for the sake of the Loliondo Wildlife Corridor.[70] The president's emphatic tweet did not make a difference on ground, however, as mentioned previously. In February 2015, the Serengeti National Park rangers burned down 114 Maasai settlements, which rendered two thousand to three

67. Homewood et al. 2012, 598.
68. Adam Ihucha, "No End in Sight to Loliondo Conflict as Protagonists Dig In," *The East African*, December 23, 2014, http://asokoinsight.com/news/end-sight-loliondo-conflict-protagonists-dig/.
69. Personal electronic communication, Susanna Nordlund, July 3, 2016. See also, Susanna Nordlund, The Tanzanian Government Insists on Grabbing Maasai Land in Loliondo, *Just Conservation*, March 24, 2013, including a number of updates from various sources available at http://www.justconservation.org/the-tanzanian-government-insists-on-grabbing-maasai-land-in-loliondo.
70. Jakaya Kikwete, Twitter handle: @jmkikwete, November 23, 2014.

thousand Maasai men, women, and children without food, a place to live, or medical supplies.[71] Despite these disappointing outcomes, it is important to recall that Maasais have mounted a formidable challenge to Tanzania's land reforms on account of "a long tradition of enrolling outsiders in their cause."[72] As I discussed in Chapter 4, some Maasai groups have developed a repertoire of links with national political leaders, as well as national and international NGOs, whose support they draw upon when their land rights are threatened.

The Maasais' predicament constitutes one extreme of an uneasy tussle of power that pervades the country's forested regions. Peasants in East Usambara Mountains in northeastern Tanzania, who lost part of their land to the village forest reserves, equated the village council's authority to that of the central government. They argued, "You cannot compete with the government, it is impossible . . . the government starts from the bottom to the top."[73] This is especially true for East Usambara, which remains a stronghold of the ruling party. Similar to forest leaders among the peasants in Indian forests, young leaders in Tanzania use their appointments to local forest management committees as a means to expand their network of influence both within the village and outside of it. Even so, under an appropriate balance of power within the village, political influences may sometimes prove useful for the protection of land rights. For example, the residents of Mitini (Zanzibar) successfully enrolled the assistance of the House of Representatives (HoR) in the run-up to the 2010 elections. The HoR convinced the Department of Forestry to "release" some areas from the region's national park for agricultural purposes.[74] Noticeably, the HoR did not adhere to provisions that would allow peasants to be compensated for lost access to land and forests. Such interventions thus remain ad hoc, without long-term gains for rural residents.

Careful examination of such negotiations suggests that rural residents' actions reflect their best assessment about the political viability of their demands for and assertion of land rights. A comparative study of elite capture and counter-resistance in Tanzania and India showed that disadvantaged, forest-dependent groups often exploited inter-elite competition to advance their own interests within a situation of entrenched power asymmetries.[75] Even so, in the case of Mitini mentioned above, the next time the community hit a roadblock in its negotiations with forestry agencies, it did not seek the assistance of the HoR representative. Because the next election was not due

71. Anon, "Tanzania breaks promise—thousands of Maasai evicted to make way for lion hunt," *The Ecologist,* February 27, 2015, http://www.theecologist.org/News/news_analysis/2771261/tanzania_breaks_promise_thousands_of_maasai_evicted_to_make_way_for_lion_hunt.html.
72. Igoe 2006, 399; Hodgson 2011.
73. Quoted by Rantala and German 2013, 362.
74. Benjaminsen 2014, 388–89.
75. Lund and Saito-Jensen 2013.

for another three years, Mitini residents did not believe that the HoR representative would be helpful in this case.[76]

Peasants in Tanzania have come a long way from their reverential attitude
toward President Julius Nyerere and elected leaders in general. As the findings
of 2014–2015 Afrobarometer surveys show, 89 percent of Tanzanians interviewed reject the "one-man rule," which shows the weakening of the support
for the strong authority that the president exercises.[77] At the same time, only
57.2 percent of Tanzanians believe that "democracy is preferable to any other
kind of government."[78] Similarly, surveys show that Tanzania is among the
countries where the demand for democracy is much lower than is the supply
of democratic institutions, which gives political elites a great deal of room for
policy maneuver.[79] Moreover, the poorest rural residents are often weighed
down by the "dull compulsion of economic forces" from which they can see few
avenues of escape.[80] The presence of deeply entrenched systemic inequalities
explains also why attempts to bring about institutional change have been so
weak and have seen so little success.

Mexico: Peasants' Resilience Against "Counter-Reforms"

Mexican peasants' response to the 1992 reforms occurred in the context of
a long history of very intense and sustained engagement between the state
and peasants. The contemporary effects of this history are captured in the assertions a peasant leader made at a 1985 march: "Why accept the tutelage of
the government? *Campesinos* are adults, masters of their own production . . .
The land wasn't given to us by groups of bureaucrats, it was given by Emiliano
Zapata and our ancestors."[81] Such militant arguments did not mean that peasants did not want to engage with the state. Instead, they sought to maintain
the integrity of ejidos as a means of engaging with the state. A survey conducted in the states of Michoacán and Durango between 2005 and 2007 found
that among the inter-community associations that were formed largely out of
the initiative of ejidos (as opposed to those driven by the initiative of any of
the several branches of the party state), 69 percent considered "political representation" to be an important function of the association.[82]

76. Ibid.
77. Author's online analysis of the results available at http://afrobarometer.org/
online-data-analysis/analyse-online. Last accessed July 3, 2016.
78. ibid.
79. Christine Mungai, "Africa loves 'democracy,' but also likes its military dictators, one-
party rule, and Big Men—study." *Mail & Guardian Africa*, October 21, 2014, http://
mgafrica.com/article/2014-10-20- what-the-concept-of-democracy-means-in-africa.
80. Mamdani 1985, 184.
81. Foley 1991, 68.
82. Antinori and García-López 2008, 33.

Even though there seems to be little evidence confirming political party cadres' involvement in negotiating local outcomes of PROCEDE, such involvement was highly likely because party leaders' central role on the ground is taken for granted. As one scholar comments, ejidatarios associated "agrarian changes with the power between different groups within the ejido-village or with the kindnesses of some politician and political party at a state or municipal level."[83] Others have argued that the "conflicts over nature of economic development, political rule, and social life" constitute the very essence of Mexican political life.[84] Such significant integration of party politics and agrarian issues notwithstanding, ejidatarios did not follow party diktats blindly. Instead, peasants remained skeptical of PROCEDE's implications for taxation and other types of state interference, adopting a wait-and-see philosophy.[85] Ejidatarios' engagement in the process was far richer than it would be if they had merely been recipients of patronage, as some descriptions of Mexico's peasant politics suggest was the case. Eventually, the ejidatarios responded to PROCEDE policies according to the contexts of their own specific situations. Political factors, such as party loyalty, do not seem to have determined either the timing or the outcomes of PROCEDE.[86]

Peasants actively took control of the reform process, which led to the following counterintuitive outcomes. First, instead of the anticipated loss of land, ejidos collectively increased landholdings and assets during the program. The expansion of the ejidal land is likely to explain the equalizing effects of PROCEDE cited previously. Despite the limitations imposed on parcel registration by the presence of Calakmul Biosphere Reserve discussed in Chapter 4, forty out of the sixty-three ejidos in the state of Campeche reported an average of 16 percent increase over the area they controlled prior to the implementation of PROCEDE. Research shows that the increase in ejido lands is attributable to the outcomes of PROCEDE land surveys. During these state-supported surveys, ejidatarios identified ejido boundaries in ways that included portions of protected lands.[87] More generally, even though the 1992 reforms formally ceased land redistributions in Mexico, subsequent peasant mobilization by the neo-Zapatistas and large-scale land occupations by various peasant groups led the various provincial governments and the federal land reform bureaucracy to revive land reform via the mechanism of the Agrarian Accords (*Acuerdos Agrarios*). Between 1995 and 2000, the accords led to the redistribution of 240,000 hectares, most of which became ejidos.[88] Land grants were not the only way in which ejidos benefited—as mentioned earlier, as parastatal

83. Torres-Mazuera 2013, 399.
84. Rubin 1990, 249.
85. Nuijten 2004,184.
86. Digiano et al. 2013; de Janvry et al. 2014.
87. Haenn 2006.
88. Haar 2005.

logging corporations were privatized, their assets were transferred to the neighboring ejido unions and forestry federations.[89] The longstanding peasant mobilization and organization, coupled with the presence of pro-peasant actors within the state, contributed to the effective design and implementation of the reform process.[90]

The state of affairs *within* the ejidos presents a complex picture. First, most ejido leaders did not want to give up on the powers they had enjoyed in the pre-reform days. As a former ejido commissioner said, the PROCEDE gave peasants "wings"—leaders could not control them anymore.[91] Second, despite the statutory provisions, very few ejido assemblies recognized the land rights of avecindados and posesionarios, while others changed their mind in the due course and decided to charge rents for lands granted.[92] In other ejidos, ejidatarios instituted informal and extra-legal norms that asserted the ejidatarios' "prerogative to broker access to natural resources" in such a way that non-ejidatarios are eligible for only a 50 percent share of the benefits available to ejidatarios.[93] Additionally, a large number of avecindados and posesionarios seemed to have lost access to the land they had been able to access via informal arrangements prior to the reforms. Formalization of the previously informal forms of access granted to avecindados and posesionarios would have threatened ejidatarios' control over ejido lands, including the commons. As mentioned earlier, many of these outcomes are attributable to ejidos' institutional design, which supports an exclusive regime of rights institutionalized at the time of the ejidos' founding decades ago. The limited progress ejidos made in recognizing the rights of avecindados and posesionarios points to the limitation of absolute devolution of power.[94]

Ejido leaders' economic power and political authority has weakened due to the processes of land parcelization and the decline in their support from the state. Concurrently, Mexico's high rate of urbanization and the continued growth of new communities created by former non–right holding ejido residents has engendered newer avenues of political engagement. For example, Article 41 of the 1992 agrarian law allows non–right holder ejido residents to participate in urban zonal affairs. Accordingly, the state has established smaller administrative units of "neighborhoods" that elect civil authorities in the form of block leaders, delegates, and subdelegates.[95] The communities of posesionario

---

89. Similarly, the privatization of the National Coffee Institute of Mexico (INMECAFE), which was government's coffee-buying organization, benefitted the coffee producers' federations. See Foley 1995.
90. Fox 2007.
91. Quoted by DiGiano 2011, 142.
92. Appendini 2001; Nuijten 2004.
93. Navarro-Olmedo et al. 2015, 14.
94. For a similar argument from India, see Bardhan 2002.
95. Torres-Mazuera 2013.

families, who remained on the sideline of ejido-based local agrarian structures, have been able to take advantage of these newer institutions to cultivate new political and economic relations with municipal leaders. These new means of representation also have heightened local political competition beyond the traditionally entrenched structures of ejido-based mobilization.[96] In such cases, municipal authorities have worked proactively to improve the non-ejidatarios' access to government programs.[97] While these changes are neither uniform nor universal, the exclusions that participatory reforms failed to address are now being addressed due to political parties and leaders' desire to create new constituencies out of the rapidly increasing population of *posesionarios* and *avecindados*.

Campesinos in Mexico also did a much better job than their counterparts in India and Tanzania in navigating the constraints the national bureaucracy responsible for nature conservation sought to impose on rural land reform. As mentioned in Chapter 4, ejidatarios capitalized on the implementation of PROCEDE to take control of portions of land set aside for the Calakmul Biosphere Reserve. Even more importantly, even though conversion of the reserve and NPA lands held by ejidatarios into parcels was effectively forbidden, the reform did not interfere with how ejido assemblies managed the milpa agricultural methods that some ejidatarios practiced within ejido commons. In a large number of cases, especially in southern Mexico, agrarian communities permit, manage, and regulate milpa quite autonomously.[98] While the 1992 agrarian reforms offered increased autonomy for eijidatarios, who are no longer considered the "pupil" of the state, neither the reserve administration nor forestry agencies sought to exploit the reform process to interfere with ejidal autonomy. As one prominent community forestry expert put it, Mexico's "National Forestry Commission (CONAFOR) would not care about the parcelization as long as the management plan was followed."[99] In other words, even if ejidatarios subdivided the forest commons and harvested timber individually, CONAFOR would not interfere unless ejidos violated the rules and norms laid out in the prescribed management plan.[100] Some scholars do point to the CONAFOR's use of community forestry funds to coerce inter-community associations to adopt market-based forestry management interventions.[101] Even so, as opposed to the unilateral changes the state forestry agencies introduced

96. See Navarro-Olmedo et al. 2015.
97. Ibid.
98. DiGiano et al. 2013.
99. Personal electronic communication, Mexican forest policy expert, January 8, 2015. This observation was also repeated by another social scientist working on issues related to forest rights in Mexico. Electronic communication, November 20, 2015.
100. Bray and Merino-Pérez 2002.
101. García López 2013.

in India's Joint Forest Management (JFM) or the subversion of community-based forest management (CBFM) expansion by Tanzania's forestry agencies, CONAFOR remains focused on the agenda of forest management and production, without seeking to dilute the autonomous territorial jurisdiction that ejido assemblies and councils enjoy.

6.5 CONCLUSION

As the introduction to Part II identified, each of the case study countries exhibits a puzzling pattern of reform outcomes that defied expectations. These expectations included the likely decimation of forests because of the Forest Rights Act–driven scramble for land in India, the attractiveness of land registration in Tanzania in light of increasing land competition, and large-scale privatization of ejido property in Mexico. I have argued that in each of these cases, the policy predictions assumed that peasants would behave, depending on one's ideological views, either as "lock-step communitarians" or self-interested rational beings who maximize individual land entitlements.[102] The political economy of institutions framework discussed in Chapter 1 would predict that peasants and other local actors would act based on their intimate understanding of long-entrenched power relations, contemporary political and economic contexts, and the choice set effectively accessible to them at the time of the reforms. In Chapter 5 and this chapter, I have demonstrated how these factors shaped the local outcomes of forestland rights reforms.

One of the most striking differences among the case study countries is the scope and depth of powers that forestry agencies enjoy. In both India and Tanzania, each with histories of populist socialist governments, forestry and wildlife agencies demonstrate a rather blatant disregard for statutory provisions related to forest-dependent groups' forest and land rights (also see Chapter 7). More importantly, instead of representing constituents' interests, most politicians and elected leaders in these two countries work as partners of national forestry and wildlife agencies. Compare this to Mexico in which case, despite the country's system of bureaucratic authoritarianism, forestry agencies do not interfere in agrarian communities' decision-making procedures. The analysis of Mexico's land reform outcomes within the boundaries of a biosphere reserve and NPAs showed that even in such cases, Mexican forestry and wildlife agencies' powers turned out to be highly circumscribed. The agrarian communities situated within the NPA territories successfully deployed political capital to challenge international conservation groups' influence in the country.

102. This formulation is owed to Eisenstadt 2011, 3.

In each of the case study countries, the reform process led to "creative accommodations," which reflected the cumulative effects of "local interactions with state-sponsored development initiatives over multiple decades."[103] Yet, such accommodations led to different types of outcomes, depending on the overall balance of power between forestry agencies and peasant groups. In the Indian case, despite the exclusion of forestry agencies from the formal institutional process of implementing the FRA, forestry officials successfully intervened to sabotage the act's effectiveness. Ironically, as discussed in Chapter 5, India's forestry officials and agencies wielded such disproportionate influence because the failures of previous episodes of institutional change gave them an aura of indispensability. In Tanzania, despite village councils' legal authority under the VLA to determine the contents of VLUPs, government and nongovernmental forestry and wildlife agencies took control of the process of developing the VLUPs. In Mexico, meanwhile, the net outcome of 1992 land reforms was a slight expansion in land controlled by agricultural communities, even though these communities initially viewed the reforms with suspicion. PROCEDE policies led to the creation of 1,276 new ejidos, thereby adding 387,000 hectares of land to the jurisdiction of agrarian communities, while less than 2 percent of agrarian land was privatized under the reforms.[104]

The reform outcomes from these three countries provide qualified support for an "institutional design" perspective. India's Forest Rights Act (FRA) of 2006, for example, shows the potential for fundamental institutional change. The FRA's institutional design ensured the representation of forestry officials in sub-district- and district-level committees, while the majority of these committees' members are elected leaders. Yet, even such robust institutional design could not help rein in forestry agencies' entrenched power—the political control over bureaucracy needed for ensuring forest rights under this kind of system was missing in India.[105] Tanzania's costly and unwieldy land formalization program is designed quite badly, which has led to extremely low rates of issuing household land certificates. Yet, it would be a mistake to assume that the badly designed institutions were put in place and persist because the policymakers did not know better.[106] The Tanzanian government's flagship program for land formalization has been designed and implemented in partnership with Hernando de Soto's Institute for Liberty and Democracy (ILD).[107] Even so, as the various documents and the statements of politicians

103. Wilshusen 2010, 768.
104. Assies 2008, 53.
105. See Christensen and Lægreid 2007.
106. See Onoma 2010.
107. Sundet 2008; Cf. Assies 2009.

discussed in this chapter suggest, Tanzania's formalization program has not focused on the poor.

The assessment presented in these pages stands vindicated as this book goes into press. Even though in the run-up to the October 2015 general elections the ruling party promised to focus on resolving land conflicts, the new Minister of Lands, Housing and Human Settlements Development "banned local authorities from surveying land and planning its use," because the minister believed that local government officials are dishonest.[108] The minister announced that the job would be handed over to private planning and surveying companies that would recover their costs from land buyers. In a related development, the Minister of Natural Resources and Tourism ordered citizens to remove livestock from the nation's forest reserves within two months, failing which "all owners will be brought to court while their livestock will be confiscated."[109] Evidently, the Tanzanian government's pre-poll announcements were little more than an opportunistic response to the anticipated electoral challenge mounted by a united opposition. Similarly, the conservative Bharatiya Janata Party-led government in India seems to be focused almost exclusively on promoting industrial and infrastructural projects, which has led the government to ask the Ministry of Tribal Affairs (MoTA) to relax the FRA provisions that make it necessary for the government to seek prior and informed consent of village assemblies.[110]

Compare the situation in these two countries to that in Mexico, where "the success and endurance of *ejidos*" is attributed to "territorial, and local political organizations."[111] There is an important insight here: the broad-based acceptance of ejidos as a collective political entity, authorized to mediate the relationship between ejidatarios and the state, helped peasants engage with and benefit from the country's 1992 agrarian reforms, even though the Mexican government had intended the reform to "open up" the agrarian sector. On the contrary, despite the presence of the Village Land Act, Tanzania's peasants can rarely draw on the country's extensive party-state machinery, which is controlled by local elites. In both Tanzania and India, local and regional political links often came from local political entrepreneurs who were willing

108. Anon, "Councils banned from surveying land," *The Citizen*, April 7, 2016. http://www.thecitizen.co.tz/News/-/1840340/3149496/-/krd6ri/-/index.html.
109. Anon, "Tanzania: All 'Foreign' Livestock Ordered Out of Forest Reserves," April 12, 2016. http://allafrica.com/stories/201604130823.html.
110. Suvojit Chattopadhyay, "How the state is reclaiming power over tribal communities," *Live Mint*. February 4, 2016. http://www.livemint.com/Opinion/iOlXJf8QPczHwuvuPAZiAP/How-the-state-is-reclaiming-power-over-tribal-communities.html. Nitin Sethi, "Chhattisgarh govt cancels tribal rights over forests to facilitate coal mining," *Business Standard*. February 16, 2016. http://www.business-standard.com/article/current-affairs/chhattisgarh-govt-cancels-tribal-rights-over-forest-lands-116021601327_1.html.
111. Torres-Mazuera 2013, 400, emphasis added; Gordillo 2009.

to assist government and nongovernmental actors and agencies seeking to change local resource management practices. These outcomes point to the need for examining the mechanisms of political intermediation at the local level. While such mechanisms facilitated the implementation of reforms to peasants' advantage in Mexico, they undermined the realization of rights in India and Tanzania despite the presence of statutory protections.

The legal status accorded to swidden farming provides additional comparative insights. While Mexico's agrarian communities continue to maintain decision-making autonomy regarding milpa, neither Indian nor Tanzanian laws recognizes swidden as a legitimate economic activity or a valid reason for claiming land rights. Even though most lands that used to be under swidden have transformed into sedentary farming plots, government agencies continue to describe these lands as swidden cultivation areas under de jure state ownership, while land rights activists and some scholars refer to them as collective property.[112] The popularity of such factually incorrect and outdated descriptors by state actors is attributable to swiddeners' political marginalization and forestry agencies' domination of national policymaking.

112. Personal communication, graduate researcher, Anand, July 26, 2009. A British social scientist of India shared an interesting anecdote of field research in northeast India in which a community member kept referring to a swidden field as "my field," even though the natural scientist on the team continued to refer to the field as a "community" land. Personal communication, London, May 19, 2013.

PART III

Policy Differences and Key Lessons

This concluding part comprises two chapters. Chapter 7 examines the ongoing development of national policy instruments related to the international program for forest-based carbon emission reduction. This chapter applies the political economy of institutions framework to scrutinize the popular arguments about green imperialism and the centrality of clearly defined statutory forestland tenures for securing carbon forestry benefits for local residents. Chapter 8 summarizes the book's main findings and contributions, and explains the implications for policy and research. It also outlines a research agenda to build on this book's theoretical and methodological approaches.

CHAPTER 7

✧

Public Accountability in Policy-making

Forest-Based Climate Change Mitigation

in India, Tanzania, and Mexico

R esearch and scholarship on international environmental governance have
undergone a momentous transformation over past few years; the "action"
has moved to the subnational and local levels.[1] The increasing prominence of
private and civil society initiatives, in both the practice of and scholarship on
international environmental governance, are a testimony to this trend.[2] Even
though scholars refer to the demise of Kyoto Protocol as the turning point
for this trend, international agencies and national governments continue to
dominate Reducing Emissions from Deforestation and Forest Degradation
(REDD+), which represents a suite of interventions related to forest-based
mitigation of greenhouse gas emissions.[3]

The top-down imposition and aggressive promotion of REDD+ as a means
to counter climate change has prompted a number of scholars to compare it
to carbon imperialism, green imperialism, or a "green grab."[4] Even as international indigenous rights activists have greeted REDD+ with the calls of *"Alto
al imperialismo del carbon!"* (Cease carbon imperialism!), national governments

1. Auer 2000; Lemos and Agrawal 2006; de Oliveira 2014.
2. Bernstein et al. 2010; Hoffman 2011.
3. The "plus" in REDD+ refers to the inclusion of the role of conservation, sustainable management of forests, and enhancement of forest carbon stocks in reducing
emissions.
4. Cabello and Gilbertson 2012; Fairhead et al. 2012; Allan and Dauvergne 2013.

have continued to vie for a share of international REDD+ funds.[5] As the title of a recent doctoral dissertation suggests, the REDD+ program seems to have defeated the old refrain of "Not in My Backyard" (NIMBY) with governments saying "Yes in My Backyard."[6] It has already influenced national forest policies, in many cases leading to dispossession and displacements of indigenous and other forest-dependent people from forest areas now being set aside to serve as carbon enclosures.[7] Even so, the policy and programmatic manifestations of REDD+ at the national and subnational levels have been far from uniform. This chapter examines the differences in how national governments in India, Tanzania, and Mexico have responded to the REDD+ program, specifically with regard to the recognition of forest-dependent peoples' rights within REDD+ polices that these governments have proposed. The political economy of institutions framework would suggest that national REDD+ policy proposals will reflect the fundamental features of political and policy processes examined in previous chapters, the differences in relationships between key stakeholders, and the extent to which policy processes privilege the interests and perspectives of certain actors and agencies over others.

REDD+ scholars and policymakers emphasize that clarity and security of forest tenure should be the first priority in the list of institutional reforms needed to facilitate successful implementation of REDD+ and other similar market-based arrangements. Proponents of such tenure reforms argue that they offer two types of benefits. First, security of tenure creates incentives for forest-dependent people to invest in forest conservation efforts, which REDD+ should reward.[8] Second, the presence of secured tenure rights will prompt governments to share with forest-dependent people a significant portion of economic gains that developing countries receive through REDD+. Building on these arguments, REDD+ scholars also emphasize the need for multi-level institutional arrangements that facilitate cross-scale governance of forests.[9] Overall, institutions that specify the relationship between forests and forest-dependent people are at the center of much of the current scholarship about national and international forest governance initiatives such as REDD+. Longstanding forestry decentralization programs and forestland rights debates in the case study countries provide a unique opportunity to test these arguments. In this chapter, I examine the links between tenure security and national governments' willingness to share REDD+ benefits with forest-dependent people. To this end, I seek answers to the following questions. First, under conditions of multiple and contested forestland tenure regimes,

5. Doolittle 2010.
6. Balderas Torres 2012.
7. Lunstrum et al. 2015.
8. Larson et al. 2013; Lawlor et al. 2010.
9. Doherty and Schroeder 2011; Kashwan and Holahan 2014.

which of the multiple forms of tenure constitute the basis of REDD+ benefit-sharing arrangements enshrined in national policy proposals? Second, what explains variation in the nature of benefit-sharing mechanisms outlined in national REDD+ policy proposals?

Section 7.2 introduces the case study countries' policies and programs of forestry decentralization, followed by an explanation in Section 7.3 of the REDD+ benefit-sharing arrangements that REDD+ policy documents propose in each of the three countries. Section 7.4 analyzes the links between the forestry decentralization policies and national REDD+ architectures in India and Tanzania. Subsequently, in Section 7.5 I analyze the REDD+ policy proposals of Mexico, which provides insights about the relationship between the structure of national forestry administration and pro-community REDD+ benefit-sharing proposals. This section also includes insights from India and Tanzania, which helps explain why the potential for positive Mexico-type outcomes remains unfulfilled in these two countries.

I begin in the next section with a short conceptual discussion about the importance of territoriality for policy proposals, including market-like instruments such as REDD+.

7.1 TERRITORIALITY AND ITS IMPLICATIONS FOR FOREST GOVERNANCE

The idea and ideologies of "scientific forestry," first developed in Europe to maximize timber yields, were ill-suited to societies in Asia and Sub-Saharan Africa where forests provided for homes and subsistence for a large number of forest-dependent people.[10] Ideally speaking, there is no reason why a science of forestry management cannot be deployed to serve the interests of forest-dependent people while also promoting sustainable conservation of forests, biodiversity, and wildlife.[11] However, European colonial governments imposed scientific forestry regimes in Asia and Africa through a *territorially based and legally enforced jurisdiction* of state forests dedicated to commercial forestry.[12] At the time of their independence from Great Britain, both India (1947) and Tanzania (1961) inherited forestry regimes comprising government forestry agencies that exercised territorial control over large state forests. Yet in Mexico, the global march of scientific forestry as a territorially based and legally enforced system came to a halt. These outcomes are attributable to the configuration of colonial and postcolonial political economy discussed in Chapters 2 and 3. A year before the British colonial government

10. Barton 2000.
11. Adams et al. 2004.
12. Vandergeest and Peluso 1995.

enacted the Indian Forest Act of 1927, which remains in force even to this day, the Mexican government enacted the 1926 forestry law with provisions inspired by the tenets of scientific forestry.[13] Had the 1926 forestry law, as interpreted by the then forestry service, prevailed, the history of Mexican forestry would have been dramatically different today. However, in the battle of wills between Mexico's nascent forestry agency and political actors who favored the broad-based agrarian reform in forested regions, the latter emerged as winners.[14]

The balance of power between forestry agencies and peasants demanding land rights in Mexico experienced a decisive shift during the presidency of Lázaro Cárdenas (1934–1940). Cárdenas, who gave Mexico's agrarian reforms a giant push and founded structures of peasant corporatism, was sufficiently enthusiastic about nature conservation to invite Miguel de Quevedo, known as the father of forestry in Mexico, into his administration.[15] The policies and programs that de Quevedo proposed, however, were inspired by the European philosophy of scientific forestry—which, as we have seen, was the basis for exclusionary colonial regimes in Asia and Africa.[16] The tussle between the technocratic methods of scientific forestry and the ideals of Mexico's agrarian revolution eventually prompted Cárdenas to dismiss de Quevedo, dissolve the independent Forestry Department, and move its functions over to the Agriculture Department.[17] This institutional restructuring, coupled with the redistribution of forested territories as part of the country's agrarian reforms, resulted in the transfer of large areas of forestland to the proprietary control of agrarian communities, which now hold an estimated 60 to 80 percent of the country's forests.[18]

The Tanzania Local Government (District) Authorities Act of 1982 recognizes the village assembly as "the supreme authority" in village-level policy making, with executive powers vested in elected village councils. Furthermore, the Village Land Act (VLA) of 1999 gives elected village councils wide-ranging jurisdictions over all land located within village boundaries, which include nearly 19 million hectares of unreserved forestland that stands on the village lands.[19] However, as discussed in Chapter 6, the Land Act of 1999 puts "unoccupied and unused" village lands under the category of state-owned "general lands."[20] These legal ambiguities have fueled the Tanzanian political and

13. Barton 2000.
14. Simonian 1995.
15. Klooster 2003.
16. Barton 2000.
17. Klooster 2003, 99–101.
18. Estimates vary between 60 percent (Madrid et al. 2009) to 80 percent (Bray et al. 2005).
19. Blomley 2006.
20. Purdon 2013.

economic elite's vested interest in capturing the surplus generated out of the country's lucrative wildlife tourism and trophy hunting business. These perverse incentives faced by powerful actors in and out of government have led to a remarkable expansion of Tanzania's national parks and wildlife reserves since the 1970s.[21] District councils, an important part of Tanzania's local government structures, and international conservation groups, such as the Jane Goodall Institute, argue that the "unused and unoccupied" village lands should be regarded as general land because the size and distance of these lands from villages makes it difficult for village councils to manage them. Therefore, even though the country's local government laws and one important land law afford significant territorial powers to village councils and assemblies, forestry agencies continue to vie for control of the same lands.[22]

Despite establishing some institutions that reverse the legacy of colonial-era policies, the Tanzanian government has enacted laws that compromise the autonomy of village councils and assemblies. Similarly, the Indian government has maintained and even strengthened forestry agencies' power and authority.[23] As Table 3.1 (p. 58 in Chapter 3) shows, the area of land designated as de jure state forestland in India saw nearly a 30 percent net increase between 1961 and 2011. As evident from the affidavits the MoEF submitted in the Supreme Court of India, the ministry recognizes that in many cases, forestry agencies mistakenly designated lands previously occupied and used by rural residents as state forestland.[24] Unfortunately, the scope and extent of these "mistakes" is so large that they cannot be described merely as mistakes.[25] Even so, the ministry has strong incentives to maintain the status quo. Forest officials often demand control over a greater share of the federal budget and a larger role in policymaking on the basis of their control of 23 percent of India's territory.[26] Such incentives explain why, as I discuss in this chapter, the forestry agencies resisted and successfully stalled a proposal to reform the Indian Forest Act (IFA) of 1927. The colonial-era IFA continues to be the foundation of India's contemporary forest management.

This brief overview of forestry institutions in the three case study countries is based on the power-centric perspective on institutions, which has been a running theme in this book. Even so, this perspective is not set in opposition to either the state or markets. The market-like nature of the REDD+ program should motivate national governments to rectify previous policy failures so they are in alignment with the expectations that bilateral and multilateral

21. Brockington 2002.
22. Blomley et al. 2011, 3.
23. Neumann 2001; Jayal 2001.
24. MoEF 2004.
25. Garg 2005; Roma and Chowdhury 2010.
26. MoEF 2006.

agencies have outlined in more than a decade of advocating for institutional reforms in preparation for REDD+.[27] Such expectations were especially high with regard to countries that have had longstanding forestry decentralization programs—which, if appropriately strengthened, would help facilitate REDD+ interventions.[28]

7.2 POLICIES AND PROGRAMS OF FORESTRY DECENTRALIZATION

India's forestry decentralization policies stand on two distinct pillars: a traditional state-initiated decentralization effort in the form of the Joint Forest Management (JFM), and the Forest Rights Act (FRA) of 2006, which is better described as democratic decentralization of natural resources.[29] The JFM emerged in the state of West Bengal in the late 1980s as a joint initiative of forestry officials and citizen groups who came together to find ways to ameliorate everyday conflicts related to local forest regulations.[30] In the 1990s, the Ministry of Environment and Forests issued executive orders to replicate the program at the national level. As a result of combined efforts of the ministry and donor agencies interested in supporting participatory forestry, many state governments also implemented JFM.[31]

JFM arrangements are based on a "memorandum of understanding" that forestry agencies sign with a village-level executive committee, which is outside the purview of the elected village councils.[32] The JFM participants agree to protect a designated forest in return for the promise of a share of timber revenues and authorized access for subsistence-related use of minor forest produce, such as fuel wood, fodder, and some types of medicinal herbs. A JFM forest is typically 50 hectares in size, and in most cases, forestry agencies often allowed only the poorest quality, highly degraded forests to be brought under JFM, especially in the cases of forestlands allocated to all-women groups.[33] Moreover, the participating communities could not independently harvest timber or use commercially valuable forest produce, such as bamboo, gums, seeds, and the tendu leaves used in making country cigarettes.[34] Almost all valuable forms of forest produce are nationalized,

27. Wunder 2010; cf. Sandbrook et al. 2010.
28. Agrawal and Angelsen 2009; Thompson et al. 2011; Kashwan and Holahan 2014.
29. Kumar et al. 2015; cf. Ribot et al. 2006.
30. Sivaramakrishnan 1999; Joshi 1999, 2000.
31. Sundar 2001; Lélé 2004; Springate-Baginski and Blaikie 2007.
32. For the pitfalls of promoting such committees instead of delegating power to elected local governments, see Ribot 2011.
33. Agarwal 2002; Negi et al. 2004; Auch et al. 2014.
34. Khare et al. 2000.

which means that only government agencies can trade in these products, even in forests brought under JFM.[35]

Within this general model of JFM, some variation existed between states regarding aspects of benefit-sharing mechanisms, the development of local institutions, the nature and effectiveness of conflict resolution mechanisms, and the extent to which JFM committees became part of regional- and state-level community forestry federations.[36] Even though JFM offered modest benefits to participating communities, the promises of such modest benefits were sufficient to motivate a large number of forest-dependent groups to join the program. As such, JFM promised to help alleviate conflicts and engender collaboration between local community groups and forestry agencies.[37] In Andhra Pradesh, where the program enjoyed strong political support, JFM has performed much better on outcomes regarding both environmental protection and forest-dependent people's livelihoods than it has in other states.[38]

Few scholars have investigated how the broader context of mainstream politics has shaped JFM. The state of West Bengal, which is the birthplace of JFM, constitutes a useful reference point. The Communist Party of India (Marxist) ruled the state for thirty-five long years.[39] Similar to the PRI in Mexico, the CPI (M) established corporatist organizations to incorporate labor unions, peasants, and women into the structures of the party-state.[40] The existence of a pluralistic public sphere—which brought together community leaders, politicians, party cadres, and representatives nominated by other local government institutions—contributed immensely to the success of JFM in West Bengal.[41] The pervasiveness of political activism, under the shadow of the patronage structures instituted by the party-state, gave peasants and forest-dependent groups the required confidence to contest the authority of forestry agencies, sometimes through overt and violent means. These conflicts prompted forestry officials to seek cooperation of forest-dependent people.[42] The nexus of grassroots political activism and a party-state was missing, however, in most other states where JFM was implemented—largely in the format

---

35. In recent years, some states have liberalized the minor forest produce regulations, but it has not always benefitted forest-dependent people who lack the capital and organizational resources needed to deal with high volumes of commercially valuable forest produce. See Saxena 2003.
36. Singh 2002; Vira 2005; Kashwan 2011; Springate-Baginski and Blaikie 2007; Fleischman 2012.
37. Joshi 2000; Baviskar 2001.
38. Fleischman 2012; Lélé 2000.
39. Incidentally, the CPI regime's fall has been widely attributed to the government's acquisition of fertile agricultural land for enabling India's industrial giant Tata & Sons to set up a car manufacturing plant. See Chakravorty 2013.
40. Ray 1999; Desai 2001.
41. Sivaramakrishnan 2000.
42. Joshi 2000.

of a national blueprint, leading to the formation of 112,816 local forest protection committees.[43]

This rapid implementation of JFM, which was attributed to donor "pressures," led to a number of problems.[44] Early on, scholars questioned if JFM fostered genuine collaboration between local groups and forestry agencies.[45] A World Bank study concluded subsequently that participants in JFM were "reduced to mere laborers, hired mainly to plant trees."[46] As a result, despite many successful cases of forest protection, JFM delivered few benefits for community members.[47] In states such as Madhya Pradesh and Rajasthan, forestry agencies made arbitrary, unilateral changes to the percentage of earnings from timber harvesting they had agreed to share with village JFM committees, years after the initial memoranda of understandings were signed.[48] Additionally, forestry agencies used JFM-related international aid to reinforce and even expand the boundaries of state forests. Forest departments secured such outcomes by making JFM benefits conditional on the JFM Executive Committee members successfully removing "encroachments" from forest areas. This included an estimated 37,000 hectares of lands under podu, a local variant of swidden cultivation, brought under JFM in Andhra Pradesh.[49] In other cases, forestry agencies used JFM-related agreements to redefine property rights in formerly autonomous local institutions, such as *van panchayats* (forest councils), in ways that enabled forestry departments to claim more than half of the timber revenues from forests protected by JFM committees.[50] Because the JFM vested authority in village JFM committees, most of which included community members *nominated* by government forestry officials, the program also reinforced the marginalization of elected local governments within India's fiscal and political structure.[51] Overall, JFM expanded the

---

43. A variety of international agencies helped diffuse the Indian model of JFM to Ghana, the Philippines, Senegal, Thailand, the Pacific Northwest region of the United States, and Zimbabwe, (Sivaramakrishnan 1996). Blomley and Iddi (2009) make a reference to the precedence of JFM in India, with potential effects on the introduction of JFM in Tanzania.
44. Lélé 2000; Agrawal and Ostrom 2001.
45. Saxena 1992; Sivaramakrishnan 1996; Lélé 1998; Sundar 1998.
46. World Bank 2005, 9.
47. "Promised Moon, Paid Pittance—Madhya Pradesh," *Down to Earth*, September 15, 2011, http://www.downtoearth.org.in/content/promised-moon-paid-pittance-madhya-pradesh.
48. Sundar 2001; Springate-Baginski and Blaikie 2007; *Down to Earth*, "Wealth of forests withheld," New Delhi. September 15, 2011. http://www.downtoearth.org.in/print/33942.
49. World Bank 2004, 2 cited in Springate-Baginski and Blaikie 2007, 349–51. For more examples, see Sarin 2005.
50. Soma Parthasarthi quoted in CWDS 2005, 32.
51. Sundar et al. 2001; Lélé 2004. For a broad-based discussion about the implication of prioritization of nonelected bodies over elected local governments in international development, see Ribot 2011.

scope of government forestry agencies' jurisdiction and strengthened their authority.

JFM's coverage did not extend to most productive forests and covered only a very small fraction of the country's forested areas. For the most part, forestry agencies and officials carried on with business as usual. My field research and other scholars' surveys show that forestry officials continued to hold views based on a traditional, top-down, and "fines and fences" approach to forest conservation.[52] As discussed in Chapter 5, the forestry agencies undertook a nationwide campaign to evict Adivasis and other forest-dependent peasants from state forests, ultimately precipitating the enactment of the FRA in 2006. The FRA provides for far stronger rights to local communities: in addition to the statutory protection of land rights for forest-dependent people discussed in Chapter 6, the FRA also grants forest-dependent groups collective rights to manage and benefit from community forest resources. It also guarantees much stronger rights of "ownership, access to collect, use and dispose of minor forest produce," which forest-dependent people have "traditionally collected."[53] Dozens of prominent international conservation groups, such as the International Union for Conservation of Nature and Natural Resource (IUCN) and the Rainforest Alliance, signed a petition in 2007 urging the Indian government to implement the FRA properly. These groups argued that the FRA constituted a fairer and potentially more effective approach for the conservation of India's forests.[54]

Despite such endorsements, India's forestry agencies and officials actively opposed the implementation of FRA.[55] The forestry officials cited the regulations and penalties in the colonial-era 1927 Indian Forest Act to justify the status quo. The most senior forestry official in the state of Maharashtra argued, "The *alleged* rights ... recognized under the [FRA, cannot be exercised] without permission in writing by a forest-officer."[56] The FRA does not stipulate such requirements, however. Instead, it explicitly requires that the FRA be implemented in all forests, including the protected areas (PAs). India's forestland rights regimes are thus divided into two parallel but contradictory tenure regimes. The first includes the 1927 law and its minor amendments since independence, combined with various executive orders related to JFM.

52. Kumar and Kant 2005.
53. GOI 2006, Chapter 2, Section 3.1c.
54. Anon, "Implement Forest Rights Act, PM Urged," *The Hindu*, New Delhi, December 27, 2007.
55. NCFRA 2010; Kumar and Kerr 2012; Kashwan 2013.
56. Letter No. Desk-12/Land/3/Gadchiroli/C.R.320 (10-11)/86/2011-12 dated April 24, 2011, issued by the Office of the Principle Chief Conservator of Forests (Head of Forest Force), Maharashtra State. Circulated over the Yahoo! group Forest Rights on April 24, 2011, available at http://groups.yahoo.com/group/forestrights/ (membership required).

The MoEF and local forestry agencies consider this first set of institutions to be the foundation of Indian forestry. The second type of forestland regime— favored by land rights activists, pro-community environmentalists, and increasingly by forest-dependent groups—is based on the FRA. This nascent set of institutions, as discussed previously, constitutes an integrated resolution of forest and land rights conflicts, and offers statutory protection for community-based management of forests and valuable forest produce. These two regimes of forestry institutions entail a remarkably different distribution of costs and benefits of environmental conservation, and favor different sets of actors and agencies.

Like India, Tanzania's trajectory of decentralization also has produced parallel and divergent forestry decentralization regimes. Tanzania implemented three different types of forestry decentralization policies in the 1990s: community-based forest management (CBFM), JFM, and wildlife management areas (WMAs). Considering this book's focus on forestry and forestlands, I do not discuss the WMAs at length, but the institutional arrangements under them are comparable to CBFM. CBFM—introduced via the National Forest Policy of 1998—offers statutory backing for villagers' "rights to use, manage and *own* forests on village lands."[57] Under CBFM, village councils in Tanzania have the authority to establish village land forest reserves, to levy and retain fines and proceeds from confiscated timber without paying a royalty to government forestry agencies, and to retain all income from the sale of all forest produce.[58] Furthermore, the Forest Act of 2002 recognizes village councils' authority to develop forest management bylaws and to constitute village forest committees or village environmental committees, both of which are defined as subcommittees accountable to elected local governments. As of 2008, 2.35 million hectares, which constituted 12 percent of Tanzania's unreserved forests, had been placed under CBFM in more than 1,460 villages.[59]

JFM applies to national and district government forest reserves.[60] The Forest Act of 2002, which provides for the mechanism of JFM, does not provide details about how the productive resources from the forests managed under JFM would be divided between different stakeholders. As of 2008, 1.77 million hectares, which is 13 percent of the forests reserved by Tanzania's central or local governments, had been placed under JFM in more than 863 villages. The Ministry of Natural Resources and Tourism has proposed that participant communities receive 40 percent of the timber royalties in protected forests, but this arrangement is awaiting approval from the Finance

57. Nelson and Bromley 2010, 83, emphasis added.
58. Ibid.
59. Blomley and Iddi 2009, 19.
60. Nielsen and Treue 2012.

Ministry.[61] Similar to India's JFM, the legal status of JFM in Tanzania is uncertain, which raises questions regarding whether JFM can form the basis of channeling the benefits of international policies and programs to forest-dependent people. Ironically, forestry agencies in Tanzania have reintroduced the colonial-era practice of taungya as part of the JFM program. As Erin Dean shows, taungya subverts peasant land claims as contested areas of forest-land are brought under JFM—similar to the conditions that existed following India's JFM interventions, discussed earlier in the chapter.[62] Tanzania's CBFM constitutes a more legally secured means of enlisting forest-dependent people in international forestry initiatives, such as REDD+. Accordingly, the distribution of costs and benefits of forest protection in Tanzania would vary significantly depending on which of the regimes of forestry decentralization inform the country's formulation of REDD+ policy proposals.

Mexico's 1992 land reforms, which formally ceased the country's long-standing agrarian reforms, strengthened agrarian communities' ownership rights by removing constitutional language that said that community territory and forests were only granted in usufruct.[63] Additionally, the 1992 reforms significantly cut down on the Mexican state's ability to meddle in the exercise of community rights.[64] The country's famed community forestry program, which draws on the rights of agrarian communities as enshrined in agrarian law, is well-established. Most importantly, in contrast to JFM programs in India and Tanzania—in which participating rural groups are granted subsistence-related use of firewood, minor forest products, and grazing rights within the forest—the term "community forestry" in Mexico is synonymous with community-based timber extraction.[65] Mexico's community forestry program nevertheless has some flaws. The forest rights of two groups of people who often live on ejido property—the avecindados and the posesionarios—are not fully protected under agrarian laws, including the 1992 law. Similarly, the rights of a large number of women, including the spouses of ejido members, are not recognized in Mexico's agrarian laws.

The General Law on Sustainable Forest Development of 2003, which now constitutes the foundation of Mexico's forestry administration, does not contradict the Agrarian Law of 1992. However, the country's environment regulatory agency—the Secretariat of Environment and Natural Resources (SEMARNAT)—often imposes lengthy and costly bureaucratic procedures, including the requirement that an agrarian community interested in timber

61. Blomley and Iddi 2009, 19.
62. Dean 2011.
63. I owe this formulation to David Bray, personal electronic communication, October 10, 2015.
64. Bray 2013.
65. Skutsch et al. 2013, 816.

harvesting must implement a forest management plan prepared by an authorized technical forester.[66] If the area to be logged includes parts of rainforests
and protected natural areas, the agrarian community also must obtain an environmental impact assessment. In addition, Mexico's central executive forestry agency, CONAFOR, argued that REDD+ requires that federal and state
legislation, including the technical rules (*normas oficiales mexicanas*) and forest
management plans, must be enforced *thoroughly and without hindrance*.[67]

Mexico's forestry and land tenure regimes are fragmented also along multiple dimensions and across multiple agencies. If they so desired, these agencies could have excluded non–right holders, while protecting the rights of and
maintaining the support of ejidatarios who enjoy full rights and control local
decision-making (but constitute a small percentage of population in agrarian communities). Table 7.1 presents a comparative summary of forest tenure
regimes in the three study countries and categorizes each of the statutes as
either "strong" or "weak" depending on the strength of community tenure
rights. Each of the study countries has more than one land tenure law, each of
which entails a different distribution of rights. The next section examines how
the contested terrains of forestland tenures shape REDD+ benefit-sharing arrangements in each of the study countries.

7.3 REDD+: POLICY PROPOSALS REGARDING
BENEFIT SHARING

REDD+ is premised on a results-based approach in which "developed countries pay developing countries for reductions in forest loss rates below an
established baseline and/or increases in forest carbon stocks."[68] The carbon
stocks related to reforestation on the one hand and avoided deforestation
and degradation on the other have different implications for the computation
of the amount of emission reductions, the uncertainty and risks associated
with such emission reductions, and the amount of benefits available to forest-
dependent groups.[69] However, these distinctions have yet to be reflected in
policy documents, in which REDD+ is portrayed as a unified approach that
constitutes financial incentives for any forestry-related actions that result in
net emission reductions.

A major bone of contention in REDD+ has been "benefit sharing"—that
is, how the economic benefits from REDD+ would be shared between government forestry agencies (which claim statutory ownership of more than

66. Zúñiga et al. 2012.
67. Robles and Peskett 2010, 7, emphasis added.
68. Lawlor et al. 2010, 1.
69. Skutsch et al. 2013.

Table 7.1 KEY FOREST TENURE LAWS IN CASE STUDY COUNTRIES

	Legislative framework	Forestry decentralization/ devolution program	Do communities have rights to harvest and market commercially valuable forest produce?	Strength of rights for forest-dependent people	Level of government discretion
India	Indian Forest Act 1927; National Forest Policy 1988; Joint Forest Management (executive orders) 1990 onward	Joint Forest Management (JFM)	No: Forest departments promised a share (50 to 75 percent) of net revenues. Effectively this translated into meager sum for a handful of communities over past 15 years.	Very weak: Rights limited to harvesting firewood and collecting fodder in limited quantities.	Very high
	Forest Rights Act (FRA) 2006; FRA Rules 2008; FRA Rules (Amendment) 2012	Community Forest Rights (CFR)	No: (timber rights) Yes: (All nontimber/minor forest produce) Community groups hold the rights to manage community forests, and harvest and market nontimber forest produce; timber rights unclear.	Strong: Statutory rights under the FRA are remarkably more powerful than the FD recognizes; defensible in a law of court.	Low
Tanzania	National Forest Policy of 1998; Land Act of 1999; Forest Act of 2002	JFM	No: Communities may get an unspecified share of timber royalties and other benefits.	Very weak	Very high
	National Forest Policy of 1998; Village Land Act 1999; Forest Act of 2002	Community-based forest management (CBFM)	Yes: Village councils retain all of the income from fines and the sale of forest produce.	Very strong: Unlike India's FRA, CBFM applies to all forest produce, including timber.	Low
Mexico	Agrarian Law of 1992;	Community Forestry	Yes: Agrarian communities with an approved management plan enjoy a full array of rights to forest produce. Rights restricted to ejidatarios.	Very strong: Communities have timber rights and have rights to all other commercially valuable forest produce.	Low
	General Law on Sustainable Forest Development of 2012	Community Forestry	Yes: Agrarian communities with appropriate management plans and safeguards, have rights to harvest, process, and market high value timber.	Strong: Recognizes the rights of *posesionarios legales*.	Low[1]

[1] Some level of ambiguity is inherent to the nature of international REDD+ regime (see Balderas Torres and Skutsch 2014).

85 percent of the world's forests) and forest-dependent people (who claim traditional use and rights to many of the same forests).[70] While no "official" inter-government REDD+ programs exist as of now, private foundations, UN agencies, bilateral agencies, and multilateral agencies are supporting a large number of pilot and other REDD+ projects. A recent report shows that over the past decade, private- and public-sector actors have invested a cumulative $5.1 billion to initiatives related to REDD+.[71] Recent research into a large number of donor-initiated projects shows that the pilot projects reflect the priorities of the donors to facilitate broad-based distribution of REDD+ benefits, which is not always the focus of emergent government policies regarding REDD+ benefit sharing.[72] Even though national governments have not enacted concrete REDD+ policy frameworks, the key elements of their policies are reflected in various government-issued policy planning documents. The policy documents that I reviewed for this research include REDD+ readiness proposals, REDD+ guidelines, and developing countries' submissions to the UN Framework Convention on Climate Change (UNFCCC) and other multilateral agencies, including the World Bank's Forest Carbon Facility. In this section, I summarize the policy proposals about REDD+ benefit-sharing mechanisms in the case study countries.

Considering governments' inclination to renege on policy promises,[73] and to set up "decoy" institutions "deliberately designed to preempt" forest governance,[74] government proposals need to be approached with some caution. Accordingly, the following analysis of REDD+ benefit-sharing arrangements is based on specific national contexts. Specifically, I examine whether the policy documents offer a clear and unambiguous division of benefits (carbon rights) between forest-dependent people and other stakeholders. Second, I investigate whether the benefit-sharing proposals are linked to the statutes that grant secure forestland rights to forest-dependent people. Third, this analysis leverages the distinction between formal benefit-sharing mechanisms and "social safeguards."

This point about the distinction between formal benefit sharing and more informal social safeguards requires further elaboration. The UNFCCC calls on REDD+ countries to institutionalize safeguards to protect a range of environmental and social values, such as "respect for indigenous and local communities, public participation and the protection of biodiversity."[75] While REDD+ advocates cite the near-universal acceptability of the idea of safeguards, they

70. Agrawal et al. 2011.
71. Silva-Chávez et al. 2015.
72. Larson et al. 2013; Sunderlin et al. 2014; Kashwan 2015.
73. Ribot et al. 2006.
74. Dimitrov 2005, 4.
75. McDermott et al. 2012, 64.

are nonbinding commitments regarding the relative priority of carbon versus noncarbon values.[76] REDD+ safeguards provide a set of guiding principles, but they lack "specificity and authority," and no formal sanctions are attached if one does not comply.[77] Defining some goals as safeguards relegates them to the sidelines of multilateral negotiations, pushes the related provisions to the appendices of agreements, and leaves their implementation to the discretion of government. Accordingly, when a REDD+ policy document describes certain benefits only as safeguards, they constitute a much weaker commitment than if they were discussed in terms of REDD+ benefit sharing.

Officials from India's Ministry of Environment and Forests reportedly declared that "100 percent of the funding from REDD+ will flow to local communities."[78] However, no credible mechanisms have been developed to facilitate transparent and timely flow of funds to local communities. India's REDD+ benefit-sharing proposals are linked to the country's JFM program that, as we have seen, grants government forestry agencies considerable discretionary powers.[79] A history of unfulfilled promises related to JFM makes it difficult for local actors to trust the promises now being made regarding REDD+. To make things worse, as India's top officials argue, "India does not want to have any more safeguards imposed on it by the UNFCCC . . ."[80] These officials and India's REDD+ documents mention "homegrown safeguards" such as the Forest Rights Act (FRA). Despite these pronouncements, as discussed earlier in the chapter, forestry agencies and officials have frequently violated the FRA and other progressive laws that devolve much stronger rights to forest-dependent groups than JFM and other forestry laws do.[81]

In Tanzania, the country's REDD+ strategy document describes community-based forest management (CBFM) as the "most appropriate way to achieve forest landscape restoration" because it entails the allocation of "clear forest land rights."[82] Yet, few communities have benefited from CBFM because of the extensive bureaucratic processes and approvals needed before a community can participate in CBFM. Instead of utilizing REDD+ as an opportunity to promote CBFM, Tanzania's REDD+ policy documents characterize all of the country's village lands as "open access" lands doomed to a fate of the tragedy of the commons.[83] The country's REDD+ policy proposals thus do not

76. Ibid, 63.
77. Jagger et al. 2012; Visseren-Hamakers et al. 2012.
78. Vijge and Gupta 2014, 24.
79. MoEF 2013, 64.
80. Vijge and Gupta 2014, 21 quoting the director general of MOEF.
81. Kashwan 2013, 2016b; Kumar and Kerr 2012; Kumar et al. 2015. Also see Mayank Aggarwal, "Several ministers under pressure from PMO and Environment ministry for relaxing norms in FRA act," *Daily News & Analysis*, New Delhi, October 9, 2014.
82. URT 2013, 13.
83. Westholm et al. 2011, 15.

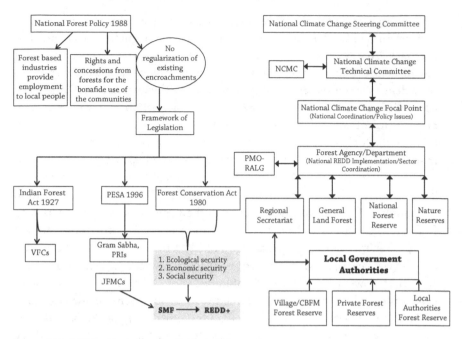

Figure 7.1 REDD+ Organograms: India and Tanzania.

advance the goal of delegating the responsibility for the management of forest resources to "the lowest possible level of local management," as outlined in the Forest Act of 2002.[84] Tanzania's REDD+ strategy posits that social and eco-logical *safeguards* will "give special consideration to livelihoods, resource use rights . . . conservation of biodiversity . . . and good governance as reflected in the Action Plan."[85] As discussed earlier, including goals under the category of safeguards pushes them to the margins of the program and leaves implemen-tation to government agencies' discretion.

In an innovative practice of policy communication, India and Tanzania's REDD+ policy documents present organizational charts to make substantive claims about some of the most contested policy questions. India's reference document for REDD+ prominently displays the following declaration within the REDD+ organogram (Figure 7.1): "No regularization of existing encroach-ments."[86] As mentioned earlier, "encroachment" is the label that government forestry agencies in India and elsewhere use for peasants' contested land claims. The REDD+ reference document thus reasserts the MoEF's claims while contravening the provisions of the FRA of 2006, which accords statutory legitimacy to these outstanding land claims. In an interesting coincidence,

84. Blomley 2006, 9.
85. URT 2013.
86. MoEF 2013, 61.

the organizational chart shown in Tanzania's REDD+ strategy document, "Institutional Structure for REDD+ Implementation and Reporting," also shows "general lands" exclusively under "Forest Agency/Department" without including any links to "Local Government Authorities."[87] This aspect of the country's forestland regimes is in violation of the provisions of Village Land Act of 1992, which, as discussed earlier, put large areas of country's forests and woodlands under village councils' jurisdiction.

Policy reports from government agencies of India and Tanzania describe REDD+ benefit-sharing mechanisms in a haphazard manner and in an ambiguous language. First, neither of these two countries explain the rationale for benefit sharing, a question that has been debated under the guise of "carbon rights" in the literature.[88] Second, the proposed benefit-sharing mechanisms center on the tenure arrangements and administrative structures that favor forestry agencies. India's policy documents link REDD+ implementation and benefit-sharing arrangements to JFM, which lacks statutory support, grants discretionary powers to forestry agencies, and has a record of unfulfilled benefit-sharing arrangements. The "Institutional Arrangement for REDD+" shown in India's REDD+ reference document simply reproduces the hierarchical structure of the ministry and state forestry departments, without even mentioning the provisions of the FRA.[89] This also holds true for the Tanzanian REDD+ policy documents discussed earlier.[90]

On the other end of the spectrum, Mexico's REDD+ strategy documents not only reassert the strong community rights contained in the country's Agrarian Law of 1992, but also explicitly attach "carbon rights" to agrarian communities' statutory rights. Mexico's Payment for Environmental Services (PES) program includes operational rules to ensure equitable and nondiscriminatory access for women and indigenous people to benefits from CONAFOR-sponsored programs, which ensures that communities not listed in the National Agrarian Registry and not surveyed under PROCEDE may also benefit from PES.[91] The General Law of Sustainable Forest Management was amended in 2012 to develop economic instruments for conservation and improvement of environmental goods and services, which result from "sustainable forest management by owners (*propietarios*) and other legitimate owners of forest land (*legítimos posesores*)."[92] Mexican forestry experts are divided in their opinions about whether avecindados and residents other than the ejidatarios will successfully

---

87. URT 2013, 22.
88. Corbera et al. 2011.
89. MoEF 2013, 64.
90. URT 2013, 22.
91. Robles and Peskett 2010.
92. Skutsch et al. 2013, 817. The phrase legítimos posesores could be interpreted as including the avecindados, especially those that have been formally recognized by ejido general assemblies.

Table 7.2 NATIONAL REDD+ BENEFIT-SHARING ARRANGEMENTS

Country national climate change program	Type	REDD+ benefit-sharing provisions	Additional provisions listed under "safeguards"	Land tenure regime that informs benefit-sharing/safeguards	Strength of tenure regime (Strong/Weak)[1]	Level of ambiguity (High/Low)
India National Action Plan on Climate Change (NAPCC)	Executive Order	"To encourage and incentivize local communities for their role in conservation by transferring the financial benefits accrued on account of REDD+ . . . based on their performance" (MoEF 2014)	"Safeguarding existing traditional rights of local communities. . . . Fair and transparent accounting and disbursement of benefits and REDD+ incentives" (MoEF 2014, 6)	Refers most frequently to JFM. Safeguards: The progressive Forest Rights Act of 2006.	Weak	High
Tanzania National REDD+ Strategy	Executive Order	"Provision of sufficient incentives/compensation to motivate stakeholders" (URT 2013a).	"Ensure environmental safeguards and possible impacts on the environment as well as livelihoods and rights of communities" (URT 2013, 53).	The Land Act 1992; Draft National REDD+ Strategy classifies village land as state forestland.	Weak	High
Mexico Climate Change Law 2012	Law	" . . . the property rights relating to . . . carbon lie with the legal owners of land (e.g. ejidos, communities, indigenous groups, individuals, firms) . . . activities that generate more social benefits and support rural sustainable development." (Balderas Torres and Skutsch 2014, p.7 citing the National REDD+ Strategy 2012)	Safeguards to respect "gender considerations and guaranteeing the *certainty over property rights and economic competitiveness*." (Balderas Torres and Skutsch 2014, p.7 citing the National REDD+ Strategy 2012)	Combines the progressive aspects of Agrarian Law of 1992 and the General Law on Sustainable Forest Development 2002 (amended in 2012).	Strong	Low[2]

[1] Based on the assessment presented in Table 2.
[2] Some level of ambiguity is inherent to the nature of international REDD+ regime (see Balderas Torres and Skutsch 2014).

secure access to a variety of forestry benefits under REDD+.[93] Mexico's revised national REDD+ strategy (ENAREDD+) released in November 2014 reiterates the country's commitment to "equitable benefit-sharing; certainty regarding and respect for property rights; free, prior, and informed consent (FPIC) for both rural and indigenous communities."[94] The increasing political salience of the emergent neighborhood groups that recognize the political and economic rights of non-ejidatarios, as discussed in Chapter 6, is likely to give further impetus to their participation in decision-making via both political and policy processes.

Faced with ambiguities and multiple tenure laws, REDD+ policymakers in India, Tanzania, and Mexico selectively deploy aspects of national tenure laws in REDD+. The security of citizens' forestland rights does not seem to be the main concern for government agencies in India and Tanzania. The forestry agencies in these countries have not based REDD+ benefit-sharing mechanisms on tenure laws that offer security of benefits to forest-dependent people. In Mexico, however, forestry agencies not only respect the community forest rights enshrined in the country's agrarian laws, but have also arguably taken steps to make REDD+ even more inclusionary.[95] This approach shows that a *lack* of clearly defined tenure regimes is not the main reason why major forested countries like India and Tanzania fail to allot a significant proportion of REDD+ benefits to forest-dependent people. Instead, REDD+ policy positions reflect a carefully curated mix of provisions from among contending laws that serve the interests of actors and agencies that wield power in the policymaking process.[96] The following section analyzes national REDD+ policy processes to propose one additional explanation of variation between the case study countries.

7.4 NATIONAL REDD+ ARCHITECTURES IN INDIA AND TANZANIA

India's strategy vis-à-vis climate change is captured in the country's National Action Plan on Climate Change (NAPCC), which the prime minister released

93. Electronic communication, Expert 1 of Mexican community forestry, January 23, 2015; electronic communications, Expert 2 of Mexican community forestry, February 6, 2015.
94. Baker et al. 2014, 5.
95. Even though some commentators based in Mexico criticize the Mexican government about its REDD+ policies, they do so from a much higher reference level of the recognition and respect for the rights of agrarian and indigenous communities than is the norm in most of the countries in Asia and Africa. Compare for instance, the approach of civil society groups in Tanzania (Kweka 2013) or of environmental NGOs, such as TERI in India.
96. Larson et al. 2013.

in June 2008. NAPCC is not a law or an ordinance that needs the backing of Parliament, but an executive plan prepared under the guidance of the Prime Minister's Council on Climate Change. This council comprises senior government bureaucrats from the key ministries, diplomats, noted journalists, environmentalists, and businesspeople, but no representatives from the land rights movements or peasants' groups.[97] Moreover, climate change debates and policymaking are conducted as an entirely apolitical and technocratic exercise. For instance, instead of being debated in Parliament, an Environment Ministry official announced India's intention to establish a National REDD+ Coordinating Agency (REDD+ Cell) at a global deforestation conference held in Oslo in 2010.[98] While many policy practitioners and some scholars in environmental and forest management decry political interference, no policy process operates in a political vacuum.[99] As recent research shows, the ostensibly technocratic processes dominated by experts often promote the interests of specific actors in the policy process.[100]

The NAPCC identifies eight core "national missions" and directs ministries to submit detailed implementation plans to the Prime Minister's Council.[101] The missions are organized through intersectoral groups, which include "experts from industry, academia and civil society."[102] Climate change policies and programs related to the forestry sector, including the REDD+, are tied to the government's "Green India Mission," which aims to restore 20 million hectares of forestland in the next ten years at a cost of approximately $10 billion.[103] These afforestation plans, which will entail planting fast-growing tree species, are expected to sequester 43 million tons of carbon annually. The MoEF's National REDD+ Cell is responsible for REDD+ policy design and implementation.[104] The MoEF also calls for the creation of REDD+ cells at the state level, within the jurisdiction of state forest departments. The state

97. The Globe International Report on climate change legislation includes NAPCC, but it is not even a formal executive order. The plans and provisions of NAPCC are entirely at the discretion of the ministry.
98. "National REDD+ agency may be set up," *The Hindu,* May 28, 2010, http://www.thehindu.com/news/national/national-redd-agency-may-be-set-up/article439989.ece.
99. See, for instance, Tim Trench, "In Mexico, it's the politics . . ." *CIFOR Forests News,* August 19, 2015, http://blog.cifor.org/32106/in-mexico-its-the-politics?
100. For an economist's perspective, see Easterly 2014; see also Baviskar 2004; Li 2007.
101. The missions are: the National Solar Mission, the National Mission for Enhanced Energy Efficiency, the National Mission on Sustainable Habitat, the National Water Mission, the National Mission for Sustaining the Himalayan Ecosystem, the National Mission for a Green India, the National Mission for Sustainable Agriculture, and the National Mission on Strategic Knowledge for Climate Change.
102. GOI 2008, 5.
103. Keya Acharya, "Climate Change: REDD at Cancun Causes Angst in India," *Inter Press Service,* December 4, 2010.
104. The MoEF has recently been rechristened to the Ministry of Environment and Forests and Climate Change.

REDD+ cells will, in turn, work with forest divisions (territorial jurisdictions that correspond to forest districts in other countries) and the village JFM committees, which function under the direct control of forest departments, as discussed earlier.[105] The core institutional structure of REDD+ as implemented through national- and state-level REDD+ cells mimics the organogram of the MoEF and state forestry departments put together. The "Reference Document on REDD+," prepared by a group of apparently independent experts, suggests that the country's forest management structure "does not require any major change to support implementation of REDD+."[106] Instead, the document argues that the current forest management regime needs to be strengthened to support REDD+ implementation.

Instead of inviting genuine engagement from India's diverse civil society and forestland rights movements, the MoEF asks for the *cooperation* of other national-level stakeholders to "ensure sustainable management of forests, to address drivers of forest degradation, and to improve the livelihoods of forest dependent communities."[107] Even though livelihoods are mentioned in REDD+ policy documents, the MoEF does not engage with the Ministries of Tribal Affairs or Rural Development, or any of the prominent NGOs and academics that have worked for decades in this field.[108] The MoEF has enlisted experts and representatives from select research institutions and civil society organizations, most of which function under the MoEF's jurisdiction.[109] These agencies' role is limited to "technical and capacity building support," or to inform regional forestry officials and environmental NGOs about *the* REDD+ architecture, as if national and international REDD+ institutional arrangements were already finalized. The only NGO involved significantly in the process—the Energy and Resources Institute, headed until recently by former IPCC chairperson R.K. Pachauri—is too close to the ministry to be regarded as a representative of the country's large and diverse civil society sector. The ministry and its collaborators seem to define their task as advertising REDD+ to government officials and NGOs.

A number of prominent civil society groups opposed the Indian government's support for REDD+ proposals put forth at the sixteenth Conference of Parties (COP) held in Cancún, Mexico, in 2010. Civil society groups criticized

---

105. See the "Institutional Arrangement for REDD+," MoEF 2013, 64.
106. Ibid., 48.
107. MoEF 2014, 11.
108. More than 1,500 concerned citizens, including conservation experts and advocates, led by a national group called Conservation India signed a petition to draw attention to the government's plans to dedicate public funds to "meaningless tree planting projects." See "Urgent! The Compensatory Afforestation (CAF) Bill 2015 Must be Recast—Act Now!" August 10, 2015. http://www.conservationindia.org/campaigns/why-the-compensatory-afforestation-bill-2015-must-be-recast.
109. These include the Forest Survey of India, the Indian Council of Forestry Research and Education, the Indian Institute of Forest Management, and the Wildlife Institute of India.

India's 2008 submission to the UNFCCC for ignoring forest-dependent peoples' statutory rights, even as agri-business plantations were recognized as "plantations" eligible for REDD+ payments.[110] Today, the MoEF continues to ignore these major concerns to such an extent that rights groups consider it futile to engage any further with the REDD+ policy process.[111]

Tanzania is part of the REDD+ Readiness program (sponsored by the World Bank's Forest Carbon Partnership Facility), is one of the UN-REDD+ countries, and has received significant and sustained bilateral funding from Norway. The Office of the Vice President is the supreme authority overseeing the country's engagement with the REDD+ process. In operational terms, two inter-ministerial/inter-departmental committees—the National Climate Change Steering Committee (NCCSC) and the National Climate Change Technical Committee (NCCTC)—are responsible for the development of strategy and the implementation of climate change policies, respectively. Within this broad multisectoral, multi-stakeholder approach to REDD+, Tanzania Forest Services Agency of the Ministry of Natural Resources and Tourism is responsible for the implementation of REDD+.[112] The NCCTC—which comprises one representative each from civil society, the private sector, and research institutions—is charged with overseeing technical issues and the implementation of the National Strategy for REDD+.

In general, Tanzania's REDD+ institutional structure has facilitated engagement with civil society groups in ways that have been more effective than similar efforts in India. A REDD+ policy advisory group constituted by the national government sought the participation of civil society organizations and community groups, including the Community Research and Development Services (CORDS). Similarly, the Association for Law and Advocacy for Pastoralists (ALAPA), which was one of the indigenous rights groups that signed a petition demanding that the World Bank rethink its decision to change its safeguards policy, participates in the REDD+ technical working group related to legal issues, governance, and safeguards.[113] Edward Loure, a Tanzanian indigenous rights activist, won the 2016 Goldman

---

110. Keya Acharya, "Climate Change: REDD at Cancun Causes Angst in India," *Inter Press Service*, December 4, 2010.

111. Telephone interview, researcher and national policy observer, June 12, 2014. For a recent critique, see Ashish Aggarwal, "Managing forests for carbon," *Daily O*, July 10, 2015, http://www.dailyo.in/politics/teri-climate-change-greenhouse-gas-redd-cdm-cifor-green-india-mission-unfccc-deforestation-biodiversity/story/1/4906.html; "Our Forests are not for Sale! Stop Privatizing India's Forests! A Press Release by All India Forum of Forest Movements (AIFFM)," September 21, 2015, http://www.redd-monitor.org/2015/09/24/india-plans-to-hand-over-degraded-forests-to-plantation-companies/.

112. Tanzania Forest Services Agency Web site, http://www.tfs.go.tz/about/category/the-organisation.

113. Anon. "This statement is made by Tanzania indigenous peoples' civil societies on their Significant concerns on the proposed World Bank Environmental and

Environmental Prize for helping indigenous groups secure community land titles (CCROs as discussed in Chapter 6) for more than 200,000 acres of land.[114] Loure also brokered a deal in 2013 between the indigenous Hadzabe group and the REDD+ project Carbon Tanzania (CT), which has enabled the Hadzabe to earn $60,000 in carbon offset sales.[115]

Tanzania's national REDD+ strategy document refers to extensive multi-actor, multilevel institutional arrangements that link the Vice President's Office to village councils, which hold statutory authority over village forest reserves. Tanzania's strategy document cites clear allocation of forest land rights under CBFM, and recognizes the importance of "traditional knowledge and practices."[116] Notwithstanding such declarations and the increased participation of civil society groups, research on the ground shows that communities' and NGOs' participation in forest management was limited to "consultations and awareness meetings, [and] the local communities were left out of most of the planning and decision-making process."[117] These observations are supported by other researchers who have followed the policy process over time.[118] In recent times, a number of serious conflicts have been associated with Tanzania's REDD+ pilot and preparedness projects.[119] The next section offers an explanation about why the REDD+ policy proposals in these countries vary so significantly.

7.5 REDD+ POLICY PROPOSALS: POLITICAL AND ADMINISTRATIVE DRIVERS OF RESPONSIVE POLICYMAKING

Scholars of forest policy and REDD+ attribute Mexico's progressive policy successes to the country's radical patterns of forestland ownership.[120] Indeed, as discussed earlier, the history of the Mexican Revolution of 1910 and the

Social Framework," December 5, 2014, http://www.bankinformationcenter.org/wp-content/uploads/2015/03/Statement-from-Tanzanian-Indigenous-Peoples-organizations-on-the-proposed-Environmental-and-Social-Framework-27-endorsing-organizations.pdf.

114. Alpha Nuhu, "Tanzanian wins global recognition for protecting natural environment," *Daily News*, April 19, 2016, http://www.dailynews.co.tz/index.php/features/48969-tanzanian-wins-global-recognition-for-protecting-natural-environment.

115. Ibid.

116. URT 2013, 13. N

117. Manyika and Nantongo 2012, 67.

118. Rantala 2012. Email communication, Tanzanian graduate researcher, June 10, 2014.

119. Beymer-Farris and Bassett 2012.

120. Bray 2013; Corbera et al. 2011.

redistribution of land it engendered have had a remarkable influence over the country's forestry institutions.[121] Unlike India and Tanzania, Mexico's forestry agencies do not exercise territorial control over large areas of the hinterlands. Even so, it is important to recall that the state's commitment to agrarian reforms began to weaken in the late 1970s, which culminated in the Mexican state officially ending agrarian reforms in 1992.[122] In light of these political developments, this section examines the effect of national and subnational politics in the REDD+ policy process to inductively identify other factors that contributed to the pro-community REDD+ benefit-sharing policy proposals in Mexico.

CONAFOR, Mexico's national forestry commission, is the main executive agency responsible for the country's forestry programs, including REDD+. While CONAFOR is a semi-autonomous agency closely tied to the environment ministry SEMARNAT, it has often acted quite independently of SEMARNAT. The Federal Attorney of Environmental Protection (PROFEPA—Procuraduría Federal de Protección al Ambiente, in Spanish) is responsible for auditing, inspecting, and enforcing forestry laws and management programs approved by SEMARNAT.[123] While PROFEPA is often short of resources, it has acted against improprieties in logging and other projects that SEMARNAT has sanctioned.[124] Even though CONAFOR is responsible for implementing REDD+, PROFEPA has been working with agrarian communities to set up local environmental watchdog committees (CVAP). The CVAPs function under ejidos or comunidades general assemblies, which hold proprietary rights over much of Mexico's forests.[125]

The CVAPs are not a new idea at all. Mexico's agrarian laws provide for the existence of an oversight committee (*Consejo de Vigilancia*), which is an elected committee responsible for monitoring and supervising ejido accounts, budgets, expenditures, and ensuring that ejido commissioners function according to the General Assembly's wishes. The oversight committees have been ineffective in states such as Durango,[126] and problematic in the Calakmul Biosphere Reserve insofar as they have tended to align with environmental groups against the interests of peasants.[127] However, in the state of Oaxaca, which has a more fully developed community forestry sector, the supervisory committees are quite active and effective.[128] Similar structures aimed to

121. Bray 2013; Mathews 2011.
122. The Echeverria administration (1970–76) witnessed the last round of land redistributions.
123. PROFEPA's mandate extends to all environmental programs in the country. See Healy et al. 2014.
124. Mitchell 2006.
125. IDLO 2011.
126. Personal electronic communication, scholar of Mexican community forestry, January 17, 2015.
127. Haenn 2003, 91.
128. Skype interview, Mexican scholar and community forestry activist, January 23, 2015.

facilitate policy deliberations and accountability also exist at the municipal and regional levels.[129]

At this point, it is useful to examine the roots of the divided jurisdictions within Mexico's national environmental and forestry administration, which have resulted from a combination of donor interventions and political considerations. The founding of PROFEPA, the federal environmental attorney's office, can be traced to an initiative by a Boston-based consulting firm contracted to the U.S. Agency for International Development (USAID)—an initiative that predates the birth of Mexico's new federal environmental ministry, SEMARNAT.[130] Most importantly, the relative autonomy of CONAFOR, the forestry executive agency, from SEMARNAT can be traced to political considerations of the National Action Party (PAN), the conservative party which took control of Mexico's presidency in 2000. Removing forestry from the environmental ministry and placing it under the control of an executive agency with a mandate of "developing, promoting, and carrying out activities related to the productivity, conservation and restoration of forests," was part of the PAN's efforts to strengthen its ties to the peasant sector.[131] The PAN continued to use forestry as a means of employment and economic development for some of country's poorest peasants. The trio of PAN leaders who led these efforts—Vicente Fox, Alberto Cárdenas, and Felipe Calderon—came from Mexico's hinterlands, states such as Michoacán and Jalisco with large areas of forestland, which were also sources of income and employment for large numbers of people.[132]

Subsequently, Mexico established the Inter-Ministerial Climate Change Commission (CICC) in 2005 to coordinate the development of the country's climate change policies, programs, and strategies. The CICC, comprising senior representatives from ten key ministries, also receives input from the Consultative Council on Climate Change (C4), which includes scientists and representatives from Mexico's civil society organizations and the private sector.[133] Most importantly, the Mexican Senate established a multiparty special commission on climate change to write a climate change law in 2010, becoming the first country to do so.[134] The commission organized more than seventy brainstorming sessions and meetings with scientists, scholars, government representatives, NGOs, and international organizations. More recently, in advance of 2012 presidential elections, the environmental advocates had an important ally in Congress—José Ignacio Pichardo Lechuga, chair of the Special Commission on

129. IDLO 2011.
130. Mumme 2007.
131. Meirovich 2014, 133.
132. Ibid.
133. The REDD-Desk, "REDD in Mexico," May 2013, http://theredddesk.org/countries/mexico.
134. USAID 2010.

Forests. This fortuitous political opportunity structure led to the enactment of the General Law on Climate Change and amendments to the General Law for Sustainable Forest Development in 2012, which provides the basis for Mexico's REDD+ benefit-sharing policies discussed earlier.[135] Party politics continue to shape institutional structures, which also forces national agencies to be more responsive to popular mobilization.

Mexican activists and scholars have questioned the dominance of big international NGOs (BINGOs) in REDD+ and other climate change–related consultations.[136] For instance, an initial program document draft that CONAFOR submitted to the World Bank's Forest Carbon Partnership Facility proposed to divert agrarian communities' share of REDD+ proceeds to "activities that diminish deforestation and degradation."[137] Civil society groups forced the commission to drop this proviso in favor of transferring resources directly to agrarian communities. CONAFOR also previously sought to exclude the well-established ejido unions from being part of the "official" silviculturalist association—National Confederation of Organizations of Silviculturists (CONASIL in Spanish), even though civil society mobilization played an important role in the founding of CONASIL.[138] CONAFOR's ability to impose its will on these negotiations also is constrained by the involvement of other powerful government agencies— including the Ministry of Agriculture, Livestock and Rural Development, Fisheries and Food (SAGARPA), the Ministry of Agrarian, Territorial and Urban Development (SEDATU), and the National Commission for the Development of Indigenous Peoples (CDI). The involvement of these various agencies is much more than symbolic, as Mexico's REDD+ program is situated *within* the broader frame of sustainable rural development.[139] This is also a reflection, in part, of campesinos' control over agrarian properties, which house more than 70 percent of Mexico's forests, and agrarian and indigenous communities' enduring political importance.[140]

Mexico's approach to REDD+ stands in remarkable contrast to India, where forestry agencies have refused to respect the provisions of the country's Forest Rights Act, which granted forest-dependent people the right to take control of and benefit from management of forests. India's forestry establishment—the Ministry of Environment and Forests, as well as state

---

135. Purple S. Romero, "This goes far beyond REDD+—Mexico's legal preparedness and cultural take on REDD+ Safeguards," October 18, 2013, http://reddplussafe-guards.com/mexico/.
136. Skype interview, Mexican academic and community forestry activist, January 23, 2015.
137. Anon 2014, 3–6.
138. García-López 2012, 112.
139. See USAID 2010; CONAFOR 2013.
140. Gordillio 2009.

forestry departments—are organized into one monolithic agency, in which every important decision is taken by the officers of the elite cadre of Indian Forest Service.[141] The executive-heavy policymaking process predominates in India because a majority of India's forest-dependent people are not mobilized into an electorally salient voting constituency.[142] Their lack of political salience also has undermined efforts to reform India's forestry administration.

The former Minister of Environment and Forests Jairam Ramesh (2009–11) proposed to reform the colonial-era Indian Forest Act (IFA) of 1927. Even though his senior colleagues from the Congress party had cited the indiscriminate application of forest laws as one of the root causes of the Maoist unrest in India's forested regions and had demanded major reforms in the past, the party failed to put its weight behind Ramesh's proposal for institutional reforms.[143] Additionally, senior forest officials openly opposed and successfully stalled the proposal; the IFA continues to be the foundation of India's contemporary forest management.[144] Ramesh's failure to reform the IFA also influenced his vision for reforming the MoEF, as evident in the following qualifier that appears alongside each of the four different models of divided jurisdictions that Ramesh proposed for the MoEF's environment department: "Forestry and wildlife continue to be functions of the MoEF and are beyond the scope of this document."[145]

Even so, the MoEF is not the only agency in India that has jurisdiction over forests. The FRA of 2006 gives the Ministry of Tribal Affairs (MoTA) jurisdiction over FRA-related forestlands, including forests brought under collective forest rights. In the decade since the FRA was enacted, the MoTA has frequently sounded alerts whenever any of the government ministries violated the FRA provisions.[146] Instead of acting responsibly, however, the MoEF has disregarded the MoTA's directives on most occasions. In the discussions I had with the minister of tribal affairs and in comments he made publicly toward the end of his tenure, he described his helplessness to counter the

141. Hannam 2000; Kumar and Kant 2005.
142. Chhatre and Saberwal 2005.
143. Vivek Deshpande, "Jairam plans changes in Forest Act, depts unaware," *The Indian Express*, April 20, 2011, Nagpur, http://archive.indianexpress.com/news/jairam-plans-changes-in-forest-act-depts-unaware/778477/.
144. Richard Mahapatra, "Losers again," *Centre for Science and Environment's Fortnightly News Bulletin*, May 16, 2012 http://www.downtoearth.org.in/blog/losers-again-38199.
145. Ramesh 2015, 305–10.
146. "Deo locks horns with environment min over clearance to Mahan," *The Daily News and Analysis*, July 19, 2013, http://www.dnaindia.com/india/report-deo-locks-horns-with-environment-min-over-clearance-to-mahan-1863210;   Jay Mazoomdar, "Don't Violate Forest Rights Act, MoEF Told," *The Indian Express*, December 19, 2014, http://indianexpress.com/article/india/india-others/dont-violate-forest-rights-act-moef-told/.

onslaught of industrial and mining projects. He said, "While we empower the forest dwellers through the [FRA, the MoEF] ... gives clearances to industrial projects in forest areas. We should have a say here."[147] Such inter-ministerial violations have increased significantly since the change of government in May 2014 when the conservative Bharatiya Janata Party (BJP)-led National Democratic Alliance came into power.[148] The present minister of tribal affairs, Jual Oram, also has stated publicly that the MoEF's policies violate the FRA provisions, but this has not swayed the MoEF's policy decisions.[149] In other words, the potential for checks and balances that exists within the present institutional set-up has been undermined repeatedly by the government in New Delhi, which favors economic development at the expense of forest-dependent peoples' interests.[150]

Unlike India, where the donor community has little leverage, donors have been far more influential in Tanzania.[151] Recently, donors helped the country carve a semi-autonomous Tanzania Forest Services (TFS) Agency out of the Forestry and Beekeeping Division (FBD), which used to be the umbrella executive agency. What remains of the FBD is responsible for policy planning, research, training, licensing, and quality control. Tanzania National Parks (TANAPA), a parastatal body, manages the country's national parks and wildlife reserves. This separation of regulatory and executive powers between the FBD, the TFS, and TANAPA, combined with heightened electoral competition between political parties in recent years, increases the potential for improving accountability.[152] Whether these goals will be realized remains to be seen because the transition has been managed poorly so far. Researchers argue that the process has led to "blurred lines of responsibility," "competing incentives," and "creation of parallel structures"—thereby weakening the accountability and effectiveness of government personnel

147. Prasad Nichenametla, "Ministry Has Limited Scope To Empower Tribals, Says KC Deo," *The Hindustan Times*, May 16, 2013, http://www.hindustantimes.com/newdelhi/ministry-has-limited-scope-to-empower-tribals-says-kc-deo/article1-1061293.aspx.

148. Mayank Aggarwal, "Several ministers under pressure from PMO and Environment ministry for relaxing norms in FRA act," *Daily News & Analysis*, October 9, 2014.

149. Jay Mazoomdar, "Don't Violate Forest Rights Act, MoEF Told," *The Indian Express*, December 19, 2014, http://indianexpress.com/article/india/india-others/dont-violate-forest-rights-act-moef-told/.

150. Similar debates also preceded the enactment of the Mines and Minerals (Development and Regulation) (Amendment) Bill (MMDR) in 2015 in Parliament. See Srestha Banerjee, "Parliament passes controversial mining bill," *Down to Earth*, March 20, 2015. http://www.downtoearth.org.in/content/rajya-sabha-passes-controversial-mining-bill.

151. For India, see Vira 2005; for Tanzania, see Harris et al. 2011.

152. Nelson et al. 2012.

on the ground.[153] Tanzania's forestry administration stands at a crucial juncture, but the task of steering it in the right direction is hampered by Tanzanian leaders' single-minded focus on the goals of economic growth without ensuring that a majority of the country's population actually benefits from such economic growth. The same also applies to REDD+, which is seen as an opportunity to attract investment, and not as a reward to local communities' contributions to forest conservation.[154]

Political leaders' indifference has facilitated forestry agencies' continuing dominance and the perpetuation of the problematic forestry rights status quo in both India and Tanzania.[155] The supposedly depoliticized functioning of forestry agencies in these two countries has only disguised entrenched political and economic actors' interest in perpetuating state control over forests and forestland.

7.6 CONCLUSION

Clearly defined and secure tenure rights continue to be an important goal in international forestry. The security of tenure that agrarian communities in Mexico enjoy is one of the reasons Mexican peasants stand to benefit from REDD+ more than their counterparts in other countries. But security of tenure, while necessary, is not sufficient to ensure that international forestry and wildlife conservation helps forest-dependent groups. Both India and Tanzania, for example, have statutory provisions that government forestry agencies and ministries could have used to ensure a fairer distribution of benefits from REDD+. But they chose not to do so.

Forestry policymakers in the case study countries have been able to choose from among multiple tenure systems that are available to them.[156] An examination of their choices contributes important insights into the intent, speed, and direction of tenure reforms that REDD+ advocates and international agencies have sought to promote for more than a decade. First, it is evident that forestland tenure reforms cannot be "programmed and incentivized ... to achieve dramatic top-down changes in global forest management within two decades."[157] While acknowledging this reality, it is equally important to offer deeper explanations about why governments have not responded to calls for tenure reforms. What other institutional and political factors may explain why

---

153. Harris et al. 2011, 12–13; personal interview, Tanzania forest policy expert, June 20, 2014.
154. Kweka 2013.
155. Harris et al. 2011.
156. Steinberg 2015.
157. Westholm et al. 2011.

some governments have performed much better than others have? A systematic examination of how national policymakers have repackaged different forest tenure options into REDD+ policy proposals reinforces the well-rehearsed arguments about the political economy of natural resource policies and institutions. Governments in India and to a lesser extent Tanzania are evidently not interested in extending significant REDD+ benefits to forest-dependent groups.

The immense amount of international investment in REDD+ preparedness is intended to build government agencies' capacity to implement new forest management practices. While the need for capacity-building cannot be denied, poor enforcement of resource regulations is "as much a choice as an intrinsic limitation."[158] Bill Ascher identified developing country ruling elites' concern with their own political and economic interests as the proximate cause of poorly designed and executed resource management policies and programs, while identifying structural or institutional problems as the root causes.[159] This book has systematically traced how institutional structures in three developing countries emerged from the configuration of power relations among actors and agencies with a direct stake in the design of property regimes and forest policy institutions. An especially insightful case is India's forestry decentralization program JFM, which was formalized in the year 1990. Soon after these JFM guidelines came into existence, policy experts pointed to major flaws inherent in JFM's institutional structure: its insecure legal or statutory basis; its lack of properly defined relationships with village councils; and the fact that the formal JFM arrangements reinforced the already very heavily skewed balance of power between forestry agencies and village groups.[160] India's forestry service, one of the strongest in the world, has been unable to respond to these concerns, which scholars have reiterated incessantly.[161] This long perpetuation of the problematic status quo in India's forestry sector prompted the United Progressive Alliance (UPA) government to ask the Ministry of Tribal Affairs (MoTA) to enact a new law.

The resulting legislation, India's Forest Rights Act of 2006, epitomizes the type of tenure reforms that REDD+ advocates often demand. The FRA devolves strong, secure, and relatively clearly defined rights to rural residents. But because India's REDD+ policy process is disconnected from the country's mainstream political process, it does not reflect the FRA's provisions. The outcomes would be different if the MoTA could actively participate in the REDD+ policy deliberations.[162] In addition, India would likely have developed a more

---

158. Ascher 2000, 10.
159. Ibid, 14.
160. Saxena 1992; Sivaramakrishnan 1996; Corbridge and Jewitt 1997; Sarin 1998; Lélé 1999.
161. For a recent nuanced assessment of the Indian Forest Service, see Fleischman 2012.
162. The MoTA's interventions have helped prevent the violation of forest-dependent peoples' rights in the context of the Indian government's establishment of large

robust REDD+ policy framework if the Indian government had worked to have Parliament enact a climate change law.[163]

The theoretical concept of REDD+ unites a number of complex ideas in science (the amount and pace of carbon stored in different types of forests), economics (the counterfactual scenarios of avoided deforestation and degradation), and politics (the distribution of costs and benefits that different institutional arrangements entail). Such complexity, often identified with the so-called "wicked problems," creates further opportunities—either for anchoring policy debates in principles that policymakers consider foundational, or for equivocation and disguising of interests in the cloak of complexity and uncertainty.[164] The policy documents analyzed in this chapter demonstrated that, to a great extent, Mexican policymakers have translated the promises of statutory laws into actual policy documents, which reiterate that ejidos and other communities hold "carbon rights."[165] The Rights and Resources Researchers show that of the twenty-three countries with large forest areas they examined, only Mexico and Guatemala passed national legislation defining tenure rights regarding carbon.[166] Mexican policymakers are continuing to brainstorm about how the carbon stored in specific forests should be rewarded through a combination of market-based and incentive-based mechanisms.

The question of carbon rights needs to be distinguished from the financial instruments used to value forest-based carbon stocks—as these instruments reflect contentious decisions about how to determine the financial value of avoided deforestation and degradation. Such accounting requires an appreciation for economies of scale and a larger geographic scope—as carbon stocked in one site could lead to "leakages" in neighboring sites, with attendant consequences for emission reduction credits.[167] Moreover, a clear distinction between economic rights related to forest-based carbon and the financial instrumentation of carbon credits may also help insure forest-dependent groups against risks inherent to financial markets. On the other hand, forestry agencies in India and Tanzania have sought to cleverly obfuscate the question of carbon rights while making noncredible commitments in the guise of REDD+ safeguards. The techno-managerial solution of REDD+ takes on very different

industrial projects financed through foreign direct investment. Kumar and Kerr 2012.

163. For comparative analyses of climate change-related legislation, see Nachmany et al. 2014.

164. Moeliono et al. 2014.

165. The relevant statute is the Sustainable Forest Development Law of 2012, Article 134bis read in conjunction with Article 7 (XXXIX) & Article 33 (IX).

166. RRI 2014.

167. The distinction between "economic instruments" and "financial instruments" is the root of much confusion in the literature on Mexico's REDD+ policies and proposals. Personal electronic communication, Mexico forest policymaker (via David Bray), October 10, 2015.

lives in these countries, depending on the nature of political and administrative landscapes, which determine how much space forest-dependent people have in the policy process and the extent to which government forestry agencies and ministries are held to account by equally powerful but independent government agencies.

The success of REDD+ and other similar environmental conservation initiatives requires that the purview of reforms be broadened—from a relatively narrow focus on tenure reforms to more substantive reforms in the structure of national forestry administrations and ministries.

CHAPTER 8

✧

Conclusion

Toward Social Justice and Enduring Nature Conservation

Institutions are the by-products of competing impulses within a society; they represent specific configurations of interests and ideas about the desirability of some actions over others. Because institutional change is often fraught with conflicts and confrontations, "institutions have embedded in them the sediments of earlier struggles."[1] In addition to these sediments of the past, institutions also reflect the intricate layers of social, economic, and political inequalities within a society. Natural resources and environmental politics are deeply intertwined with these inequalities, which is why environmental conservation and social justice—the two most important issues of our times invoked at the beginning of this book—present a set of interconnected social dilemmas of the grandest scale.

Forests are crucial for local and global environmental protection, and they are also critical to the lives and livelihoods of nearly a fifth of humanity. Forests, and natural landscapes which house them, also evoke a multitude of images and emotions, which range from the raw and intense greed of "carbon cowboys" on the one hand to well-intentioned wildlife activists on the other. These considerations lie at the core of the political contestation over environmental issues that are inextricably linked to—but sit uncomfortably in the company of—questions of social justice. Questions of competing claims to forests and forestlands, which directly affect an estimated seven hundred and

1. Mallon 1994, 69.

fifty million to one billion people within forested regions around the globe, epitomize the red-green politics of this day and age.

This book's examination of the development of forestland regimes in India, Tanzania, and Mexico provided insights into the origins of specific types of forestland regimes—state-controlled territories in India and Tanzania, and largely community-controlled landscapes in Mexico.[2] Because each of these countries has also introduced forest and land reforms during the 1990s and 2000s, my purposively selected sample of countries also offers comparative insights about contemporary institutional reforms. In addition, the confrontations over land rights through peasant mobilizations of varying strengths that emerged in each of these countries offered opportunities to study how political elites handled these tensions between questions of social justice and environmental conservation. The political mediation of these tensions has been the main focus of this book.

The next section offers a summary of the book's findings, followed by a discussion of its contributions to theory and policy in Section 8.2. Section 8.3 considers implications for resolving the tensions between the goals of social justice and nature conservation. Section 8.4 offers an outline of proposed future research.

8.1 KEY ARGUMENTS

The analyses presented in this book were organized into three parts corresponding to three distinct combinations of scale and subject matter.

Part I (Chapters 1–4) explored the origins of forestland regimes in the three case study countries during the colonial era and their evolution during the post-independence era. Chapter 2 showed that forestland regimes in independent India and Tanzania continued to reflect the colonial regimes' projects of resource exploitation and control over native populations. In Mexico, meanwhile, the colonial-era political and economic context, especially the relationship between the conquistadors and the crown, worked against the establishment of a colonial forestland regime.[3] While haciendas (landed estates, some of which also contained mines or plantations) emerged as a formidable center of social and economic power in colonial-era Mexico, they

---

2. Not all state-owned forests are "enclosed" in India and Tanzania, because according to the countries' laws, local residents are allowed to make subsistence use of forest products. Yet most forest laws give forestry officials enough discretionary power to make this kind of resource use contingent and risky for the user, thereby creating opportunities for rent-seeking by the officials.
3. The reference here is to the difference between forestland regimes as described in this book and a forestry regime devoted to the monitoring and regulation of forests without a focus on territorial control.

proved less resilient in the long run than did the colonial-era state forestland regimes in post-independence India and Tanzania. Mexico's post-revolutionary forestry regimes evolved primarily because of national elites' interest in commercial exploitation, and to a lesser extent because of their concerns for forest conservation. In both India and Tanzania, many native chiefs and leaders acted as colonial intermediaries in forestry-related issues. Similar micro-level political and economic relations devoted to forest exploitation did not take strong hold in Mexico until the evolution of community forestry in the mid-1980s.

The state's control of the "commanding heights" of national economies in the post–World War II period, which led to the concentration of political and economic authority in central governments, was a major driving force in the consolidation of forestland regimes in post-independence India and Tanzania, as shown in Chapter 3. The combined forces of colonial-era institutional infrastructure, the legitimacy that political elites earned from their leadership in the national struggles for freedom, and the hierarchical nature of society in these two countries contributed to the central state's control of the hinterlands, control that did not provoke significant resistance. Mexican political elites also sought to exploit forests to pursue economic development, but the Mexican government was forced to resort to large-scale redistributions of forestlands because of landed elites' continued power in the country's post-revolution years. This chapter also showed that the models of economic development these countries adopted entailed varying degrees of concern for poor peasants, which in turn affected the extent of centralization of forestland regimes in these countries. Lastly, incentivized by international nature and wildlife conservation groups, national political elites in these countries developed political and economic interests that were aligned with the promotion of nature conservation. Even so, because of differences in these countries' domestic politics, conservation programs in India and Tanzania largely exclude forest-dependent people, while forest-dependent groups in Mexico are at the center of Mexican forestry and conservation programs.

These outcomes can be attributed to the historical and contemporary differences between these countries, specifically the nature of political engagement between a country's elite and its peasant groups as discussed in Chapter 4. These differences mean that the interests of forest-dependent groups have commanded little political and policy attention in Tanzania, while they have enjoyed greater success in India due to the much stronger mobilization among peasants and the emergence of a truly multiparty system beginning in the late 1980s. In Mexico, a combination of inter-elite competition and strong peasant mobilization compelled the country's political leaders to undertake the costly investments needed to establish and maintain corporatist peasant organizations and to authorize these groups to work closely with government agencies tasked with peasant welfare. Even though Mexican politics has experienced significant changes over the past two decades, it is still quite accessible to Mexican indigenous and peasant groups, which bodes well for attempts to facilitate "community engagement" in the newer agendas of climate change mitigation and adaptation.

Part II (Chapters 5–6) examined the politics of cross-scale links related to forestland reforms. Chapter 5 mapped the multilayered politics and convoluted policymaking process leading to the enactment of India's Forest Rights Act (FRA) in 2006, followed by a discussion of the highly uneven and generally disappointing implementation of the act to date. Forestry agencies' dominance and the marginalization of the interests of Adivasis (India's indigenous people) and other forest-dependent people undermined the FRA at both national and local levels; yet, those were not the only challenges the FRA encountered. For example, elected representatives—who were formally responsible for representing the interests of their constituents in FRA committees at the subdistrict and district levels—viewed the FRA as a government land-grant program, rather than a law that recognized Adivasi forest and land *rights*. Decades of living, working, and thriving under the shadows of a heavily governed and governmentalized political sphere have inculcated a deeply cynical and patronizing outlook among most of the country's elected leaders, especially at the state level.[4] The effects of such political intimacy are visible in the subjective understanding elected representatives have of their role; instead of representing their constituents *to* the state, they think of themselves as authoritative representatives *of* the state. Moreover, the pragmatic legitimacy that the state commands in India undermines efforts to bring about a progressive change in the institutional status quo. In Tanzania, the ruling party and political elites maintain an even stronger hold over local politics than do their counterparts in India, which makes the large-scale mobilization of demand for land rights in Tanzania even more difficult. But in Mexico, despite the semiauthoritarian nature of the state, the ideological space that peasant welfare occupies within Mexican politics, coupled with peasant groups' ability to shape electoral outcomes, means that elected leaders and parties were *relatively* more responsive to peasant groups' demands.

Part III of the book (Chapters 7–8) brings the findings of the previous two parts to bear on an analysis of contemporary policy outcomes. A key question is whether the influence of the international community's engagement in the decade-long deliberations over carbon forestry interventions of REDD+ influenced the national policymaking process to provide additional benefits for forest-dependent people in the case study countries. Chapter 7 demonstrated

---

4. For a discussion of links between governmentality, political representation, and participatory development, see Williams 2004; Agrawal 2005a; Carr 2013.

that, by and large, international deliberations and the supposed incentives regarding REDD+ have made very little difference to the nature of policy outcomes in developing countries. If anything, national governments have negotiated their way out of enacting meaningful land tenure reforms while writing lengthy reports about "social safeguards," which are only nonbinding commitments against trampling peasant land rights. What does this mean for the infusion of energy into international environmental policy community following the Paris Climate Conference of 2015? First, scholars now recognize that the Kyoto Protocol, the predecessor to the Paris agreements and perhaps the strongest international environmental governance agreement ever, failed because "it didn't take into account domestic politics."[5] Even though most scholars of environmental governance have focused primarily on domestic politics in developed countries, domestic politics in developing countries also greatly influences the outcomes of international conservation, as this book's findings demonstrate. Additionally, there are important feedback effects that international environmental policymakers must consider.

Ken Conca has long argued that the discourses and resources devoted to global environmental governance may reinforce the authority, power, and legitimacy of national governments.[6] This book's findings show that international conservation has indeed produced such effects. International conservation has shaped state-society relations in important ways, as Paige West demonstrates in her vividly titled monograph, *Conservation Is Our Government Now: The Politics of Ecology in Papua New Guinea*.[7] Equally importantly, global environmental governance may create perverse incentives for state agencies to promote unsustainable and wasteful environmental policies and programs that they would otherwise find difficult to impose because of domestic political constraints.[8] This suggests that while the international environmental community has to engage with domestic political actors, such engagements should be broad-based—engagements with a plurality of actors and voices, with the goal of fostering public demands for global environmental quality.[9] The comparative findings in this book offer specific recommendations about the importance of inter-bureau checks and balances in domestic policymaking,

5. Jessica F. Green, "Wondering what's different about the Paris climate change negotiations? Here's what you need to know," MonkeyCage Blog, *Washington Post*, December 1, 2015. https://www.washingtonpost.com/news/monkey-cage/wp/2015/12/01/wondering-whats-different-about-the-paris-climate-change-negotiations-heres-what-you-need-to-know/. See also Josh Bushy, "Domestic Politics, Climate Change, and International Ambition," *Duck of Minerva* (blog), January 17, 2015, http://duckofminerva.com/2015/01/domestic-politics-climate-change-and-international-ambition.html.
6. Conca 1994.
7. West 2006.
8. Kashwan and Bussey forthcoming. cf. Ascher 1999.
9. Auer 2000.

the presence of which explains the encouraging REDD+ policy outcomes in Mexico.[10] This particular aspect of institutional structure also explains why the policymaking process in Tanzania was more open to a variety of civil society perspectives compared to the process in India, which did not involve its much stronger civil society sector. Tanzania's model of divided jurisdictions between forestry agencies and wildlife parastatals meant that national agencies' interests in promoting REDD+ are far more diversified than they are in India, which has a relatively monolithic forestry establishment led by the elite Indian Forest Service at every level of forestry administration.

These findings complement the theories of policy diffusion and epistemic communities, which emphasize the importance of policy knowledge and international expert networks in facilitating the development and adoption of policy reforms. Despite the presence of a strong and diverse civil society community in the fields of forest policy and forestland rights in India, however, the Indian government did not solicit this community's input in the policy-making process. Government agencies' continued hold over the policymaking process meant that these epistemic communities' knowledge remained unutilized. Consequently, it is clear that epistemic communities can only play a meaningful role in policy diffusion if national-level institutional arrangements foster accountability among all key actors involved in environmental governance, including government agencies.

8.2 SCHOLARLY CONTRIBUTIONS: INTERDISCIPLINARY AND MULTI-SCALE ANALYSIS

The motivation driving this book has been a desire to inform the discussion regarding the simultaneous pursuit of social justice and environmental conservation. Instead of relying on any one theory, I outlined the political economy of institutions framework comprised of conceptual tools drawn from historical institutionalism, institutional analysis, development studies, and comparative politics. Because of the inherent diversity and complexity of the processes of institutional origin and institutional change, eclectic frameworks like the one developed in this book may work better than any attempt to develop a unified theory of institutional change or environmental sustainability.

A second methodological contribution of this book relates to the demonstration of the utility of combining the investigation of an interrelated set of empirical phenomena over time (in this case, the colonial, post-independence,

---

10. For similar arguments from the decentralization literature, see Agrawal and Ribot 1999; Agrawal and Ostrom 2001.

and contemporary eras) and across different levels (in this case, the national and local levels). Such an analysis spanning temporal scales, political boundaries, or administrative levels is helpful for separating out the effects of path dependence from contemporary institutional structures that shape policy-making, for determining the political and economic factors that affect the motivations and aspirations of main actors, and for analyzing the extent to which peasant groups' interests are represented in the political and policy processes.

The application of the political economy of institutions framework to examine the evolution of forestland regimes and the analysis of contemporary policy outcomes has broader policy implications. Consider, for example, the ongoing international efforts related to climate change mitigation, which are geared almost exclusively to strengthening the capacity of national governments and government agencies. As Bill Ascher pointed more than a decade and half ago, international policymakers continue to be driven by an assumption that policymaking is flawed because national governments lack resources or do not know better.[11] Such a long history of misplaced international policy efforts requires a more engaged examination of *why* such failures persist. The statements and actions of political leaders—Tanzania's Julius Nyerere and India's Indira Gandhi in the past, and Mexican President Carlos Salinas de Gortari in more recent times—show that national leaders behave opportunistically and strategically to take advantage of such naïve assumptions on the part of the international community. Such a contextualized and multi-scale analysis contributes to a finer understanding of international and national environmental governance in the context of the heightened urgency for environmental protection in the Anthropocene.[12] Research about institutional reforms necessary for dealing with the changed realities requires that scholars go beyond specific "reform sectors" to also study the political and economic struggles for access to control over environmental resources.[13]

8.3 POLICY IMPLICATIONS: POLITICAL ECONOMY OF INSTITUTIONS

State dominance of forest ownership and forest tenures around the world, despite decades of advocacy for the decentralization of forest rights to benefit forest-dependent groups, is indicative of the political and economic drivers of forest property rights institutions. Globally, more than 85 percent of forests are under state ownership—including almost 97 percent of forests in sub-Saharan Africa, more than 90 percent in Asia, and 70 percent in Latin

11. Ascher 1999.
12. I thank an anonymous Oxford University Press reviewer for this formulation.
13. Fox 1985.

America. Forestland regimes in India and Tanzania are representative of a large number of countries in Asia and sub-Saharan Africa.

The deep political and economic roots of national forestland regimes in a large number of former colonies mean that institutional reform is not likely to come about without a strong political impetus for change. The rather disappointing outcomes of more than a decade of advocacy for tenure reforms under the still-ongoing UN Framework Convention on Climate Change (UNFCCC) negotiations supports this observation. Even so, it would be unwise to treat these failures as "implementation failures." International actors and agencies are by no means disinterested actors extorting uncooperative national leaders to introduce reforms.[14] Despite their exhortations for tenure reforms, international REDD+ advocates have done little to prevent the ongoing centralization of forest policymaking in a number of countries—including Nepal, which has had a model community forestry program in place.[15]

International Drivers of Twenty-First Century Enclosures

David Kaimowitz, a prominent international forest policy expert, argues that fundamental reforms pertaining to the root causes of deforestation require addressing questions of land conflicts and poverty alleviation. However, because introducing such reforms is politically difficult, international agencies have helped national governments implement activities that only "give the impression that they are responding to the public's concerns over forest destruction," Kaimowitz argues.[16] Forest reservations have become the instrument of choice for developing country leaders to show their commitment to forest and wildlife conservation. The global community of nations surpassed the target of bringing 10 percent of the planet's surface under protected areas (PAs) that the World Parks Commission set in 1990. The PAs are lands devoted exclusively to the protection of forests, wildlife, and biodiversity. At the tenth meeting of the Conference of Parties to the Convention on Biological Diversity in October 2010 in Nagoya, Japan, delegates from 193 countries resolved to bring 17 percent of global landmass under PAs by 2020.[17] This new benchmark

14. Sociologist Charles Geisler argues that non-Africans justify the present transformation of African landscapes by ". . . reasserting terra nullius narratives of the past, . . . couched in security needs of the global North and referenced to the low density of Africa's rural population . . . [and] the ambiguity of its land tenure . . ." (Geisler 2012, 15; see also Larson and Ribot 2007).
15. Gallemore and Munroe 2013; Brockhaus and Gregorio 2014; Thuy et al. 2014; Vijge and Gupta 2014.
16. Kaimowitz 2000, 230. For a very similar argument about institutional reforms in international development, see Andrews 2013.
17. Convention on Biological Diversity http://www.cbd.int/sp/targets/rationale/target-11/.

is well within reach, with more than 15.6 percent of the world's land already set aside as PAs. The International Union for Nature Conservation (IUCN) also announced the launching of the Bonn Challenge in 2011 to restore 150 million hectares of "destroyed forests."[18] The 2014 New York Declaration on Forests expanded the Bonn Challenge with a new goal of restoring 350 million hectares by 2030.

The keenness with which governments accept these numerous "challenges" must be seen in the context of the government control of state forests, which account for nearly a quarter of the planet's total land surface.[19] These massive "land banks" maintained under state ownership are one source of new enclosures. From time to time, however, governments must bring additional areas of land under state ownership to compensate for the loss of forest areas due to large-scale development projects such as mega-dams, highways, mining projects, industrial corridors, and, more recently, special economic zones.[20] As a result, governments often claim control over village lands (as in the case of Tanzania) or lands under contested tenure (as in the case of India) for forest restoration projects.[21] As new research by Forrest Fleischman shows, forest restoration projects often result in fast-growing forest plantations, which is indicative of forestry agencies' failure to develop substantive ecosystem restoration initiatives.[22] Governments' ability to control the movement of land from one legal category to another explains why, despite rapid economic growth in dozens of large developing countries since 1990, no country in the world has witnessed a *net* decline in the proportion of land they maintain as PAs. Figure 8.1 shows the rapid increase in the amount of land in protected areas throughout the world.

The expansions of PAs and other state forests often deprive forest-dependent people of subsistence-related use of forests and other natural resources. Yet, the celebrations that followed the announcements of forest restoration

18. IUCN, "World on track to meet ambitious forest restoration goal," Bonn, Germany, March 21, 2015. http://www.iucn.org/news_homepage/?19085/World-on-track-to-meet-ambitious-forest-restoration-goal.

19. Nearly 30 percent of the world's landmass is in forests, out of which nearly 86 percent is under state ownership. Agrawal et al. 2011.

20. German et al. 2013; Rahmato 2011. For an investigative report on land-banking strategies by private conservation groups, see Ottaway and Stephens 2003.

21. As this book went to press, India's Minister for Environment, Forests, and Climate Change (MOEFC) released data on forest "encroachments," which include the micro-farm parcels over which the FRA recognizes the ownership of forest-dependent people. Mayank Aggarwal. "Nearly 1.9 million hectares of forest land in India encroached upon: Prakash Javadekar." April 29, 2016. *Live Mint.* http://www.livemint.com/Politics/75gTa1ikLOy7MSspIeOsJK/Nearly-19-million-hectares-of-forest-land-in-India-encroach.html.

22. Fleischman 2014. Such failures are evident in the fact that only 11.5 percent of land designated as state forests (and under the jurisdiction of the MOEFCC) has very dense forests with a canopy density of 70 percent or more. See Forest Survey of India (FSI) 2015.

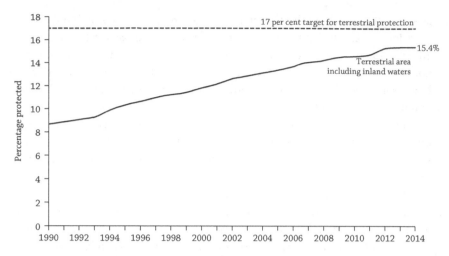

Figure 8.1 Growth in Percentage of Nationally and Internationally Designated Terrestrial Protected Areas (1990–2014).
Source: Juffe-Bignoli et al. 2014, 9.

goals from the conferences and roundtables in Aichi (Japan), Bonn (Germany), and New York suggest that conservationists consider the state-supported enclosures to be a conservation success story.[23] The clichéd conflict between the environment and economic development thus disguises a systematic but discriminatory mediation of access to and control over large areas of forested landscapes. Quite anachronistically, the contemporary state imitates the postcolonial developmentalist state—facilitating large-scale economic development and the use of market-like policy instruments while evicting millions of peasants from their lands.[24] State and many nonstate actors, whose interests in centralizing control over land align in a variety of ways, are unlikely to be willing partners in promoting the security of "ownership and control over land and other forms of property, inheritance, natural resources" as the international community promises under the 2030 Sustainable Development Goals (SDGs) enshrined recently under the aegis of the UN.[25]

One way in which national governments could be forced to act would be through international agreements that impose binding requirements about domestic forest tenure reforms. Such a strategy seems feasible in the context of the anticipated infusion of international finance after the culmination of ongoing deliberation for the development of a formal international agreement related to forest-based carbon emission reductions. In an international

23. For a theoretical discussion of the conflict between environmental values and political values, see Jayal 2001.
24. Gupta and Sivaramakrishnan 2011; McElwee et al. 2014; Hellwig 2015; cf. Gupta 2014.
25. UN General Assembly 2015, 15.

system that recognizes the rights of nation-states as sovereign actors, however, "binding" agreements are not really binding. This is particularly true when international environmental conservation campaigns are often compromised because of the dominant actors' political and economic interests.[26] The very limited effectiveness of intergovernmental institutions to bring about positive policy change suggests that we redirect forest reforms efforts to national level political and policy processes. This relates to the second important policy implication of this book's emphasis on the importance of political institutions.

Political Institutions to Facilitate Peasant Engagement

To the extent that democratic institutions are meant to ensure that elected representatives and governments are responsive and accountable, national political institutions play a critical role in mediating the tensions between the goals of social justice and environmental conservation.[27] The evidence about REDD+ outcomes presented in Chapter 7 echoes Rosemary Lyster's argument that effective participation in REDD+ decision-making depends heavily on the "political space and freedom that civil society enjoys in any given jurisdiction."[28] As discussed previously, development studies scholars tend to equate "political space" to a civil society–driven social mobilization of the poor and marginalized groups, often outside of electoral politics.[29] This book joins an existing body of literature, which has emerged mainly from scholars of Latin America, that emphasizes the importance of *political* mobilization aimed to facilitate citizen engagement with elected representatives and governments at national, provincial, and local levels.[30] While political mobilization is necessary, it is often not sufficient for bringing about policy and institutional changes. In this book, I have argued for the importance of structures of political intermediation, especially when they are established by political parties and leaders as a response to the domestic political environment.[31] Accordingly, this book emphasizes the importance of formally structured venues designed to facilitate sustained political engagement between policymakers, political leaders, and citizen groups.

26. Larson 2011; Kashwan and Holahan 2014.
27. See Steinberg 2015, 127–60.
28. Lyster 2011, 126.
29. Webster and Engberg-Pedersen 2002.
30. Fox 2007; Bebbington et al. 2008; Chhatre 2008; Grammont et al. 2009..
31. For arguments about the importance of political mobilization, see Wolford 2003; Chhatre and Saberwal 2006; Walker 2012.

Unless peasant groups and their supporters find a foothold in the high echelons of provincial- and national-level policymaking, and are able to substantively influence policymakers' behavior, promises made in the political arena may not come to fruition.[32] The importance of a "system of representation" responsible for the "aggregation of general and political demands" cannot be emphasized more strongly.[33] Donor agencies and international advocacy groups moving in the direction of "thinking and working politically" should consider facilitating formal and systematic engagement with political parties and policymaking agencies.[34] As such, the international community needs to extend support for strengthening peasant groups' organizational and political capacities to engage more productively in the national policymaking processes.[35] This would help peasant groups and other marginalized communities utilize democratic institutions to hold governments and government leaders accountable.[36] Such partnerships would help promote international environmental goals and bolster subordinate groups' ongoing struggles to improve access to and control over resources, which will also advance the implementation of the property rights goals in the 2030 SDGs.[37] Carefully devised strategies of external support are becoming even more important in light of recent findings that neoliberal political and economic reforms have undermined poor people's participation in the political process.[38] Despite the immense potential that strategic partnerships of the type proposed here offer, it would be naïve to ignore the micropolitics of struggles that feed on external support for local resource management interventions.

Micropolitics, Institutional Reforms, and Cross-Scale Political Mobilization

The political economy of institutions framework outlined in Chapter 1 is designed to facilitate cross-temporal and cross-scale analyses of institutional

32. Fox 2005, 2007. For similar arguments in the context of middle-class feminists in the United States of the 1980s, see Katzenstein 2003.
33. Garretón, 2002, 9 cited in Grammont et al. 2009, 22.
34. Duncan Green, "Thinking and Working Politically: an exciting new aid initiative," November 27, 2013 http://oxfamblogs.org/fp2p/thinking-and-working-politically-an-exciting-new-aid-initiative/.
35. For recent scholarship on inter-sectoral civil society collaborations to target domestic laws and the institutions of the state, see Peluso et al. 2008.
36. For the important role played by Malaysian civil society in its political transformation, see Weiss 2006.
37. Li 1996; Leach et al. 1999; Ribot and Peluso 2003; Wollenberg et al. 2006; Sikor and Stahl 2011.
38. Holzner 2010.

outcomes—for example, by explaining how the differences in colonial lega-cies of national forestland regimes in India, Tanzania, and Mexico shape con-temporary policy reforms. Similarly, this analytical framework, coupled with insights from comparative politics, also facilitates a concrete analysis of how national-level contemporary political contexts and the structures of political intermediation shape the grassroots outcomes of institutional reforms—in-cluding the Forest Rights Act in India, the land formalization programs in Tanzania, and the 1992 counter-reforms in Mexico. As the political ethnog-raphy presented in Chapters 5 and 6 shows, such an approach also facilitates conversation across methods and disciplines. The study of state-society inter-action is especially suited for such a dialogue.

Consider an insightful finding from a multinational study of REDD+ pilot proj-ects conducted by the social scientists at the Center for International Forestry Research (CIFOR). They found that donors and research agencies, are "pro-ac-tively attuned to tenure challenges that are not (always) perceived as problematic locally . . ."[39] These authors do not reflect any more on this observation, which certainly requires further investigation. Based on the exploration of micropolitics of forestland reforms in India and Tanzania in Chapters 5 and 6, I would argue that one way to understand this puzzling CIFOR finding is to see it from the per-spective of strategically motivated villagers who are interested in getting whatever support they can from NGOs and donors—support that national political actors might jeopardize if such projects become sites for criticizing national policies and the policymakers. Such an interpretation of the CIFOR findings mentioned above also is supported by extensive ethnographic research about property relations.

Dennis Galvan's ethnography of fertility rituals called Raan among the Serer ethnic group in rural Senegal offers an insightful illustration of how rural groups have adapted to the profound political changes of recent times.[40] By 1993, representatives of postcolonial state in Senegal have become an integral part of the Raan, replacing the region's Mande kings as the party designated "to receive . . . admonitions, complaints, and . . . ridicule at the hands of the masters of fire . . . This is a moment to make . . . the state, listen, to vent frus-tration at its alien rules and arbitrary behavior."[41] By inviting the state into one of its most sacred spaces, the Serer have an opportunity to engage with the state and possibly to hold it accountable, which is the symbolic essence of this age-old ritual. At the same time, recognizing the state's authority in this contemporary variation on Serer rituals also legitimizes the state's authority to intervene in local affairs.[42] Additionally, if the sacred spaces are also imbued with an unequal distribution of power between the traditional leaders and the

39. Sunderlin et al. 2014, 7.
40. Galvan 2004.
41. Ibid., 8.
42. Sikor and Lund 2009.

villagers, the state-society engagement evident from Galvan's work would further reinforce those inequalities.

Galvan's findings resonate strongly throughout the scholarship on micropolitics of property rights in Africa and elsewhere. Christian Lund similarly presents numerous examples of the paradoxical coexistence of citizens' resistance to and cooperation with the state. According to Lund, rural residents recognized the state for its power "to authorize and name, nominate, endorse, and acclaim."[43] Despite the contemporary emphasis on neoliberalism and the withdrawal of the state, forested regions in the Global South continue to be territories of major state interventions. As discussed previously, poverty alleviation is often a central plank in election campaigns, which invoke popular sentiments of nationalism with the subtext of promises of widespread prosperity.[44] High levels of poverty, somewhat ironically, enable political elites to use economic development or promises of development as a means of promoting state legitimacy in the Global South.[45] Indeed, because of the income, resources, and influence attached to the projects of environmental conservation, local leaders are often keen to host environmental conservation projects.[46] Political leaders tap into these local aspirations to promote the hybrid environment-development projects as multifaceted engagements with the countryside.[47]

For all of these reason, rural residents often only demand reforms in settings they think are reasonably well-suited to such demands.[48] Indeed, even elite actors, such as the judges in Tanzania who refused to hear land cases that brought them into direct conflict with the presidential administration, may be reluctant to take action that will invite political confrontation.[49] Subnational inequalities are a crucial piece in the configuration of issues that need to be addressed in order to hold the local state accountable.[50] The intimate nexus between national political elites' tactics and the compulsions of marginality that shape the lived experiences of the masses has important implications for arguments that noted development economist Bill Easterly makes in a recent book. Easterly offers a scathing critique of the conventional approach to economic development that pays little

43. Lund 2008, 132.
44. Jaffrelot 1999; Chhatre and Saberwal 2005; Kashwan 2014.
45. The literature on "developmental state" alludes to such links between "development" and state legitimacy, thereby strengthening the critique of bold statements made by some contemporary political scientists who argue that "the *only* serious source of legitimacy is democracy" (see Fukuyama 2004, 26; italics added for emphasis).
46. Kashwan 2011, 2016a; McElwee 2012; McElwee et al. 2014.
47. Haenn 2003; Chhatre and Saberwal 2006; Shapiro-Garza 2013.
48. For an insightful discussion of a similar instance in the context of India's JFM, see Kumar 2002. The author worked as a divisional forest officer before pursuing his doctoral research on the politics and political economy of India's forest reforms.
49. Igoe 2003, 868.
50. Corbridge et al. 2005.

attention to the foundations of "liberty, freedom, equality, rights, or democracy," and seeks to pursue development via "nonideological evidence-based
policies."[51] Adding that such techno-managerial approaches end up reinforcing the power and legitimacy of the state, Easterly advocates for "spontaneous solutions in politics, markets, and technology."[52] Even though Easterly
rightly argues for prioritization of local peoples' rights, the comparative
analyses in this book show that a rights-based spontaneous order can be built
only on the strong foundations of political spaces that need to be carved out
from the bottom up and that facilitate mass engagement with politics and
policymaking.[53]

Let us consider the evidence about introduction of neoliberal policies in
Mexico and India, which helps illustrate the intimate nexus of political and
economic processes with reference to Easterly's argument above, and also
with regard to contemporary Marxist political economy arguments scruti-
nized briefly in Chapter 1. Legacies of the revolutionary past, coupled with
a very real threat of peasant rebellion, forced the Mexican political elites to
negotiate the introduction of neoliberal economic reforms in the late 1970s
and early 1980s with peasant groups, often by resorting to new rounds of
land redistributions. These negotiations were visible even more prominently
during the introduction of the "counter-reforms" in the Mexico of the early
1990s, as I discussed in Chapter 6.[54] Around the same time, though, Indian
political elites successfully introduced neoliberal reforms "by stealth" without
having to negotiate with popular constituencies, as one would expect to witness in democratic politics.[55] Both India and Tanzania have since witnessed
some political churnings, which have brought the contentious questions of
economic transformation to the forefront of domestic politics, yet the eman-
cipatory potential remains limited because of a lack of articulation between
popular and elite sectors.[56]

8.4 AGENDA FOR FURTHER RESEARCH

This book has offered comparative qualitative analysis of the settings of institutional change in India, Tanzania, and Mexico. While it is not my intention to make broad-sweeping generalizations, the study's findings—read in

51. Easterly 2013, 4–6.
52. Ibid., 10.
53. Johnson and Forsyth 2002; Joshi 2010; Kashwan 2013; Ruparelia 2013.
54. In a paper with interesting implications for the debate about the state-capitalism
    dialectic, authors argue that the constituent elements of the so-called Washington
    Consensus emerged from the work of political leaders and technocrats in Latin
    America (Birdsall et al. 2010, 6).
55. Jenkins 1999
56. Nelson et al. 2012; Ruparelia 2013.

conjunction with emerging regional patterns of economic and political outcomes—may resonate beyond these three countries. For example, a review of
scholarship trends conducted as part of this research pointed to a pattern in
the cross-national variation in peasant land rights—forested regions in Latin
American countries consistently witnessed higher levels of political mobilization and are often host to some of the most progressive forestland regimes.
An important example is the practice of shifting cultivation or swidden, which
is illegal in most Asian countries, but is protected under various laws in Latin
American countries such as Brazil, Guatemala, Honduras, Mexico, Nicaragua,
and Panama.[57] While the regional patterns are hardly controversial, the causal
mechanisms that might explain these regional differences certainly are.
Preliminary evidence emerging from various sources seems to converge on a
political explanation for these cross-national differences.

Presentations made at the State of Rights and Resources 2013–2014 conference of the Rights and Resources Initiative (RRI), a prominent global think
tank, suggested that most Latin American countries are far ahead on forest
tenure reforms.[58] A RRI researcher provided the following explanation about
the regional differences, which offers an independent corroboration of my
findings:

> The relative progress of forest tenure reform in Latin America is often linked
> to the broader land reform movements and democratization movements that
> gained traction in the region through the 1970s, 80s, [and] 90s. The momen-
> tum provided by conservation efforts for the Amazon forests have also been an
> important tool for creating the *political space* to discuss forest tenure reform . . .
> While the outcomes varied tremendously in terms of the recognition of rights
> by extent, the quality of the rights recognized, and the enforcement and pro-
> tection of rights, one feature is particularly consistent throughout South and
> Central America—that communities achieved unprecedented gains.[59]

Such an explanation begs an obvious question—why haven't similar interventions for forest conservation in other regions led to the creation of political space for community groups? Before getting into a discussion about causal
mechanisms, which follows at the end of this section, let us consider studies
from other fields of policy and politics. Neoliberal economic reforms in East
Asia and Latin America have been part of a number of comparative studies.
In one of the first studies, Cristóbal Kay compares newly industrializing East
Asian countries, which experienced spectacular economic development, to

---

57. Colfer et al. 2015, 65.
58. Thanks to the webcast services made available by RRI, I was able to participate and
    engage with the panelists via Skype.
59. RRI researcher, personal electronic communication, March 10, 2014.

Latin America countries, which had industrialized much earlier but experienced less economic success. Kay attributes the successes of East Asia's economic reforms to 1) state capacity and policy performance, or "statecraft"; 2) the character of agrarian reform and its impact on equity and growth; and 3) interactions between agriculture and industry in development strategies.[60] The regional trends Kay posited are inverted when the analysis focuses instead on income inequality. As David Dollar and his colleagues at the World Bank show: "Latin America in the 2000s had pro-poor growth with [the] income of the poor rising significantly faster than mean income, while Asia had the opposite, pro-rich growth."[61]

Additionally, it is instructive to examine the regional patterns of inequality-adjusted Human Development Index (HDI) values for 2014, included in Appendix IV. Even though Latin America and the Caribbean have a higher HDI value (of 0.748) than South Asia (0.607) and sub-Saharan Africa (0.518), the latter two regions are even farther behind in terms of inequalty-adjusted HDI scores. This is surprising considering that the level of inequality is much higher among Latin American countries as opposed to countries in the other two regions. Could one attribute these counterintuitive outcomes to the ways in which peasant groups and other mass movements engage with the political process, which forces national governments to continue to invest in the social and rural sectors? This is a hypothesis worth examining, as there is some evidence to suggest that such an inquiry would contribute new insights.

For example, Anthony Bebbington and colleagues attribute the relative success of poverty alleviation efforts in Latin America, among other factors, to mass social protests, which created a political space for institutional reforms.[62] Prior experiences with state-led service provisions of social welfare, including in authoritarian societies, have helped produce widespread expectations among citizens that "the state is obliged to provide social services that are sufficient to enable every citizen . . . to live with dignity."[63] Instead of being carved out in a top-down manner, political space is thus often a product of the political and discursive struggles waged by marginalized groups. Other scholars have emphasized the importance of social and political capital, networks, and cross-sector coalition.[64] However, most of these studies portray these processes as *social* processes driven by various actors and agencies. This book demonstrates the importance of an added *political* element—the mechanisms of political intermediation between peasant groups and dominant political parties. Future comparative analyses should examine the relative importance

60. Kay 2002.
61. Dollar et al. 2013.
62. Bebbington et al. 2008, 16.
63. McGuire 2010, 11.
64. Fox 2007; Bebbington et al. 2008.

and influence of, and interactions among, these various factors in shaping institutional outcomes. Such studies will create the foundation for systematic accumulation of knowledge about the politics of simultaneously pursuing multiple societal goals—such as social justice, economic development, and environmental protection.

8.5 CONCLUSION: PURSUING SOCIAL JUSTICE AND ENVIRONMENTAL CONSERVATION

Both social justice and environmental conservation are important normative concerns of the contemporary era. However, these two concerns have often collided—primarily, I would argue, due to the nature-society dichotomy that continues to dominate thinking among the ardent advocates of each of the two concerns. This notion of two separate social and natural worlds has come under significant scrutiny, most notably through the nascent but increasingly volatile discussions of the Anthropocene, a new geological time period that marks the "Age of Man."[65] In this concluding section, I reflect on the certain biases inherent in the production of scholarly knowledge and provide an illustration related to forestland conflicts, which also yields wider lessons about researching environmental change in the Anthropocene.

Let us return for a moment to the subject of swidden farming. More than one hundred million people throughout the Global South continue to rely, either partially or fully, on this form of smallholder and subsistence farming. It is clear that, except for Latin America, swidden farmers do not have rights to the land they farm. While some might argue that this lack of land rights has to do with the "shifting" or rotating form of the farming system, this belief is incorrect. In many cases, including in India's northeast region where farming practices have transitioned into sedentary farming, those lands continue to be recorded in government records as being under "shifting" cultivation. Moreover, considering India's reasonably strong civil society and research communities, the question of securing land rights of swidden farmers have been debated on numerous occasions. It is clear that the neglect of land rights of swidden farmers is owed, almost certainly, to what Sharachchandra Lélé and co-authors describe as the "three-fold squeeze" peculiar to the Adivasi; these authors argue the Adivasis lack political and economic power, do not have access to political and economic organizations that shape their life chances, and lack control over the productive resources they need for subsistence.[66] Even within Latin America, groups that are affected by similar political and

65. Dalby 2007; Lövbrand et al. 2009; Palsson et al. 2013.
66. Lélé and Rao 1996b, 77.

economic disadvantages have not always benefited from the region's revolutions and reforms.

The historical, cultural, political, and economic dynamics associated with the conversion of land at the forest frontier often contributes to the "demonization" of peasant colonists.[67] However, such prejudices are not limited to the hinterlands or to the political actors responsible for making laws and policies. Outside of a specialized group of scholars who study contemporary swidden, researchers' disciplinary backgrounds shape how they portray this form of agriculture and the people who engage in it.[68] When swidden is discussed or analyzed, the focus remains on its biophysical characteristics. Often scientists and policymakers ignore the existence of swidden altogether, making swiddeners disappear from the storyline. For instance, consider the reflections that Carol Colfer and her co-authors share vis-à-vis the Center for International Forestry Research (CIFOR)'s Landscape Mosaics project in Tanzania. Though swidden was the primary agricultural method at all five of CIFOR's research sites, and was responsible for the creation of the "mosaics" being studied, only one scientist talked about the role this farming system had played in that outcome.[69] On the other extreme are scientists who seek to apply "indigenous and scientific knowledge of swidden cultivation to tropical forest restoration."[70] Both of these approaches—either ignoring swidden as an actual and longstanding land use, or eulogizing its potential to solve the contemporary crisis of forest conservation—produce the same effect of disregarding the agency and rights of more than one hundred million swiddeners internationally and of the "hundreds of millions families" who live inside forest areas.[71]

The impacts of swidden are neither uniformly destructive nor uniformly good for the environment. Instead, its effects depend on the size of the forest catchment, length of fallow period, external pressures on the forest when farm parcels are left fallow, and above all, the overall livelihood security of the swiddeners. All in all, swidden is a complex system with varying effects, and broad-brush explanations are unlikely to be accurate. Having said that, and precisely because of the great diversity of the system's effects, I argue that the land rights related to swidden farming are a political issue that should be resolved before concerned environmentalists or indigenous rights activists work with practitioners of swidden to pursue goals of social justice or environmental conservation. To understand the logical validity of this argument about the politics of swiddeners' "property rights," it is instructive to compare

---

67. Larson 2010, 49.
68. For holistic discussions of swidden, see Mertz 2009; Mertz et al. 2013; Vliet et al. 2013.
69. Colfer et al. 2015, 64.
70. This is the title of a recently published paper by Wangpakapattanawong et al. 2010.
71. Alcorn and Royo 2015, 292.

even the most destructive form of swidden to the example of an industry contributing acid rain–causing emissions to the atmosphere. Until recently, there have been no restrictions on the dumping of industrial pollutants into the atmosphere, which was seen as an open-access sink. Not very long ago, the international community recognized that it was important to protect the atmospheric sink. Despite concerns about the misuse and overuse of the atmosphere, governments do not ban polluting industries. Instead, the industries that emitted the acid-rain causing pollutant sulfur dioxide, for example, were "grandfathered" into the market-based SO_2 emission reduction program.[72] For instance, in the United States, a certain number of "emission permits" were distributed free of charge to the polluting industries, even though evidence shows that auctioning those permits would have made the program economically more efficient.[73] The "rights" to pollute or to use up atmospheric sinks established by prior practices were recognized in the new property regime, even though such practices were conclusively destructive to the environment.

Now consider REDD+, the program for rewarding forest-based carbon emissions reduction that connects the actions of swidden farmers and industrial polluters. In many emerging programs, industrial polluters are able to buy forest-based carbon emission reduction offsets to continue their industrial production processes. On the contrary, swidden farmers whose activities sometimes cause carbon emissions and damage forests have few opportunities to carry on with their activities. In any case, there is little discussion of the property rights of swidden farmers. Even if one were to not consider the moral and ethical implications of this distinction between industries and swidden farmers, the property rights of swidden farmers are, analytically speaking, not any different from the rights of a polluting industry. Instead of being grandfathered into the program, peasants must often discontinue the practice of swidden, or suffer at the hands of predatory governments or "carbon cowboys" that are involved in a scramble for carbon credits.[74] This shows how our prejudices favoring industrialization over peasant livelihoods shape the design of academic research and policy proposals on these topics, each of which reinforces the status quo of power differences between different classes of users of environmental resources.[75]

The absence of objective and dispassionate policy analyses drawing attention to these anomalies is difficult to explain.[76] From an institutional

72. Stavins 1998; Ellerman 2005.
73. Stavins 2012.
74. Lederer 2011; Nerlich 2012. For a similar report from Indonesia, see Simon Pollock, "Will REDD+ help save Indonesia's forest, or create 'carbon cowboys' instead?" Mongabay Series: Global Forest Reporting Network, August 20, 2015, http://news.mongabay.com/2015/08/will-redd-help-save-indonesias-forest-or-create-carbon-cowboys-instead/.
75. For a similar argument about the tools employed in the field of environmental economics, see Bromley 2004.
76. For a nuanced discussion, see Larson 2010.

perspective, statutory rights are necessary, even if insufficient, for progressive structural transformations. Therefore, the recognition of swiddeners' de facto resource rights to forestland should precede a multifaceted engagement over questions of how best to manage the transition to organic but sedentary farming. This becomes especially important because, in many cases, swidden cycles are now too short to be sustainable. I have used this particularly difficult form of the forestland conflicts pertaining to swidden to illustrate the ways in which normative ideals that we hold dear, either of justice or environmental protections, intersect with the historical legacies of institutions, policies, and knowledge-producing practices. The process and the outcomes of the contemporary forest enclosures have evoked familiar references to dispossession and primitive accumulation, with the addition of "green grab" to this vocabulary.[77] More importantly, the contemporary enclosures are carried out with the stated intention of conserving nature, while other destructive uses of forested landscapes—for the development of mines, dams, and industrial infrastructure—continue apace.[78]

Amidst the complexity and enormity of the task of reconciling social justice and environmental conservation concerns within forestland rights regimes, it might be difficult to decide what role outsiders—activists, journalists, researchers, and scholars—might play. The arguments that this book makes assist in pursuing answers to that question. Anyone in the business of representing the concerns of peasants and other marginalized groups by advocating for change, or working to actually make change happen, needs to be careful about the direct and indirect impact their actions might have on the lives and livelihoods of hundreds of millions forest-dependent people. The best one can do is to help peasants formulate and articulate their concerns, and enable them to demand change from elected leaders and governments. Helping create the organizational spaces and institutional mechanisms for the articulation of citizen concerns will prove immensely useful in fostering progressive change.

Changes in individual attitudes and consumption patterns, as well as collective action to resolve social dilemmas, are all important steps toward a more secured future for the humanity. We must remember though, it is not *just* about the relationship between humanity and nature. The more important task is to reset our relations with one another, which is made complicated by the divisions of gender, caste, class, and national boundaries. To restructure social and political relations, vis-à-vis the questions of access to and control over nature and environmental resources, we will

77. Peluso 2007 and other essays in Heynen et al. 2007; Fairhead et al. 2012; Fairbairn 2013; Levien 2013.
78. Watts 2000.

need to change the underlying institutions, i.e. the rules of the game. Such institutional transformations can be accomplished *mainly* through political means. Well-structured and enduring mechanisms of political intermediation that enable citizen groups to articulate their interests, in ways that favorably influence political and policy processes, seem to be indispensable to the pursuit of an environmentally resilient and socially just world.

APPENDIX I

Number of People Affected
by Forestland Conflicts

Country/ Region	Type of Land Rights Conflicts	Number of People Affected	Data Period	Source
Global	Swidden	35 million to 1 billion	2001	Mertz et al. 2009
Global	Swidden	500 million	1980	Lawrence et al. 2010
Global	Swidden	190 million	2000	Plagge et al. 2008
Indonesia	Tradition land rights (adat); Government sets aside land as forest reserves	40 million	1999–2013	Butt 2014, 59
Africa	People living in areas set aside for nature conservation	900,000 to 14.4 million*	2002	Geisler 2002
Thailand	Population inside protected areas	11 million	1995	Leblond 2010
India	Population set to be displaced from wildlife areas	4 million	2004	Sekhsaria and Vagholikar 2004
Cambodia	Illegal land grabbing	1.7 million	2006	Wallace and Conca 2012.

Note: The data above are not exhaustive, but are meant to represent different types of land conflicts within forested areas. Accordingly, they are not meant to be aggregated, but interpreted as an indication of overall scope and magnitude of the problem.
* The coverage of protected areas and wildlife reserves has doubled since after 2002 when Geisler computed his estimates.

APPENDIX II

A Sample of Specific Events Related to Forestland Conflicts

Year	Country	Number of People Affected (*) by Displacements	Status: Threatened/ Displaced/ Evicted Resettled/ Returned	Reason (Project, Program, or Policy)
1990's	Botswana	2,200[1]	Relocated	Central Kalahari Game Reserve
1996	Kenya	1,050[2]	Threatened	Central Kenya Wildlife Corridor—Lekiji
1990s–2000	Bangladesh	200,000[3]	Threatened	Chittagong Hill Tracts reforestation plans
2000's	Tanzania	20,000[4]	Displaced/ Threatened	Serengeti National Park
2000	Cameroon	1,465[5]	Displaced	Korup National Park
2000	Republic of Congo	5,802[5]	Displaced	Noubale-Ndoki National Park
2000	Republic of Congo	9,750[5]	Displaced	Odzala National Park
2001	Cameroon	8,000[5]	Displaced	Lake Lobeke National Park
2001	Equatorial Guinea	10,197[5]	Displaced	Nsoc National Park
2001	Nigeria	2,876[5]	Displaced	Cross River National Park Okwangwo Division
2009	Tanzania	3,000[6]	Displaced/	Usangu Game Reserve
2009	Uganda	4,000[7]	Displaced	Mount Elgon National Park

Year	Country	Number of People Affected (*) by Displacements	Status: Threatened/ Displaced/ Evicted Resettled/ Returned	Reason (Project, Program, or Policy)
2010	Uganda	20,000[8]	Displaced	Mubende and Kiboga districts for the plantations carried out by the UK based New Forests Company (NFC)
2011	Tanzania	7,000[6]	Displaced	Usangu Game Reserve
2011	Kenya	2,000[9]	Displaced/ Homeless	Laikipia National Park
2011	India	118,000[10]	Threatened	Greater Talacauvery National Park
2011	Uganda	2,201[11]	Displaced	Mount Elgon National Park
2011	Guatemala	1000s[12]	Violently evicted	Polochic valley
2013	Tanzania	70,000[13]	Returned	Loliondo Reserve
2013	Botswana	3,500[1]	Resettled	Central Kalahari Game Reserve
	Gabon	12,600 [5]	Displaced	Gamba Complex of Protected Areas
2014	Kenya	7000–15,000[14]	Displaced/ threatened	Cherangani Hills
2014	Thailand	1000s[15]	Threatened	Buriram Province

[1] Robert K. Hitchcock, "Conservation, Culture, and Land Use Conflicts in the Central Kalahari, Botswana," June 30, 2012. Just Conservation. http://www.justconservation.org/conservation-culture-and-land-use-conflicts-botswana#sthash.U7Esobhx.dpuf

[2] Harrison Ole Kisio, "Lekiji: a Village in a Wildlife Corridor. Conservation and Corruption—A deadly combination in Lekiji, Laikipia," March 30, 2013. Just Conservation. http://www.justconservation.org/lekiji-a-village-in-a-wildlife-corridor#sthash.4mdM7vJ9.dpuf

[3] Roy 2005, 118, 126.

[4] Blomley et al. 2013.

[5] Schmidt-Soltau 2003.

[6] Walter Hicks, "Tanzania's Troubling Trend of Land Rights Violations And Evictions," Ecology Global Network, September 10, 2012. http://www.ecology.com/2012/09/10/tanzanias-land-rights-violations/.

[7] Chris Lang, "Uganda: Wildlife Authority Evicts 2,200 From Elgon," Just Conservation, June 08, 2011. http://www.justconservation.org/uganda-wildlife-authority-evicts-2,200-from-elgon/

[8] Zagema 2011

[9] Clar Nichonghaile and David Smith, "Kenya's Samburu people 'violently evicted' after US charities buy land." The Guardian, December 14, 2011. http://www.theguardian.com/world/2011/dec/14/kenya-samburu-people-evicted-land

[10] Anon, "Greater Talacauvery project may displace 2.20 lakh people," The Hindu, October 12, 2011. http://www.thehindu.com/news/cities/Mangalore/greater-talacauvery-project-may-displace-220-lakh-people/article2530535.ece

[11] Chris Lang "2,201 people in Manafwa District have been rendered landless after Uganda Wildlife Authority (UWA) evicted them from Mt. Elgon National Park," Just Conservation, June 8, 2011. http://www.justconservation.org/uganda-wildlife-authority-evicts-2,200-from-elgon/

[12] Anon, "Guatemala: Biofuels Production Leads to Violent Evictions," March 22, 2011. http://www.wilderutopia.com/international/guatemala-biofuels-production-leads-to-violent-evictions/

[13] Marc Nkwame "Tanzania: PM Ends Loliondo Long-Running Land Conflict," Just Conservation, September 25, 2013 http://www.justconservation.org/tanzania-pm-ends-loliondo-long-running-land-conflict

[14] John Vidal, "Kenyan families flee Embobut forest to avoid forced evictions by police," The Guardian, January 7, 2014. http://www.theguardian.com/global-development/2014/jan/07/kenya-embobut-forest-forced-evictions-police. Note: Estimates from the original source, or computed with the assumption of a five-member family, for data reported in the number of families affected.

[15] Anon, "Thailand: Military Forcibly Evicts Forest Residents Arbitrary Arrests, Threats, Poor Relocation Sites in Buriram Province," Human Rights Watch, July 19, 2014. https://www.hrw.org/news/2014/07/19/thailand-military-forcibly-evicts-forest-residents/

Major Socioeconomic and Political Indicators in Case Study Countries

Country	Gross National Income Per Capita, Purchasing Power Parity (Current International $), 2013 [1]	Multidimensional Poverty Index (MPI = H*A) [2]	Headcount Ratio: Population in Multidimensional Poverty (H) [2]	Intensity of Deprivation Among the Poor (A) [2]	Gini WDI [3] (Reference Year)	Gini Land Concentration Index [4] (Reference Period)	Political Rights (1–7) [5]	Civil Liberties (1–7) [5]
India	5,350	0.283	53.7	52.7	33.9 (2009)	0.5924 (1981–1990)	2	3
Tanzania	2,430*	0.332	65.6	50.7	37.8 (2011)	0.7899 (1971–1980)	3	3
Mexico	16,020	0.015	4.0	38.9	48.1 (2012)	0.747 (1961–1970)	3	3**

[1] World Bank 2015.
[2] Oxford Poverty and Human Development Initiative (2013).
[3] World Development Indicators 2015 (World Bank 2015): Distribution of Income or Consumption, Table 2.9. Accessed Online http://wdi.worldbank.org/table/2.9.
[4] IFAD 2001, 117–19.
[5] Freedom House 2015. One represents the most free and seven the least free.
* Covers Mainland Tanzania only.
** According to Freedom House, the civil liberties trend is going down overall.

APPENDIX IV

————⌁————

Inequality-Adjusted Human Development Index for Selected Regions

Region	Human Development Index (HDI) Value	Inequality-Adjusted HDI Value	Loss Due to Inequality (%)
Sub-Saharan Africa	0.518	0.345	33.3
South Asia	0.607	0.433	28.7
Arab States	0.686	0.512	25.4
Latin America and the Caribbean	0.748	0.570	23.7

Source: Human Development Report, United Nations Development Programme 2015.

APPENDIX V

Statistical Analysis of Forestland Claims in Gujarat, India

The key focus of the analysis in this appendix is to explain how political and economic interdependence between village leaders and government forest officials in India influences the assertion of land rights through village forest rights committees (FRCs). As part of the research at the village level, I surveyed sixty forest rights committees.[1] The sample size was driven by an attempt to balance the need for an adequate number of observations with my interest in pursuing an in-depth qualitative inquiry that would contribute new insights about the complexity of the question under investigation. While the relevant qualitative evidence was presented and analyzed in Chapter 5, this appendix presents the quantitative analysis of household land claims. The total number of communities surveyed was split nearly equally along each of the two dimensions shown in Table A5.3.

Table A5.3 SAMPLING OF VILLAGES FOR CROSS-SECTIONAL SURVEYS

	With Prior Forest Conservation Arrangements	Without Prior Forest Conservation Arrangements	Total
Low Electoral Competition	18	15	33
High Electoral Competition	13	14	27
Total	31	29	60

1. This corresponds to fifty-nine villages, as in one village there were two FRCs, which is allowed under the definition of "community" provided in the FRA.

Dependent/Outcome Variable: The key outcome variable in this case is the natural log of the total area of forestland claimed for household land rights under India's Forest Rights Act (FRA).[2] The logarithmic transformation of the dependent variable standardizes the results across communities with different areas of village land under the de jure public forest category.

Explanatory/Independent Variables

Electoral Competition: Electoral competition accounts for the level of competition for an elected position and is measured by the effective number of candidates[3]

$$Effective\ number\ of\ candidates = 1/\Sigma k^2$$

Where k is the share of votes secured by a candidate in the 2007 elections to the Gujarat legislative assembly.[4]

Past Forest Conservation Arrangements: Half of the communities were selected randomly from among a list of communities with prior forest protection arrangements.[5] Each of the communities in the group with a consistent track record of forest protection, was matched with another community in close proximity that did not have pre-existing forest conservation arrangements. The definitions of and measurements for the outcome and the explanatory variables are summarized in Table A5.4. The summary statistics of these variables are presented in Table A5.5.

Hypothesis I: The higher the level of electoral competition, the larger the proportion of village forestland claimed under forestland cultivation.

Causal Logic: Greater electoral competition incentivizes candidates to cater to popular issues such as forestland titles.

---

2. The outcome variable is censored at zero—i.e. it cannot take a negative value, which violates the assumptions of ordinary least square regressions. Therefore, this analysis uses Tobit models, which produce unbiased estimates in cases where the key outcome variables cannot take a negative value (Tobin 1958).
3. Chhibber and Nooruddin 2004.
4. Election Commission of India; http://eci.gov.in/StatisticalReports/Election Statistics.asp.
5. This list was created through detailed consultation with local social workers who have been active in the region for more than two decades and who are very familiar with the communities' records on forest protection.

Variable	Explanation	Data Sources
Forestland Cultivation Claimed (ln)	Natural logarithmic transformation of the total area of forestland claimed under cultivation by individuals/households in a village.[a]	FRC records
Electoral Competition	Dichotomous variable indicating the level of electoral competition (high or low). A constituency with three or more effective candidates is regarded as one with high electoral competition (1), otherwise it is regarded as a case of low electoral competition (0) (see, Chhibber and Nooruddin 2004).	Election Commission data: 2007 elections to Gujarat State Legislative Assembly.
History of Forest Protection	This dichotomous variable is based on the reputation a community carried for having made significant forest protection efforts over the past ten to fifteen years. The reputation assessment was conducted through detailed discussions with senior social activists who have been engaged with the agenda of forest protection for more than two decades.[b]	Based on detailed discussions; followed by triangulation on the ground
Forest Leaders	An ordinal variable denoting if none, one, or both of the two key FRC positions are occupied by leaders who also have been or are represented on the executive committee of the village forest protection committee.	Village survey
Association with Social Movement	Dichotomous variable recording whether the community members interviewed reported that their village was associated closely with forestland rights movements.	Village survey
Percentage Irrigation	Percentage of total area of agricultural land under irrigation in a village.	Calculated based on census data
Land Heterogeneity	Index measure of heterogeneity in legal ownership of agricultural land in a village, which is the probability that two randomly selected households do not belong to the same landholding class, and is equivalent to the Gini index for discrete variables (Naidu 2009, 678).	Village survey
Per Capita Agricultural Land	Per capita legal agricultural holding.	Calculated based on census data

[a] The FRA recognizes the joint ownership of husband and wife for all married claimants. Accordingly, most claims are made on behalf of a household.

[b] The potential for some bias cannot be negated in this kind of a methodology. Therefore, I exercised significant caution in choosing whom to consult. The activists I consulted had engaged with questions of forest conservation, more or less on a voluntary basis, such that I did not see them having a vested interest in giving inflated assessments of the success of forest protection projects. Moreover, I personally visited many of the communities to verify the assessments, which I found to be accurate.

Table A5.5 SUMMARY STATISTICS

Variable	Observations	Mean	Standard Deviation	Minimum	Maximum
Forestland Cultivation Claimed (Ln)	56	3.85	1.43	0	6.32
Electoral Competition	56	0.46	0.50	0	1
Forest Protection Arrangements	56	0.50	0.50	0	1
Forest Leaders	56	0.50	0.76	0	2
Association with Social Movements	56	0.51	0.50	0	1
Heterogeneity in Land Ownership	56	0.20	0.09	0	0.39
Per Capita Legal Agricultural Holding	56	1.10	0.58	0	3.27
Land Heterogeneity	56	0.19	0.09	0	0.39
Percent of Agricultural Land under Irrigation	56	38.62	38.00	0	99.43

Hypothesis II: A community's "close association" with social movements is associated with a larger area of forestland claimed under cultivation.[6]

Causal Logic: Social movements actively mobilize forest dwellers not to give up their existing farming and have contributed greatly to the dissemination of information regarding the provisions of the FRA.

Hypothesis III: The election of "forest leaders" as office holders in FRCs is associated with a lower area of forestland claimed under the FRA.[7]

Causal Logic: Because of a prior engagement with Forest Department officials, forest leaders will likely minimize the area of forestland claimed under household land rights of the FRA, thereby leading to a lower area of forestland claimed for household land rights in comparison to the villages in which the FRCs are not led by "forest leaders."

6. The variable "close association" with social movements is explained in Table A5.4 above.
7. "Forest leader" as defined here has a very specific meaning, which is explained in Table A5.4 above.

Table A5.6 TOBIT RESULTS FOR LAND RIGHTS CLAIMED
UNDER THE FRA

Variable	M1	M2
Electoral Competition	0.74*	0.952***
	0.39	0.338
Forest Protection Arrangements	−0.75***	−0.81***
	0.22	0.23
Forest Leaders	−0.29**	−0.34**
	0.13	0.14
Association with Social Movements	1.02***	1.04***
	0.24	0.24
Village Land under Irrigation	−0.007	−0.012**
	0.006	0.005
Per Capita Legal Agricultural Landholding	−0.43***	
	0.15	
Heterogeneity in Land Ownership		−0.53
		0.19
_cons	4.25***	3.79***
	0.26	0.30
sigma		
_cons	0.89***	0.92***
Statistics		
N[1]	56	56
F	9.76	6.48
Prob > F	0.00	0.00

Notes: [1] Four observations exerting undue leverage (i.e. DFBettas >1) dropped from
this analysis;
The asterisks above indicate the level of significance: ***significant at 1 percent,
**significant at 5 percent, *significant at 10 percent.

Table A5.6 presents the results of two models that differ in the type of control variable related to income and wealth effects. Each of the two models employs the "proportion of agricultural land under irrigation" as the key control variable reflecting wealth effects. In the first model (M1), I also control for legal agricultural holdings per capita. The second model (M2) uses land heterogeneity—i.e., inequality in legal agricultural landholding—as a control variable.

The results of the Tobit regressions presented in Table A5.6 support the hypotheses that the pre-existing institutions and political economy variables contribute to significant variation in outcomes of institutional change. In this case, the beta coefficient for any given independent variable indicates a percent change in the area of forestland claimed in response to a one-unit change in an independent variable. In the case of dichotomous independent variables, it yields percentage change in the area of forestland claimed when the value of the variable changes from zero to one. In the discussion below, I interpret the results from the first model, M1.

The results of cross-sectional statistical analysis presented in Table A5.6 offer strong support for Hypotheses II and III proposed above, and contingent support for Hypothesis I. Electoral competition has a positive effect, but has a weak statistical significance (only significant at 10 percent margin of error). A village located in a high electoral competition constituency is likely to claim more than 74 percent more forestland under cultivation than a village that is located in a constituency with low levels of political competition. Various iterations of this model run by the author suggest that the effects of electoral competition are contingent on income and wealth effects.[8] These variations imply that the effects of electoral competition are embedded within the local political economy and the entrenched economic inequities. While electoral incentives have been effective in motivating politicians to encourage a greater number of forestland cultivations in the past, they did not translate into politicians exerting their influence during the subsequent policy implementation processes—which, by most accounts, has been poor.[9]

Hypothesis II about the effect of the association of a community with social movements is strongly supported. The coefficient related to the presence of social movements is highly significant (at 1 percent margin of error), and has a strong effect of a 102 percent increase in the area of forestland claimed under household land rights in comparison to a similar village that is not associated with a social movement. It must be noted that the high percentage increase is due to the very low area of forestland claimed in control villages.[10] These results also hold in the models with alternative measures of income effects. Notwithstanding the strong effects of social movements in facilitating land rights claims, these results do not fully reflect the nature of the barriers that social movements encountered in encouraging peasants to claim land rights under the FRA (see Chapter 5).

The hypothesized expectations regarding forest leaders' influence on the area claimed under private land rights in a village (Hypothesis III) also are met in each of the two variants of the model. In cases when one of the two key positions of FRC leadership—either the president or the secretary—is held by a

8. For instance, electoral competition has a much stronger statistical significance (at 1 percent) in Model 2 included in the table.
9. NCFRA 2010.
10. The average aggregate forestland claimed in the villages without an active engagement with a social movement is 63.05 hectares, while the figure is 108.50 hectares in villages that did not associate closely with social movements. The average land claimed per household in this sample was 1.63 hectares (see Table 5.2).

forest leader, the area of forestland claimed by households is lower by 30 percent when compared to a village in which neither of the two key FRC leaders had previous engagements with forestry agencies. Readers should note that the effects of forest leaders in key FRC positions is over and above the effect that village level forest protection arrangements may have had in controlling or reducing the amount of farming within state forests. When everything else is held constant, the existence of past forest conservation arrangements in a community was associated with a 75 percent decline in the area of forestland claimed under the FRA (compared with villages without successful forest protection arrangements).

Lastly, it is important to understand the effects of the economic factors mentioned above. Among the socioeconomic variables, per capita agricultural landholding has a highly significant effect on land claims. An increase of 1 hectare in per capita agricultural holding leads to a 44 percent decline in the area of forestland claimed under household land rights established by the FRA. The aggregate amount of privately claimed land is greater in the villages with a smaller total amount of legal agriculture landholdings, which is a reflection of peasant households' efforts to find ways to secure landholdings they need for minimum subsistence. If the FRA had triggered a land scramble, we would have witnessed larger private land claims from land-rich villages. These results indicate a micro-level tradeoff between the goals of food security in the forested regions and the agenda of securing de jure forest areas set aside for conservation.

REFERENCES

Adams, William, and Jon Hutton. 2007. "People, Parks and Poverty: Political Ecology and Biodiversity Conservation." *Conservation and Society* 5: 147–83.

Adams, William, and Martin Mulligan. 2002. *Decolonizing Nature Strategies for Conservation in a Post-Colonial Era*. London: Earthscan.

Adams, William. M., Ros Aveling, Dan Brockington, Barney Dickson, Jo Elliott, Jon Hutton, Dilys Roe, Bhaskar Vira, and William Wolmer. 2004. "Biodiversity Conservation and the Eradication of Poverty." *Science* 306: 1146–49.

Agarwal, Bina. 2002. "The Hidden Side of Group Behaviour; a Gender Analysis of Community." In *Group Behaviour and Development: Is the Market Destroying Cooperation?* eds. Judith Heyer, Frances Stewart and Rosemary Thorp. New York: Oxford University Press. 185–208.

———. 1992. "The Gender and Environment Debate: Lessons from India." *Feminist Studies* 18: 119–58.

Agoramoorthy, Govindasamy, and Minna J. Hsu. 2008. "Small Size, Big Potential: Check Dams for Sustainable Development." *Environment: Science and Policy for Sustainable Development* 50: 22–35.

Agrawal, Arun. 2005a. *Environmentality: Technologies of Government and the Making of Subjects*. New Delhi: Oxford University Press.

———. 2005b. "Environmentality: Community, Intimate Government, and the Making of Environmental Subjects in Kumaon, India." *Current Anthropology* 46: 161–90.

———. 2001a. "Common Property Institutions and Sustainable Governance of Resources." *World Development* 29: 1649–72.

———. 2001b. "State Formation in Community Spaces? Decentralization of Control over Forests in the Kumaon Himalaya, India." *Journal of Asian Studies* 60: 9–40.

Agrawal, Arun, and A. Angelsen. 2009. "Using Community Forest Management to Achieve REDD+ Goals." In *Moving Ahead with REDD: Issues, Options, and Implications*, eds. A. Angelsen, M. Brockhaus, M. Kanninen, E. Sills, W.D. Sunderlin and S. Wertz-Kanounnikoff. Bogor, Indonesia: Center for International Forestry Research (CIFOR).

Agrawal, Arun, Daniel Nepstad, and Ashwini Chhatre. 2011. "Reducing Emissions from Deforestation and Forest Degradation." *Annual Review of Environment and Resources* 36: 373–96.

Agrawal, Arun, and Elinor Ostrom. 2001. "Collective Action, Property Rights, and Decentralization in Resource Use in India and Nepal." *Politics and Society* 29: 485–514.

Agrawal, Arun, and Jesse C. Ribot. 1999. "Accountability in Decentralization: A Framework with South Asian and West African Cases." *The Journal of Developing Areas* 33: 473–502.

Agrawal, Arun, and K. Sivaramakrishnan. 2000. *Agrarian Environments: Resources, Representations, and Rule in India*. Durham, NC: Duke University Press.

Aiyar, Mani Shankar. 2003. "Can the Congress Find a Future?" *Seminar* 526. Accessed online at http://www.india-seminar.com/2003/526/526%20mani%20shankar%20 aiyar.htm.

Alcorn, Janis Bristol, and Antoinette G. Royo. 2007. "Conservation's Engagement with Human Rights: 'Traction,' 'Slippage,' or Avoidance." *Policy Matters* 15: 115–39.

Alix-Garcia, Jennifer. 2008. "An Exploration of the Positive Effect of Inequality on Common Property Forests." *Journal of Development Economics* 87: 92–105.

Allan, Jen Iris, and Peter Dauvergne. 2013. "The Global South in Environmental Negotiations: The Politics of Coalitions in REDD+." *Third World Quarterly* 34: 1307–22.

Alonso-Mejía, Alfonso, and Leeanne E. Alonso. 1999. "Scientific Research and Social Investigation Priorities for the Monarch Butterfly Special Biosphere Reserve: Recommendations." In *1997 North American Conference on the Monarch Butterfly*, eds. Jürgen Hoth, Leticia Merino, Karen Oberhauser, Irene Pisanty, Steven Pricey, and Tara Wilkinson. Montréal (Québec): Commission for Environmental Cooperation. 183–94.

Alston, Lee J., Gary D. Libecap, and Bernardo Mueller. 2000. "Land Reform Policies, the Sources of Violent Conflict, and Implications for Deforestation in the Brazilian Amazon." *Journal of Environmental Economics and Management* 39: 162–88.

Amelung, Torsten. 1993. "Tropical Deforestation as an International Economic Problem." In *Economic Progress and Environmental Concerns*, ed. Herbert Giersch. Berlin: Springer-Verlag. 233–53.

Andrews, Matt. 2013. *The Limits of Institutional Reform in Development: Changing Rules for Realistic Solutions*. Cambridge: Cambridge University Press.

Ankersen, Thomas T., and Thomas Ruppert. 2006. "Tierra Y Libertad: The Social Function Doctrine and Land Reform in Latin America." *Tulane Environmental Law Journal* 19: 69.

Anon. 2014. "Comments on the Draft ER-PIN for the Mexico REDD+ ER Program." Washington, DC: The Bank Information Center.

Anon. 1995. *Jungle Amaru Amey Jungle Na – Sangharsh Thee Sahkar Sudhi (Jungle Is Ours and We Are of the Jungle: From Conflict to Cooperation)*. Ranpur: Anand Niketan Ashram.

Anon. 1954. "The Aboriginal Population of India." *Civilisations* 4: 423–43.

Antinori, Camille, and David Barton-Bray. 2005. "Community Forest Enterprises as Entrepreneurial Firms: Economic and Institutional Perspectives from Mexico." *World Development* 33: 1529–43.

Antinori, Camille, and Gustavo A. Garcia-López. 2008. "Cross-Scale Linkages in Common-Pool Resource Management: The Evolution of Forest Associations in the Mexican Forest Commons." Paper presented at the 12th IASC 2008 Biennial Conference, University of Gloucester, Cheltenham.

Appendini, Kirsten. 2001. "Land Regularization and Conflict Resolution: The Case of Mexico." Document prepared for Food and Agriculture Organizations (FAO), Rural Development Division, Land Tenure Service, Mexico City.

Arneil, Barbara. 1996. "The Wild Indian's Venison: Locke's Theory of Property and English Colonialism in America." *Political Studies* 44: 60–74.

Arrow, Kenneth J. 1951. *Social Choice and Individual Values*. New Haven: Yale University Press.

Ascher, William. 1999. *Why Governments Waste Natural Resources: Policy Failures in Developing Countries*. Baltimore & London: The John Hopkins University Press.

Asher, Mansi, and Nidhi Agarwal. 2007. *Recognising the Historical Injustice: Campaign for the Forest Rights Act 2006*. Pune: National Centre for Advocacy Studies.

Askew, Kelly, Faustin Maganga, and Rie Odgaard. 2013. "Of Land and Legitimacy: A Tale of Two Lawsuits." *Africa* 83: 120–41.

Assembe-Mvondo, Samuel, Carol J.P. Colfer, Maria Brockhaus, and Raphael Tsanga. 2014. "Review of the Legal Ownership Status of National Lands in Cameroon: A More Nuanced View." *Development Studies Research* 1: 148–60.

Assies, Willem. 2009. "Land Tenure, Land Law and Development: Some Thoughts on Recent Debates." *Journal of Peasant Studies* 36: 573–89.

———. 2008. "Land Tenure and Tenure Regimes in Mexico: An Overview." *Journal of Agrarian Change* 8: 33–63.

Auch, Eckhard, Jürgen Pretzsch, and Holm Uibrig. 2014. "Organizational Changes in Forest Management." In *Forests and Rural Development*, eds. Jürgen Pretzsch, Dietrich Darr, Holm Uibrig, and Eckhard Auch. Berlin and Heidelberg: Springer. 111–44.

Auer, M.R. 2000. "Who Participates in Global Environmental Governance? Partial Answers from International Relations Theory." *Policy Sciences* 33: 155–80.

Auyero, Javier. 2006. "Introductory Note to Politics under the Microscope: Special Issue on Political Ethnography I." *Qualitative Sociology* 29: 257–59.

Avritzer, Leonardo. 2009. *Participatory Institutions in Democratic Brazil*. Baltimore, MD: Johns Hopkins University Press.

Baden-Powell, B.H. 1893. *Forest Law: A Course of Lectures on the Principles of Civil and Criminal Law and on the Law of the Forest (Chiefly Based on the Laws in Force in British India)*. London: Bradbury, Agnew, & Co.

Baiocchi, Gianpaolo, Patrick Heller, and Marcelo Kunrath Silva. 2008. "Making Space for Civil Society: Institutional Reforms and Local Democracy in Brazil." *Social Forces* 86: 911–36.

Baker, Rachel, Juan Carlos Carrillo, and Allison Silverman. 2014. *The Development of a National Safeguard System for REDD+ in Mexico: A Case for the Value of International Guidance*. Washington, DC: Bank Information Center.

Bakshi, Aparajita. 2008. "Social Inequality in Land Ownership in India: A Study with Particular Reference to West Bengal." *Social Scientist* 36: 95–116.

Balderas Torres, Arturo. 2012. "Yes in My Backyard: Market Based Mechanisms for Forest Conservation and Climate Change Mitigation in La Primavera, México." Enschede, Netherlands: University of Twente.

Balderas Torres, Arturo, and Margaret Skutsch. 2012. "Splitting the Difference: A Proposal for Benefit Sharing in Reduced Emissions from Deforestation and Forest Degradation (REDD+)." *Forests* 3: 137–54.

Banerjee, Abhijit, and Lakshmi Iyer. 2005. "History, Institutions, and Economic Performance: The Legacy of Colonial Land Tenure Systems in India." *The American Economic Review* 95: 1190–213.

Bardhan, Pranab. 2002. "Decentralization of Governance and Development." *Journal of Economic Perspectives* 16: 185–205.

Barnes, Clare, Frank van Laerhoven, and Peter P.J. Driessen. 2016. "Advocating for Change? How a Civil Society-Led Coalition Influences the Implementation of the Forest Rights Act in India." *World Development* 84: 162–75.

Barnes, Grenville. 2009. "The Evolution and Resilience of Community-Based Land Tenure in Rural Mexico." *Land Use Policy* 26: 393–400.

Barsimantov, James A., Alexis E. Racelis, Grenville Barnes, and Maria DiGiano. 2009. "Tenure, Tourism and Timber in Quintana Roo, Mexico: Land Tenure Changes in Forest Ejidos after Agrarian Reforms." *International Journal of the Commons* 4: 293–318.

Barton, G.A. 2000. "Empire Forestry and American Environmentalism." *Environment and History* 6: 187–203.

Barton, Gregory. 2001. "Empire Forestry and the Origins of Environmentalism." *Journal of Historical Geography* 27: 529–52.

Bartra, Armando, and Gerardo Otero. 2005. "Contesting Neoliberal Globalism and Nafta in Rural Mexico: From State Corporatism to the Political-Cultural Formation of the Peasantry?" *Journal of Latino/Latin American Studies* 1: 164–90.

Bartra, Roger. 1982. "Capitalism and the Peasantry in Mexico." *Latin American Perspectives* 9: 36–47.

———. 1975. "Peasants and Political Power in Mexico: A Theoretical Approach." *Latin American Perspectives* 2: 125–45.

Baru, Sanjaya. 2014. *The Accidental Prime Minister: The Making and Unmaking of Manmohan Singh*. New Delhi: Penguin Books India.

Basu, Amrita. 1987. "Grass Roots Movements and the State: Reflections on Radical Change in India." *Theory and Society* 16: 647–74.

Basu, Ipshita. 2012. "The Politics of Recognition and Redistribution: Development, Tribal Identity Politics and Distributive Justice in India's Jharkhand." *Development & Change* 43: 1291–312.

Bates, Crispin. 1988. "Congress and the Tribals." Paper presented at the Indian National Congress.

Bates, Robert, Avner Greif, Margaret Levi, Jean-Laurent Rosenthal, and Barry Weingast. 2000. "Analytic Narratives Revisited." *Social Science History* 24: 685–96.

Bauer, J.R., ed. 2006. *Forging Environmentalism: Justice, Livelihood, and Contested Environments*. Armonk, NY: M.E. Sharpe.

Baviskar, Amita. 2005. "Adivasi Encounters with Hindu Nationalism in MP." *Economic and Political Weekly* 40: 5105–13.

———. 2004. "Between Micro-Politics and Administrative Imperatives: Decentralisation and the Watershed Mission in Madhya Pradesh, India." *European Journal of Development Research* 16: 26–40.

———. 2003. "States, Communities and Conservation: The Practice of Ecodevelopment in the Great Himalayan National Park." In *Battles over Nature. Science and the Politics of Conservation*, eds. V. Saberwal and M. Rangarajan. New Delhi: Permanent Black. 267–99.

———. 2001. "Forest Management as Political Practice: Indian Experiences with the Accommodation of Multiple Interests." *International Journal of Agricultural Resources, Governance and Ecology* 1: 243–63.

———. 1997. "Tribal Politics and Discourses of Environmentalism." *Contributions to Indian Sociology* 31: 195–223.

———. 1995. *In the Belly of the River: Tribal Conflicts over Development in the Narmada Valley*. New Delhi and New York: Oxford University Press.

———. 1994. "Fate of the Forest: Conservation and Tribal Rights." *Economic and Political Weekly* 39: 2493–501.

Baviskar, Amita, and Nandini Sundar. 2008. "Democracy Versus Economic Transformation?" *Economic and Political Weekly* 43: 87–89.

Baviskar, Amita, Subir Sinha, and Kavita Philip. 2006. "Rethinking Indian Environmentalism: Industrial Pollution in Delhi and Fisheries in Kerala." In *Forging Environmentalism: Justice, Livelihood, and Contested Environments*, ed. J.R. Bauer. New York: East Gate Book. 189–256.

Bebbington, Anthony. 2005. "Theorizing Participation and Institutional Change: Ethnography and Political Economy." In *Participation: From Tyranny to*

Transformation?: Exploring New Approaches to Participation in Development, eds. Samuel Hickey and Giles Mohan. New York, NY: Zed Books. 278–83.

Bebbington, Anthony J., Anis A. Dani, Arjan de Haan, and Michael Walton, eds. 2008. *Institutional Pathways to Equity: Addressing Inequality Traps*. Washington, DC: World Bank Publications.

Becker, Laurence C. 2001. "Seeing Green in Mali's Woods: Clonial Legacy, Forest Use, and Local Control." *Annals of the Association of American Geographers* 91: 504–26.

Behar, Amitabh. 2002. *Peoples' Social Movements: An Alternative Perspective on Forest Management in India*. London: Overseas Development Institute.

Bénit-Gbaffou, Claire, and Sophie Oldfield. 2014. "Claiming 'Rights' in the African City: Popular Mobilisation and the Politics of Informality in Nairobi, Rabat, Johannesburg and Cape Town." In *The Routledge Handbook on Cities of the Global South*, eds. Sue Parnell and Sophie Oldfield. Oxon, U.K. and New York: Routledge. 281–95.

Benjaminsen, Grete. 2014. "Between Resistance and Consent: Project–Village Relationships When Introducing REDD+ in Zanzibar." *Forum for Development Studies* 41: 377–98.

Benjaminsen, Tor A., and Ian Bryceson. 2012. "Conservation, Green/Blue Grabbing and Accumulation by Dispossession in Tanzania." *The Journal of Peasant Studies* 39: 335–55.

Benjaminsen, Tor A., F.P. Maganga, and J.M. Abdallah. 2009. "The Kilosa Killings: Political Ecology of a Farmer–Herder Conflict in Tanzania." *Development and Change* 40: 423–45.

Benjaminsen, Tor A., Mara J. Goldman, Maya Y. Minwary, and Faustin P. Maganga. 2013. "Wildlife Management in Tanzania: State Control, Rent Seeking and Community Resistance." *Development and Change* 44: 1087–109.

Bergius, Mikael. 2014. *Expanding the Corporate Food Regime: The Southern Agricultural Growth Corridor of Tanzania. Current and Potential Implications for Rural Households*. Ås, Norway: Norwegian University of Life Science.

Bernstein, Steven, Michele Betsill, Matthew Hoffmann, and Matthew Paterson. 2010. "A Tale of Two Copenhagens: Carbon Markets and Climate Governance." *Millennium-Journal of International Studies* 39: 161–73.

Beyene, Atakilte, Claude Gasper Mung'ong'o, Aaron Atteridge, and Rasmus Kløcker Larsen. 2013. "Stockholm Environment Institute, Working Paper 2013–03."

Beymer-Farris, Betsy A., and Thomas J. Bassett. 2012. "The REDD Menace: Resurgent Protectionism in Tanzania's Mangrove Forests." *Global Environmental Change* 22: 332–41.

Bhaduri, Amit, and Romila Thapar. 2009. "Will the Mindset from the Past Change?" *The Hindu*. http://www.hindu.com/2009/11/09/stories/2009110955350800.htm.

Bhukya, Bhangya. 2013. "Enclosing Land, Enclosing Adivasis: Colonial Agriculture and Adivasis in Central India, 1853-1948." *Indian Historical Review* 40: 93–116.

Bhullar, Lovleen. 2008. "The Indian Forest Rights Act 2006: A Critical Appraisal." *Law, Environment and Development Journal* 4: 20–34.

Bhushan, Prashant. 2009. "Misplaced Priorities and Class Bias of the Judiciary." *Economic and Political Weekly* 44: 32–37.

Bijoy, C.R. 2011. "The Great Indian Tiger Show." *Economic and Political Weekly* XLVI: 36–41.

———. 2008. "Forest Rights Struggle: The Adivasis Now Await a Settlement." *American Behavioral Scientist* 51: 1755.

———. 2003. "Injustice in God's Country: The Adivasi Uprising in Kerala." *Himal South Asian*.

Bijoy, C.R., and K. Ravi Raman. 2003. "Muthanga: The Real Story: Adivasi Movement to Recover Land." *Economic and Political Weekly* 38: 1975–82.

Birdsall, Nancy, Augusto De la Torre, and Felipe Valencia Caicedo. 2010. "The Washington Consensus: Assessing a Damaged Brand." Working Paper No. 213. Washington, DC: Center for Global Development.

Bishop, John Douglas. 1997. "Locke's Theory of Original Appropriation and the Right of Settlement in Iroquois Territory." *Canadian Journal of Philosophy* 27: 311–37.

Blomley, T., K. Lukumbuzya, and G. Brodnig. 2011. *Participatory Forest Management and REDD+ in Tanzania*. Washington, DC: World Bank.

Blomley, Tom. 2006. *Mainstreaming Participatory Forestry within the Local Government Reform Process in Tanzania*, Gatekeeper Series 128. London: International Institute for Environment and Development.

Blomley, Tom, and Said Iddi. 2009. *Participatory Forest Management in Tanzania 1993-2009: Lessons Learned and Experiences to Take*. Dar es Salaam: Ministry of Natural Resources and Tourism, Forestry and Beekeeping Division.

Blomley, Tom, Dilys Roe, Fred Nelson, and Fiona Flintan. 2013. "'Land Grabbing': Is Conservation Part of the Problem or the Solution?" IIED Briefing. London: International Institute for Environment and Development.

Boone, Catherine. 2013. *Property and Political Order: Land Rights and the Structure of Politics in Africa*. New York, NY: Cambridge University Press.

——. 2012. "Territorial Politics and the Reach of the State: Unevenness by Design." *Revista de Ciencia Política (Santiago)* 32 (3): 623–41.

Boone, Catherine, and Lydia Nyeme. 2015. "Land Institutions and Political Ethnicity in Africa: Evidence from Tanzania." *Journal of Comparative Politics* 48: 67–86.

Booth, David, Flora Lugangira, Patrick Masanja, Abu Mvungi, Rosemarie Mwaipopo, Joaquim Mwami, and Alison Redmayne. 1993. *Social, Cultural and Economic Change in Contemporary Tanzania. A People-Oriented Focus*. Stockholm: Swedish International Development Authority.

Borras, Saturnino M. Jr. 2006. "Redistributive Land Reform in 'Public' (Forest) Lands? Lessons from the Philippines and Their Implications for Land Reform Theory and Practice." *Progress in Development Studies* 6: 123–45.

Bose, I. 2010. "How Did the Indian Forest Rights Act, 2006, Emerge?" *Institutions and Pro-Poor Growth (IPPG) Discussion Papers 39*. University of Manchester.

Boyer, Christopher R. 2005. "Contested Terrain: Forestry Regimes and Community Responses in Northeastern Michoacán, 1940-2000." In *The Community Forests of Mexico: Managing for Sustainable Landscapes*, eds. David Barton Bray, Letieia Merino-Pérez and Deborah Barry. Austin, TX: University of Texas Press. 27–48.

Boyer, Christopher R., and Emily Wakild. 2012. "Social Landscaping in the Forests of Mexico: An Environmental Interpretation of Cardenismo, 1934-1940." *Hispanic American Historical Review* 92: 73–106.

Brara, Rita. 2006. *Shifting Landscapes: The Making and Remaking of Village Commons in India*. New Delhi: Oxford University Press.

Brass, Paul R. 1968. "Coalition Politics in North India." *The American Political Science Review* 62 (4): 1174–91.

Bray, David Barton. 2013. "When the State Supplies the Commons: Origins, Changes, and Design of Mexico's Common Property Regime." *Journal of Latin American Geography* 12: 33–55.

——. 1995. "Peasant Organizations and 'the Permanent Reconstruction of Nature:' Grassroots Sustainable Development in Rural Mexico." *The Journal of Environment & Development* 4: 185–204.

Bray, David Barton, and Leticia Merino-Pérez. 2002. "The Rise of Community Forestry in Mexico: History, Concepts, and Lessons Learned from Twenty-Five Years of Community Timber Production." Report prepared for the Ford Foundation.

Bray, David Barton, Leticia Merino-Pérez, and Deborah Barry. 2005. *The Community Forests of Mexico: Managing for Sustainable Landscapes*. Austin, TX: University of Texas Press.

Brechin, Steven R., Peter R. Wilshusen, Crystal L. Fortwangler, and Patrick C. West. 2002. "Beyond the Square Wheel: Toward a More Comprehensive Understanding of Biodiversity Conservation as Social and Political Process." *Society & Natural Resources* 15: 41–64.

Brockhaus, Maria, and Monica Di Gregorio. 2014. "National REDD+ Policy Networks: From Cooperation to Conflict." *Ecology and Society* 19: 14.

Brockington, Dan. 2007. "Forests, Community Conservation, and Local Government Performance: The Village Forest Reserves of Tanzania." *Society & Natural Resources* 20: 835–48.

———. 2006. "The Politics and Ethnography of Environmentalisms in Tanzania." *African Affairs* 105: 97–116.

———. 2002. *Fortress Conservation: The Preservation of the Mkomazi Game Reserve, Tanzania*. Bloomington: International African Institute in association with Indiana University Press.

Brockington, Daniel, and James Igoe. 2006. "Eviction for Conservation: A Global Overview." *Conservation and Society* 4 (3): 424–70.

Bromley, Daniel W. 2004. "Reconsidering Environmental Policy: Prescriptive Consequentialism and Volitional Pragmatism." *Environmental and Resource Economics* 28: 73–99.

Bryant, R.L. 1994. "The Rise and Fall of Taungya Forestry: Social Forestry in Defence of the Empire." *Ecologist* 24: 21–26.

Burnett, G. Wesley, and Richard Conover. 1989. "The Efficacy of Africa's National Parks: An Evaluation of Julius Nyerere's Arusha Manifesto of 1961." *Society & Natural Resources* 2: 251–60.

Butt, Simon. 2014. "Traditional Land Rights before the Indonesian Constitutional Court." *Law, Environment and Development Journal* 10: 1.

Byamugisha, F. 2014. *Agricultural Land Redistribution and Land Administration in Sub-Saharan Africa: Case Studies of Recent Reforms*. Washington, DC: World Bank Publications.

Cabello, Joanna, and Tamra Gilbertson. 2012. "A Colonial Mechanism to Enclose Lands: A Critical Review of Two REDD+-Focused Special Issues." *ephemera* 12: 162.

Campaign for Survival and Dignity. 2004. "Endangered Symbiosis: Evictions and India's Forest Communities." Report of the Jan Sunwai (Public Hearing). New Delhi: CSD.

Carr, Edward R. 2013. "Livelihoods as Intimate Government: Reframing the Logic of Livelihoods for Development." *Third World Quarterly* 34: 77–108.

Centre for Women's Development Studies (CWDS). 2005. "Report of Seminar on Globalization and the Women's Movement in India." New Delhi, January 20–22.

Chakravorty, Sanjoy. 2013. *The Price of Land: Acquisition, Conflict, Consequence*. New Delhi and Oxford: Oxford University Press.

Chamarbagwala, Rubiana. 2006. "Economic Liberalization and Wage Inequality in India." *World Development* 34: 1997–2015.

Chance, John K. 1996. "The Caciques of Tecali: Class and Ethnic Identity in Late Colonial Mexico." *Hispanic American Historical Review* 76 (3): 475–502.

Chandhoke, Neera. 1994. "Why People Should Have Rights." *Economic and Political Weekly* 29: 2697–700.

Chandra, Kanchan. 2015. The New Indian State. *Economic & Political Weekly* 50 (41): 47.

Chandra, Uday. 2015. "Rethinking Subaltern Resistance." *Journal of Contemporary Asia* 45: 563–73.

———. 2013a. "Liberalism and Its Other: The Politics of Primitivism in Colonial and Postcolonial Indian Law." *Law & Society Review* 47: 135–68.

———. 2013b. "Negotiating Leviathan: Statemaking and Resistance in the Margins of Modern India." Ph.D. dissertation. Yale University.

Chatterjee, P. 2011. *Lineages of Political Society: Studies in Postcolonial Democracy.* New York: Columbia University Press.

Chatterjee, Partha. 2012. "The Debate over Political Society." In *Re-Framing Democracy and Agency in India: Interrogating Political Society*, ed. Ajay Gudavarthy. New York: Anthem Press. 305–22.

———. 2004. *The Politics of the Governed: Reflections on Popular Politics in Most of the World.* New York: Columbia University Press.

———. 1993. *The Nation and Its Fragments: Colonial and Postcolonial Histories.* Princeton, NJ: Princeton University Press.

Chaudhuri, B.B. 2008. *Peasant History of Late Pre-Colonial and Colonial India.* New Delhi: Pearson Longman, an imprint of Pearson Education: Project of History of Indian Science, Philosophy, and Culture.

Chhatre, Ashwini. 2008. "Political Articulation and Accountability in Decentralisation: Theory and Evidence from India." *Conservation and Society* 6: 12–23.

———. 2003. "The Mirage of Permanent Boundaries: Politics of Forest Reservation in the Western Himalayas, 1875–97." *Conservation and Society* 1: 137–59.

Chhatre, Ashwini and Vasant Saberwal. 2006. *Democratizing Nature: Politics, Conservation, and Development in India.* New Delhi: Oxford University Press.

———. 2005. "Political Incentives for Biodiversity Conservation." *Conservation Biology* 19: 310–17.

Chhibber, Pradeep, and Irfan Nooruddin. 2004. "Do Party Systems Count?: The Number of Parties and Government Performance in the Indian States." *Comparative Political Studies* 37: 152–87.

Chhibber, Pradeep K., and John R. Petrocik. 1989. "The Puzzle of Indian Politics: Social Cleavages and the Indian Party System." *British Journal of Political Science* 19: 191–210.

Chhotray, Vasudha. 2007. "The Anti-Politics Machine in India: Depoliticisation through Local Institution Building for Participatory Watershed Development." *Journal of Development Studies* 43: 1037–56.

Chowdhury, Ashok, and Roma Malik. 2009. "A Case Study of the National Forum of Forest People and Forest Workers' (NFFPFW) Struggle for Rights of Forest Workers." New Delhi: NFFPFW.

Chowdhury, Rinku Roy. 2014. "The Intersection of Independent Lies: Land Change Science and Political Ecology." In *Land Change Science, Political Ecology and Sustainability: Synergies and Divergences*, eds. C. Brannstrom and J. M. Vadjunec: Routledge. 224–40.

Christensen, Tom, and Per Lægreid. 2007. "The Whole-of-Government Approach to Public Sector Reform." *Public Administration Review* 67: 1059–66.

Clark, G., M. Waite, G. Boyd, E. Kallonga, A. Ligson, and P. Connelly. 2007. *Poor People's Wealth: Plain Language Information About Tanzania's Property and Business Formalisation Programme Mkurabita.* Dar es Salaam: MKURABITA.

Colchester, Marcus. 1994. "Sustaining the Forests: The Community-Based Approach in South and South-East Asia." *Development and Change* 25: 69–100.

Coleman, E.A. 2009. "Institutional Factors Affecting Biophysical Outcomes in Forest Management." *Journal of Policy Analysis and Management* 28: 122–46.

Colfer, Carol J Pierce, Janis B Alcorn, and Diane Russell. 2015. "Swiddens and Fallows." In *Shifting Cultivation and Environmental Change: Indigenous People, Agriculture and Forest Conservation*, eds. Malcolm F. Cairns Oxon, UK and New York: Routledge. 62–86.

Collier, George Allen, and Elizabeth Lowery Quaratiello. 2005. *Basta!: Land and the Zapatista Rebellion in Chiapas*. Oakland, CA: Food First Books.

Collier, R.B., and S. Handlin. 2009. *Reorganizing Popular Politics: Participation and the New Interest Regime in Latin America*. University Park, PA: Pennsylvania State University Press.

CONAFOR. 2013. *Carbon Fund Emission Reductions Program Idea Note (Er-Pin)*. Washington, DC: Forest Carbon Partnership Facility (FCPF), The World Bank.

Conca, Ken. 1994. "Rethinking the Ecology-Sovereignty Debate." *Millennium-Journal of International Studies* 23: 701–11.

Conte, Christopher Allan. 2004. *Highland Sanctuary: Environmental History in Tanzania's Usambara Mountains*. Athens, OH: Ohio University Press.

———. 1999. "The Forest Becomes Desert: Forest Use and Environmental Change in Tanzania's West Usambara Mountains." *Land Degradation & Development* 10: 291–309.

Corbera, E., M. Estrada, P. May, G. Navarro, and P. Pacheco. 2011. "Rights to Land, Forests and Carbon in REDD+: Insights from Mexico, Brazil and Costa Rica." *Forests* 2: 301–42.

Corbridge, S. 2002. "The Continuing Struggle for India's Jharkhand: Democracy, Decentralisation and the Politics of Names and Numbers." *Commonwealth & Comparative Politics* 40: 55–71.

———. 2000. "Competing Inequalities: The Scheduled Tribes and the Reservations System in India's Jharkhand." *The Journal of Asian Studies* 59: 62–85.

———. 1988. "The Ideology of Tribal Economy and Society: Politics in the Jharkhand, 1950-1980." *Modern Asian Studies* 22: 1–42.

Corbridge, Stuart, John Harriss, and Craig Jeffrey. 2013. *India Today Economy, Politics and Society*. Cambridge, U.K., and Malden, MA: Polity Press.

Corbridge, S., and S. Jewitt. 1997. "From Forest Struggles to Forest Citizens? Joint Forest Management in the Unquiet Woods of India's Jharkhand." *Environment & Planning* 29: 2145–64.

Corbridge, S., and S. Kumar. 2002. "Community, Corruption, Landscape: Tales from the Tree Trade." *Political Geography* 21: 765–88.

Corbridge, Stuart, and Manoj Srivastava. 2013. "Mapping the Social Order by Fund Flows: The Political Geography of Employment Assurance Schemes in India." *Economy and Society* 42: 455–79.

Corbridge, S., G. Williams, M. Srivastava, and R. Véron. 2005. *Seeing the State: Governance and Governmentability in India*: Cambridge: Cambridge University Press.

Cornelius, Wayne A., and David Myhre. 1998. *The Transformation of Rural Mexico: Reforming the Ejido Sector*, Us-Mexico Contemporary Perspectives Series. Boulder, CO: Lynne Rienner Publishers.

Corson, Catherine. 2011. "Territorialization, Enclosure and Neoliberalism: Non-State Influence in Struggles over Madagascar's Forests." *The Journal of Peasant Studies* 38: 703–26.

Coulson, Andrew. 1982. *Tanzania: A Political Economy*. Oxford: Oxford University Press.

Cousins, Ben. 1997. "How Do Rights Become Real?: Formal and Informal Institutions in South Africa's Land Reform." *IDS Bulletin* 28: 59–68.

Crawford, Beverly, and Arend Lijphart. 1995. "Explaining Political and Economic Change in Post-Communist Eastern Europe Old Legacies, New Institutions, Hegemonic Norms, and International Pressures." *Comparative Political Studies* 28: 171–99.

Cronon, William. 1983. *Changes in the Land: Indians, Colonists, and the Ecology of New England*. New York: Macmillan.

Dalby, Simon. 2007. "Anthropocene Geopolitics: Globalisation, Empire, Environment and Critique." *Geography Compass* 1: 103–18.

Damodaran, A. 2006. "Tribals, Forests and Resource Conflicts in Kerala, India: The Status Quo of Policy Change." *Oxford Development Studies* 34: 357–71.

Dandekar, Ajay, and Chitrangada Choudhury. 2010. "Pesa, Left-Wing Extremism and Governance: Concerns and Challenges in India's Tribal Districts." New Delhi: Ministry of Panchayati Raj, Government of India.

de Alba, Iván González. 2012. *Mexico's "Official" Multidimensional Poverty Measure: A Comparative Study of Indigenous and Non-Indigenous Populations*. Oxford Poverty & Human Development Initiative: University of Oxford.

de Ita, Ana. 2006. "Land Concentration in Mexico after Procede." In *Promised Land: Competing Visions of Agrarian Reform*, eds. Peter Rosset, Raj Patel, and Michael Courville. Oakland, CA: Food First Books. 148–64.

de Janvry, A., N.D. Key, and E. Sadoulet. 1997. *Agricultural and Rural Development Policy in Latin America: New Directions and New Challenges*. Rome: Food and Agriculture Organization of the United Nations.

de Janvry, Alain, Céline Dutilly, Carlos Muñoz-Piña, and Elisabeth Sadoulet. 2001. "Liberal Reforms and Community Responses in Mexico." In *Communities and Markets in Economic Development*, eds. M. Aoki and Y. Hayami. Oxford: Oxford University Press. 318–44.

de Janvry, Alain, Marco Gonzalez-Navarro, and Elisabeth Sadoulet. 2014. "Are Land Reforms Granting Complete Property Rights Politically Risky? Electoral Outcomes of Mexico's Certification Program." *Journal of Development Economics* 110: 216–25.

de Oliveira, José Antônio Puppim. 2014. "The Mismatch of Implementation Networks in International Environmental Regimes." In *Improving Global Environmental Governance: Best Practices for Architecture and Agency*, eds. Norichika Kanie, Steinar Andresen, and Peter M. Haas. New York: Routledge. 108–29.

De Schutter, Olivier. 2011. "Green Rush: The Global Race for Farmland and the Rights of Land Users." *Harvard International Law Journal* 52: 503.

de Soto, H. 2000. *The Mystery of Capital: Why Capitalism Triumphs in the West and Fails Everywhere Else*. New York: Basic Books.

de Soto, Hernando 1989. *The Other Path: The Economic Answer to Terrorism*. New York: Basic Books.

Dean, Erin. 2011. "Birds of One Tree: Participatory Forestry and Land Claims in Tanzania." *Human Organization* 70: 300–09.

Deaton, Angus. 2003. "Adjusted Indian Poverty Estimates for 1999-2000." *Economic and Political Weekly*: 322–26.

Deaton, Angus, and Jean Drèze. 2002. "Poverty and Inequality in India: A Re-Examination." *Economic and Political Weekly* 37 (36): 3729–48.

Debnath, Biswanath. 1999. "Crisis of Indian Anthropology." *Economic and Political Weekly* 34: 3110–14.

Deininger, Klaus, and Fabrizio Bresciani. 2001. "Mexico's Second Agrarian Reform: Implementation and Impact." Washington, DC: World Bank.

Demarest, Arthur Andrew. 2004. *Ancient Maya: The Rise and Fall of a Rainforest Civilization*. Cambridge: Cambridge University Press.

Desai, Manali. 2001. "Party Formation, Political Power, and the Capacity for Reform: Comparing Left Parties in Kerala and West Bengal, India." *Social Forces* 80: 37–60.

Diamond, L. 1999. *Developing Democracy: Toward Consolidation*. Baltimore and London: Johns Hopkins University Press.

DiGiano, Maria, Edward Ellis, and Eric Keys. 2013. "Changing Landscapes for Forest Commons: Linking Land Tenure with Forest Cover Change Following Mexico's 1992 Agrarian Counter-Reforms." *Human Ecology* 41: 707–23.

DiGiano, Maria Louise. 2011. "Privatizing the Commons? A Political Ecology of Mexico's 1992 Agrarian Reform in Quintana Roo, Yucatan Peninsula." Ph.D., University of Florida.

Dimitrov, R.S. 2005. "Hostage to Norms: States, Institutions and Global Forest Politics." *Global Environmental Politics* 5: 1–24.

Doherty, Emma, and Heike Schroeder. 2011. "Forest Tenure and Multi-Level Governance in Avoiding Deforestation under REDD." *Global Environmental Politics* 11: 66–88.

Dollar, David, Tatjana Kleineberg, and Aart Kraay. 2013. *Growth Still Is Good for the Poor*, World Bank Policy Research Working Paper. Washington, DC: World Bank.

Doniger, Wendy. 2010. *The Hindus: An Alternative History*. Oxford: Oxford University Press.

Doolittle, Amity A. 2010. "The Politics of Indigeneity: Indigenous Strategies for Inclusion in Climate Change Negotiations." *Conservation and Society* 8: 286.

Dove, M. 1993. "A Revisionist View of Tropical Deforestation and Development." *Environmental Conservation* 20: 17–24.

Dressler, W. 2009. *Old Thoughts in New Ideas: State Conservation Measures, Livelihood and Development on Palawan Island, the Philippines*. Quezon City: Ateneo de Manila University Press.

Drèze, Jean. 2005. "Tribal Evictions from Forest Land." National Advisory Council. http://econpapers.repec.org/paper/esswpaper/id_3a201.htm.

Drèze, Jean, and Amartya Sen. 2013. *An Uncertain Glory: India and Its Contradictions*. Princeton, NJ: Princeton University Press.

Drèze, Jean, Meera Samson, and Satyajit Singh. 1997. *Displacement and Resettlement: Ecological and Political Issues on the Narmada Valley Conflict*. New Delhi and Oxford: Oxford University Press.

Du Toit, J.T., and D.H.M. Cumming. 1999. "Functional Significance of Ungulate Diversity in African Savannas and the Ecological Implications of the Spread of Pastoralism." *Biodiversity & Conservation* 8: 1643–61.

Durand, Leticia, and Luis Bernardo Vázquez. 2011. "Biodiversity Conservation Discourses. A Case Study on Scientists and Government Authorities in Sierra De Huautla Biosphere Reserve, Mexico." *Land Use Policy* 28: 76–82.

Dwivedi, Ranjit. 2002. "Models and Methods in Development–Induced Displacement (Review Article)." *Development and Change* 33: 709–32.

Dyngeland, C., P. Vedeld, and A. Vatn. 2014. "REDD+ at Work? Implementing Consistent REDD+ Policies at Local Levels—A Case from Kilosa District, Tanzania." *International Forestry Review* 16: 549–62.

Easterly, W. 2013. *The Tyranny of Experts: How the Fight against Global Poverty Suppressed Individual Rights*. New York: Basic Books.

Eckersley, Robyn. 1995. "Liberal Democracy and the Rights of Nature: The Struggle for Inclusion." *Environmental Politics* 4: 169–98.

Eisenstadt, Todd A. 2011. *Politics, Identity, and Mexico's Indigenous Rights Movements.* New York: Cambridge University Press.

———. 2009. "Agrarian Tenure Institution Conflict Frames, and Communitarian Identities: The Case of Indigenous Southern Mexico." *Comparative Political Studies* 42: 82–113.

———. 2003. *Courting Democracy in Mexico: Party Strategies and Electoral Institutions.* New York: Cambridge University Press.

Ellerman, A. Denny. 2005. "US Experience with Emissions Trading: Lessons for Co2 Emissions Trading." In *Emissions Trading for Climate Policy: US and European Perspectives,* ed. Bernd Hansjürgens. New York: Cambridge University Press. 78–95.

Elliott Armijo, Leslie, and John Echeverri-Gent. 2014. "Brave New World? The Politics of International Finance in Brazil and India." In *The Financial Statecraft of Emerging Powers: Shield and Sword in Asia and Latin America,* ed. Leslie Elliott Armijo. New York: Palgrave Macmillan. 47–76.

Elmore, Richard F. 1979. "Backward Mapping: Implementation Research and Policy Decisions." *Political Science Quarterly* 94: 601–16.

Engel, U., G. Erdmann, and A. Mehler. 2000. *Tanzania Revisited: Political Stability, Aid Dependency, and Development Constraints.* Hamburg: Institut für Afrika-Kunde.

Evans, Susan T. 1990. "The Productivity of Maguey Terrace Agriculture in Central Mexico During the Aztec Period." *Latin American Antiquity* 1: 117–32.

Fairbairn, Madeleine. 2013. "Indirect Dispossession: Domestic Power Imbalances and Foreign Access to Land in Mozambique." *Development and Change* 44: 335–56.

Fairhead, James, Melissa Leach, and Ian Scoones. 2012. "Green Grabbing: A New Appropriation of Nature?" *The Journal of Peasant Studies* 39: 237–61.

Fairley, Elizabeth. 2013. "Upholding Customary Land Rights through Formalization? Evidence from Tanzania's Program of Land Reform." Ph.D. dissertation. University of Minnesota.

———. 2012. "Upholding Customary Land Rights through Formalization: Evidence from Tanzania's Program of Land Reform." Paper presented at the Annual World Bank Conference on Land and Poverty, Washington, DC.

Farley, K.A., L. Ojeda-Revah, E.E. Atkinson, B.R. Eaton-González. 2012. "Changes in Land Use, Land Tenure, and Landscape Fragmentation in the Tijuana River Watershed Following Reform of the Ejido Sector." *Land Use Policy* 29, 187–197.

Faust, Betty Bernice. 2001. "Maya Environmental Successes and Failures in the Yucatan Peninsula." *Environmental Science & Policy* 4: 153–69.

Fay, Chip and Genevieve Michon. 2005. "Redressing Forestry Hegemony When a Forestry Regulatory Framework Is Best Replaced by an Agrarian One." *Forests, Trees and Livelihoods* 15: 193–209.

Fay, Chip, Martua Sirait, and Ahmad Kusworo. 2000. "Getting the Boundaries Right: Indonesia's Urgent Need to Redefine Its Forest Estate." Southeast Asia Policy Research Working Paper, No. 25, World Agroforestry Center, Bogor, Indonesia.

Fay, P.C., and Martua Sirait. 2002. "Reforming the Reformists in the Post-Soeharto Indonesia." In *Which Way Forward?: People, Forests, and Policymaking in Indonesia,* ed. Carol Colfer. Washington, DC: Resources for Future. 126–43.

Feierman, Steven. 1990. *Peasant Intellectuals Anthropology and History in Tanzania.* Madison, WI: University of Wisconsin Press.

Felix, Mwema. 2015. "Future Prospect and Sustainability of Wood Fuel Resources in Tanzania." *Renewable and Sustainable Energy Reviews* 51: 856–62.

Ferguson, James. 1990. "The Anti-Politics Machine." In *The Anti-Politics Machine*: '*Development*,' *Depoliticization, and Bureaucratic Power in Lesotho*. Cambridge, UK: Cambridge University Press.

Flannery, Kent V., and Joyce Marcus. 1976. "Formative Oaxaca and the Zapotec." *American Scientist* 64: 374–83.

Fleischman, Forrest Daniel. 2014. Why do Foresters Plant Trees? Testing Theories of Bureaucratic Decision-Making in Central India. *World Development* 62: 62–74.

———. 2012. "Public Servant Behavior and Forest Policy Implementation in Central India." Ph.D. dissertation. Indiana University, Bloomington.

Foley, Michael W. 1995. "Privatizing the Countryside: The Mexican Peasant Movement and Neoliberal Reform." *Latin American Perspectives* 22 (1): 59–76.

Foley, Michael W. 1991. "Agenda for Mobilization: The Agrarian Question and Popular Mobilization in Contemporary Mexico." *Latin American Research Review* 26: 39–74.

Forsyth, Tim. 2008. "Political Ecology and the Epistemology of Social Justice." *Geoforum* 39: 756–64.

Foweraker, J., and A.L. Craig. 1990. *Popular Movements and Political Change in Mexico*. Boulder, CO and London: Lynne Rienner Publishers.

Foweraker, Joe. 2001. "Grassroots Movements and Political Activism in Latin America: A Critical Comparison of Chile and Brazil." *Journal of Latin American Studies* 33: 839–65.

Fox, Jonathan. 2007. *Accountability Politics: Power and Voice in Rural Mexico*, Oxford Studies in Democratization. Oxford, UK, and New York: Oxford University Press.

———. 2005. "Empowerment and Institutional Change: Mapping 'Virtuous Circles' of State-Society Interaction." In *Power, Rights, and Poverty: Concepts and Connections*, ed. Ruth Alsop. Washington, DC: World Bank. 68–82.

———. 1996. "How Does Civil Society Thicken? The Political Construction of Social Capital in Rural Mexico." *World Development* 24: 1089–103.

———. 1994. "The Difficult Transition from Clientelism to Citizenship: Lessons from Mexico." *World Politics* 46: 151–84.

———. 1985. "Agrarian Reform and Populist Politics: A Discussion of Stephen Sanderson's Agrarian Populism and the Mexican State." *Latin American Perspectives* 12 (3): 29–41.

Fox, Jonathan A., and Luis Hernández. 1989. "Offsetting the 'Iron Law of Oligarchy': The Ebb and Flow of Leadership Accountability in a Regional Peasant Organization." *Grassroots Development* 13: 8–15.

Fox, Sean. 2013. "The Political Economy of Urbanisation and Development in Sub-Saharan Africa." Working Paper No. 13–146. London: The London School of Economics and Political Science (LSE).

Fratkin, Elliot M., and Tiffany Sher-Mei-Wu. 1997. "Maasai and Barabaig Herders Struggle for Land Rights in Kenya and Tanzania." *Cultural Survival Quarterly* 21: 55–61.

Forest Survey of India (FSI). 2015. *India: State of Forest Report 2015*. New Delhi. FSI.

Fukuyama, Francis. 2004. *State-Building: Governance and World Order in the 21st Century*. Ithaca, NY: Cornell University Press.

Gabrielson, Teena. 2008. "Green Citizenship: A Review and Critique." *Citizenship Studies* 12: 429–46.

Gadgil, Madhav, and Ramachandra Guha. 1992. *This Fissured Land: An Ecological History of India*. Berkeley: University of California Press.

Gaikwad, V. 1995. "Tribal and the Tiger: A Case Study of the Kanha National Park." Centre for Management in Agriculture, Indian Institute of Management, Ahmedabad.

Gallemore, Caleb, and Darla K. Munroe. 2013. "Centralization in the Global Avoided Deforestation Collaboration Network." *Global Environmental Change* 23: 1199–210.

Galvan, Dennis Charles. 2004. *The State Must Be Our Master of Fire How Peasants Craft Sustainable Development in Senegal.* Berkeley: University of California Press.

Ganapathy, Nirmala. 2005. "Environment Ministry Strikes at Root of Tribal Land Rights Bill." *Indian Express*, April 14, 2005.

Gandhi, Indira. 1992. *Of Man and His Environment.* New Delhi: Abhinav Publications.

García-Frapolli, Eduardo, Gabriel Ramos-Fernández, Eduardo Galicia, and Arturo Serrano. 2009. "The Complex Reality of Biodiversity Conservation through Natural Protected Area Policy: Three Cases from the Yucatan Peninsula, Mexico." *Land Use Policy* 26: 715–22.

García-López, Gustavo A. 2014. "Explaining the Emergence and Evolution of Multi-Level Forest Governance: Inter-Community Organisations in Mexico." Unpublished Manuscript.

———. 2013. "Scaling up from the Grassroots and the Top Down: The Impacts of Multi-Level Governance on Community Forestry in Durango, Mexico." *International Journal of the Commons* 7: 406–31.

———. 2012. "Scaling up from the Top Down and the Bottom Up: The Impacts and Governance of Inter-Community Forest Associations in Durango, Mexico." Ph.D. dissertation. Indiana University.

Gardner, Benjamin. 2012. "Tourism and the Politics of the Global Land Grab in Tanzania: Markets, Appropriation and Recognition." *The Journal of Peasant Studies* 39: 377–402.

Garg, Anil. 2005. *Orange Areas: Examining the Origin and Status.* Pune: National Centre for Advocacy Studies.

Garretón, Manuel Antonio. 2002. "La transformación de la acción colectiva en América Latina." *Revista de la CEPAL* 76: 7–24.

Geisler, Charles. 2012. "New Terra Nullius Narratives and the Gentrification of Africa's 'Empty Lands.'" *Journal of World Systems Research* 18: 15–29.

———. 2002. "Endangered Humans." *Foreign Policy* 130: 80–81.

Geoghegan, Jacqueline, Sergio Cortina Villar, Peter Klepeis, Pedro Macario Mendoza, Yelena Ogneva-Himmelberger, Rinku Roy Chowdhury, B.L. Turner Ii, and Colin Vance. 2001. "Modeling Tropical Deforestation in the Southern Yucatan Peninsular Region: Comparing Survey and Satellite Data." *Agriculture, Ecosystems & Environment* 85: 25–46.

George, A.L., and A. Bennett. 2005. *Case Studies and Theory Development in the Social Sciences.* Cambridge. MA: MIT Press.

German, Laura, George Schoneveld, and Esther Mwangi. 2013. "Contemporary Processes of Large-Scale Land Acquisition in Sub-Saharan Africa: Legal Deficiency or Elite Capture of the Rule of Law?" *World Development* 48: 1–18.

Gibson, Clark C. 1999. *Politicians and Poachers: The Political Economy of Wildlife Policy in Africa.* Cambridge, UK: Cambridge University Press.

Gidwani, Vinay, and Joel Wainwright. 2014. "On Capital, Not-Capital, and Development: After Kalyan Sanyal." *Economic & Political Weekly* 49: 40–47.

Gledhill, John. 1997. "Fantasy and Reality in Restructuring Mexico's Land Reform." Paper presented at the Modern Mexico session of the annual meeting of the Society for Latin American Studies, St. Andrews, Scotland.

Global Witness. 2014. *Deadly Environment: The Dramatic Rise in Killings of Environmental and Land Defenders*. London: Global Witness Ltd.

Gomez, Placido. 1985. "The History and Adjudication of the Common Lands of Spanish and Mexican Land Grants." *Public Land and Resources Law Digest* 23: 134.

Gooch, Pernille. 2009. "Victims of Conservation or Rights as Forest Dwellers: Van Gujjar Pastoralists between Contesting Codes of Law." *Conservation and Society* 7: 239–48.

Gopalakrishnan, Shankar 2010. "Conservation, Power and Democracy." *Seminar* 613. http://www.india-seminar.com/2010/613.htm.

Gordillo, Gustavo. 2009. "The Political Economy of the Agrarian Reform Process in Mexico (1991–1992)." Paper presented at the Conference on Land Governance in Support of the MDG's: Responding to New Challenges, March 9–10, 2009, Washington, DC.

Gould, Jeremy. 2006. "Strong Bar, Weak State? Lawyers, Liberalism and State Formation in Zambia." *Development and Change* 37: 921–41.

Government of India (GOI). "Agricultural Statistics at a Glance 2014." The Directorate of Economics & Statistics of the Department of Agriculture & Cooperation. New Delhi: Oxford University Press.

———. *Guidelines for Convergence between NREGS and the schemes of the Ministry of Environment and Forest (MoEF)*. 2008. Vol. N0.J-11019/2/2008-NREGA. New Delhi: Ministry of Rural Development. http://www.nrega.net/csd/convergence-guidelines/33_44.pdf.

———. 2006. "The Scheduled Tribes and Other Traditional Forest Dwellers (Recognition of Forest Rights) Act, 2006." In *No.2 of 2007*. New Delhi: The Gazette of India; Government of India.

Grammont, Hubert C. de, Horacio Mackinlay, and Richard Stoller. 2009. "Campesino and Indigenous Social Organizations Facing Democratic Transition in Mexico, 1938-2006." *Latin American Perspectives* 36: 21–40.

Greene, Kenneth F. 2008. "Dominant Party Strategy and Democratization." *American Journal of Political Science* 52: 16–31.

Grindle, Merilee S., and John W. Thomas. 1989. "Policy Makers, Policy Choices, and Policy Outcomes: The Political Economy of Reform in Developing Countries." *Policy Sciences* 22: 213–48.

Gudavarthy, Ajay. 2012. *Re-Framing Democracy and Agency in India: Interrogating Political Society*. London, New York, and New Delhi: Anthem Press.

Gudavarthy, Ajay, and G. Vijay. 2007. "Antinomies of Political Society: Implications of Uncivil Development." *Economic and Political Weekly* 52 (28): 3051–59.

Guha, Ramachandra. 2007. "Adivasis, Naxalites and Indian Democracy." *Economic and Political Weekly* 42: 3305.

———. 2002. "Anil Agarwal and the Environmentalism of the Poor." *Capitalism Nature Socialism* 13: 147–55.

———. 2001. "The Prehistory of Community Forestry in India." *Environmental History* 6: 213.

———. 1983. "Forestry in British and Post-British India: A Historical Analysis." *Economic and Political Weekly* 18: 1882–96.

Guha, Ramachandra, Nandini Sundar, Amita Baviskar, Ashish Kothari, Neema Pathak, N.C. Saxena, Sharachchandra Lélé, Don G. Roberts, Smriti Das, and K.D. Singh. 2012. *Deeper Roots of Historical Injustice*. Washington, DC: Rights and Resources Initiative.

Guha, Sumit. 1996. "Forest Polities and Agrarian Empires: The Khandesh Bhils, C. 1700-1850." *Indian Economic & Social History Review* 33: 133–53.

Gupta, A., and K. Sivaramakrishnan. 2011. *The State in India after Liberalization: Interd isciplinary Perspectives*. New York: Routledge.

Gupta, Akhil. 2014. "Viewing States from the Global South" In *Off-Centered States*, eds. Chris Krupa and David Nugent. Philadelphia: University of Pennsylvania Press.

Haan, Arjan de. 2008. "Inequalities within India's Poorest Regions: Why Do the Same Institutions Work Differently in Different Places?" In *Institutional Pathways to Equity: Addressing Inequality Traps*, eds. Anthony J. Bebbington, Anis A. Dani, Arjan de Haan, and Michael Walton. Washington, DC: World Bank Publications.

Haenn, Nora. 2010. "A 'Sustaining Conservation' for Mexico?" In *The International Handbook of Environmental Sociology*, eds. Michael R. Redclift and Graham Woodgate. Cheltenham, UK: Edward Elgar Publishing Limited. 408.

———. 2006. "The Changing and Enduring Ejido: A State and Regional Examination of Mexico's Land Tenure Counter-Reforms." *Land Use Policy* 23: 136–46.

———. 2005. *Fields of Power, Forests of Discontent: Culture, Conservation, and the State in Mexico*. Tucson: University of Arizona Press.

———. 2003. "Risking Environmental Justice: Culture, Conservation, and Governance at Calakmul, Mexico." In *Struggles for Social Rights in Latin America*, eds. Susan Eva Eckstein and Timothy P. Wickham-Crowley. New York and London: Routledge. 81.

Haeuber, R. 1993a. "Indian Forestry Policy in Two Eras: Continuity or Change?" *Environmental History Review* 17: 49.

———. 1993b. "Development and Deforestation: Indian Forestry in Perspective." *The Journal of Developing Areas* 27: 485–514.

Håkansson, Thomas. 2008. "Regional Political Ecology and Intensive Cultivation in Pre-Colonial and Colonial South Pare, Tanzania." *The International Journal of African Historical Studies* 41: 433–59.

———. 1998. "Rulers and Rainmakers in Precolonial South Pare, Tanzania: Exchange and Ritual Experts in Political Centralization." *Ethnology* 37: 263–83.

Hall, Peter A. 2008. "Systematic Process Analysis: When and How to Use It." *European Political Science* 7: 304–17.

Hall, Peter A., and Rosemary C.R. Taylor. 1996. "Political Science and the Three New Institutionalisms." *Political Studies* 44: 936–57.

Hames, Raymond. 2007. "The Ecologically Noble Savage Debate." *Annual Review of Anthropology* 36: 177–90.

Hannam, K. 2000. "Educating an Environmental Elite: The Training of the Indian Forest Service." *International Research in Geographical and Environmental Education* 9 (4): 285–95.

Haque, M.S. 1998. "The Paradox of Bureaucratic Accountability in Developing Nations under a Promarket State." *International Political Science Review* 19: 357.

———. 1997. "Incongruity between Bureaucracy and Society in Developing Nations: A Critique." *Peace & Change* 22: 432–62.

Hardiman, David. 1998. "Well Irrigation in Gujarat: Systems of Use, Hierarchies of Control." *Economic and Political Weekly* 33: 1533–44.

———. 1996. "Farming in the Forest: The Dangs 1830-1992." In *Village Voices, Forest Choices—Joint Forest Management in India*, eds. Mark Poffenberger and Betsy McGean. New Delhi: Oxford University Press.

———. 1994. "Power in the Forests: The Dangs 1820–1940." In *Subaltern Studies Viii: Essays in Honour of Ranajit Guha*, eds. D. Arnold and D. Hardiman. New Delhi: Oxford University Press.

———. 1987. *The Coming of the Devi: Adivasi Assertion in Western India*. New Delhi: Oxford University Press.

Harris, Dan, Pilar Domingo, Cassian Sianga, Enock Chengullah, and Calyst Basil Kavishe. 2011. *The Political Economy of Social Accountability in Tanzania: Anti-Logging Advocacy and the Mama Misitu Campaign*. London: Overseas Development Institute.

Harriss, J., J. Hunter, and CJ Lewis, eds. 1995. *The New Institutional Economics and Third World Development*. London: Routledge

Harvey, Neil. 1990. "Peasant Strategies and Corporatism in Chiapas." In *Popular Movements and Political Change in Mexico*, eds. Joe Foweraker and Ann L. Craig. Boulder, CO and London: Lynne Rienner Publishers. 183–98.

Havnevik, Kjell J., and Mats Hårsmar. 1999. *The Diversified Future. An Institutional Approach to Rural Development in Tanzania*. Stockholm: Expert Group on Development Issues (EGDI).

Hayes, T., and E. Ostrom. 2005. "Conserving the World's Forests: Are Protected Areas the Only Way?" *Indiana Law Review* 35: 595.

Healy, R.G., D. VanNijnatten, and M. López-Vallejo. 2014. *Environmental Policy in North America: Approaches, Capacity, and the Management of Transboundary Issues*. Toronto: University of Toronto Press.

Heller, Patrick. 2009. "Democratic Deepening in India and South Africa." *Journal of Asian and African Studies* 44: 123–49.

———. 2001. "Moving the State: The Politics of Democratic Decentralization in Kerala, South Africa, and Porto Alegre." *Politics and Society* 29: 131–63.

———. 2000. "Degrees of Democracy: Some Comparative Lessons from India." *World Politics* 52: 484–519.

Heller, Patrick, K.N. Harilal, and Shubham Chaudhuri. 2007. "Building Local Democracy: Evaluating the Impact of Decentralization in Kerala, India." *World Development* 35: 626–48.

Hellman, Judith Adler. 1983. "The Role of Ideology in Peasant Politics: Peasant Mobilization and Demobilization in the Laguna Region." *Journal of Inter-American Studies and World Affairs*: 3–29.

Hellwig, Timothy. 2015. *Globalization and Mass Politics: Retaining the Room to Maneuver*. New York: Cambridge University Press.

Herring, Ronald J. 1983. *Land to the Tiller: The Political Economy of Agrarian Reform in South Asia*. New Haven: Yale University Press.

Hertel, Shareen. 2015. "Hungry for Justice: Social Mobilization on the Right to Food in India." *Development and Change* 46: 72–94.

Heynen, Nik, James McCarthy, Scott Prudham, and Paul Robbins, eds. 2007. *Neoliberal Environments: False Promises and Unnatural Consequences*. New York: Routledge.

Higham, Rob, and Alpa Shah. 2013. "Affirmative Action and Political Economic Transformations: Secondary Education, Indigenous People, and the State in Jharkhand, India." *Focaal* 2013: 80–93.

Hirsch, Philip. 1990. "Forests, Forest Reserve, and Forest Land in Thailand." *The Geographical Journal* 156: 166–74.

Hiskes, Richard P. 2009. *The Human Right to a Green Future: Environmental Rights and Intergenerational Justice*. Cambridge, UK and New York: Cambridge University Press.

Hobley, M. 1996. *Participatory Forestry: The Process of Change in India and Nepal*.

Hochstetler, Kathryn, and Margaret E. Keck. 2007. *Greening Brazil: Environmental Activism in State and Society*. Durham, N.C. and London: Duke University Press.

Hodgson, Dorothy L., and Richard A. Schroeder. 2002. "Dilemmas of Counter-Mapping Community Resources in Tanzania." *Development and Change* 33: 79–100.

Hodgson, Dorothy Louise. 2011. *Being Maasai, Becoming Indigenous Postcolonial Politics in a Neoliberal World*. Bloomington: Indiana University Press.

Hoffmann, Matthew J. 2011. *Climate Governance at the Crossroads: Experimenting with a Global Response after Kyoto*. New York, NY: Oxford University Press.

Holden, Robert H. 1990. "Priorities of the State in the Survey of the Public Land in Mexico, 1876-1911." *The Hispanic American Historical Review* 70: 579–608.

Holzner, Claudio A. 2010. *Poverty of Democracy*. Pittsburgh, PA: University of Pittsburgh Press.

Homewood, Katherine, E.F. Lambin, E. Coast, A. Kariuki, I. Kikula, J. Kivelia, M. Said, S. Serneels, and M. Thompson. 2001. "Long-Term Changes in Serengeti-Mara Wildebeest and Land Cover: Pastoralism, Population, or Policies?" *Proceedings of the National Academy of Sciences* 98: 12544–49.

Homewood, Katherine, Ernestina Coast, and Michael Thompson. 2004. "In-Migrants and Exclusion in East African Rangelands: Access, Tenure and Conflict." *Africa: Journal of the International African Institute* 74: 567–610.

Hughes, A.J. 1969. *East Africa: Kenya, Tanzania, Uganda*. Baltimore: Penguin Books.

Huijzendveld, Frans D. 2008. "Changes in Political Economy and Ecology in West-Usambara, Tanzania: Ca. 1850-1950." *The International Journal of African Historical Studies* 41: 383–409.

Huismann, W. 2014. *Pandaleaks: The Dark Side of the WWF*. Bremen, Germany: Nordbook.

Hurst, Andrew. 2004."Not yet out of the Woods: A Political Ecology of State Forest Policy and Practice in Mainland Tanzania, 1961-1998." Ph.D. dissertation. St. Antony's College/School of Geography and the Environment, University of Oxford.

Hyden, Göran. 1999. "Top-Down Democratization in Tanzania." *Journal of Democracy* 10: 142–55.

———. 1980. *Beyond Ujamaa in Tanzania: Underdevelopment and an Uncaptured Peasantry*. Berkeley: University of California Press.

Hyden, Goran, and Donald C. Williams. 1994. "A Community Model of African Politics: Illustrations from Nigeria and Tanzania." *Comparative Studies in Society and History* 36: 68–96.

Ibhawoh, Bonny, and J.I. Dibua. 2003. "Deconstructing Ujamaa: The Legacy of Julius Nyerere in the Quest for Social and Economic Development in Africa." *African Journal of Political Science* 8: 59–83.

Igoe, Jim. 2006. "Becoming Indigenous Peoples: Difference, Inequality, and the Globalization of East African Identity Politics." *African Affairs* 105: 399–420.

———. 2005. "Global Indigenism and Spaceship Earth: Convergence, Space, and Re-Entry Friction." *Globalizations* 2: 377–90.

———. 2003. "Scaling up Civil Society: Donor Money, Ngos and the Pastoralist Land Rights Movement in Tanzania." *Development and Change* 34: 863–85.

International Development Law Organization (IDLO). 2011. "Legal Preparedness for REDD+ in Mexico: A Case Study." Rome: IDLO and Food and Agriculture Organization of the United Nations.

International Fund for Agricultural Development (IFAD). Rural Poverty Report 2001, Oxford, UK: Oxford University Press.

Iyengar, S., and N. Shukla. 1999. "Regeneration and Management of Common Property Land Resources (CPLRs) in India: A Review." Working Paper No. 110. Ahmedabad: Gujarat Institute of Development Research.

Jaffrelot, Christophe. 1999. *The Hindu Nationalist Movement and Indian Politics: 1925 to the 1990s; Strategies of Identity-Building, Implantation and Mobilisation (with Special Reference to Central India)*. New Delhi: Penguin Books.

Jagger, Pamela, Kathleen Lawlor, Maria Brockhaus, Maria Fernanda Gebara, Denis Jean Sonwa, and Ida Aju Pradnja Resosudarmo. 2012. "REDD+ Safeguards in National Policy Discourse and Pilot Projects." In *Analysing REDD+: Challenges and Choices*, eds. Arild Angelsen, Maria Brockhaus, William D. Sunderlin, and Louis V. Verchot. Bogor Barat, Indonesia: Center for International Forestry Research. 301–16.

Janu, C.K. 2003. "The South Indian Adivasi Experience in the Nagarhole National Park and the Muthanga Wild Life Sanctuary." Paper presented at the Vth World Parks Congress, Durban, 1 September, 2003.

Jayal, Niraja Gopal. 2001. "Balancing Political and Ecological Values." *Environmental Politics* 10: 65–88.

Jayasuriya, Kanishka. 2005. "Beyond Institutional Fetishism: From the Developmental to the Regulatory State." *New Political Economy* 10: 381–87.

Jeffery, Charlie. 2008. "The Challenge of Territorial Politics." *Policy & Politics* 36: 545–57.

Jenkins, J. Craig. 1983. "Resource Mobilization Theory and the Study of Social Movements." *Annual Review of Sociology* 9: 527–53.

Jenkins, Rob. 1999. *Democratic Politics and Economic Reform in India*. Cambridge, UK: Cambridge University Press.

Jewitt, Sarah. 2008. "Political Ecology of Jharkhand Conflicts." *Asia Pacific Viewpoint* 49: 68–82.

———. 1995. "Europe's 'Others'? Forestry Policy and Practices in Colonial and Postcolonial India." *Environment and Planning D: Society and Space* 13: 67–90.

Jodha, N.S. 1986. "Common Property Resources and the Rural Poor in Dry Regions of India." *Economic and Political Weekly* 21: 1169–81.

Johansson, Tino. 2008. "Beasts on Fields. Human-Wildlife Conflicts in Nature-Culture Borderlands." Ph.D. dissertation. University of Helsinki.

Johnson, Craig. 2004. "Uncommon Ground: The 'Poverty of History' in Common Property Discourse." *Development and Change* 35: 407–34.

Johnson, Craig, and Timothy Forsyth. 2002. "In the Eyes of the State: Negotiating a 'Rights-Based Approach' to Forest Conservation in Thailand." *World Development* 30: 1591–605.

Joireman, Sandra Fullerton. 2011. *Where There Is No Government: Enforcing Property Rights in Common Law Africa*. Oxford and New York: Oxford University Press.

Joseph, G.M., T.J. Henderson, R. Kirk, and O. Starn. 2009. *The Mexico Reader: History, Culture, Politics*. Durham and London: Duke University Press.

Joseph, S. 2006. "Power of the People: Political Mobilisation and Guaranteed Employment." *Economic and Political Weekly* 41: 5149.

Joshi, Anuradha. 2010. "Do Rights Work? Law, Activism, and the Employment Guarantee Scheme." *World Development* 38: 620–30.

———. 2000. "Roots of Change: Front Line Workers and Forest Policy Reform in West Bengal." Ph.D. dissertation. Massachusetts Institute of Technology.

———. 1999. "Progressive Bureaucracy: An Oxymoron? The Case of Joint Forest Management in India." Rural Development Forestry Network Paper 24a Winter 98/99. London: Overseas Development Institute.

Joshi, Anuradha, and Mick Moore. 2000. "Enabling Environments: Do Anti-Poverty Programmes Mobilise the Poor?" *Journal of Development Studies* 37: 25–56.

Joshi, Sapan. 2003. "Deep in the Woods." *Down to Earth* January 15.

Juffe-Bignoli, D., N.D. Burgess, H. Bingham, E.M.S. Belle, M.G. de Lima, M. Deguignet, B. Bertzky, A.N. Milam, J. Martinez-Lopez, E. Lewis, A. Eassom, S. Wicander, J. Geldmann, A. van Soesbergen, A.P. Arnell, B. O'Connor, S. Park, Y.N. Shi, F.S. Danks, B. MacSharry, N. Kingston. 2014. *Protected Planet Report 2014*. Cambridge, UK: The United Nations Environment Programme World Conservation Monitoring Centre (UNEP-WCMC).

Jung, Courtney. 2008. *The Moral Force of Indigenous Politics: Critical Liberalism and the Zapatistas*. Cambridge, UK, and New York: Cambridge University Press.

Kaimowitz, D. 2000. "Forestry Assistance and Tropical Deforestation: Why the Public Doesn't Get What It Pays For." *International Forestry Review* 2: 225–31.

Kaimowitz, David. 2002. "Amazon Deforestation Revisited." *Latin American Research Review* 37: 221–35.

Kalpavriksh. 2000. *Adivasi Rights, Environment and the Law: Selected Readings*. National Conference on Human Rights, Social Movements, Globalisation, and the Law, Panchgani, India.

———. 2002. "The Forest Encroachment Issue: A Briefing Note." Kalpvriksh, New Delhi.

Kangalawe, Richard Y.M., and Christine Noe. 2012. "Biodiversity Conservation and Poverty Alleviation in Namtumbo District, Tanzania." *Agriculture, Ecosystems & Environment* 162: 90–100.

Kashwan, Prakash. 2016a. "Integrating Power in Institutional Analysis: A Micro-Foundation Perspective." *Journal of Theoretical Politics* 28: 5–26.

———. 2016b. "Power Asymmetries and Institutions: Landscape Conservation in Central India." *Regional Environmental Change*: 1–13. doi: https://doi.org/10.1007/s10113-015-0925-8.

———. 2015. "Forest Policy, Institutions, and REDD+ in India, Tanzania, and Mexico." *Global Environmental Politics* 15: 95–117.

———. 2014. "Botched-up Development and Electoral Politics in India." *Economic & Political Weekly* XLIX 48–55.

———. 2013. "The Politics of Rights-Based Approaches in Conservation." *Land Use Policy* 31: 613–26.

———. 2011. "Democracy in the Woods: The Politics of Institutional Change in India's Forest Areas." Ph.D. dissertation. Indiana University, Bloomington.

Kashwan, Prakash, and Robert Holahan. 2014. "Nested Governance for Effective REDD+: Institutional and Political Arguments." *International Journal of the Commons* 8: 554–75.

Kashwan, Prakash, and Timothy R. Bussey. 2017. "Taming a Machiavellian State? International Environmental Governance and Domestic Policymaking in India and Mexico." In *Handbook of Environmental Governance*, ed. Alka Sapat. New York, NY: Routledge.

Kashwan, Prakash, and Viren Lobo. 2014. "Of Rights and Regeneration: The Politics of Governing Forest and Non-Forest Commons" In *Democratizing Forest Governance*, eds. Sharachchandra Lélé and Ajit Menon. New Delhi: Oxford University Press. 349–75.

Katzenstein, Mary Fainsod. 2003. "Redividing Citizens Divided Feminisms: The Reconfigured U.S. State and Womens Citizenship." In *Women's Movements Facing the Reconfigured State*, eds. Lee Ann Banaszak, Karen Beckwith, and Dieter Rucht. Cambridge, UK: Cambridge University Press. 203–18.

Katznelson, Ira, and Barry R. Weingast. 2005. *Preferences and Situations: Points of Intersection between Historical and Rational Choice Institutionalism*. New York: Russell Sage Foundation.

Kauffman, Paul Richard. 1983. "Brokers of Status: The Development of Bhakti (Devotion) and Sarkar (Government) by Bhils of Southern Rajasthan." Ph.D. dissertation. Australian National University.

Kay, Cristóbal. 2002. "Why East Asia Overtook Latin America: Agrarian Reform, Industrialisation and Development." *Third World Quarterly* 23: 1073–102.

Kelly, Alice B. 2011. "Conservation Practice as Primitive Accumulation." *Journal of Peasant Studies* 38: 683–701.

Kelly, James J. 1994. "Article 27 and Mexican Land Reform: The Legacy of Zapata's Dream." *Columbia Human Rights Law Review* 25: 541.

Kelsall, Tim. 2000. "Governance, Local Politics and Districtization in Tanzania: The 1998 Arumeru Tax Revolt." *African Affairs* 99: 533–51.

———. 2002. "Shop Windows and Smoke-Filled Rooms: Governance and the Re-Politicisation of Tanzania." *The Journal of Modern African Studies* 40: 597–619.

Khare, A., M. Sarin, N.C. Saxena, S. Palit, S. Bathla, F. Vania, and M Satyanarayana. 2000. "Joint Forest Management: Policy, Practice and Prospects." London: International Institute for Environment and Development.

Kijima, Yoko. 2006. "Caste and Tribe Inequality: Evidence from India, 1983-1999." *Economic Development and Cultural Change* 54: 369–404.

Kingstone, Peter. 2011. *The Political Economy of Latin America: Reflections on Neoliberalism and Development*. New York and London: Routledge.

Kitschelt, H., and S. Wilkinson. 2007. *Patrons, Clients, and Policies: Patterns of Democratic Accountability and Political Competition*. New York: Cambridge University Press.

Kitschelt, Herbert. 2000. "Linkage between Citizens and Politicians in Democratic Polities." *Comparative Political Studies* 33: 845–79.

Kjosavik, Darley J. 2006. "Articulating Identities in the Struggle for Land: The Case of the Indigenous People (Adivasis) of Highland Kerala, South India." Paper presented at the International Symposium–At the Frontier of Land Issues: Social Embeddedness of Rights and Public Policy, Montpellier, France.

Kleinman, P.J.A., D. Pimentel, and R.B. Bryant. 1995. "The Ecological Sustainability of Slash-and-Burn Agriculture." *Agriculture, Ecosystems & Environment* 52: 235–49.

Klemm, Cyrille de, and Clare Shine. 1993. *Biological Diversity Conservation and the Law: Legal Mechanisms for Conserving Species and Ecosystems*, Environmental Policy and Law Paper No. 29: IUCN—The World Conservation Union.

Klooster, Dan. 2003. "*Campesinos* and Mexican Forest Policy During the Twentieth Century." *Latin American Research Review* 38: 94–126.

———. 2000. "Institutional Choice, Community, and Struggle: A Case Study of Forest Co-Management in Mexico." *World Development* 28: 1–20.

Klooster, Daniel, and Omar Masera. 2000. "Community Forest Management in Mexico: Carbon Mitigation and Biodiversity Conservation through Rural Development." *Global Environmental Change* 10: 259–72.

Knight, Alan. 1994. "Peasants into Patriots: Thoughts on the Making of the Mexican Nation." *Mexican Studies/Estudios Mexicanos* 10: 135–61.

Knight, Jack. 1992. *Institutions and Social Conflict*. New York: Cambridge University Press.

Kohli, A. 2016. *The State and Development in the Third World: A "World Politics" Reader*. Princeton, NJ: Princeton University Press.

Kohli, Atul. 1987. *The State and Poverty in India*. Cambridge, UK: Cambridge University Press.

Kothari, Rajni. 1970. *Politics in India*. New Delhi, India: Orient Blackswan.

———. 1964. "The Congress 'System' in India." *Asian Survey* 4 (12): 1161–73.

Krishan, Shree. 2005. *Political Mobilization and Identity in Western India: 1934-1947*. New Delhi: Sage Publications.

Krishna, Sankaran. 2015. "Number Fetish: Middle-Class India's Obsession with the GDP." *Globalizations* 12 (6): 859–71.

Kubik, Jan. 2009. "Ethnography of Politics: Foundations, Applications, Prospects." In *Political Ethnography: What Immersion Contributes to the Study of Power*, ed. Edward Schatz. Chicago: University of Chicago Press. 25–52.

Kulkarni, Sharad. 1987. "Forest Legislation and Tribals: Comments on Forest Policy Resolution." *Economic and Political Weekly* 22: 2143–48.

———. 1982. "Encroachment on Forests: Government Versus People." *Economic and Political Weekly* 17: 55–59.

Kumar, Kundan, and John M. Kerr. 2013. "Territorialisation and Marginalisation in the Forested Landscapes of Orissa, India." *Land Use Policy* 30: 885–94.

———. 2012. "Democratic Assertions: The Making of India's Recognition of Forest Rights Act." *Development and Change* 43: 751–71.

Kumar, Kundan, Neera M. Singh, and John M. Kerr. 2015. "Decentralisation and Democratic Forest Reforms in India: Moving to a Rights-Based Approach." *Forest Policy and Economics* 51: 1–8.

Kumar, Sanjay. 2002. "Does 'Participation' in Common Pool Resource Management Help the Poor? A Social Cost-Benefit Analysis of Joint Forest Management in Jharkhand, India." *World Development* 30: 763–82.

Kumar, Sushil and Shashi Kant. 2005. "Bureaucracy and New Management Paradigms: Modeling Foresters' Perceptions Regarding Community-Based Forest Management in India." *Forest Policy and Economics* 7: 651–69.

Kurtz, Marcus J. 2006. *Free Market Democracy and the Chilean and Mexican Countryside.* Cambridge, U.K. and New York: Cambridge University Press.

Kurup, Apoorv. 2008. "Tribal Law in India: How Decentralized Administration Is Extinguishing Tribal Rights and Why Autonomous Tribal Governments Are Better." *Indigenous Law Journal* 7: 87.

Kweka, D. 2013. *REDD+ Politics in the Media: A Case Study from Tanzania.* Bogor, Indonesia: Center for International Forestry Research (CIFOR).

Lane, Charles R. 1994. "Pastures Lost: Alienation of Barabaig Land in the Context of Land Policy and Legislation in Tanzania." *Nomadic Peoples* 34/35: 81–94.

Lange, Matthew K. 2004. "British Colonial Legacies and Political Development." *World Development* 32: 905–22.

Lange, Matthew, James Mahoney, and Matthias vom Hau. 2006. "Colonialism and Development: A Comparative Analysis of Spanish and British Colonies." *American Journal of Sociology* 111 (5): 1412–62.

Lange, Siri. 2008. "The Depoliticisation of Development and the Democratisation of Politics in Tanzania: Parallel Structures as Obstacles to Delivering Services to the Poor." *Journal of Development Studies* 44: 1122–44.

Larson, Anne M. 2011. "Forest Tenure Reform in the Age of Climate Change: Lessons for REDD+." *Global Environmental Change* 21: 540–49.

———. 2010. "The 'Demonization' of Rainforest Migrants, Or: What Conservation Means to Poor Colonist Farmers" In *Beyond the Biophysical*, eds. Laura A. German, Joshua J. Ramisch, and Ritu Verma. Dordrecht, Heidelberg, London, and New York: Springer. 49–71.

Larson, Anne M., D. Barry, and Ganga Ram Dahal. 2010. "New Rights for Forest-Based Communities? Understanding Processes of Forest Tenure Reform." *International Forestry Review* 12: 78–96.

Larson, Anne, and Jesse Ribot. 2007. "The Poverty of Forestry Policy: Double Standards on an Uneven Playing Field." *Sustainability Science* 2: 189–204.

Larson, Anne M., Maria Brockhaus, William D. Sunderlin, Amy Duchelle, Andrea Babon, Therese Dokken, Thu Thuy Pham, I.A.P. Resosudarmo, Galia Selaya, Abdon Awono, and Thu-Ba Huynh. 2013. "Land Tenure and REDD+: The Good, the Bad and the Ugly." *Global Environmental Change* 23: 678–89.

Lawlor, Kathleen, Erika Weinthal, and Lydia Olander. 2010. "Institutions and Policies to Protect Rural Livelihoods in REDD+ Regimes." *Global Environmental Politics* 10: 1–11.

Lawrence, Deborah, Claudia Radel, Katherine Tully, Birgit Schmook, and Laura Schneider. 2010. "Untangling a Decline in Tropical Forest Resilience: Constraints on the Sustainability of Shifting Cultivation across the Globe." *Biotropica* 42: 21–30.

Leach, Melissa, and Robin Mearns. 1996. *The Lie of the Land: Challenging Received Wisdom on the African Environment.* Oxford and Portsmouth, NH: International African Institute in association with James Currey.

Leach, Melissa, Robin Mearns, and Ian Scoones. 1999. "Environmental Entitlements: Dynamics and Institutions in Community-Based Natural Resource Management." *World Development* 27: 225–47.

Leblond, Jean-Philippe. 2010. "Population Displacement and Forest Management in Thailand." Working Paper No. 8. Montreal. Canada Research Chair in Asian Studies--Université de Montréal.

Leblond, Jean-Philippe, and Thanh Hai Pham. 2014. "Recent Forest Expansion in Thailand: A Methodological Artifact?" *Journal of Land Use Science* 9: 211–41.

Lederer, Markus. 2011. "From CDM to REDD+ — What Do We Know for Setting up Effective and Legitimate Carbon Governance?" *Ecological Economics* 70: 1900–07.

Lélé, Sharachchandra. 2007. "A 'defining' moment for Forests?" *Economic and Political Weekly* 42 (25): 2379–83.

———. 2004. "Beyond State-Community Polarisations and Bogus 'Joint'Ness: Crafting Institutional Solutions for Resource Management." In *Globalisation, Poverty and Conflict: A Critical "Development" Reader*, ed. Max Spoor. Dordrecht: Kluwer Academic Publishers.

———. 2000. *Godsend, Sleight of Hand, or Just Muddling Through: Joint Water and Forest Management in India.* London: Overseas Development Institute.

———. 1999. "Institutional Issues in (J)Fm (and R)." Paper presented at the National Workshop on JFM organized by Vikram Sarabhai Centre for Development Interaction (VIKSAT), Ahmedabad.

———. 1998. "Why, Who, and How of Jointness in Joint Forest Management: Theoretical Considerations and Empirical Insights from the Western Ghats of Karnataka." Paper presented at the International Workshop on Shared Resource Management in South Asia, Anand, Gujarat.

Lélé, Sharachachandra, and Ajit Menon, eds. 2014. *Democratizing Forest Governance.* New Delhi: Oxford University Press.

Lélé, Sharachachandra, and R. Jagannath Rao. 1996a. "Re-Lighting Lamps: A Draft Action Plan for Revitalizing the Tribal Cooperatives in Karnataka." In *Rediscovering Cooperation*, ed. R. Rajagopalan. Anand, Gujarat: Institute of Rural Management. 92–105.

———. 1996b. "Whose Co-Operatives and Whose Produce? The Case of Lamps in Karnataka." In *Rediscovering Cooperation*, ed. R. Rajagopalan. Anand: Institute of Rural Management, 53–97.

Lemos, Maria Carmen, and Arun Agrawal. 2006. "Environmental Governance." *Annual Review of Environment and Resources* 31: 297–325.

Levien, Michael. 2013. "The Politics of Dispossession Theorizing India's 'Land Wars'." *Politics & Society* 41 (3): 351–94.

Levine, Arielle. 2002. "Convergence or Convenience? International Conservation Ngos and Development Assistance in Tanzania." *World Development* 30: 1043–55.

Levy, Santiago, and Michael Walton. 2009. *No Growth without Equity?: Inequality, Interests, and Competition in Mexico.* Washington, DC: World Bank Publications.

Lewis, G. Malcolm. 1998. *Cartographic Encounters: Perspectives on Native American Mapmaking and Map Use.* Chicago: University of Chicago Press.

Lewis, Michael. 2003. "Cattle and Conservation at Bharatpur: A Case Study in Science and Advocacy." *Conservation and Society* 1: 1.

Li, Tania Murray. 2010. "To Make Live or Let Die? Rural Dispossession and the Protection of Surplus Populations." *Antipode* 41: 66–93.

———. 2007. "Practices of Assemblage and Community Forest Management." *Economy and Society* 36: 263–93.

———. 2005. "Beyond 'the State' and Failed Schemes." *American Anthropologist* 107: 383–94.

———. 1996. "Images of Community: Discourse and Strategy in Property Relations." *Development and Change* 27: 501–27.

Lobo, Brian. 2011. *A Status of Adivasis/Indigenous: Maharashtra.* Vol. 3, Peoples Land Series. New Delhi: Aakar Books.

Locke, J. 1986 (1690). *Second Treatise of Government.* London: Prometheus Books.

Lockhart, James. 1969. "Encomienda and Hacienda: The Evolution of the Great Estate in the Spanish Indies." *Hispanic American Historical Review* 49 (3): 411–29.

Lofchie, Michael F. 2014. *The Political Economy of Tanzania: Decline and Recovery.* Philadelphia: University of Pennsylvania Press.

———. 2013. "The Roots of Civic Peace in Tanzania." In *The Economic Roots of Conflict and Cooperation in Africa*, eds. William Ascher and Natalia Mirovitskaya. New York: Palgrave Macmillan. 107–39.

Louis, P. 2006. "The Scheduled Tribes." In *Alternative Economic Survey, India 2005–06: Disempowering Masses.* New Delhi: Daanish Books.

Lövbrand, Eva, Johannes Stripple, and Bo Wiman. 2009. "Earth System Governmentality: Reflections on Science in the Anthropocene." *Global Environmental Change* 19: 7–13.

Lovett, Jon C. 2003. "The Forest Act, 2002 (Tanzania)." *Journal of African Law* 47: 133–35.

Ludden, D. 1999. *An Agrarian History of South Asia.* New York: Cambridge University Press.

Luna, Juan P., and Elizabeth J. Zechmeister. 2005. "Political Representation in Latin America: A Study of Elite-Mass Congruence in Nine Countries." *Comparative Political Studies* 38: 388–416.

Lund, C. 2008. *Local Politics and the Dynamics of Property in Africa.* New York: Cambridge University Press.

Lund, Jens Friis, and Moeko Saito-Jensen. 2013. "Revisiting the Issue of Elite Capture of Participatory Initiatives." *World Development* 46: 104–12.

Lunstrum, Elizabeth, Pablo Bose, and Anna Zalik. 2015. "Environmental Displacement: The Common Ground of Climate Change, Extraction and Conservation." *Area* 48 (2): 130–133.

Lyster, Rosemary. 2011. "REDD+, Transparency, Participation and Resource Rights: The Role of Law." *Environmental Science and Policy* 14: 118–26.

MacKenzie, John M. 1997. *The Empire of Nature: Hunting, Conservation and British Imperialism*. Manchester and New York: Manchester University Press.

MacLean, Lauren M. 2010. *Informal Institutions and Citizenship in Rural Africa: Risk and Reciprocity in Ghana and Cote D'Ivoire*. New York: Cambridge University Press.

MacLeod, Murdo J. 2008. *Spanish Central America: A Socioeconomic History, 1520-1720*. Austin, TX: University of Texas Press.

Macura, Biljana, Francisco Zorondo-Rodríguez, Mar Grau-Satorras, Kathryn Demps, Marie Laval, Claude A. Garcia, and Victoria Reyes-García. 2011. "Local Community Attitudes toward Forests Outside Protected Areas in India. Impact of Legal Awareness, Trust, and Participation." *Ecology and Society* 16: 10.

Maddox, G.H, and James L. Giblin, eds. 2006. *In Search of a Nation. Histories of Authority & Dissidence in Tanzania*. Oxford: James Currey.

Madrid, L., J.M. Núñez, G. Quiróz, and Y. Rodríguez. 2009. "La propiedad social forestal en México." *Investigaciones Ambientales* 1(2): 179–96.

Madrid, Miguel de la. 1984. "Mexico: The New Challenges." *Foreign Affairs* 63: 62–76.

Magaloni, Beatriz, Alberto Diaz-Cayeros, and Federico Estévez. 2007. "Clientelism and Portfolio Diversification: A Model of Electoral Investment with Applications to Mexico." In *Patrons, Clients, and Policies: Patterns of Democratic Accountability and Political Competition*, eds. H. Kitschelt and S. Wilkinson. New York: Cambridge University Press. 182–205.

Magaloni, Beatriz, and Ruth Kricheli. 2010. "Political Order and One-Party Rule." *Annual Review of Political Science* 13: 123–43.

Mahoney, James. 2000. "Path Dependence in Historical Sociology." *Theory and Society* 29: 507–48.

Mahoney, James, and Kathleen Ann Thelen. 2010. *Explaining Institutional Change: Ambiguity, Agency, and Power*. New York: Cambridge University Press.

Mallon, Florencia E. 1994. "Reflections on the Ruins: Everyday Forms of State Formation in Nineteenth-Century Mexico." In *Everyday Forms of State Formation: Revolution and the Negotiation of Rule in Modern Mexico*, eds. G.M. Joseph and Daniel Nugent. Durham, NC: Duke University Press.

Malloy, J. 1976. *Authoritarianism and Corporatism in Latin America*. Pittsburg: University of Pittsburgh Press.

Mallya, Ernest T. 2009. *Promoting the Effectiveness of Democracy Protection: Institutions in Southern Africa Tanzania's Commission for Human Rights and Good Governance*. Johannesburg: Electoral Institute for Sustainable Democracy in Africa.

———. 1999. "Civil Society and the Land Question in Tanzania." Report for the Department of Political Science and Public Administration, University of Dar es Salaam, Tanzania.

Mamdani, Mahmood. 1996. *Citizen and Subject: Contemporary Africa and the Legacy of Late Colonialism*. Princeton, NJ: Princeton University Press.

———. 1985. "A Great Leap Backwards: A Review of Goran Hyden's No Shortcut to Progress." *Ufahamu: A Journal of African Studies* 14 (2): 178–94.

Manor, James. 2004. "The Congress Defeat in Madhya Pradesh." *Seminar* 534. http://www.india-seminar.com/2004/534/534%20james%20manor.htm.

Manyika, Kanizio Fredrick, and Mary Gorret Nantongo. 2012. "Emerging Institutional Structures for Implementing REDD+ at National and Local Level in Tanzania." Term paper for the 2nd Thor Heyerdahl Summer School in Environmental Governance, June 26–6 July 2012. Ås, Norway: Norwegian University of Life Sciences.

March, James G., and Johan P. Olsen. 1996. "Institutional Perspectives on Political Institutions." *Governance* 9: 247–64.

———. 1984. "The New Institutionalism: Organizational Factors in Political Life." *The American Political Science Review* 78: 734–49.

Marcus, George E. 1995. "Ethnography in/of the World System: The Emergence of Multi-Sited Ethnography." *Annual Review of Anthropology* 24: 95–117.

Martinez-Alier, Joan. 2014. "The Environmentalism of the Poor." *Geoforum* 54: 239–41.

Mathews, Andrew S. 2011. *Instituting Nature: Authority, Expertise, and Power in Mexican Forests*. Cambridge, MA: MIT Press.

Mathews, Andrew Salvador. 2002. "Mexican Forest History." *Journal of Sustainable Forestry* 15: 17–28.

Mathur, Hari Mohan. 2009. "Investor-Friendly Development Policies: Unsettling Consequences for the Tribal People of Orissa." *The Asia Pacific Journal of Anthropology* 10: 318–28.

Matland, R.E. 1995. "Synthesizing the Implementation Literature: The Ambiguity-Conflict Model of Policy Implementation." *Journal of Public Administration Research and Theory* 5: 145.

Matose, Frank. 1997. "Conflicts around Forest Reserves in Zimbabwe: What Prospects for Community Management?" *IDS Bulletin* 28: 69–78.

Mawdsley, Emma, Deepshikha Mehra, and Kim Beazley. 2009. "Nature Lovers, Picnickers and Bourgeois Environmentalism." *Economic and Political Weekly*: 49–59.

McAfee, Kathleen, and Elizabeth N. Shapiro. 2010. "Payments for Ecosystem Services in Mexico: Nature, Neoliberalism, Social Movements, and the State." *Annals of the Association of American Geographers* 100: 579–99.

McAuslan, Patrick. 1998. "Making Law Work: Restructuring Land Relations in Africa." *Development & Change* 29: 525.

McBride, George McCutchen. 1923. *The Land Systems of Mexico*. New York: American Geographical Society.

McDermott, Constance L., Lauren Coad, Ariella Helfgott, and Heike Schroeder. 2012. "Operationalizing Social Safeguards in REDD+: Actors, Interests and Ideas." *Environmental Science & Policy* 21: 63–72.

McDowell, Chris. 1996. *Understanding Impoverishment: The Consequences of Development-Induced Displacement*. Vol. 2. Providence, RI and Oxford: Berghahn Books.

McEldowney, Philip. 1980. "Colonial Administration and Social Developments in Middle India: The Central Provinces, 1986-1921." Ph.D. dissertation. Virginia Tech.

McElwee, Pamela D. 2012. "Payments for Environmental Services as Neoliberal Market-Based Forest Conservation in Vietnam: Panacea or Problem?" *Geoforum* 43: 412–26.

McElwee, Pamela, Tuyen Nghiem, Hue Le, Huong Vu, and Nghi Tran. 2014. "Payments for Environmental Services and Contested Neoliberalisation in Developing Countries: A Case Study from Vietnam." *Journal of Rural Studies* 36: 423–40.

McGuire, James W. 2010. *Wealth, Health, and Democracy in East Asia and Latin America*. New York: Cambridge University Press.

Meadowcroft, James. 2005. "From Welfare State to Ecostate." In *The State and the Global Ecological Crisis*, eds. J. Barry and R. Eckersley. London and Cambridge, MA: MIT Press. 3–24.

Meirovich, Hilen Gabriela. 2014. "The Politics of Climate in Developing Countries: The Case of Mexico." Ph.D. dissertation. Georgetown University.

Melville, Elinor G.K. 1994. *A Plague of Sheep: Environmental Consequences of the Conquest of Mexico*. Cambridge, UK: Cambridge University Press.

Menon, Ajit. 2007. "Engaging with the Law on Adivasi Rights." *Economic and Political Weekly* 42 (24): 2239–42.

———. 2004. "Colonial Constructions of 'Agrarian Fields' and 'Forests' in the Kolli Hills." *Indian Economic Social History Review* 41: 315–37.

Menon, Ajit, and C.R. Bijoy. 2014. "The Limits to Law, Democracy and Governance." *Yojana* 58: 9–12.

Menon, Ajit, Christelle Hinnewinkel, and Sylvie Guillerme. 2013. "Denuded Forests, Wooded Estates: Statemaking in a Janmam Area of Gudalur, Tamil Nadu." *Indian Economic & Social History Review* 50: 449–71.

Merino-Perez, Leticia. 2013. "Conservation and Forest Communities in Mexico: Experiences, Visions, and Rights." In *Community Action for Conservation: Mexican Experiences*, eds. Luciana Porter-Bolland, Isabel Ruiz-Mallén, Claudia Camacho-Benavides, and Susannah R. McCandless. New York: Springer. 25–44.

Merton, Robert King. 1949. "On Sociological Theories of the Middle Range." In *Classical Sociological Theory*, ed. Craig Calhoun. Malden, MA: Blackwell Publishing. 531–42.

Mertz, Ole. 2009. "Trends in Shifting Cultivation and the REDD Mechanism." *Current Opinion in Environmental Sustainability* 1: 156–60.

Mertz, Ole, Kelvin Egay, ThildeBech Bruun, and TinaSvan Colding. 2013. "The Last Swiddens of Sarawak, Malaysia." *Human Ecology* 41: 109–18.

Mertz, Ole, Stephen J. Leisz, Andreas Heinimann, Kanok Rerkasem, Thiha, Wolfram Dressler, Van Cu Pham, Kim Chi Vu, Dietrich Schmidt-Vogt, Carol J.P. Colfer, Michael Epprecht, Christine Padoch, and Lesley Potter. 2009. "Who Counts? Demography of Swidden Cultivators in Southeast Asia." *Human Ecology* 37: 281–89.

Migdal, Joel S. 2001. *State in Society: Studying How States and Societies Transform and Constitute One Another*, Cambridge Studies in Comparative Politics. Cambridge, UK, and New York: Cambridge University Press.

Migdal, Joel Samuel, Atul Kohli, and Vivienne Shue. 1994. *State Power and Social Forces: Domination and Transformation in the Third World*. New York: Cambridge University Press.

Ministry of Environment and Forests (MoEF). 2014. *National REDD+ Policy & Strategy: Zero Draft*.

———. 2013. *Reference Document for REDD+ in India*.

———. 2006. *Report of the National Forest Commission*.

———. 2004. "Affidavit on Behalf of Ministry of Environment and Forests." Government of India, in the Supreme Court of India. I.A. No.1126 in Writ Petition (Civil) No. 202 of 1995.

Ministry of Tribal Affairs (MoTA). 2016. Status Report on Implementation of the Scheduled Tribes and Other Traditional Forest Dwellers (Recognition of Forest Rights) Act, 2006 [for the period ending 30th April 2016].

———. 2014. Status Report on Implementation of the Scheduled Tribes and Other Traditional Forest Dwellers (Recognition of Forest Rights) Act, 2006 [for the period ending 31st December 2014].

———. 2012. Status Report on Implementation of the Scheduled Tribes and Other Traditional Forest Dwellers (Recognition of Forest Rights) Act, 2006 [for the period ending 30th April, 2012].

Mirchandani, G.G. 1977. *Subverting the Constitution*. New Delhi: Abhinav Publications.

Mitchell, Ronald B. 2001. "Institutional Aspects of Implementation, Compliance, and Effectiveness." In *International Relations and Global Climate Change*, eds. Urs Luterbacher and Detlef F. Sprinz. Boston, MA: MIT Press. 221–44.

Mitchell, Ross E. 2006. "Environmental Governance in Mexico: Two Case Studies of Oaxaca's Community Forest Sector." *Journal of Latin American Studies* 38: 519–48.

Mitchell, T. 2002. *Rule of Experts: Egypt, Techno-Politics, Modernity.* Berkeley, Los Angeles, and London: University of California Press.

Moe, T.M. 2005. "Power and Political Institutions." *Perspectives on Politics* 3: 215.

Moeliono, Moira, Caleb Gallemore, Levania Santoso, Maria Brockhaus, and Monica Di Gregorio. 2014. "Information Networks and Power: Confronting the 'Wicked Problem' of REDD+ in Indonesia." *Ecology and Society: a journal of integrative science for resilience and sustainability* 19 (2): 9. http://www.ecologyandsociety.org/vol19/iss2/art9/.

Mombeshora, Solomon. 2000. *Agrarian Change in Tanzania.* Avondale, Zimbabwe: Mond Books.

Moore, Sally Falk. 1973. "Law and Social Change: The Semi-Autonomous Social Field as an Appropriate Subject of Study." *Law & Society Review* 7: 719–46.

Moosvi, Shireen. 2011. "The World of Labour in Mughal India (C.1500-1750)." *International Review of Social History* 56: 245–61.

Morse, Yonatan L. 2014. "Party Matters: The Institutional Origins of Competitive Hegemony in Tanzania." *Democratization* 21: 655–77.

Mosse, David. 2010. "A Relational Approach to Durable Poverty, Inequality and Power." *Journal of Development Studies* 46: 1156–78.

Mosse, David, Sanjeev Gupta, Mona Mehta, Vidya Shah, and Julia Rees. 2002. "Brokered Livelihoods: Debt, Labour Migration and Development in Tribal Western India." *Journal of Development Studies* 38: 59–88.

Mountfort, Guy. 1983. "Project Tiger: A Review." *Oryx* 17: 32–33.

Mulé, Rosa. 1999. "New Institutionalism: Distilling Some 'Hard Core' propositions in the Works of Williamson and March and Olsen." *Politics* 19: 145–51.

Mumme, Stephen P. 2007. "Trade Integration, Neoliberal Reform, and Environmental Protection in Mexico Lessons for the Americas." *Latin American Perspectives* 34: 91–107.

Muñoz-Piña, Carlos, Alain deJanvry, and Elisabeth Sadoulet. 2003. "Recrafting Rights over Common Property Resources in Mexico." *Economic Development & Cultural Change* 52: 129–58.

Nachmany, Michal, Samuel Fankhauser, Terry Townshend, Murray Collins, Tucker Landesman, Adam Matthews, Carolina Pavese, Katharina Rietig, Philip Schleifer, and Joana Setzer. 2014. *The Globe Climate Legislation Study: A Review of Climate Change Legislation in 66 Countries.* London: GLOBE International and Grantham Research Institute, London School of Economics.

Nagesh, H.V. 1981. "Forms of Un-Free Labour in Indian Agriculture." *Economic and Political Weekly* 16: A109-A15.

Naidu, Sirisha C. 2009. "Heterogeneity and Collective Management: Evidence from Common Forests in Himachal Pradesh, India." *World Development* 37: 676–86.

Nash, Roderick Frazier. 2014 (1967). *Wilderness and the American Mind.* New Haven and London: Yale University Press.

National Committee on Forest Rights Act (NCFRA). 2010. "Manthan: Report of the National Committee on Forest Rights Act (NCFRA)." New Delhi: Ministry of Environment and Forests and Ministry of Tribal Affairs.

Navarro-Olmedo, Santana, Nora Haenn, Birgit Schmook, and Claudia Radel. 2015. "The Legacy of Mexico's Agrarian Counter Reforms: Reinforcing Social Hierarchies in Calakmul, Campeche." *Journal of Agrarian Change* 16 (1): 145–67.

Nayar, Baldev Raj. 2005. "India in 2004: Regime Change in a Divided Democracy." *Asian Survey* 45: 71–82.

Negi, Neeraj Kumar, Radhey Shyam Sharma, and Bhim Raj. 2004. "Joint Forest Management in Rajasthan: Its Spread, Performance and Impact." In *Joint Forest Management in India: Spread, Performance and Impact*, eds. N.H. Ravindranath and P. Sudha. Hyderabad: Universities Press. 122–44.

Negretto, Gabriel L. and José Antonio Aguilar-Rivera. 2000. "Rethinking the Legacy of the Liberal State in Latin America: The Cases of Argentina (1853-1916) and Mexico (1857-1910)." *Journal of Latin American Studies* 32: 361–97.

Nehru, J. 1967. *Jawaharlal Nehru's Speeches*. Vol. 2. New Delhi: Publications Division, Ministry of Information and Broadcasting.

Nelson, Fred. 2011. "Blessing or Curse? The Political Economy of Tourism Development in Tanzania." *Journal of Sustainable Tourism* 20: 359–75.

———. 2004. "The evolution and impacts of community-based ecotourism in northern Tanzania." Drylands Programme Issue Paper 131. London: International Institute of Environment and Development.

Nelson, Fred, and Arun Agrawal. 2008. "Patronage or Participation? Community-Based Natural Resource Management Reform in Sub-Saharan Africa." *Development and Change* 39: 557–85.

Nelson, Fred, Emmanuel Sulle, and Edward Lekaita. 2012. "Land Grabbing and Political Transformation in Tanzania." Paper presented at the International Conference on Global Land Grabbing II, Ithaca, NY.

Nelson, Fred, and Sinandei Ole Makko. 2005. "Communities, Conservation, and Conflicts in the Tanzanian Serengeti." In *Natural Resources as Community Assets—Lessons from Two Continents*, eds. Martha West Lyman and Brian Child. Madison, WI: Sand County Foundation and the Aspen Institute.

Nelson, Fred, and Tom Blomley. 2010. "Peasants' Forests and the King's Game? Institutional Divergence and Convergence in Tanzania's Forestry and Wildlife Sectors." In *Community Rights, Conservation and Contested Land. The Politics of Natural Resource Governance in Africa*. London and Washington, DC: Earthscan. 79–106.

Nerlich, Brigitte. 2012. "'Low Carbon' Metals, Markets and Metaphors: The Creation of Economic Expectations About Climate Change Mitigation." *Climatic Change* 110: 31–51.

Neumann, Roderick P. 2002. "The Postwar Conservation Boom in British Colonial Africa." *Environmental History* 7: 22–47.

———. 2001. "Disciplining Peasants in Tanzania: From State Violence to Self-Surveillance in Wildlife Conservation." In *Violent Environments*, eds. Nancy Peluso and Michael Watts. Ithaca, NY: Cornell University Press. 305–27.

———. 2000. "Land, Justice, and the Politics of Conservation in Tanzania." In *People, Plants, and Justice: The Politics of Nature Conservation*, ed. Charles Zerner. New York: Columbia University Press. 117–33.

———. 1998. *Imposing Wilderness: Struggles over Livelihood and Nature Preservation in Africa*. Berkeley: University of California Press.

———. 1997. "Primitive Ideas: Protected Area Buffer Zones and the Politics of Land in Africa." *Development and Change* 28: 559–82.

———. 1995. "Local Challenges to Global Agendas: Conservation, Economic Liberalization and the Pastoralists' Rights Movement in Tanzania." *Antipode* 27: 363–82.

———. 1992. "Political Ecology of Wildlife Conservation in the Mt. Meru Area of Northeast Tanzania." *Land Degradation & Development* 3: 85–98.

Newell, Peter. 2005. "Race, Class and the Global Politics of Environmental Inequality." *Global Environmental Politics* 5: 70–94.

Newell, Peter, and Joanna Wheeler, eds. 2006. *Rights, Resources and the Politics of Accountability*. London and New York: Zed books.

Nielsen, Martin Reinhardt, and Thorsten Treue. 2012. "Hunting for the Benefits of Joint Forest Management in the Eastern Afromontane Biodiversity Hotspot: Effects on Bushmeat Hunters and Wildlife in the Udzungwa Mountains." *World Development* 40: 1224–39.

Nilsen, Alf Gunvald. 2012. Adivasis in and Against the State. *Critical Asian Studies* 44 (2): 251–82.

Noronha, Ligia, Nidhi Srivastava, Divya Datt, and P.V. Sridharan. 2009. Resource Federalism in India: The Case of Minerals. *Economic and Political Weekly* 44 (8): 51–59.

North, D.C. 1990. *Institutions, Institutional Change and Economic Performance*. Cambridge, UK: Cambridge University Press.

Nuijten, Monique. 2004. "Peasant 'Participation', Rural Property and the State in Western Mexico." *The Journal of Peasant Studies* 31: 181–209.

———. 2003. "Family Property and the Limits of Intervention: The Article 27 Reforms and the Procede Programme in Mexico." *Development and Change* 34: 475–97.

O'Donnell, G.A. 1998. "Horizontal Accountability in New Democracies." *Journal of Democracy* 9: 112–26.

O'Donnell, Guillermo. 1993. "On the State, Democratization and Some Conceptual Problems: A Latin American View with Glances at Some Postcommunist Countries." *World Development* 21: 1355–69.

O'Dwyer, Conor. 2006. *Runaway State-Building: Patronage Politics and Democratic Development*. Baltimore, MD: Johns Hopkins University Press.

O'Malley, Marion Elizabeth. "Cattle and Cultivation: Changing Land Use and Labor Patterns in Pastoral Maasi Livelihoods, Loliondo Division, Ngorongoro District, Tanzania." Ph.D., University of Colorado at Boulder, 2000.

Odgaard, Rie. 2002. "Scrambling for Land in Tanzania: Process of Formalisation and Legitimisation of Land Rights." *European Journal of Development Research* 14: 71.

Olson, Mancur. 1965. *The Logic of Collective Action. Public Goods and the Theory of Groups*. Vol. CXXIV, Harvard Economic Studies. Cambridge, MA: Harvard University Press.

Omvedt, Gail. 2006. *Dalit Visions: The Anti-Caste Movement and the Construction of an Indian Identity*. Hyderabad: Orient Longman.

———. 1984. "Ecology and Social Movements." *Economic and Political Weekly* 19: 1865–67.

Onoma, Ato Kwamena. 2010. *The Politics of Property Rights Institutions in Africa*. New York: Cambridge University Press.

Orlove, Benjamin S. and Stephen B. Brush. 1996. "Anthropology and the Conservation of Biodiversity." *Annual Review of Anthropology*: 329–52.

Oskarsson, Patrik. 2013. "Dispossession by Confusion from Mineral-Rich Lands in Central India." *South Asia: Journal of South Asian Studies* 36: 199–212.

Ostrom, Elinor. 2011. "Background on the Institutional Analysis and Development Framework." *Policy Studies Journal* 39: 7–27.

———. 2010. "Beyond Markets and States: Polycentric Governance of Complex Economic Systems." *American Economic Review* 100: 641–72.

———. 2007. "Institutional Rational Choice: An Assessment of the Institutional Analysis and Development Framework." In *Theories of the Policy Process*, ed. Paul A. Sabatier. Boulder, CO: Westview Press.

————. 2005. *Understanding Institutional Diversity*. Princeton, NJ: Princeton University Press.

————. 1990. *Governing the Commons: The Evolution of Institutions for Collective Action*. New York: Cambridge University Press.

Ottaway, David B., and Joe Stephens. 2003. "Nonprofit Land Bank Amasses Billions: Charity Builds Assets on Corporate Partnerships." *The Washington Post*, May 4, 2003.

Oxford Poverty and Human Development Initiative (OPHI). 2013. *Global Multidimensional Poverty Index Databank*. Oxford, UK: University of Oxford.

Pai, Sudha. 2009. *The Developmental State and the Dalit Question: Congress Response*. New Delhi and London: Routledge India.

Palsson, Gisli, Bronislaw Szerszynski, Sverker Sörlin, John Marks, Bernard Avril, Carole Crumley, Heide Hackmann, Poul Holm, John Ingram, and Alan Kirman. 2013. "Reconceptualizing the 'Anthropos' in the Anthropocene: Integrating the Social Sciences and Humanities in Global Environmental Change Research." *Environmental Science & Policy* 28: 3–13.

Patel, P.M. 2001. "Politics and Mobilization of Lower Classes." Unpublished Manuscript. Department of Political Science, MS University of Baroda.

Pathak, Akhileshwar. 1994. *Contested Domains: The State, Peasants and Forests in Contemporary India*. New Delhi: Sage Publications.

Pathak, Shekhar. 1991. "The Begar Abolition Movements in British Kumaun." *Indian Economic & Social History Review* 28: 261–79.

Pati, R.N., and J. Dash. 2002. *Tribal and Indigenous People of India: Problems and Prospects*: A.P.H. Publishing Corp.

Pearce, Fred. 2016. *Common Ground: Securing Land Rights and Safeguarding the Earth*. Oxford, UK: Oxfam GB.

Pedersen, Rasmus Hundsbæk. 2014. "Tanzania's New Wave Land Reform: A Matter of Institutionalisation." In *Land Justice for Sustainable Peace in Tanzania*, eds. D. Kimaro, A. Munga, A. Mollel, A. Maganya, and G. Walalaze. Lushoto, Tanzania: Sebastian Kolowa Memorial University. 249–67.

Pellegrini, Lorenzo, and Anirban Dasgupta. 2011. "Land Reform in Bolivia: The Forestry Question." *Conservation and Society* 9: 274.

Peluso, N.L. 1992. *Rich Forests, Poor People: Resource Control and Resistance in Java*. Berkeley: University of California Press.

————. 2007. "Enclosure and Privatization of Neoliberal Environments." In *Neoliberal Environments: False Promises and Unnatural Consequences*, eds. Nik Heynen, James McCarthy, Scott Prudham, and Paul Robbins. London and New York: Routledge. 51–62.

Peluso, Nancy Lee, and Michael Watts, eds. 2001. *Violent Environments*. Ithaca, NY: Cornell University Press.

Peluso, Nancy Lee and Peter Vandergeest. 2011. "Political Ecologies of War and Forests: Counterinsurgencies and the Making of National Natures." *Annals of the Association of American Geographers* 101: 587–608.

————. 2001. "Genealogies of the Political Forest and Customary Rights in Indonesia, Malaysia, and Thailand." *The Journal of Asian Studies* 60: 761–812.

Peluso, Nancy Lee, Suraya Afiff, and Noer Fauzi Rachman. 2008. "Claiming the Grounds for Reform: Agrarian and Environmental Movements in Indonesia." *Journal of Agrarian Change* 8: 377–407.

People's Union for Democratic Rights (PUDR). 1982. *Undeclared Civil War: A Critique of the Forestry Policy*. New Delhi: PUDR.

Perramond, Eric P. 2008. "The Rise, Fall, and Reconfiguration of the Mexican Ejido." *Geographical Review* 98: 356–71.

Peters, Pauline E., and Kambewa Daimon. 2007. "Whose Security? Deepening Social Conflict over 'Customary' Land in the Shadow of Land Tenure Reform in Malawi." *The Journal of Modern African Studies* 45: 447–72.

Philip, Kavita. 2001. "Seeds of Neo-Colonialism? Reflections on Ecological Politics in the New World Order." *Capitalism Nature Socialism* 12: 3–47.

Pierson, Paul. 2000. "Increasing Returns, Path Dependence, and the Study of Politics." *The American Political Science Review* 94: 251–67.

Plagge, C.E., S. Frolking, L.P. Chini, and G. Hurtt. 2008. "Slash and Burn Agriculture: A Dynamic Spatio-Temporal Model of Shifting Cultivation Locations and Areas." Paper presented at the American Geophysical Union, Fall Meeting 2008.

Pole, Christopher, and Marlene Morrison. 2003. *Ethnography for Education.* Maidenhead, UK: Open University Press.

Poteete, Amy R., Marco Janssen, and Elinor Ostrom. 2010. *Working Together: Collective Action, the Commons, and Multiple Methods in Practice.* Princeton, NJ: Princeton University Press.

Prakash, Amit. 2011. "Politics, Development and Identity: Jharkhand: 1991–2004." In *The Politics of Belonging in India: Becoming Adivasi*, eds. Daniel J. Rycroft and Sangeeta Dasgupta. New York: Taylor & Francis. 175–89.

Prakash, Aseem. 2003. "Re-Imagination of the State and Gujarat's Electoral Verdict." *Economic and Political Weekly* 38: 1601–10.

Prasad, Archana. 2006. "Unravelling the Forms of 'Adivasi' Organization and Resistance in Colonial India." *Indian Historical Review* 33: 225–44.

———. 1999. "Military Conflict and Forests in Central Provinces, India: Gonds and the Gondwana Region in Pre-Colonial History." *Environment and History* 5: 361–75.

———. 1998. "The Baiga: Survival Strategies and Local Economy in the Central Provinces." *Studies in History* 14: 325–48.

Prasant, Kumar, and Dip Kapoor. 2010. "Learning and Knowledge Production in Dalit Social Movements in Rural India." In *Learning from the Ground Up: Global Perspectives on Social Movements and Knowledge Production*, eds. Aziz Choudry and Dip Kapoor. New York: Palgrave. 193–210.

Przeworski, Adam, Susan Carol Stokes, and Bernard Manin. 1999. *Democracy, Accountability, and Representation*, Cambridge Studies in the Theory of Democracy. Cambridge, UK, and New York: Cambridge University Press.

Puddington, Arch. 2015. "Discarding Democracy: A Return to the Iron Fist." In *Freedom in the World 2015*. Washington, DC: Freedom House.

Purdon, Mark. 2013. "Land Acquisitions in Tanzania: Strong Sustainability, Weak Sustainability and the Importance of Comparative Methods." *Journal of Agricultural and Environmental Ethics* 26: 1127–56.

Rahmato, Dessalegn. 2011. *Land to Investors: Large-Scale Land Transfers in Ethiopia.* Addis Ababa, Ethiopia: Forum for Social Studies.

Rajshekhar, Maddipatla. 2012. "The Law That Disagreed with Its' Preamble: An Enquiry into the Drafting of the Scheduled Tribes and Other Traditional Forest Dwellers (Recognition of Forest Rights) Act, 2006." Paper presented at the International Workshop on Livelihoods and the Environment: Debating Interdisciplinary Perspectives, New Delhi, October 15–16, 2009.

Ramakrishna, Kilaparti. 1984. "The Emergence of Environmental Law in the Developing Countries: A Case Study of India." *Ecology Law Quarterly* 12: 907.

Ramakrishnan, Venkitesh. 2008. "Hope & Fear." *Frontline* 25. http://www.frontline.in/static/html/fl2504/stories/20080229500100400.htm.

Ramanathan, Usha. 2002. "Common Land and Common Property Resources." In *Land Reforms in India- Issues of Equity in Rural Madhya Pradesh*, ed. Praveen K. Jha. Vol. 7. New Delhi: Sage Publications. 204.

Ramesh, J. 2015. *Green Signals: Ecology, Growth, and Democracy in India*. New Delhi: Oxford University Press.

Randeria, Shalini. 2007. "The State of Globalization: Legal Plurality, Overlapping Sovereignties and Ambiguous Alliances between Civil Society and the Cunning State in India." *Theory Culture Society* 24: 1–33.

———. 2006. "Entangled Histories: Civil Society, Caste Solidarity, and Legal Pluralism in Post-Colonial India." In *Civil Society: Berlin Perspectives*, ed. J. Keane. Berlin: Berghahn Books. 213–42.

Rangan, Haripriya. 1997. "Property vs. Control: The State and Forest Management in the Indiana Himalaya." *Development and Change* 28: 71–94.

Rangan, Haripriya, and Marcus B. Lane. 2001. "Indigenous Peoples and Forest Management: Comparative Analysis of Institutional Approaches in Australia and India." *Society & Natural Resources* 14: 145–60.

Rangarajan, M. 2003. "The Politics of Ecology: The Debate on Wildlife and People in India, 1970–95." In *Battles over Nature. Science and the Politics of Conservation*, eds. V.K. Saberwal and M. Rangarajan. Vol. 31. New Delhi: Permanent Black. 2391–409.

———. 2001. *India's Wildlife History: An Introduction*. New Delhi: Permanent Black.

Rangarajan, Mahesh. 2009. "Striving for a Balance: Nature, Power, Science and India's Indira Gandhi, 1917-1984." *Conservation & Society* 7: 299–312.

———. 1996a. *Fencing the Forest-Conservation and Ecological Change in India's Central Provinces 1860-1914*. New Delhi: Oxford University Press.

———. 1996b. "Environmental Histories of South Asia: A Review Essay." *Environment and History* 2: 129–43.

Rantala, S., 2012. "Knowledge and brokerage in REDD+ policy making: A Policy Networks Analysis of the case of Tanzania." Sustainability Science Program Working Paper 2012-03. Cambridge, MA: Sustainability Science Program, Kennedy School of Government, Harvard University.

Rantala, S., and L.A. German. 2013. "Exploring Village Governance Processes Behind Community-Based Forest Management: Legitimacy and Coercion in the Usambara Mountains of Tanzania." *International Forestry Review* 15: 355–67.

Rao, Nitya. 2007. "Custom and the Courts: Ensuring Women's Rights to Land, Jharkhand, India." *Development & Change* 38: 299–319.

Ray, Raka. 1999. *Fields of Protest: Women's Movements in India*. Minneapolis, MN: University of Minnesota Press.

Ray, Rita Ghosh. 1996. "The Attitude of Kautilya to Aranya." *Environment and History* 2: 221–29.

Read, Daniel J. 2015. "Legitimacy, Access, and the Gridlock of Tiger Conservation: Lessons from Melghat and the History of Central India." *Regional Environmental Change*: 1–11. doi: 10.1007/s10113-015-0780-7.

Reddy, M. Gopinath, K. Anil Kumar, P. Trinadha Rao, and Oliver Springate-Baginski. 2010. "Obstructed Access to Forest Justice: An Institutional Analysis of the Implementation of Rights Reform in Andhra's Forested Landscapes." Institutions and Pro-Poor Growth (IPPG) Discussion Papers No. 47. Norwich, UK: School of International Development, University of East Anglia.

Ribot, J.C. 2011. *Choice, Recognition and the Democracy Effects of Decentralization*. Working Paper No. 5. Visby, Sweden: Swedish International Center for Local Democracy.

———. 2007. "Representation, Citizenship and the Public Domain in Democratic Decentralization." *Development* 50: 43–49.

———. 2006. "Choose Democracy: Environmentalists' Socio-Political Responsibility." *Global Environmental Change* 16: 115–19.

———. 2004. *Waiting for Democracy: The Politics of Choice in Natural Resource Decentralization*. Washington, DC: World Resources Institute.

Ribot, Jesse C., and Anne Larson. 2011. "Affirmative Policy on an Uneven Playing Field: Implications for REDD." In *Forests and People: Property, Governance, and Human Rights*, eds. Thomas Sikor and J. Stahl. London and New York: Routledge.

Ribot, Jesse C., Arun Agrawal, and Anne M. Larson. 2006. "Recentralizing While Decentralizing: How National Governments Reappropriate Forest Resources." *World Development* 34: 1864–86.

Ribot, Jesse C., and Nancy L. Peluso. 2003. "A Theory of Access." *Rural Sociology* 68 (2): 153–181.

Rights and Resources Initiative (RRI). 2014. *Status of Forest Carbon Rights and implications for Communities, the Carbon Trade, and REDD+ Investments*. Washington, DC: Rights and Resources Initiative.

———. 2012. *What Rights? A Comparative Analysis of Developing Countries' National Legislation on Community and Indigenous Peoples' Forest Tenure Rights*. Washington, DC: Rights and Resources Initiative.

Rittel, Horst W.J., and Melvin M. Webber. 1973. "Dilemmas in a General Theory of Planning." *Policy Sciences* 4: 155–69.

Robbins, Paul. 1998. "Authority and Environment: Institutional Landscapes in Rajasthan, India." *Annals of the Association of American Geographers* 88: 410–35.

Robles, Francesca Felicani, and Leo Peskett. 2010. *Carbon Rights in Mexico*. Washington, DC: World Bank.

Rogers, Peter J. 2002. "Global Governance/Governmentality, Wildlife Conservation, and Protected Area Management: A Comparative Study of Eastern and Southern Africa." Paper presented at the African Studies Association 45th Annual Meeting, Washington, DC.

Roma, and Ashok Chowdhury. 2010. "India: Forest Protection is a Matter of Ecological Justice." Bulletin No. 159. Montevideo, Uruguay: World Rainforest Movement.

Rose, Carol M. 1985. "Possession as the Origin of Property." *University of Chicago Law Review* 52: 73–88.

Rosencranz, A., and Sharachchandra Lélé. 2008. "Supreme Court and India's Forests." *Economic and Political Weekly* 43: 11.

Rosset, Peter, Raj Patel, and Michael Courville. 2006. *Promised Land Competing Visions of Agrarian Reform*. Oakland, CA: Food First books.

Roth, Robin. 2004. "On the Colonial Margins and in the Global Hotspot: Park–People Conflicts in Highland Thailand." *Asia Pacific Viewpoint* 45: 13–32.

Roy, Chandra. 2005. "Economic Solutions to Political Problems: The Case of the Chittagong Hill Tracts Patrick Thornberry." In *Minorities, Peoples and Self-Determination: Essays in Honour of Patrick*, eds. Nazila Ghanea-Hercock, Alexandra Xanthaki, and Patrick Thornberry. Leiden and Boston: Martinus Nijhoff Publishers.

Rubin, Jeffrey W. 1990. "Popular Mobilization and the Myth of State Corporatism." In *Popular Movements and Political Change in Mexico*, eds. Joe Foweraker and Ann L. Craig. Boulder, CO: Lynne Rienner Publishers. 247–67.

Rudolph, Lloyd I. and Susanne Hoeber Rudolph. 1987. *In Pursuit of Lakshmi: The Political Economy of the Indian State*. Chicago: University of Chicago Press.

——. 1960. "The Political Role of India's Caste Associations." *Pacific Affairs* 33: 5–22.

Ruiz, Luis. 2007. "From Marxism to Social History: Adolfo Gilly's Revision of the Mexican Revolution." *A Contracorriente* 4 (2): 243–54.

Ruparelia, Sanjay. 2013. "India's New Rights Agenda: Genesis, Promises, Risks." *Pacific Affairs* 86: 569–90.

Ruparelia, Sanjay, Sanjay Reddy, John Harriss, and Stuart Corbridge. 2011. *Understanding India's New Political Economy: A Great Transformation?* Oxon, U.K. and New York: Routledge.

Ruttan, Lore M. and Monique Borgerhoff Mulder. 1999. "Are East African Pastoralists Truly Conservationists? 1." *Current Anthropology* 40: 621–52.

Rycroft, D.J., and S. Dasgupta. 2011. *The Politics of Belonging in India: Becoming Adivasi*. Oxon, UK and New York: Routledge.

Saberwal, Vasant K. 2000. "Conservation as Politics: Wildlife Conservation and Resource Management in India." *Journal of International Wildlife Law and Policy* 3: 166.

——. 1999. *Pastoral Politics: Shepherds, Bureaucrats, and Conservation in the Western Himalaya*. New Delhi: Oxford University Press.

——. 1998. "Science and the Desiccationist Discourse of the 20th Century." *Environment and History* 4: 309–43.

Saberwal, V.K., and M. Rangarajan. 2003. *Battles over Nature: Science and the Politics of Conservation*. New Delhi: Permanent Black.

Sachedina, Hassanali Thomas. 2008. "Wildlife Is Our Oil: Conservation, Livelihoods and Ngos in the Tarangire Ecosystem, Tanzania." Ph.D. dissertation. University of Oxford.

Sack, Robert David. 1986. *Human Territoriality: Its Theory and History*. Cambridge, UK, and New York: Cambridge University Press.

Sahgal, Bittu, and Jennifer Scarlott. 2010. "This Heaven and This Earth: Will India Keep Its Promise to Panthera Tigris?" In *Tigers of the World : The Science, Politics, and Conservation of Panthera Tigris*, eds. Ronald Lewis Tilson and Philip J. Nyhus. Boston: Elsevier/Academic Press. 301–14.

Sahoo, Niranjan. 2011. "In Search of a Model Land Legislation the New Land Acquisition Bill and Its Intractable Challenges." New Delhi: Observer Research Foundation.

Sainath, P. 1996. *Everyone Loves a Good Drought*. New Delhi: Penguin India.

Samoff, Joel. 1979. "The Bureaucracy and the Bourgeoisie: Decentralization and Class Structure in Tanzania." *Comparative Studies in Society and History* 21: 30–62.

Sanderson, S.E. 1981. *Agrarian Populism and the Mexican State: The Struggle for Land in Sonora*. Berkeley, Los Angeles, and London: University of California Press.

Saldaña-Portillo, María Josefina. 2003. *The Revolutionary Imagination in the Americas and the Age of Development*. Durham, NC: Duke University Press.

Sandbrook, C., F. Nelson, W.M. Adams, and A. Agrawal. 2010. "Carbon, Forests and the REDD Paradox." *Oryx* 44: 330–34.

Sanyal, K.K. 2007. *Rethinking Capitalist Development: Primitive Accumulation, Governmentality and Post-Colonial Capitalism*. New Delhi and Oxon, UK: Routledge.

Saravanan, Velayutham. 2009. "Political Economy of the Recognition of Forest Rights Act, 2006: Conflict between Environment and Tribal Development." *South Asia Research* 29: 199–221.

Sarin, M. 2005. *Laws, Lore and Logjams: Critical Issues in Indian Conservation.* The Gatekeeper Series 116. London,: Institute of Environment and Development.

———. 1998. *Who Is Gaining? Who Is Losing? Gender and Equality Concerns in Joint Forest Management.* New Delhi: Society for Promotion of Wastelands Development (SPWD).

Sarin, Madhu. 2005a. "Scheduled Tribes Bill 2005: A Comment." *Economic and Political Weekly* 40: 2131–34.

Sarker, Debnarayan. 2011. "The Implementation of the Forest Rights Act in India: Critical Issues." *Economic Affairs* 31: 25–29.

Sau, Ranjit. 2006. "Scheduled Tribes Bill: For Whom and for What?" *Economic and Political Weekly* 41 (48): 5009–11.

Saxena, N.C. 2003. "Livelihood Diversification and Non-Timber Forest Products in Orissa: Wider Lessons on the Scope for Policy Change?" Working Paper 223. London: Overseas Development Institute.

———. 1997. *The Saga of Participatory Forest Management in India.* Jakarta, Indonesia: Center for International Forestry Research (CIFOR).

———. 1992. *Joint Forest Management: A New Development Bandwagon in India?* Nottingham: Rural Development Forestry Network (RDFN).

Schabel, Hans G. 1990. "Tanganyika Forestry under German Colonial Administration, 1891–1919." *Forest & Conservation History* 34: 130–41.

Schatz, Edward. 2009. *Political Ethnography : What Immersion Contributes to the Study of Power.* Chicago: The University of Chicago Press.

Schlager, E. 2007. "A Comparison of Frameworks, Theories, and Models of Policy Processes." In *Theories of the Policy Process,* ed. Paul Sabatier. Boulder, CO: Westview Press.

Schlager, Edella, and Elinor Ostrom. 1992. "Property-Rights Regimes and Natural Resources: A Conceptual Analysis." *Land Economics* 68: 249–62.

Schmidt-Soltau, Kai. 2003. "Conservation-Related Resettlement in Central Africa: Environmental and Social Risks." *Development and Change* 34: 525–51.

Schmitter, Philippe C. 1974. "Still the Century of Corporatism?" *The Review of Politics* 36 (1): 85–131.

Schroeder, R.A. 1999. "Geographies of Environmental Intervention in Africa." *Progress in Human Geography* 23: 359–78.

Scott, James C. 2009. *The Art of Not Being Governed : An Anarchist History of Upland Southeast Asia.* New Haven: Yale University Press.

———. 1998. *Seeing Like a State: How Certain Schemes to Improve the Human Condition Have Failed.* New Haven and London: Yale University Press.

———. 1985. *Weapons of the Weak: Everyday Forms of Peasant Resistance.* New Haven: Yale University Press.

Sekhar, Nagothu Udaya, and Ivar Jørgensen. 2003. *Social Forestry in South Asia: Myths and Realities,* Noragric Working Paper No. 30. Ås: Agricultural University of Norway.

Sekhsaria, P., and N. Vagholikar. 2004. "Forced Displacement from Protected Areas: The Spectre Looms Large." InfoChange News & Features. http://infochangeindia. org/environment/features/forced-displacement-from-protected-areas-the-spectre-looms-large.html.

Seymour, Frances, Tony La Vina, and Kristen Hite. 2014. *Evidence Linking Community-Level Tenure and Forest Condition: An Annotated Bibliography.* San Francisco: Climate and Land Use Alliance.

Shah, Amita, and O.G. Sajitha. 2009. "Dwindling Forest Resources and Economic Vulnerability among Tribal Communities in a Dry/Sub-Humid Region in India." *Journal of International Development* 21: 419–32.

Shah, Ghanshayam. 1972. "Voting Behaviour of Adivasi and Harijan Leaders: A Study of the 1971 Elections." *The Indian Journal of Political Science* 33: 431–42.

Shah, M., D. Banerji, P.S. Vijayashankar, and P. Ambasta. 1998. *India's Drylands—Tribal Societies and Development through Environmental Regeneration.* New Delhi: Oxford University Press.

Shapiro-Garza, Elizabeth. 2013. "Contesting the Market-Based Nature of Mexico's National Payments for Ecosystem Services Programs: Four Sites of Articulation and Hybridization." *Geoforum* 46: 5–15.

Sharma, B.D. 1989. "Report of the Commissioner for Scheduled Castes and Scheduled Tribes." Report No. 29. New Delhi: Government of India.

Sharma, K.L. 1976. "Jharkhand Movement in Bihar." *Economic and Political Weekly* 11: 37–43.

Sheth, D.L. 2002. "The Politics of Communal Polarisation: A Precursor to the Gujarat Carnage." *Manushi* 129: 15–21.

Shivji, Isha G. 1998. *Not yet Democracy: Reforming Land Tenure in Tanzania.* London: International Institute of Environment and Development, /HAKIARDHI - Land Rights Research and Resources Institute, and Faculty of Law, University of Dar es Salaam.

Shivji, Issa G. 1991. "The Democracy Debate in Africa: Tanzania." *Review of African Political Economy* 18: 79–91.

Shrivastava, A., and A. Kothari. 2012. *Churning the Earth: The Cost of India's Growth.* New Delhi: Penguin Books Limited.

Siaroff, A. 2011. "Regime (comparative politics)." In *International encyclopedia of political science*, eds. B. BadieD. Berg-Schlosser & L. Morlino. Thousand Oaks, CA: SAGE Publications Ltd. doi: 10.4135/9781412959636.n511.

Sikor, Thomas. 2010. "Forest Justice: Towards a New Agenda for Research and Practice?" *Journal of Integrative Environmental Sciences* 7: 245–50.

———. 2006a. "Politics of Rural Land Registration in Post-Socialist Societies: Contested Titling in Villages of Northwest Vietnam." *Land Use Policy* 23: 617–28.

———. 2006b. "Analyzing Community-Based Forestry: Local, Political and Agrarian Perspectives." *Forest Policy and Economics* 8: 339–49.

Sikor, Thomas, and Christian Lund. 2009. "Access and Property: A Question of Power and Authority." *Development and Change* 40: 1–22.

Sikor, Thomas, and J. Stahl. 2011. *Forests and People: Property, Governance, and Human Rights.* London and New York:: Routledge.

Silva-Chávez, Gustavo, Brian Schaap, and Jessica Breitfeller. 2015. *REDD+ Finance Flows 2009-2014: Trends and Lessons Learned in Reddx Countries.* Washington, DC: Forest Trends.

Simonian, L. 1995. *Defending the Land of the Jaguar: A History of Conservation in Mexico.* Austin, TX: University of Texas Press.

Simpson, E.N. 1937. *The Ejido: Mexico's Way Out.* Chapel Hill: The University of North Carolina Press.

Singh, Chhatrapati. 2000. *India's Forest Policy & Forest Laws.* Dehradun: Natraj Publishers.

———. 1986. *Common Property and Common Poverty: India's Forests, Forest Dwellers, and the Law.* New Delhi and New York: Oxford University Press.

Singh, Digvijaya. 2005. "The Real Issues." *Seminar* 552.

Singh, Neera M. 2013. The Affective Labor of Growing Forests and the Becoming of Environmental Subjects: Rethinking Environmentality in Odisha, India. *Geoforum* 47: 189–98.

———. 2002. Frederations of Community Forest Management Groups in Orissa: Crafting New Institutions to Assert Local Rights. *Forest, Trees and People* 46: 35–45.

Singh, S. 1985. "Some Aspects of the Ecological Crisis in India." *Social Scientist* 13: 82.

Sinha, Aseema. 2012. "A Story of Four Revolutions: Mechanisms of Change in India." *Asia Policy* 14: 122–26.

Sivaramakrishnan, K. 2011. "Environment, Law, and Democracy in India." *The Journal of Asian Studies* 70: 905–28.

———. 2000. "Crafting the Public Sphere in the Forests of West Bengal: Democracy, Development, and Political Action." *American Ethnologist* 27: 431–61.

———. 1999. *Modern Forests: Statemaking and Environmental Change in Colonial Eastern India*. Stanford, California: Stanford University Press.

———. 1996. "Co-Management for Forests: Are We Overly Preoccupied with Property Rights?" *Common Property Resource Digest* 37: 6–8.

Skaria, Ajay. 1997. "Shades of Wildness Tribe, Caste, and Gender in Western India." *Journal of Asian Studies*: 726–45.

Skutsch, Margaret, Cecilia Simon, Alejandro Velazquez, and José Carlos Fernández. 2013. "Rights to Carbon and Payments for Services Rendered under REDD+: Options for the Case of Mexico." *Global Environmental Change* 23: 813–25.

Smardon, Richard C. and Betty B. Faust. 2006. "Introduction: International Policy in the Biosphere Reserves of Mexico's Yucatan Peninsula." *Landscape and Urban Planning* 74: 160–92.

Spear, Thomas. 2003. "Neo-Traditionalism and the Limits of Invention in British Colonial Africa." *The Journal of African History* 44: 3–27.

Spear, Thomas T. 1997. *Mountain Farmers: Moral Economies of Land & Agricultural Development in Arusha & Meru*. Berkeley and Los Angeles: University of California Press.

Springate-Baginski, Oliver, and Piers M. Blaikie. 2007. *Forests, People and Power: The Political Ecology of Reform in South Asia*. London and Sterling, VA: Earthscan.

Sreerekha, M.S. 2010. "Challenges before Kerala's Landless: The Story of Aralam Farm." *Economic and Political Weekly* 45 (21): 55–62.

Stavins, Robert N. 2012. *Economics of the Environment: Selected Readings*. New York: WW Norton.

———. 1998. "What Can We Learn from the Grand Policy Experiment? Lessons from So _2 Allowance Trading." *The Journal of Economic Perspectives* 12: 69.

Stein, Howard. 2014. "Formalization, Dispossession and the G8: Land Agenda in Africa." Paper presented at the "Imagining Land: Significance of Land in African Economics, Politics and Culture," Trinity International Development Initiative-Africa Day Event, Dublin: Trinity College.

Stein, Howard, and Kelly Askew. 2009. "Embedded Institutions and Rural Transformation in Tanzania: Privatizing Rural Property and Markets." Paper Prepared for the Fourth Meeting of the Africa Task Force, Initiative for Policy Dialogue (Columbia University), Pretoria, South Africa 9–10 July.

Steinberg, Paul F. 2015. *Who Rules the Earth?: How Social Rules Shape Our Planet and Our Lives*. New York, NY: Oxford University Press.

Stephen, L. 2010. *Women and Social Movements in Latin America: Power from Below*. Austin, TX: University of Texas Press.

Stevens, Caleb, Robert Winterbottom, Jenny Springer, and Katie Reytar. 2014. *Securing Rights, Combating Climate Change: How Strengthening Community Forest Rights Mitigates Climate Change*. Washington, DC: World Resources Institute and Rights and Resources Initiative.

Strahorn, Eric A. 2009. *An Environmental History of Postcolonial North India: The Himalayan Tarai in Uttar Pradesh and Uttaranchal*. New York: Peter Lang.

Sturgeon, Janet, and Thomas Sikor. 2004. "Post-Socialist Property in Asia and Europe: Variations on 'Fuzziness'." *Conservation and Society* 2: 1–17.

Sud, N. 2007. "From Land to the Tiller to Land Liberalisation: The Political Economy of Gujarat's Shifting Land Policy." *Modern Asian Studies* 41: 603–37.

Sulle, Emmanuel, and Fred Nelson. 2009. *Biofuels, Land Access and Rural Livelihoods in Tanzania*. London: International Institute for Environment and Development.

Sundar, Nandini. 2010. "The Rule of Law and the Rule of Property: Law-Struggles and the Neo-Liberal State in India." In *The State in India after Liberalization: In terdisciplinary Perspectives*, eds. A. Gupta and K. Sivaramakrishnan. New York: Routledge.

———. 2009. *Legal Grounds: Natural Resources, Identity, and the Law in Jharkhand*. New Delhi: Oxford University Press.

———. 2006. "Bastar, Maoism and Salwa Judum." *Economic and Political Weekly* 41: 3187–92.

———. 2005. "'Custom' and 'Democracy' in Jharkhand." *Economic and Political Weekly* 40: 4430–34.

———. 2004. "Devolution, Joint Forest Management and the Transformation of Social Capital." In *Interrogating Social Capital the Indian Experience*, eds. Dwaipayan Bhattacharya, Prof Niraja Gopal Jayal, Bishnu N Mohapatra and Sudha Pai. New Delhi: Sage Publications. 203–32.

———. 2001. "Is Devolution Democratization?" *World Development* 29: 2007–23.

———. 1998. *Subalterns and Sovereigns—An Anthropological History of Bastar, 1854-1996*. New York: Oxford University Press.

———. 1997. *Subalterns and Sovereigns- an Anthropological History of Bastar, 1854-1996*. New York: Oxford University Press.

Sundar, Nandini, Roger Jeffery, and Neil Thin. 2001. *Branching Out: Joint Forest Management in India*. New Delhi: Oxford.

Sundberg, Juanita. 2003. "Conservation and Democratization: Constituting Citizenship in the Maya Biosphere Reserve, Guatemala." *Political Geography* 22: 715–40.

Sunderlin, W.D., A.D. Ekaputri, E. Sills, A.E. Duchelle, D. Kweka, R Diprose, N. Doggart, S. Ball, R. Lima, A. Enright, J. Torres, H. Hartanto, and A Toniolo. 2014. *The Challenge of Establishing REDD+ on the Ground: Insights from 23 Subnational Initiatives in Six Countries*. Bogor, Indonesia: Center for International Forestry Research (CIFOR).

Sundet, Geir. 2008. "Getting to Grips with Realities. Is It Possible to Realign Mkurabita to Empower the Poor." A report prepared for Norwegian People's Aid-Tanzania. Asker, Norway: Daylight Initiatives.

———. 2004. "The Politics of Land in Tanzania." Unpublished Manuscript. http://landportal.info/sites/landportal.info/files/the_politics_of_land_in_tanzania_december_2004.doc.

Sunseri, Thaddeus Raymond. 2009. *Wielding the Ax : State Forestry and Social Conflict in Tanzania, 1820-2000*. Athens, OH: Ohio University Press.

———. 2007. "'Every African a Nationalist': Scientific Forestry and Forest Nationalism in Colonial Tanzania." *Comparative Studies in Society and History* 49: 883–913.

————. 2005. "'Something Else to Burn': Forest Squatters, Conservationists, and the State in Modern Tanzania." *The Journal of Modern African Studies* 43: 609–40.

Swamy, Arun R. 2004. "Back to the Future: The Congress Party's Upset Victory in India's 14th General Elections." Occasional Paper. Honolulu, Hawaii: Asia Pacific Center for Security Studies.

Tarrow, Sidney. 2003. *Power in Movement Social Movements, Collective Action and Politics.* New York: Cambridge University Press.

Taylor, William B. 1974. "Landed Society in New Spain: A View from the South." *Hispanic American Historical Review* 54 (3): 387–413.

Teichman, Judith. 2012. *Social Forces and States Poverty and Distributional Outcomes in South Korea, Chile, and Mexico.* Palo Alto: Stanford University Press.

Thachil, Tariq, and Ronald Herring. 2008. "Poor Choices: De-Alignment, Development and Dalit/Adivasi Voting Patterns in Indian States." *Contemporary South Asia* 16: 441–64.

Thapar, Romila. 2001. "Perceiving the Forest: Early India." *Studies in History* 17: 1–16.

Thelen, Kathleen. 1999. "Historical Institutionalism in Comparative Politics. " *Annual Review of Poltical Science* 2: 369–404.

————. 1991. *Union of Parts: Labor Politics in Postwar Germany.* Ithaca, NY: Cornell University Press.

Thiesenhusen, William C. 1995. *Mexican Land Reform, 1934 to 1991: Success or Failure?* Madison, WI: Land Tenure Center, University of Wisconsin-Madison.

Thompson, Mary C., Manali Baruah, and Edward R. Carr. 2011. "Seeing REDD+ as a Project of Environmental Governance." *Environmental Science & Policy* 14: 100–10.

Thompson, Michael, and Katherine Homewood. 2002. "Entrepreneurs, Elites, and Exclusion in Maasailand: Trends in Wildlife Conservation and Pastoralist Development." *Human Ecology* 30: 107–38.

Thomson, Guy P.C. 1991. "Popular Aspects of Liberalism in Mexico, 1848–1888." *Bulletin of Latin American Research* 10: 265–92.

Thuy, P.T., M. Moeliono, and L.N. Dung. 2014. *REDD+ Policy Networks in Vietnam.* Infobrief No. 78. Bogor, Indonesia: Center for International Forestry Research (CIFOR).

Tillin, Louise. 2008. "Politics in a New State: Chhattisgarh." *Seminar* 591.

Tilly, Charles. 2006. "Afterword: Political Ethnography as Art and Science." *Qualitative Sociology* 29: 409–12.

————. 1978. *From Mobilization to Revolution.* Reading, MA: Addison-Wesley.

Tobin, James. 1958. "Estimation of Relationships for Limited Dependent Variables." *Econometrica* 26: 24–36.

Torres-Mazuera, Gabriela. 2013. "Geopolitical Transformation in Rural Mexico: Toward New Social and Territorial Boundaries in an Indigenous Municipality of Central Mexico." *The Journal of Peasant Studies* 40: 397–422.

Tripp, Aili Mari. 2000. "Political Reform in Tanzania: The Struggle for Associational Autonomy." *Comparative Politics* 32: 191–214.

Tropp, Jacob. 2003. "Displaced People, Replaced Narratives: Forest Conflicts and Historical Perspectives in the Tsolo District, Transkei." *Journal of Southern African Studies* 29: 207–33.

Tucker, Catherine M. 2004. "Community Institutions and Forest Management in Mexico's Monarch Butterfly Reserve." *Society & Natural Resources* 17: 569–87.

Tucker, Richard P. 2012. *A Forest History of India.* New Delhi: Sage Publications.

————. 1988. "The Depletion of India's Forests under British Imperialism: Planters, Foresters, and Peasants in Assam and Kerala." In *The Ends of the Earth: Perspectives on Modern Environmental History.* New York: Cambridge University Press. 118–40.

Tully, James. 1994. "Aboriginal Property and Western Theory: Recovering a Middle Ground." *Social Philosophy and Policy* 11: 153–80.

Turner, Allen, Peter Riwa, Christopher William, and Edward Kigenza. 2014. *Landscape-Scale Community Centered Ecosystem Conservation Project in Western Tanzania: Evaluation Report.* Arlington, Virginia: USAID.

Tutino, John. 1975. "Hacienda Social Relations in Mexico: The Chalco Region in the Era of Independence." *The Hispanic American Historical Review* 55: 496–528.

United Nations Development Programme (UNDP). 2015. *Human Development Report 2015: Work for Human Development.* New York: UNDP.

UN General Assembly. 2015. "Transforming Our World: The 2030 Agenda for Sustainable Development." New York: United Nations General Assembly.

United Republic of Tanzania (URT). 2013. "National Strategy for Reduced Emissions from Deforestation and Forest Degradation (REDD+)." Vice President's Office.

Upadhyay, Carol. 2009. "Law, Custom and Adivasi Identity: Politics of Land Rights in Chhotanagpur." In *Legal Grounds: Natural Resources, Identity, and the Law in Jharkhand,* ed. Nandini Sundar. New Delhi: Oxford University Press. 30–55.

USAID. 2010. *Low Emission Development Strategy: Pre-Scoping Mission Assessment Mexico.* Washington, DC: United States Agency for International Development.

Uvin, Peter. 1996. "Tragedy in Rwanda: The Political Ecology of Conflict." *Environment: Science and Policy for Sustainable Development* 38: 7–29.

Vaidya, Anand. 2016. "'Word Traps' and the Drafting of India's Forest Rights Act." In *Staking Claims: The Politics of Social Movements in Contemporary Rural India,* eds. Uday Chandra and Daniel Taghioff. New Delhi: Oxford University Press.

Van Der Haar, Gemma. 2005. "Land Reform, the State, and the Zapatista Uprising in Chiapas." *The Journal of Peasant Studies* 32: 484–507.

Van Dusen, M.E. 2006. "Missing Markets, Migration and Crop Biodiversity in the Milpa System of Mexico: A Household Farm Model." In *Valuing Crop Biodiversity: On Farm Genetic Resources and Economic Change,* ed. Melinda Smale. Cambridge, MA: CABI Publishing. 63–77.

Van Hoyweghen, Saskia. 1999. "The Urgency of Land and Agrarian Reform in Rwanda." *African Affairs* 98: 353–72.

Vandergeest, Peter and Nancy Lee Peluso. 2006. "Empires of Forestry: Professional Forestry and State Power in Southeast Asia, Part 1 & Part 2." *Environment and History* 12: 31–64; 359–93.

———. 1995. "Territorialization and State Power in Thailand." *Theory and Society* 24: 385–426.

Varshney, A. 2014. *Battles Half Won: India's Improbable Democracy.* Gurgaon, India: Penguin Books.

Vasan, Sudha. 2009. "Forest Law, Ideology and Practice." In *Legal Grounds: Natural Resources, Identity, and the Law in Jharkhand,* ed. Nandini Sundar. New Delhi: Oxford University Press.

Venkataraman, Meena. 2010. "'Site'ing the Right Reasons: Critical Evaluation of Conservation Planning for the Asiatic Lion." *European Journal of Wildlife Research* 56: 209–13.

Véron, R., S. Corbridge, G. Williams, and M. Srivastava. 2003. "The Everyday State and Political Society in Eastern India: Structuring Access to the Employment Assurance Scheme." *Journal of Development Studies* 39: 1–28.

Véron, René, and Garry Fehr. 2011. "State Power and Protected Areas: Dynamics and Contradictions of Forest Conservation in Madhya Pradesh, India." *Political Geography* 30: 282–93.

Vihemäki, Heini. 2009. "Participation or Further Exclusion? Contestations over Forest Conservation and Control in the East Usambara Mountains, Tanzania." Doctoral Dissertation, University of Helsinki, Finland.

Vijge, Marjanneke J., and Aarti Gupta. 2014. "Framing REDD+ in India: Carbonizing and Centralizing Indian Forest Governance?" *Environmental Science & Policy* 38: 17–27.

Vira, Bhaskar. 2005. "Deconstructing the Harda Experience—Limits of Bureaucratic Participation." *Economic and Political Weekly* 40: 5068–75.

Visseren-Hamakers, Ingrid J., Constance McDermott, Marjanneke J. Vijge, and Benjamin Cashore. 2012. "Trade-Offs, Co-Benefits and Safeguards: Current Debates on the Breadth of REDD+." *Current Opinion in Environmental Sustainability* 4: 646–53.

Vitz, Matthew. 2010. "Revolutionary Environments: The Politics of Nature and Space in the Valley of Mexico, 1890-1940s." Ph.D. dissertation. New York University.

Vliet, N., O. Mertz, T. Birch-Thomsen, and B. Schmook. 2013. "Is There a Continuing Rationale for Swidden Cultivation in the 21st Century?" *Human Ecology* 41: 1–5.

von Benda-Beckmann, Franz, Keebet von Benda-Beckmann, and Melanie Wiber. 2009. *Changing Properties of Property*. New York and Oxford: Berghahn Books.

Wagemans, M., and J. Boerma. 2000. "The Implementation of Nature Policy in the Netherlands: Platforms Designed to Fail." In *Facilitating Sustainable Agriculture: Participatory Learning and Adaptive Management in Times of Environmental Uncertainty*, eds. N.G. Roling and M.A.E. Wagemakers. Cambridge, UK: Cambridge University Press. 250–71.

Waggener, Thomas R. 2001. "Logging Bans and the Asia-Pacific: An Overview." In *Forests out of Bounds: Impacts and Effectiveness of Logging Bans in Asia-Pacific*. eds. P. Durst, Thomas Waggener, Thomas Enters and Tan Ley Cheng. Bangkok, Thailand: Asia-Pacific Forestry Commission and Food and Agriculture Organization of the United Nations. 1–42.

Wakild, Emily. 2007. "Resources, Communities, and Conservation: The Creation of National Parks in Revolutionary Mexico under President Lázaro Cárdenas, 1934-1940." Ph.D. dissertation. University of Arizona.

———. 2006. "'It Is to Preserve Life, to Work for the Trees': The Steward of Mexico's Forests, Miguel Angel De Quevedo, 1862–1946." *Forest History Today*. Spring/Fall: 4–14.

Walker, A. 2012. *Thailand's Political Peasants: Power in the Modern Rural* Economy. Madison, WI: University of Wisconsin Press.

Wallace, Jennifer, and Ken Conca. 2012. "Peace through Sustainable Forest Management in Asia: The Usaid Forest Conflict Initiative." *High-value natural resources and post-conflict peacebuilding*, eds. Päivi Lujala and Siri Aas Rustad. Oxon, UK: Earthscan.

Wangpakapattanawong, Prasit, Nuttira Kavinchan, Chawapich Vaidhayakarn, Dietrich Schmidt-Vogt, and Stephen Elliott. 2010. "Fallow to Forest: Applying Indigenous and Scientific Knowledge of Swidden Cultivation to Tropical Forest Restoration." *Forest Ecology and Management* 260: 1399–406.

Watson, R.T., Ian R. Noble, Bert Bolin, N.H. Ravindranath, David J. Verardo, and David J. Dokken. 2000. *Land Use, Land-Use Change, and Forestry. A Special Report of the Intergovernmental Panel on Climate Change (IPCC)*. Intergovernmental Panel on Climate Change. Cambridge, UK: Cambridge University Press.

Watts, Michael J. 2000. "Contested Communities, Malignant Markets, and Gilded Governance: Justice, Resource Extraction, and Conservation in the Tropics." In *People, Plants, and Justice: The Politics of Nature Conservation*, ed. Charles Zerner: Columbia University Press. 21–51.

Webster, N., and L. Engberg-Pedersen. 2002. *In the Name of the Poor: Contesting Political Space for Poverty Reduction*. London and New York: Zed Books.

Weiss, Meredith Leigh. 2006. *Protest and Possibilities: Civil Society and Coalitions for Political Change in Malaysia*. Stanford, California: Stanford University Press.

West, Paige. 2006. *Conservation Is Our Government Now: The Politics of Ecology in Papua New Guinea*. Durban and London: Duke University Press.

West, Paige, James Igoe, and Dan Brockington. 2006. "Parks and Peoples: The Social Impact of Protected Areas." *Annual Review of Anthropology* 35: 251–77.

Westholm, Lisa, Robin Biddulph, Ida Hellmark, and Anders Ekbom. 2011. "REDD+ and Tenure: A Review of the Latest Developments in Research, Implementation and Debate." Report No. 2. Gothenburg, Sweden: Focali - Forest, Climate and Livelihood Research Network.

Weyland, Kurt. 2002. "Limitations of Rational-Choice Institutionalism for the Study of Latin American Politics." *Studies in Comparative International Development* 37 (1): 57–85.

Whitehead, Richard. 2011. "Historical Legacies, Clientelism and the Capacity to Fight: Exploring Pathways to Regime Tenure in Tanzania." *Democratization* 19: 1086–116.

Wiarda, Howard J. 1996. *Corporatism and Comparative Politics: The Other Great Ism*. Armonk, NY and London: M.E. Sharpe.

Williams, Glyn. 2004. "Evaluating Participatory Development: Tyranny, Power and (Re)Politicisation." *Third World Quarterly* 25: 557–78.

Williamson, Peter J. 1989. *Corporatism in Perspective*. London, Newbury Park, California and New Delhi: Sage Publications.

Wilshusen, Peter. R. 2012. "A Review of 'Instituting Nature: Authority, Expertise, and Power in Mexican Forests.'" *Annals of the Association of American Geographers* 102: 1531–33.

———. 2010. "The Receiving End of Reform: Everyday Responses to Neoliberalisation in Southeastern Mexico." *Antipode* 42: 767–99.

———. 2009. "Shades of Social Capital: Elite Persistence and the Everyday Politics of Community Forestry in Southeastern Mexico." *Environment and Planning A* 41: 389–406.

———. 2003. "Negotiating Devolution: Community Conflict, Structural Power, and Local Forest Management in Quintana Roo, Mexico." Ph.D. dissertation. University of Michigan.

Wily, L.A. 2001. *Forest Management and Democracy in East and Southern Africa: Lessons from Tanzania*. London: International Institute for Environment and Development.

Wolf, E.R. 1969. *Peasant Wars of the Twentieth Century*. New York: Harper and Row.

Wolford, Wendy. 2010. *This Land Is Ours Now: Social Mobilization and the Meanings of Land in Brazil*. Durham: Duke University Press.

———. 2003. "Producing Community: The MST and Land Reform Settlements in Brazil." *Journal of Agrarian Change* 3 (4): 500–20.

Wollenberg, E., M. Colchester, G. Mbugua, and T. Griffiths. 2006. "Linking Social Movements: How International Networks Can Better Support Community Action About Forests." *International Forestry Review* 8: 265–72.

Wood, Stephanie. 1990. "The Fundo Legal or Lands Por Razón De Pueblo: New Evidence from Central New Spain." In *The Indian Community of Colonial Mexico Fifteen Essays on Land Tenure, Corporate Organizations, Ideology and Village Politics*, eds. Arij Ouweneel and Simon Miller. Amsterdam: Centre for Latin American Research and Documentation (CEDLA).

World Bank. 2015. *World Development Indicators 2015*. Washington, DC: World Bank. doi:10.1596/978-1-4648-0440-3.

————. 2005. *India: Unlocking Opportunities for Forest-Dependent People in India (In Two Volumes) Volume I: Main Report*. New Delhi: World Bank.

————. 2001. *Mexico—Land Policy: A Decade after the Ejido Reform*. Washington, DC: World Bank. http://documents.worldbank.org/curated/en/2001/06/1671279/mexico-land-policy-decade-after-ejido-reform.

Wunder, Sven. 2010. "Forest Decentralization for REDD? A Response to Sandbrook Et Al." *Oryx* 44: 335–37.

WWF. 2005. *Conservation with Communities in the Biodiversity 'Hotspots' of India*. New Delhi: Forests & Biodiversity Conservation Programme, World Wide Fund for Nature—India.

Wyatt, Andrew. 2005. "Building the Temples of Postmodern India: Economic Constructions of National Identity." *Contemporary South Asia* 14: 465–80.

Xaxa, V. 2001. "Protective Discrimination: Why Scheduled Tribes Lag Behind Scheduled Castes." *Economic and Political Weekly* 36: 2765–72.

————. 1999. "Tribes as Indigenous People of India." *Economic and Political Weekly* 34: 3589–95.

Yagnik, Achyut. 2002. "Search for Dalit Self Identity in Gujarat." In *The Other Gujarat*, ed. Takashi Shinoda. Mumbai: Popular Prakashan. 22–37.

Yergin, D., and J. Stanislaw. 2008. *The Commanding Heights: The Battle between Government and the Marketplace*. New York: Simon & Schuster.

Ylhäisi, Jussi. 2003. "Forest Privatisation and the Role of Community in Forests and Nature Protection in Tanzania." *Environmental Science & Policy* 6: 279–90.

Zagema, Bertram. 2011. "Land and Power: The Growing Scandal Surrounding the New Wave of Investments in Land." *Oxfam Policy and Practice: Agriculture, Food and Land* 11: 114–64.

Zebich-Knos, Michele. 2008. "Ecotourism, Park Systems, and Environmental Justice in Latin America." In *Environmental Justice in Latin America: Problems, Promise, and Practice*. London: MIT Press. 185–211.

Zimmerer, Karl S. 2011. "'Conservation Booms' with Agricultural Growth." *Sustainability and Shifting Environmental Governance in Latin America* 46: 82–114.

Zúñiga, Iván, Sergio Madrid, and Claudio Garibay. 2012. "Background: Mexico's Tenure Reform Experience, 1992–2012." Washington, DC: Rights and Resources Initiative.

INDEX

Note: Tables and figures are indicated by an italic *t* or *f* following the page number.